# LOITERING WITH INTENT

## THE APPRENTICE

OTHER BOOKS BY PETER O'TOOLE

LOITERING WITH INTENT: THE CHILD

*Peter O'Toole*

# LOITERING
# WITH INTENT

## THE APPRENTICE

New York

Library of Congress Cataloging-in-Publication Data
O'Toole, Peter
Loitering with intent / Peter O'Toole. — 1st ed.
p.   cm.
ISBN 0-7868-6065-0
1. O'toole, Peter.  2. Actors—Great Britain—Biography.
I. Title.
PN2598.O7A2  1992
792'.092—dc20
[B]    92-43478
CIP


10 9 8 7 6 5 4 3 2 1

FOR HOPE

AND IN MEMORY OF

SIR KENNETH BARNES

# LOITERING
# WITH INTENT

## THE APPRENTICE

UNCOMMONLY NIPPY is it in this old house where you find me loitering at the base of the stairway in the hall, glum and with iced trotters unhappy in their station on the cold slabs of black and white chequered floor. Here, though, where the wooden banister curves to loop round and end in a carved coil, is a handy spot on which to lean, where a man muffled as I in wool and fur and felt may for a moment take his shuddering ease and lean back a little to gaze at the rails rising up the stairwell, roaming in rounded oblongs through the chill deserted floors of this forsaken house. Dismal. Look away. Look towards the front door, to the left of the door, to the traces on the wall where the painting of the Tinkerman had hung. Bold the tall dark Tinker had stood, glorious, grinning, hands stuffed into the pockets of a great long rosy red and billowing overcoat he was wearing.

To the right of the door, now. Only a stain remains where once was the gentle watercolour with its warm tints picking out the pinks in the granite of the cottage where it stood long and low on the hazy saffron hill dappled green and blue and lovely to look on. Peep under the fanned-out glass above the slender metal arch in the hall. High on the wall the violence of the huge and primitive thorn tree had alarmed up there, oils and colours raving in its frame. Once one had got used to it, though, its old threat became quite dottily warm and even welcoming. To some. Through the arch, that's the way, to your left imagine, mounted on her green marble pedestal, my dainty white stone sea maiden, sculpted so bravely, feminine and fanciful. Gone, alas, as are her companion oils; the pure faint gold deceit of a false morning's promise, the warm darks and reds of the tidy docker's hearth, and the blue spume and white clamour where the waterfall had tumbled. No, not gone; removed merely from their fixed places and living now in brilliancy as matters of my mind. It is true, however, that I do sorely miss the young and unfortunate pregnant nun. She was a writhing curving carved chestnut wood form which could be twisted round and round where she stood on her plinth. Strokable too. A splendid girl to fondle and to twiddle and to wonder at. Nor, you should know, was she a nun, nor pregnant, nor young. That had been a fancy only bestowed on her by Jeremiah Slattery MB when first he had made her acquaintance. She had arrived in the old house a couple of decades ago, mounted, brass-based and twirlable, the texture of her deep dark wood all sheen and shaped fantastical, a present from Buzz and Gino at Venice. Commonly believed by sods and soddesses who tripped in and out the premises to be an abstract sculpture in the manner, say, of a Frink or a Butler or a Moore, titles of all sorts had been scattered on her, my favoured one being Jeremiah MB's maidenly bride of Christ big with child, she was in fact a rowlock. A gondola rowlock. A complex, ancient device, your rowlock of a gondola. Her curves and contours providing a gondolier with precise purchase to propel the gondola for'ard, aft, larboard, starboard, to twist, to turn, yes, to brake, to skim the shallows, to dig the deep, to prod away the approaching palazzos.

With Toio at the prow this chestnut baby had aided Gino to skid his gondola from Venice to Trieste and back, splashing to victory three times in that annual little frolic, and had been his reins boots heels and hands in innumerable Legers, Guineas and Derbys up and down and round the grand old canal, most of which Gino had pissed: won. Eventually, of course, after many years' gallant ploughing of the waterways seas and lagoons of La Serenissima her old heart had cracked. Alive, though, living and lovely and cherished, Gino and Buzz had lifted her tenderly, placed her in my arms and there she had rested at her place in the hall, a confusion and a delight over many years for my family, friends and visitors.

Take your peepers away from that mark on the chessboard floor where the old girl had stood and swung and pop them across the way to where the little pigs had turned into buckets, the ducks had played their fiddles and the sheep had worn her richly embroidered wedding dress. Figurines of a light biscuit clay all moulded before me as I had sat on the earth and watched, occasionally blowing my conch, in a little spot down Oaxaca way where no conquistador had trod and little Spanish was spoken. The sculptress had been an extraordinarily elderly nimble of finger Indian lady whose preferred tongue had been Nahuatl but who could say in English, '*Time* magazine,' and with whom I had breakfasted on dawn plucked fungi and, throughout that timeless enchanted shadeful sun spilled day, as the artist had easily, skilfully, kneaded and soothed and rolled and shaped with slip, I the privileged overseer and herself the creator, had lifted up our spirits and our strengths with sweet crunchy munchables and draughts and whiffs of the local nerve tonic and herbal remedy. The kangaroo for the sheep's wedding dress had taken my gentle old Indian lady time, but the frog weaving baskets had hopped into life within seconds.

All gone now in this hall and the bitter nip has crept into my bones and heart. What cheer? Oh, we have that right enough for there before me is the door to the Green Room and my hand will willingly brave itself from out its glove happily to fetch from an overcoat pocket Edmund Kean's ring.

There you are, my beauty, my treasure, you are gold and moonstone and diamonds. Yes, some deluded souls not fully understanding the property of a stage ring may believe you to be copper and paste, to be exquisitely fashioned costume jewellery but, my brother and sister actors and actresses, we know that you are a matchless adornment for the finger of a monarch. I know that; Griffith the Untouchable whose gift to me the ring had been knows that; and King Bloody Dick the whoreson bastard of Old Drury, Kean, E., he knew that. 'Poor, great Edmund Kean,'

3

grieved his lifelong friend the dramatist Sheridan Knowles in the year of Kean's death, 1833, 'that noble, fine little fellow.' Yes, think of that: the actor whose prodigious versatility, blistering power and mighty genius had amazed, amused, stilled, startled, enraptured, moved and terrified his audiences in England Ireland Scotland Wales and the United States of America had been only a scrap of a bloke standing five foot four inches high.

Come to me now and his ring in my hand while I tell you. Do you see, in the wonky old business of putting on plays for public performances on the stages of playhouses, much of what for centuries had been just ordinary practice has quite disappeared from the modern English theatre, including, alarmingly, the sovereignty we actors and actresses held over our brightly lit and painted canvas, cardboard and timber domains. We have abdicated our plywood thrones, or have been deposed, or usurped, and theatrical royalty now lives on the brow of that pernicious breed of pillock your Barnstormführer itself: your theatre director. Have the hoor for I don't want her. Many do, alas, but many do.

True it is, too, that for many many centuries when, say, mustering readies for to put our shaky enterprise once again on to its shameless feet, or in copping a licence, or a permission, or a patronage, a prestige, a gathering of the wherewithal, the use of the hall, you get the drift, we have had perforce to put ourselves in the employ and thrall of a brewer or an admiral or a dangerous clown of some or other sort. From Roscius to the time of these my scratchings, it is recorded how often and how deeply we theatrical folk have been indebted to these worthies, these highnesses, these rabid toerags, but, put aside your Nero, your Great Herod, your Duke of Saxe-Meiningen, your Alexeyev and Co., seldom have they troubled their estimable selves with the actual doing of the mummery, opining, quite rightly, that the business of the learning of the jokes and of the telling them nicely, the skipping on and the skipping off the greengage, stage, the grouping and moving of ham bones in a symmetry, the giving of your hornpipe, your clog dance, the warbling of your ditties, indeed, the very traffic of actors and actresses, to be better conducted by the more experienced among us who do the bloody work for a living. Odd, do you not find, that it is the fashion at present that we who do the business should be considered and encouraged to be ignorant of the business that we do. That others, who do not do the business, are unable to do the business, are invited to instruct, counsel and superintend us in the doing of our own business. There is nazification here. There is your Barnstormführer. There is, Lord love us, a dog in the office. But what of that, but what of that, what is there left to say? On.

The Green Room, too, is gone, had, indeed, more or less gone by the time I joined back in 1953. For three hundred years it had been a familiar and cheerful little nook to be found backstage in all the theatres of these islands. A room painted and curtained and carpeted green, with chairs, sofas and a bar sprawling in it, a spot where players could meet their guests and friends before a show, could congregate before their entrances or after their exits during a show and where after a show, having doffed makeup and costume, players could again meet their guests and friends and in comfort kiss each other, kick each other, fall in love, get drunk and discuss the price of turnips. In Kean's time, between 1814 and 1830 at the Theatre Royal, Drury Lane, the Green Room there had been regularly stuffed with bloods royal, belles, beaux, movers and shakers of government, the law, the military, the aristocracy, of industry, of commerce, the greats of literature, science, music, painting, architecture, and the playwrights, actors and actresses whose work the beautiful and mighty had come to see. A cheerful habitation and refuge for theatre folk and theatre goers your little room painted green backstage of a theatre, one that had come to us and our playhouses in about 1660.

What had happened, I fancy, was that in 1642 the Lords and Commons of Parliament then assembled, noting the distracted state of England and the distressed state of her subject countries Scotland Wales and Ireland, had called for all possible means to appease and avert the wrath of God and had thought it fit that while these sad causes and set times of humiliation continued, public stage plays should cease and be forborne. All theatres had been closed. Now, we all know that in the theatre the devil displays his pomp with so many charms and seductive graces that the most solid virtue can hardly withstand it, which is as good and gamey a reason as you may need for being a lively member of the audience; and it will do quite nicely, thank you, for my being an actor.

Imagine then, back in 1642, the peoples of these islands, deprived as they were of the intemperance and impurity to be embraced in a playhouse, where could they dig some salty action? Civil War looked promising; what with the King ignoring Parliament and Parliament resenting this; what with Scotland reeling around all frisky, Ireland being rebellious again and Wales thoroughly Welsh; what with notions of a Republic a Democracy a Commonwealth being bruited abroad, why Civil War seemed the answer and so it proved. Patriot slew Patriot in a Civil War that was so popularly successful that, no sooner had conclusions of the war been reached, than it was deemed right to fight another one. Two Civil Wars, England Scotland and Wales riven and blood-soaked, Ireland boiling up nicely and Parliament the winner. What next? Chop off the King's head, that's what was next. Abolition of Kingship and the House of Lords followed hard upon. England then tried its hand at being a Commonwealth with Mr Oliver Cromwell serving as Lord General. Lord General Oliver Cromwell, having already put hard grips on the unruly of England Scotland and Wales, now turned his full attention on to Ireland. My Lord General appeased and averted the wrath of God by slaughtering between one third and one half of the Catholic population of my country and for a while Ireland lay pacified. Lord Generalship and Commonwealthdom didn't have a kingly enough ring in their titles, didn't, perhaps, reflect the real politics of the situation, didn't suit, and so my Lord General became our Lord Protector and the Commonwealth a Protectorate.

Still not enough. Still much to do. Naval adventures in the Channel, the Atlantic, the Mediterranean, the Caribbean. Naughty, unruly and Highland Scots to be hammered. War with the Dutch. War with Spain. Military alliance with France. Thousands and thousands of Irish Scots and Welsh prisoners-of-war to be shackled in irons and transported as slaves to the Indies and the Americas. Religious, military, civil and political unrest at home, indeed the House of Commons, buttressed by the Army, had seen or tried or considered a Short Parliament, a Long Parliament, a Perpetual one, a Rump and a Barebones Parliament, while Regicides, Royalists, Parliamentarians, Roundheads, Cavaliers, yeomen, serfs and villeins cavilled and caballed, grouped and galloped, muttered and plotted and feared. Our Lord Protector Cromwell died and was succeeded by his son Richard. This proved to be not to the popular taste. The son of the executed King was summoned, answered the call, entered London and the Monarchy was restored. We had a Kingdom once again. Cromwell was dug up, his head was chopped off and the wrath of God thus, I fancy, appeased and averted it was mooted fit that the theatres should again be opened.

Sixteen sixty, and eighteen years had thundered by since their closing, eighteen years during which Edmund Kean and I had been jobless and unwanted. We had, of course, kept our heads down, so avoiding all that fuss, palaver and faction-fighting going on among real people, had indeed from furtive time to time managed to scrape an illicit crust doing the clog dance, gems from the Bard and a burst of 'The Cuckoo' in secluded pubs and barns and the backs of police stations but, all in all, it had been a shaky old time and if nabbed, well, fines, whippings, pressgangs or the squeezer had been very much on the cards. Now, however, we could freely saunter into gainful employment through the stage doors of our reopened theatres, saunter, what's more, in the company of women who would play the parts of women; actresses in short, females, a sex unknown and forbidden on the stages of English drama since the gamesters, scôps and gleemen of the earlier medieval times. Imagine it. Hey diddle de dee, sipping champagne all day and dressing with the actresses! More. Our reborn popularity with the court meant not only protection and encouragement from His Royal Nibs but also attendance at the theatre of an altogether better class of riff-raff.

Your courtiers, rakes, nobs, dandies, gallants all with their fancy women, all bedight in fine fripperies, all enthusiastically rubbing bacons together with lawyers, schoolteachers and whores, merchants and their tidy wives, the whole leavened by the faithfully constant worse class of riff-raff: your knife-grinders, bottlewashers, blacksmiths, apprentices and whores, soldiery, weavers, tanners, shop assistants and suchlike with their missuses and wanton women. The reconstituted King, too, Charles II, onions deep in lust and love for sulky Nelly Gwynn, actress, orange hawker and mistress royal, took his purple place among the punters. All for their delight, the fare offered on the lighted stage, too, had brought its everlasting changes. As front runners, Shakespeare, Marlowe and Jonson were given a few decades off while comedies of 'manners' and 'intrigue' became the flavour. Thomas Betterton, with greasepaint anointed king of leading men, and, perhaps more importantly, Mrs Barry, Elizabeth Farley, Anne Bracegirdle, similarly dubbed leading ladies, femininely strutted their juicy hour upon the stage in these new-fangled plays whose matter amusingly concerned the plots and ploys, the stratagems and deceptions, the sweet-talking oratory all politically employed by men and women in the unrelenting pursuit of sexual conquest.

Commentators suggest, and my poke is with them, that the novel and the very presence of the like of Gwynn, Farley, Barry, Bracegirdle wandering loose about the playhouse, women, yes, inexplicable gorgeous dangerous women, was a reckonable force behind before and within the narrative and deadly dance of loves

8

and lusts which form the smoking matter of what we call Restoration comedy. A spotlight bared on what anthropologists would have us know to be opportunities for reproductive success politically engineered within society.

Etherege, G., is considered to have been first off the mark with his *Love in a Tub*, his *She Would if She Could*, while Mrs Aphra Behn, Wycherley, Buckingham, Dryden, Congreve, Tuke, Vanbrugh, Shadwell, Otway, Farquhar and all they followed hard upon. Follow, do, the bloodlines of plays born in 1660, when the women rejoined the drama, and you may find, mutated and beautiful in the last gasps of this our twentieth bloody century, their noble progeny muttering tales of dalliance, amorousness and despair in, say, the plays of Tennessee Williams or Terence Rattigan.

'The stage being the representation of the world and the actions in it,' said Dryden, J., in 1664, 'how can it be imagined that the picture of human life can be more exact than life itself is?' Quite. And what better way, surely, to examine, to scrutinize this question, to lay peepers and fingers on these representations, these exactitudes than for me and Edmund Kean, Jimbo, Griffith, Bletchley and the Open Razor to follow the example of that gracious majesty Charlie the Deuce and his heap? Kings Lords and Commons who shuffled backstage and took their ease in this addition to the reopened theatre, dreamt of, nailed up and painted even as His Majesty was being fitted for his throne, the very hub of matters, the Green Room.

Here we go into what once was ours, mine and my widow's, a fancy we both had shared for the way a room should behave when first we had moved into this old house, and the world was only a pup.

Twiddle away, do, with the fine eighteenth-century lockery knobs, twist them, spin them, grind them left or right, they have minds of their own, the door won't budge. Much the better way is two-handedly to grab the larger centre knob, give it a fierce wrench to starboard and immediately fling your entire person sideways against the bastard and, yes, smoothly juddering she flies open to reveal my beloved old chamber.

There is warmth in the hush and jumble of the room, Edmund, while a click of the switch pops on the overhead light. Back into my pocket goes your ring, little Ned, as we pick our way through the remainder chattels of this one-time over-furnished house, the bits and bobs of two generations stored now for safety in our raving green old room. On to the dainty quarter moon of the maplewood stage that we had built for us in the grand bay of the bow windows. The shutters are an easier proposition than the door. Merely press the tit in on the flat iron strut in the shutters' centre, raise it from its socket, let it swing down till the hook on it drives itself into your foot, wince, then you simply ripple the folding wooden shutters to tuck them into their places provided on the sides of the room-high bowing windows, only badly jamming your fingers the while. The gloves help, I find. By the time you have unbuttoned the third window, the knack usually has been found. Or not. But what of that? A dab of iodine, a refreshing light ale, these minor entry wounds bleed unheeded, as daylight streams into the eyes and you gaze through the Green Room windows at the rare view of the workhouse and the condemned hospital. Turn from these London sights and let's have a shufti at this bedlam chamber of ours, its walls stiff with playbills, posters, photos, props, framed and dangling bygones announcing memories and old thoughts. Hello! Irving's gloves are there but where's Peggy and me, in love and fair dancing together in the *Shrew*? Where the fuck is *King Lear*? Eric Porter's, 1956, Theatre Royal Bristol, my name at the bottom on the left-hand side of the list of runners and riders, when giving the Duke of Cornwall? Oh, yes, of course, I, too, have daughters. Daughters have been in here, that I know. They will have peeled themselves keepsakes. Cherish them, children, cherish my much loved snaps and tat. And you will snugly keep them safe for your dear old daddy, won't you now.

You're all right, Kean, you're still here. You're on the floor, though, for some dingy reason, down on the floor not high up where you belong, and on display. That will be fixed. You're a fine rare shape in the writing and signature on this document. There can't be many more like you. You are requesting that a fair chunk of your change should actually be put into a bank not withdrawn from one. No, there can be few, if any, of you. Yes, King Bloody Dick, didn't the bed you died in have to be sold to pay for your burial? You, you hopeless little pillock, who had earned prodigious wages for nearly twenty years, snuffed it and left not a pot to piss in. Yes, I know, sweet Ned, it's only a commonplace between our lot. Leave it be. Brighten up. Look.

To our left the huge Provençal dresser, home for thirty and more years to the flowing bar. Beside it the cupboards whose shelves held, on the top, records and tapes, in the middle, apparatus for playing the above, down below, the fridge, a preserving and temperate booth for champagne and beer. Above our heads, right and left of the stage, amplifiers to sound out great din when the joint, as regularly it had, transmogrified itself into a leaping dance hall. There is not an inch of floor nor furniture nor shelf nor stage nor piano nor radiator but in its time has been hefty host to the soles and heels of your dancing trotter. Jigs and twists and reeling chorus lines, rain dance, war dance, tap dance, your abandoned solitary gallop, your twosome, your threesome, yet your eightsome scrimmage and hoof-pounding bloodbath and the night we failed to kick the place to splinters.

Finchy gave his famed flamenco even on that low lacquered Japanese table there. Stamping and clapping and thrashing about, the while howling oaths made in Australia. Here young Rudi took off to hover in the air for a while, seemingly to gaze, amused, at his gawpers, before deciding to set himself down again, a crooked grin on his gob, God's grace in every fibre of the man. Gone, now, both. Peace to them and joy of the worm. Here and there old scout Jack MacGowran, Siobhán McKenna, wild and lovely, stripped more than the willow, while great Máire Kean, taking lots of no notice, stepped out a lonesome hornpipe on the lid of the piano as Maloney sounded through the town and the speakers.

Us? What did we do? Why, James and Ronald and I we did what we always have done. What Pringle and Mellor and Burton, Big Nance Neville, Reggie and Louis and Keith and Willis and fair throngs of our sort always have done. Calmly we mounted this little stage, demurely we lowered our strides and melodiously to our customers uttered we 'The Cuckoo'.

Oh yes, Edmund Kean Esq., we sucked melancholy out of a song in this room, old and plain songs, love songs, love songs for we cared not for good life. Sad songs, mad songs, nonsense bawdy and sweet songs. MacNeice shakily sank to the floor fluting out his 'Goodbye Lily and Goodbye Kate'. Clamping a hand over his deafening left ear, Dominic Behan, a matchless street singer and brother of Brendan, sundered hearts with 'The Trees are Growing Tall' and rattled windows at 'Tim Finnegan's Wake' even as O'Liver ended his inimitable confusing honk 'In the Vinter, in the Vintertime', and Siân's husky brooding ineffably beautiful 'David of the White Rock' still lilts hauntingly about this ridiculous old chamber. I fancy.

'Music to hear, why hear'st thou music sadly'? Why, yes, of course, all was not always riot, though much had been, times there had been of only listening quietly, of reflective foot tapping, of piped-up accompaniment, some conducting, even a brass-bowelled bellow to join in at the chorus as Beethoven blew his best down the blaster and Jelly Roll Morton came tinkling after. Pergolesi's songsters, pure and less their testicles, poured gender-less liquid dainties into ears relieved of sex and cursing but came the Kings Armstrong and Oliver, all the rugs in wig city lifted, jazz roused up in skirts and trousers when men and women sweated as they sucked the salty orange.

This land is your land sang in the eyes of slim Woody Guthrie as he handed on his banjo to a boy blowing a mouth organ. Bob Dylan took it, plucked it, picked it, stroked it, tormented it and yet further along the century came the authentic sound of gringo minstrelsy as he opened his gob and let loose that sublime whine of discontent. Bitter joy, true brother, bitter joy, and it ain't me babe neither. Elsie Randolph yearns for a someone to have a drink with her down at the Old Bull and Bush, Bailey rasps out wondering has she let her flowers down, Caruso and Ruffo heave their very tripes down the recording horns in a ferocious, singing battle between Otello and Iago. Blood! Blood! Blood! Don't tell me of the nice restraint in your behaviourism, you the tedious among our actors and actresses who, Lord love you, always have been with us. You have the bit and the bridle, dear toerags, but where's the bloody horse! Find among you the he and the she that own individual voice, flair, stance, command. Follow them. Support them. They will take you far and high. Further and higher by far than will all the downcast attention you so obediently plaster on the blatherings of such some or other supervisory windbag as at present quite litters up our scene.

Actor, author, audience, a trinity of indispensables in the one heart one soul one body of a living playhouse. To be sure, a cunning entrepreneur, a well-woven wig, a spangled shift, a glim properly spotted, consonance of setting and a muscular flyman, these and suchlike elements can bring ornament into our arena but don't confuse confection with practical pudding nor the fine spectacle of Mother Courage going one way while the set goes another, to be any more than a bright trick, a welcome and distractionary flapdoodle for a customer paying witness to our business of providing bare boards and a passion; our beginning and our end.

We can see the wheel, Edmund, though we cannot hinder the

turning, and mediocrity, which is always at its best, is the fashion
and functionaries rule. Happily, though, as we both know, our
bitch mistress theatre is a merciless whore who never forgives and
when she lifts her skirt we must thrill her with our performance
or we shall die. A playhouse dies when an audience stays away in
its thousands, preferring rather the delights offered by animated
scenery lifting and spinning about penny-dreadful plots and
persons whose central dramatic matter is held in singable jingles
honked by nobodies in particular to the accompaniment of lush
orchestras.

Leadbelly had twelve strings on his big guitar and didn't he
bang them as he rambled howling bitter blues. Bessie Smith
moaned mightily and sad sister Billie told her tunes how to sing.
Moonycrooners, too, old Ned, the sweet swinging evening bells
which swung and moved you so in your time that, sozzled, you
wept all over your piano, in our time mooned and swung and
moved us too. Bowlly, Bingo, smoky Peggy Lee, Dino, Bennett,
Sinatra, Judy, sweet warblers all. And the brave defiance of Piaf
and Brel cut deep into our souls.

Now: regard the spot below Mr Creswick's *Hamlet*, under Teatro
Olympico Vicenza, right to where *King Lear*, Theatre Royal,
Bristol, 1956, my name at the bottom on the left-hand column of
the list of runners and riders, once was nailed up, why there sat a
huge red sofa. A present bed for many, Ned, one which bore
much brunt. One which in its sprawling lolling bouncing comforting and thirty and more long years stretching tenure of this room
gave buoyant support to bums, bodies and legions of parked
carcasses. A role not unknown to its relative on the right, a smaller
version wrapped in a doggy brown, immediately below the twopence coloureds in their maple frames and Davy Garrick at
Ballinasloe where, that time in the eighteenth century, his customers could pay in coin or kind. A gold guinea for a box, a sack
of spuds for the pit, or a pound or two of fresh churned butter to
seat you cosily in the circle. Under *Juno and the Paycock* and *Man*

*and Superman* was Daddy's chair. A wing-armed old cracked leather number on which, during the long and peaceful stretches when the room knew only quiet domesticity, I would sit and read and drink and smoke and listen and chat and brood and age in considerable style and comfort. Before me, on the dogshelf below, there was Scobie's ground. Scobie, my bulldog, for thirteen years my awkward-born brute, my snorting grunting farting bulky big bowlegged pal, my broad-shouldered and mighty darling with his old head a huge blood-guttered squashed block of ancient pugnacity. Snoozing now or purposefully plodding round to sniff the customers, aware, always, of a self-appointed duty as keeper and enforcer of his one sacred Green Room rule: no acting allowed. In frolic puppyhood he had determined this stern commandment, in arthritic antiquity none had yet dared impugn his law. Thirteen years' guardianship of the sanctity of the joint and many there had been who innocently, ill-advisedly had started up a note from the throat bearing acting in its tone. All had been silenced. All. In speechless horror where they had sat or stood or perched or clung, for some had sought safety on the top of the piano, cupboards, dresser, through the window, silenced all from this acting by the frightful sight and sound of lawgiver Scobie, risen, terrible and unforgiving. 'Bulls and bears in old time have I sported with and chewed,' he rumbled through his terrible massive jaws. 'Fornication, madness, murder, drunkenness, shouting, shrieking, leaping, polite conversation and the breaking of bones, such jollities constitute acceptable behaviour in this my master's Green Room, but no acting is allowed. It is insufferable and will by me savagely be put down.'

As Scobie lay dying in his place at the foot of my chair, he rolled an admonitory eye around the room, fixed it on me, received my assurance that his will for ever would be obeyed, grinned horribly, cheesily released a final, farewell fart, closed his loving peepers and went off to bite his Maker.

Yonder stood, ricketedly, Slattery's chair, the leather and wood

Eames number with the plush footstool. Wholly busted, split and cracked, listing in several directions, handy to the bar and the television set, a twisted wrecked heap of moveable, witness to his weight, restlessness, vigour and emphatic enthusiasms.

There. A prattling spin around the room and the view we have of it from the stage. Time to put Kean's ring back in its box, time to muffle up against the cold sighing through this empty house, time to leave while the warm memories tumble and chuckle in my mind. One colourful recollection will do, I fancy, to bob about inside my head and keep me cheerful company while I clamber, switch off, shove, shut, lock, bolt and bar the house. Whose idea it had been to turn up to a party here wearing uniforms to which we were entitled quite eludes me now but, if you will, picture it and imagine, if you can, the way that it had been.

A symmetry of strawberry and white small squares decorate the Arab headdress flowing athwart the features and resting on the shoulders of the khaki uniform containing that amplitude of a man, Dewsbury. He is in the outfit of the Arab Legion. Thus bedight, in the early fifties, he rode camel through the harsh wildernesses of the Negev and the Arabian deserts in his days as a young officer of Abu Knick's disciplined and daring Anglo-Bedouin fighting force. At present, he is clearing his throat, sipping a little kaolin and morphine, thoughtfully puffing a smoke and arranging his noble features into a soulful, passionate demeanour. Something's about to be up. The white-flannelled Indian cricketer has requisitioned an enormous Mexican sombrero and, wearing it, has embarked on the hazard of circumnavigating the Green Room without touching the floor. Many have attempted this artful and difficult journey. Some have succeeded. More have failed, and with a frightful old crash. It were a good stratagem to ingest a quart or so of green Chartreuse before setting out to clamber so around the room. It tones up the questing mind, lends courage to the tricky negotiation between dresser gramophone radiator and window ledge, gives heart to the endeavour and when the fall comes, as come it inevitably does, cushions in coma the hurtling head as it crunches into the unyielding dogshelf here. Who knows, though, mayhap the sombrero will take the pace off the tumble? Mayhap. He has chosen the dumb waiter under *Waiting for Godot* for his point of departure. This is a mistake. Brave, mind you, for the area from there to the bar is dangerously dodgy and not in a quarter of a century have I seen the peril mastered at a first attempt. So it's a hundred to plenty against this Mexican cricketer making it and odds on that he'll wind up with a faceful of floor. The Open Razor, in part amused by this, in other part is giving what passes in these days as his full attention to a scrumptious little dumpling of a darling, writhing about in the uniform of her former girls' school. Not all of her fits into it. The all that doesn't doubtless has matured since its days in the fifth form, has become fuller, more rounded, shapely, tapering, ripe with feminine gender and altogether reveals a form which is wholly, wantonly edible. The Open Razor has eschewed rightful wearing of the uniform of his old Seaforth Highlanders regiment, rather preferring a frilled stock, bumfreezer jacket and the proud kilt of his family, the clan Fraser. His *sgian dubh*, the little black knife that slots into the stockings filled by Scotch and hairy wee legs, is lost. This loss, at first, caused him consternation but is now a matter of no importance as he seeks to find a toothsome part of this sexily prim schoolgirl swaying about before him, a part that he will bite. Nor does he heed the plummeting Mexican cricketer as down goes he to try a mouthful of plank.

Griffith untouchably swills a mouthful of black porter down his Welsh throat, the while debating a fine point. What power, goes the point, entitles him to shimmer where he stands inside the red coat, black trousers and white pith helmet of the uniform worn by the 24th Regiment of the South Wales Borderers when they were massacred by the Zulus at the Battle of Isandlwana in 1879? 'Well, my duck,' points out Griffith to his victim, a tall fair haughty lady, tipsy and more or less dressed in hockey strip, 'the documentary film of the battle that I made somewhat startled the British television company who were my employers because it was firmly on the side of the Zulus. However, while wholeheartedly attacking the wretched greed and barbarous inhumanity shown by the instigators of British imperialism in Africa, I hope it was perfectly clear that I deeply sympathized with the poor bloody soldiers of the 24th Regiment who were slaughtered in great numbers when obeying the grossly incompetent orders of British High Command. Any road, the South Wales Borderers gave me a lunch, the band played and the Colonel made me an honorary private of the 24th. In my view, then, and indeed, you may now think it to be so, my lovely, I am entitled to wear this glorious uniform. My youngest unmarried daughter thinks I look dishy in it. O'Toole thinks I look a right eyes front. Now you're reassured about the propriety of my wearing it, my dainty duck, don't you think it suits me? Don't you fancy me in it? If not, why, I could always take it off, but fair's fair, if I take off my lovely uniform, you must take off your hockey frock, but not by here, by here's all crowded and noisy, nasty and drunken. Somewhere tidy and quiet. Now, I have a dirty little spot in Islington. Not far away. Candid is what I am, I have no secrets, I tell the truth. You should therefore know that I am also an Untouchable. The Untouchables of India made me an honorary Untouchable, you see. I was making a documentary on Pandit Nehru for the Indian government and found my sympathies moving towards the caste of Untouchables, euphemistically known these days as the Children of God, and who, incidentally, make ferociously purposeful coppers on the streets of Delhi.'

The lovely tipsy ducky listens on, amazed, as do the Naval Commander, the Girl Guide, the Basque terrorist and the green sweatered jodhpur-limbed Land Girl; but not Bletchley. Bletchley is gracefully, intensely and nonchalantly preoccupied on a lightsome matter of his own. Having found and put on the player a little Beethoven, a quartet, your Rasumovsky; having found a tin tray which he has placed downside up upon the stage, having lightly stepped on to the tray and, uniformed all in the Green-jacket of the Rifles, has waited for the appropriate passage in the music which, when it comes, is an achingly beautiful stretch of solo violin yearning to the bow, and, tip, tap, tippety tippety top, Bletchley is now gently, expertly tap dancing to the music. Musing, I fancy, aloud the while, 'As a verse is a measured speech, I believe Francis Bacon wrote, so is a dance a measured pace and what better composer could there be, I ask you, to give a little shuffle to than a measure by Big Lud the Beetroot?' And a one two tippety tappety top.

Bellbottoms are cumbersome numbers. One's foot is like to go up the flopping flap of leg, pitch one violently over to find oneself flailing about on the prone body of a bleeding Mexican cricketer. Mine will shortly have to come off. Off as has my thick wool jersey. It, too, proved to be hot, prickly and, if not a liability as are my billowing strides, certainly unsuitable for a shrieking knees-up in my Green Room. Off with the buggers, I say, and soon. Even sooner should that gorgeous drum majorette with endlessly long legs, tinselled tassels prinking around her lush swaying bottom and tits like chapel hat pegs, continue so invitingly to ogle me. One only has to look at Mr Jim to realize how unsuitable for this occasion is one's seagoing Jolly Jack Tar set. Look at James. Look at the long article draped and lolling quite all over a sofa, gin and cigars to either hand, dressed in what, as uniforms go, he has considered himself properly to be entitled. His Jimness is dressed in loose white muslin pyjamas, wrapped around in a dark silk dressing gown. Cool, comfy, consonant to the proceedings and no chain mail worn by knights at arms was ever more pertinent to his purposes than pyjamas and dressing gown are to Jimbo's. Remark the time, long ago, when James, close to death from pneumonia and pleurisy, had been safely popped into hospital by concerned and loving friends. How these friends, glad that their chum was now in healing hands and antiseptic surroundings, had cheerfully repaired to a neighbouring boozer, chosen their light refreshments, sucked a brace down, when, yes, the door of the pub flew open, there stood the looming length of James, cap-a-pie in pyjamas and dressing gown, stiff with pre-operational medicaments, and who had boomingly announced to awed customers, 'The sterilisation unit at the Royal Free Hospital is on the blink, so I said to the surgeon, fuck it, lovey, I'm going for a stroll and very probably a cocktail. Large gin, landlord, soda and a kiss of lime.'

'"C'était pendant l'horreur d'une profonde nuit."' Hello, Dewsbury has gone off. Off with a roar and in agonized throaty French. Off, what's more, in declamatory fashion, lustily to pronounce a passage of Racine. That's acting, which is not allowed here. French acting, at that, which is a sin. Acting by Dewsbury who is not an actor compounds this hideousness because those who are not actors or actresses and yet act in the Green Room is as understandable as it is intolerable. The pain of it. '"Ma mère Jezabel devant moi s'est montrée,    Comme au jour de sa mort pompeusement parée."' Hark at Jimbo. 'What in the name of all that's chaste and sacred are you at, Bilberry? Sitting there with that curiously spotted Arabian *mouchoir* wrapped around your kisser, spouting out great gobfuls of diseased old Froggy text. Desist at once, Dewlap, acting is not permitted in Pedro's Green Room. It is uncivil, disagreeable, quite horrid and if Scobie were alive he would have had your dangling knackers bitten off and thoroughly chewed by now. Who is that limpidly lovely woman sitting at your side? Not your wife, surely. Are you still slipping it into her, Dogberry, my old sausage? Don't strike me, madam, rather turn your exciting fury on that chubby Arab with whom you seem to be in some way associated and biff him in the moosh. Oh Lordy, this is deeply unpleasant.' '"Ses malheurs n'avaient point abattu sa fierté;    Même elle avait encor set éclat emprunté    Dont elle eut soin de peindre et d'orner son visage,    Pour réparer des ans l'irréparable outrage."' Dewsbury rasps on, rasps on and Griffith shows commendable poise. 'It's to be expected, my duck,' says he to his tipsy deary, 'to be expected. He is, after all, an amateur, of course you may wear my pith helmet, there, suits you lovely, perhaps he has not heard, or has not understood, the unspoken rule that no one acts in O'Toole's Green Room. As an amateur, Dewsbury acted for recreation. For us, my haughty ducky, acting is a cognate profession, and our art. When I was deported from South Africa in 1952 for having an affair with a blacky, Oh, cor blimey, he's away!' '"Tremble, m'a-t-elle dit, fille digne de moi".' 'Oh, do put a sock in it, for fuck's sake, lovey!' It is the kilted Razor. 'Leave it out, my petal. You may have given your Clytem-fucking-nestra at university, when you were up and a member of the Oxford University Dramatic Society, but these are Pedro's chambers, sweetheart, we don't have any of that palaver here. You're acting. And in French. That's deeply depressing. You have also startled this beautiful young lady, with whom I was conducting a dialogue, which dialogue would have led, in a wee while, to my dropping my kilt and sticking my filthy little winky into her front bottom. You may have queered my pitch. Leave out the fucking French howling, lovey!'

He's game, that Mexican cricketer, game as a beagle. He's under *Hamlet* and about to attempt the dresser, gramophone, radiator, window ledge face of this room-rimming. Many have come unstuck. Many. He's bleeding from the ear. That's a first. Lips plenty, noses galore but from an ear? I think a first. And the gyrating flesh of my majorette is stilled. There's an artfully arranged lot of her and she has draped some of it in a languidly attentive arrangement across the piano, listening to the Racine, which is not half bad, if unexpected, and she looks at me as though I were on a piece of buttered toast. Trouble. '"Le cruel dieu des Juifs l'emporte aussi sur toi.    Je te plains de tomber dans ses mains redoutables,    Ma fille."'

'Were I French, Dogsend,' says Big Jim, 'not being which has in no way yet distressed me, I would pelt you with oeufs, heave at you all the various legumes, and fit a poubelle of merde over your head. This is intolerable, sir. In-fucking-tolerable. Defenestration may be the only answer. Watch it, Bletchley, you old chorus girl. That's an amazingly pretty young nurse you have watching you do your running on the spot. You're in shtuck, lovey. Little squelchy nursie will be wanting you to slip it into her every five minutes. You won't be up to it, you poor old blighter. You'll wind up in the knacker's yard with Ginger from *Black Beauty*.'

'Hark at Jim,' says Razor, 'hark at fucking Jim. He's got his young bird parked somewhere for the night, so that he can come to Pedro's drum, get pissed, spread pages of naughty dialogue at every one in sight and not have the burden of giving his child bride a seeing-to! Five minutes out from under the cosh and he's handing out dreadful warnings. Leave it out, you silly old humbug. Stick some Vera down your cakehole and assist me in persuading this here geezer that this French acting has to stop immediately.' '"En achevant ces mots epouvantables"' 'Oh for fuck's sake' '"Son ombre vers mon lit a paru se baisser;    Et moi je lui tendais les mains pour l'embrasser."'

Down goes the Mexican cricketer, gone down a down a down. Last seen heading in the direction of the dogshelf having gone out of the front door attempting the radiator under *The Long and the Short and the Tall* and *Baal*. Thud. There, he's landing now, half on and half off the stage and close to where Bletchley is a-tap a-tapping. No Beethoven, not now, just Johnny Bletchley whistling 'Don't Put Your Daughter on the Stage, Mrs Worthington' and rat-a-tat-tatting with his trotters.

Unfazed by any din of disapproval, if aware of it, and untroubled by his inability to grasp an audience into a breathless silence, the Arab croaks thickly, passionately on. '"Mais je n'ai plus trouvé qu'un horrible mélange    D'os et de chairs meurtris, et traînés dans la fange,    Des lambeaux pleins de sang, et des membres affreux    Que des chiens dévorants se disputaient entre

eux,"' he gasps at last, slumping where he perches, spent, fulfilled
and, mercy, silent. Dewsbury of Arabia has reached his terminus.
Relieved applause there is from an ageing Boy Scout, a mess
jacket and a gymslip; polite, appreciative murmurings from a
chubby lady tennis player and a cassock and surplice; muttered
curses from the Redcoat and the kilted Razor; and the perturbed
spirit of Scobie waddles back to deserved, snuffling rest. A merry
Englishness returns to Dewsbury's merry English mouth as he
bares his tusks in a merry English smile and grunts no more in
French.

My majorette unwraps herself from the keyboard, sways her
pompoms, tassels, silk and sexuality over to Dewsbury, tosses him
a penn'orth of praise, lazily undulates in my direction, tells me of
her wish to pluck off the saucy plumes of her yesteryears, to
wriggle into more sophisticated togs and there is that in her
demeanour which provokes in me a desire to emulate her in this
practice. We could, perhaps, be of assistance to each other in this
business of unbuckling, unbelting and unbuttoning rigid uniforms. Helpful and in no rush at all when once unpicked from
these our shells worn in days of duty and loyal service, we could
linger in our liberation and, before assuming other gear, mayhap
could try each other on for size. Harmony of intention, I fancy,
exudes from her inviting frame as we wrap our arms around our
persons and ooze towards the door.

'Blessed relief it is,' says James, 'that Dangleberry has seen fit to
cease his hideous French acting clamour, but close on forty years
of friendship demand that I address myself to Pedro and to
Ronald. Pedro, you're about to slide upstairs bearing armfuls of
flesh and usherette and, once up there, that fine chunk of a lady
will insist that you slip it into her. There's no avoiding it, lovey,
and you'll rue it. Rue it, that is, if you are still able to muster up
what is appropriate in these troublesome situations. It's folly,
Pedro, and the best hope is that you're past it, which I don't
doubt. Put him down, you naughty pair of red bloomers and

tiddly poms, he's a silly old sod who needs no more grief. And, Ronald, at least have the courtesy to tell your head prefect that the poor cow is on a loser. Yes, my bumpy beauty squeaking about there in your school colours, no doubt that once you were a lump in your games mistress's throat but any further dalliance with the Open Razor will prove a failure. To be sure, once you're cornered you will anticipate his slipping it in to you but Uncle Jim is here to tell you that it won't happen. In no conceivable way. Under that kilt these days is nothing but rust and faint recollections. Of Griffith I say nothing. He is not only an Unspeakable but also Welsh. This has always meant that communication between us has been at best difficult, not to be encouraged. Bletchley, stop stamping out dog-ends under the gaze of your nursing nymphet and pay attention. Better it is for us by far, surely, that these notions of hanky-panky be for a while set aside and that we address ourselves in good order to praise and bless this gaudy green chamber. This kip, grill, pisshole and knocking shop. This sanctuary, strip-joint, lunatic asylum, pub, retreat and pillowed limbo. Gentlemen, I charge you. In honour of this room and the hospitality it has ever afforded, and to scare off those who cannot bear the sound nor sight of it, we shall give a burst of "The Cuckoo".'

As we decorously lower strides, pyjamas and kilt, I spot the Mexican cricketer poised between window ledge and *Ride a Cock Horse.* He is summoning up the blood and rubbing his elbows. Probably he cracked them on the timber when he hit the stage. It hurts woefully unless one is very pissed. Let's hope the lad has been sensible. Bletchley twirls a brolly, property to his shuffling, but switches it off as we form our line, and even the Redcoat holds his peace. One, two, three, we melodiously sing.

> A queer bird the cuckoo
> It sits in the grass,
> Its wings neatly folded

Its beak up its arse.
From this queer position
It seldom doth flit,
For it's hard to sing Cuckoo
With a beak full of shit


## KING HENRY THE FOURTH, PART TWO
*Gloucestershire, before Justice Shallow's house*

In fact, we are in the drawing room of the old house some hours after our party cracked up. Most guests are filtered away but a remainder few are piled up in odd rooms about the place. Some are alive, some less so, some are either in or out of a uniform, Ron, Jim and I we sit and sip and puff and chunter out our paraphrased version of this scene from Shakespeare, playing Falstaff, Shallow, Bardolph, Silence and all, a scene which throughout this past decade and more we have found ourselves often rehearsing.

SHALLOW: And I may say to you we knew where the best bona robas were, and had the best of them at all commandment. Then was Jack Falstaff, now Sir John, a boy. I see him break Scoggins' head at the court gate, when 'a was a crack not thus high; and the very same day did I fight with one Sampson Stockfish, a fruiterer, behind Gray's Inn. Jesu, Jesu, the mad days that I have spent! and to see how many of my old acquaintance are dead!
SILENCE: We shall all follow, cousin.
SHALLOW: Certain, 'tis certain; very sure, very sure. Death, as the Psalmist saith, is certain to all; all shall die. Is old Double of your town living yet?
SILENCE: Dead, sir.
SHALLOW: Jesu, Jesu, dead! 'A drew a good bow; and dead! 'A

shot a fine shoot. John a Gaunt loved him well and betted much money on his head. And is old Double dead?

FALSTAFF: I am glad to see you well, good Master Robert Shallow. Come, I will drink with you. I am glad to see you, by my troth, Master Shallow.

SHALLOW: Oh, Sir John, do you remember since we lay all night in the windmill in St George's Field?

FALSTAFF: No more of that, Master Shallow, no more of that.

SHALLOW: Ha, 'twas a merry night. And is Jane Nightwork alive?

FALSTAFF: She lives, Master Shallow.

SHALLOW: Doth she hold her own well?

FALSTAFF: Old, old, Master Shallow.

SHALLOW: Nay, she must be old; she cannot choose but be old; certain she's old. Ha, Cousin Silence, that thou had'st seen that that this knight and I have seen! Ha, Sir John, said I well?

FALSTAFF: We have heard the chimes at midnight, Master Shallow.

SHALLOW: Peter Finch, lives he?

JIMSTAFF: Dead, sir.

RONALD: Jesu, is 'a gone? By the rood, Finchy gone. 'A took a fine snap of your cow in the dark a.m. with Monty Clift as his photographic assistant.

ALL: He did, by the rood, he did, Goddamn and pass the paint thinner.

RONALD: The brute did grin in its stall and bare its gnashers so, its eyes wide and perplexed. 'Twas a rare snap. And is old Finchy brownbread?

ALL: Brownbread, sir, dead, and is worm meat.

RONALD: He gave a brave account of your kangaroo to the Los Angeles Police Department. He did bound and leap so, with his paws pressed under his chops and singing, 'Tie Me Kangaroo Down, Sport,' that the coppers pulled their pistols on him. I played a blinder that night, let me tell you, pleading with the nasties not to shoot the mad bugger. It was lucky that he was let live to die at all.

ALL: 'Twas, Ron, 'twas. This stuff has no effect on me whatsoever.

RONALD: When did we three meet, did you say?

JIMBO: One didn't. But it would have been nineteen fifty-three ish. There or thereabouts ish. Has some uncivil bastard spiked my Vera?

RONALD: Where, by the Rood, where?

ME: Anywhere between Muriel's club, the RADA, the Mandrake, the tavern at Lords cricket ground and Momma Fischer's boozer in Store Street.

RONALD: True. Olivelli's? Still there?

ME: Still.

RONALD: Not a Pizza Hut?

ME: Not yet.

RONALD: Rudolf Nureyev, prances he yet?

JIMBO: Dead, lovey, well dead.

RONALD: Jesu! is 'a gone? He shook a fine hoof, by the Rood, when he sashayed from roof to roof on the cars stacked up in a traffic jam in New York City, with dainty little Margot jetting after.

ALL: Fair flew, he did. That pleased the bogies of New York about as well as Finchy's capers did the filth in Los Angeles. Tell her to piss off.

RONALD: Who?

ALL: Whoever she is.

RONALD: Piss off, darling. And Rudy dead. A pint of plum vodka cheered him up no end. Weren't you and he, Pedro, back in the early sixties, heaved out of some nitery, some pisshole in Soho, for romping on the tables plucking wigs off the heads of dancing hostesses?

ME: We were, Ronald, we were. But 'twasn't Soho. 'Twas a town house in Belgravia and the wigs had been on the heads of rather grand ladies who were friends of the Royal Ballet.

JIMBO: Why were they wearing wigs?

ALL: 'Twas the fashion, then.

JIMBO: Well, I do wish someone had had the goodness to tell me. That may account for the difference in their appearance one noticed when they glared at one from the pillow.

RONALD: We have heard the chimes at midnight.

ALL: That we have, that we have, that we have; in faith, Sir Ronald, we have.

RONALD: Nineteen fifty-three, you say?

ALL: We do, Ronnie, we do.

RONALD: James Villiers? Does he live?

JIMBO: He does, Ron, he does.

RONALD: Peter O'Toole?

ME: Alive, Uncle Ron, alive.

RONALD: Ronald Fraser?

ALL: Difficult to say.

SHALLOW: Jesus, the days that we have seen! 'Fifty-three, you say? Come, come.

———————

BERNARD SHAW gave me a welcome wag of his green whiskers, of that you may be sure, when I wandered through the door under the glower and the grin of Melpomene and Thalia and nodded to the Epstein head of him on its plinth below the branching staircase in the hall of the Royal Academy of Dramatic Art.

Nineteen fifty-three and whooping, 'We done the bugger!' the Nepalese Sherpa Tensing had shimmied up the remainder few feet of Everest, had joined his companion climber perching on its top, the New Zealander Edmund Hillary, and there they both had stood; conquerors of the highest mountain on earth. Refreshed, perhaps, by a sprinkle from the fountain of honour, the first jockey to be knighted, Sir Gordon 'Bighead' Richards, up on the five to one favourite Pinza, had scampered home to clock up his first win in the Derby. His cap at the tilt, the great sportsman of my childhood, Len Hutton, had skippered England to victory at cricket over Australia in this year of my young manhood, stuffing them in the final Test and thus retaining the Ashes. In two disputes over his title, the Rock himself, Marciano, had in short order put to bye-byes Jersey Joe Walcott and Roland La Starza to remain heavyweight champion of the world and here in my donkey jacket stand I, ten days late for my first term at the RADA, and trying to listen as Sergeant very kindly marks my card on such matters as what forms I should fill in, where I should present myself, to whom I should report and the location of the hook on which I should hang up my donkey jacket but, alas, there is that about which distracts my concentration from his precise flow of information.

Nor is it merely my noticing for the first time the works of art which keep GBS company. The paintings of Henry the Eighth, Queen Katherine, Irene Vanbrugh, Sarah Bernhardt and Herbert Beerbohm Tree playing the fiddle. No. Fine objects though they be, there are yet other works of both art and nature wandering through this hall from the side, underneath and in front of these wholly splendid daubings. One such is a beautiful Indian girl flowing gracefully about the place, wrapped all in a sari of fine pink silk. Another is a pair of jeans, the first I ever saw, exquisitely occupied by a fair-haired and pretty American lady amply filling a heaving red sweater, too, and who smiles at me as she passes by having softly yelped a friendly 'Hi'. Who's this? Green-eyed and tall, tossing a long mane of vivid black curls about the shoulders of her expensively tailored, charcoal-coloured suit, bright gold gleaming from her hands ears and neck, an astonishingly elegant young woman has entered the hall and now confidently walks across it on the highest of high heels.

Sergeant is, perhaps, repeating helpful instructions to me but, really, I ask you, could you if you were me properly take it all in? Could you? All of it? Do you see, hadn't I only days ago been spewing my ring up into a bucket when protecting innocent codfish from lawless predators? Hadn't my poor young body been heaving about aboard an armed corvette lurching through rough, black and Icelandic waters? My retching vigils over fishes done, hadn't I been pitched ashore, been given asylum in a grim naval barracks, read with joy the telegram from my parents telling of my scholarship to the RADA, shared this happy news with my companions, mariners all, salt-soaked, hairy-arsed, and listened to the crude tunes of their responses? 'Didn't realize you were a brown hatter, skin.' 'Opportunities for getting your end away should, horse, increase considerably.' 'Have tits grafted on your shoulderblades, lofty, you'll earn a fortune.'

Putting aside this lewdness and irrelevance to my proper purposes and realizing I was a week and more adrift from the kick-off of the autumn term, I had jumped on the first rattler going up the line to London and clocked in at a seamen's hostel there. Not having the ghost of a notion of what went on in dramatic academies, royal or otherwise, perhaps I had mused on possible methods employed in them to reveal latent histrionic abilities. To be sure, perhaps I had thought, there would certainly be the regular rigours of voice technique, of stagecraft, of exercises in movement, of the study and learning of parts, and, perhaps I had surely thought, there would be the books, persons, disciplines which owned centuries-old formulae to construct and make whole these scattered fragments of wish and wonder and feeling which roamed unchecked around one's being, but my chief concern had been to scoop up for myself some threads.

Sailor suits were surely not the wear at academies royal, my own clothes were far far away and so, having parked my dittie bag at the Church of Turkey, as kips for sailors were by us known, I went scuttling round the alleys underneath the arches south of the river seeking presentable gear. An Army and Navy surplus store came up with sturdy underwear, socks, two pairs of loose-fitting but serviceable trousers, a belt, a transparent plastic raincoat and a couple of what were described as 'lumberjack' shirts. A trip across the river realized a brace of jackets, one corduroy the other flannel, a bit cheery but affordable and they nearly fitted. A few ties joined them in their carrier bags, my sailor's shoes would do for a while, my new and unusual plumes would see me through for a week or two, and so back across the river I went tripping, aware, though, that chill winter was setting in and what I chiefly lacked was a warm topcoat.

It was between the Old Vic and Waterloo station that I found it, my donkey jacket, on display in the window of another surplus store. Toggles it had, not buttons, and it looked and felt to me as I tried it on to be a sturdy garment, black, roomy, singular in cut, raffish even, with big patch pockets, a large snug collar and ideal, surely, for a hard-working drama student to sport when wrapping up against the sleeted nip. One had seen its like before, of course, often on the fore and after decks of merchant ships and in dockyards, usually worn by men who manned auxiliary steam pumps known as donkey engines, whence the jacket took its name, and one which for some reason I had always fancied wearing. Now here stand I in the hall of the RADA, myself and my irregular finery wrapped up all in a donkey jacket, refreshed, as you may imagine, after deep kip in my cot at the Church of Turkey, followed by a long soak in the bubbling tub there and, having shaved and combed and dressed, feeling fit as I have ever felt to present myself to any and all occasions.

Not ready for this though, Sergeant, not ready at all. Yes, Sergeant, of course I'm listening, first go to Nana Brown and register and then to the bursar, yes, the principal may wish to see me so make an appointment with his secretary, yes, I've got that, have you clocked that little sweetheart with the wide blue eyes and the silver crucifix dangling down to her breasts? Rainbow Corner you call it, that nook there with the pigeon holes arranged in alphabetical order. We get our post there, do we? Hello, kitten, in your leotard and carrying a sword. This is alarming, Sergeant, alarming, and in no way could I have been ready for any of this. I see, those are little coloured oblong articles and we shove them into the slots provided when we arrive in the building, do we, and tug them out when we leave? Shouldn't be too difficult, Sergeant, but, Lord have mercy on us all, that's the loveliest woman that ever I saw in my entire puff, old stripey, she's wearing an extremely posh fur coat and has just winked at me! Could, I ask you, any of us have been ready for this? I have died and gone to heaven. Coming, Sergeant, running all the way. Good morning, Miss Brown. Forgive my arriving so late but I've been bouncing about the dip protecting fishes for the Queen.

In 1953 the Royal Academy of Dramatic Art admitted into its two-year course seventy-seven students. Forty-six men and thirty-one women chosen from eighteen different nationalities. The constituents of this total, either in gender or in nationalities, had varied little from the entrants of 1952 and the pattern would similarly be repeated in 1954. From term to term considerable winnowing would reduce these numbers of students but what it boiled down to was that between 1953 and 1955 there had been an international heap of a hundred or so men and women milling about the building in Gower Street and we blokes were outnumbered by the birds. Really, now, who could possibly have been ready for that?

My donkey jacket safely pegged up in the cloakroom, clad all in my own light and careless livery, feeling at once exhilarated, bemused, determined, and ignorantly confident, I accompanied the severe elderly tall figure of Nana Brown who led me up the stairs to the doorway of a room. We paused outside, Nana cocked an ear, I cocked an ear, we heard a rich voice from inside announcing, I fancy, 'There's no news at the court, sir, but the old news: that is, the new Duke is banished by his younger brother the old Duke; that sounds improbable; it's more likely that the old Duke was banished by his younger brother the new Duke, yes, I think Shakespeare would prefer that and so do I, so do you, so do any of us if we've any sense and so, Nell, love, I think I'd better start again, don't you?' The voice ripped into a ripe laugh, chuckles came from others to accompany it, Nana hammered at the door, opened it and into the room we both marched.

A large room, lightful, long wide windows and lit lamps, some twenty young men and women standing or sitting or lolling around, a few on the window ledges, more on chairs, three or four on the floor, their backs propped against walls, others standing, a purposeful voltage humming about but relaxed, cheerful, easy. A quiet chatter started up from the young group as Nana B. introduced me to the teacher, Miss Nell Carter, a lady of frail show, considerable seasons showing in her features and tall slender frame, but whose eyes behind their spectacles gazed out brightly blue, seeming at once to be both watchful and far, far away. Many years later it delighted me to learn that in 1905 Miss

Nell Carter had made her first appearance on the stage playing Peal-a-belle in *Bluebell in Fairyland.* Perfectly fitting, it seems to me, for despite the forthright clatter in her surname and, as I was to learn, a worldliness of manner and a sophisticated brevity in her dealings and statements to us students, I think I have not yet met anyone less earthy than Nell Carter.

Having delivered tardy me to the place deemed proper by the academy authorities, Nana Brown stamped muttering away, exited the room, and drama student O'Toole, P., twenty-one years of age, lately of oceans deep, self-consciously stood among strangers determined on only these few matters: he would be calm and would control all nervousness, awkwardness and natural impulsiveness; he would patiently observe all systems and disciplines of learning; when his time to contribute came he would bring to it all his study, all his care; in the meantime he would be keeping his eyes open and his gob shut.

Standing there, about to dispense nods, smiles, glowers or grins to the young men and women assembled, it came as a bit of a shock to hear Nell Carter saying, in effect, that we were rehearsing *As You Like It*, Shakespeare, did I know the play?; no, but I've seen a performance of it; good, well, the play has been already cast, the parts of Rosalind, Celia, the Dukes Frederick and Senior, Jaques, Orlando and Touchstone have been divided between a number of students who are each playing them in different scenes of the five acts; yes, I see, Miss Carter, give everyone a fair crack at the whip; but that other parts such as Corin, Silvius, Phebe, Audrey, etc., are being played by one student for each part, we've been wondering what you looked like; oh really?; because we've saved the part of Oliver for you; well, now, there, then that was thoughtful; you know, Oliver the unpleasant elder brother of Orlando, redeemed by the forest and his love for Celia, whom he thinks to be Aliena; yes, that's it, redeemed by the forest and his love for whatshername, yes, unpleasant elder brother of Flyblown; lovely play, don't you think?; not half; we've just reached the point at the beginning of the play where Charles the Wrestler enters your scene with Orlando and old Adam, so, students, we'll start again from the top, this is Peter O'Toole the missing Oliver, you won't have a copy so I'll loan you this Arden, much the best edition, don't you think?; it's a daisy; be sure you buy one before you go home this evening, enter from stage right and come straight down to face your brother, right everyone, Act One Scene One, curtain going up, curtain up.

About five years ago I'd seen the play, had barely understood a word of it, had been furtively trying to touch up Rita from the pie shop, and all I remembered of it was Donald Wolfit wearing motley and speaking incomprehensible sentences while waving about a bladder on a stick. Scrabbling through pages of the Arden, looking for Act One Scene One, I blundered towards the far left-hand corner of the room. Yes, there he is, Oliver, second page, 'Now, sir! What make you here?', coming after Orl says, 'Go apart, Adam, and thou shalt hear how he will shake me up.'

The room stills and there is a silence. From where I stand glaring at the book, two young men detach themselves, one has bent himself over and shuffles shakily, the other walks upright, boldly, and speaks out clearly, 'As I remember, Adam, it was upon this fashion bequeathed me by will, but poor a thousand crowns,' and on, one supposes, to the end of the speech, after which, presumably, the bent shuffler will say, 'Yonder comes my master, your brother.' Yes, on goes Orl, speaking out uninterruptedly in his clear voice and not carrying the book. He's approaching the end, it will soon be my turn. 'I will no longer endure it, though yet I know no wise remedy how to avoid it.' 'Yonder comes my master,' wheezes the bent shuffler, 'your brother.' It's my turn. Deep breath. Forward saunter I, all ease and power, shoot a stare at Adam, nail Orl with a look of hard contempt, take another deep breath and enquire, 'Now, thir! what make you here,' fucking lisp!, 'Nothing:' says Orl, 'I am not taught to make any thing.' My turn. 'What mar you then, thir?', yes; alas; on; 'Marry, sir, I am helping you to mar that which God made,' begins Orl in answer to Oli's enquiry and during which rejoinder I dart a squint at the text only to find, yes, another little bugger waiting for me, 'a poor unworthy brother of yours, with idleness' ends Orl's reply to brother Oli, and it's my turn yet again, 'Marry, thir, be better employed and be naught awhile.' Lord love him, in the opening exchanges of *As You Like It*, Shakespeare has Oliver address his brother Orlando as 'sir' no less than six times. As the scene orders between the two brothers a little scuffle, grunt and grab, suiting the action to the word, the word to the action had carefully to be arranged. This, of course, involved my thaying the word thir more timeth than theveral. Or so I believed, and as I have often found, if you believe you have it you have it. No one, it turned out, save me, had noticed my lisp. Or said they had noticed my lisp. It surely went unremarked but then it would, wouldn't it, for we all were novices, painfully self-aware and preoccupied in mustering up the courage to reveal what talent we had, or had not, and to put it down in public.

My thene with Orlando on its feet, the next number involved Oliver's chat with Charles the Wrestler, which begins with Oliver saying, 'Good Monsieur Charles, what's the new news at the new court,' and Charles responding, 'There's no news at the court, sir, but the old news', the speech which through the door Nana Brown and I had heard being so confidently, hilariously busked. It had been impossible not to notice the young chap playing Charles, even as I had entered the room dutifully trotting at the heels of Nana Brown. Tall, broad-shouldered, strong limbs moving in athletic grace, copper-nobbed with the merriest pair of blue twinklers set in square-cut attractive features, his manner easy, intelligent, larky and strong, he fair buzzed with a confident energy. Finney was his name, Albert Finney, a bold young puppy of a bloke, straight out of school, not yet eighteen, he was years younger than I, a mere lad. A gulf of three or four years between young men of twenty or so is massive and yet talent, which, as I believe the French say, is a gift secretly given to us by God and which we reveal without perceiving it, came tumbling untroubled from his frame across that wide gap of years and within minutes we had set to enjoying ourselves hugely.

Think of that. Sixty or so minutes only in the building, my eyes had been tugged from their tethers by the sight of lovely and exotic lasses wandering hither and yon, I'd officially signed on as a drama student, had been tossed into my first ever rehearsal of a play by Shakespeare, one which I scarcely knew, found my thick tongue unwilling to point up at sharp sibilances, had felt a prize ass, helped arrange a small shuffle of physical combat, rehearsed punctiliously and was now cheerfully working with this carrot-haired young rover, clearly a fine actor, one for whom I immediately felt the warmth of affection, an affection between us which has remained undiminished in despite of forty years' bruises, buffets and the often cruel vicissitudes inherent in this lovely hard old game that we both play.

---

NOT THAT ALBIE had been the only noticeable figure in the rehearsal throng, others soon came into clear focus, men as well as women, but the living fact that women made up the majority, and of that majority many there were who were handsome of form and of feature, made an unbiased view of my fellow students a difficult one successfully to balance. Without doubt, one was delighted to see that Bob, my fellow auditionee, he of the ready silver cigarette case, counsellor on matters higher educational and obliging owner of the rare motor car, too had made it. There can be no question but that one took an interest in the cut of the long slim student with the cultured voice and way who in the first act was playing the melancholy Jaques; a man, as I would learn, of charm and a contemplative intellect, but who among you would have heaved the first half brick at the lovely girl of darkling looks distributing about the room in an effortless sensuality the rounded dips and swoops of her sweet body? Not I. Certainly not I. It had taken all my trouble all my care to prevent her from snatching the eyes from my stretching sockets as she moulded her mind to will them into a frank and openly shameless gaze at her, but it would be harsh of us who are not without sin, surely, to allot all blame to her. God had made her the dainty plum she was and me to find the flesh of such fruit toothsome; a juicy prize indeed to pluck. True it is, too, that after a tugging while the lady's will had prevailed, had gently, firmly turned my noggin round and made me look into her dark eyes, under her dark hair, to find there an amused and fine regard set glowing in her high-boned face above the smile on the full lips of her mouth. Have mercy on us, my sweet laminated Jesus, we know the readiness is all but who among us, pray, could have been ready for all or, indeed, any of this?

Came lunchtime and relief as I joined the streams of boys and girls coming up or going down the stairs and pressed my way below to see the principal's secretary, who told me that her governor wished to see me. When? Now. Oh. Knock knock. 'Enter.' Sir Kenneth Barnes rose growling from his seat behind the desk, shook my hand, growled, sat down again, looked at me strangely, as though he'd never seen me before, wasn't too keen on seeing me now and wasn't wholly convinced that he wanted ever to see me again. Of respect for the theatre he growled, which insists on one respecting oneself, which argues one must know oneself in order to respect oneself or not, which demands a proper self-consciousness, yes, self-consciousness, not prattling or posing or blushing or showing off but developing a consciousness of self, to recognize one's defects, one's strengths, one's weaknesses, one's powers, one's limitations, one's possibilities, and unstintingly to put oneself to all the tests, disciplines and examinations one would encounter in the terms ahead. Make that your purpose here at the RADA, he growled, to develop a proper consciousness of self. Know yourself. The watchword of Apollo.

His face seemed to me to have gripped and gnarled itself into an expression one might easily have found in the features of a displeased medieval bishop but of a sudden it relaxed and released from its iron folds a smile of rare sweetness as he stood, shook my hand, wished me well, and then lowered himself back into his seat, the while rumbling out a series of low-pitched savage grunts.

Buoyed up by this blessing on what I had thought to be no more than a ragged nonsense in myself, this uncertainty, this doubt, these clumsy lunges at an art and craft which I could see and hear but did not know how to touch, I fair bounced out of the principal's study, into the office of his charming secretary where the pair of us cooked up a plan. Lodgings: a tidy spot, one providing modest comfort, peace, good grub and that did one's laundry was deemed necessary and the darling knew of such a place. A twiddle and a chunter on the dog and bone, phone, and the little beauty had produced what seemed the very hole. A room of my own, breakfast and an evening meal, companionship of fellow students, a trip of thirty minutes by public transport, bed and food all in, costing only a quarter of my monthly living allowance, payable in advance, laundry extra and the digs were of good report. 'Meredith, we're in!' Next, bank, bookshops, specialist shops for special togs and bobs and bits, all within walking distance of the academy, these and their addresses were jotted down for me on a piece of paper by my lady bountiful. As this and other relevant RADA literature, including my schedule of studies, was being folded into my pockets, the dear advised me to take the rest of the day off, calmly to sort myself out and to tuck myself in. Solid advice, in my view, for I had clocked in, was in shock, needed an hour or two to ingest and ponder on the intangibles and the glorious tangibles leaping about the joint and my friend the secretary assured me that the academy was a tolerant establishment, one whose teaching staff knew a good deal about young men and women fetching up in cities strange to them and looking for somewhere to lay their heads as they began the business of becoming novice actors and actresses. She would advise my teachers of what I was up to, all would be well. Lovely lady, Mary P.

Armoured in my stout donkey jacket, pennies stashed, a happy clink to keep one pocket happy, the Arden *As You Like It* in another, I skipped down the spooky spiral staircase at grubby old Goodge Street tube station, and was soon standing waiting on the dingy platform there. Underground, I had been advised, was the speedier way to navigate from A to B in London and so it proved. The rumble and the heavy press of warm air bashed on before it violently announced the imminent arrival of the hurtling electrical subway train, and seconds later, spitting sparks and clatter, out from the tunnel's throat shot the clanking great animal. It stopped, the doors swished open, I jumped on, the doors swished shut, the beast jolted, started forward and minutes later, after this nightmare funfair ride, I was plodding through the press at Waterloo station. A street map and a guide book joined Shakespeare and the Queen's yellow in my pockets, a pint of plain, a pork pie and a puff of a cigarette did me nicely for lunch, and I headed off to lay aside my old hat and to say farewell to my hairy-arsed brothers rolling about the Church of Turkey.

Forty years on, the whirling jumble of events so rapidly served up at me on that my first day at drama school still cheerfully bob about in my mind. A lot of blood has flowed under the lamp post since those fair days but the memories of all that dotty bustle live on in me, young, whole and unwounded.

Next stop had been my arrival at the recommended digs. A large house in north London, it had a civil if somewhat aloof landlady, a neat little bedroom for me, several communal bathrooms, a large airy dining room with separate tables, each wearing white tablecloths and set to accommodate four lodgers per table. The place was clearly well organized, well dusted, tidy and had plenty of rules. Rules handwritten on strategically pinned up white cards. Rules about switching on and switching off lights, rules about gas fires, bathroom boilers, turning off water taps, flushing lavatories; rigidly to be observed rules on the exact times when breakfast and dinner would be served, unbreakable commandments stating that the door admitting customers would be firmly locked at eleven p.m. and that under no circumstances would lodgers be allowed to entertain guests in this establishment. Strict, all this, but what of that? Wasn't I here to study and sleep and work and eat and think and rest, forswear misconduct, live a healthy, industrious life with companions of similar bent, law-abiding, diligent and sober?

True it is that having unpacked and hung up my scanty gear, my head was soon over the play and my part in it, breaking my brains on the scholarly introduction, the play's history, appendices, the multiplicity of notes on connotations and textual variations piled up thick at the bottom of each page, and the patient drudge of repeating and memorizing the lines. It is true, too, that I rose early, ate my breakfast at the appointed time, travelled to the academy, found a few more bearings, learned a little more of the ropes, returned to the digs, chewed my grub at the designated hour, went to my room, studied, pondered, muttered and slept. What is also true is that all my fellow lodgers were males, most of these males were from overseas, few seemed to be interested in a chat or a chuckle or a game of gangster poker, many appeared to be prim, perhaps inhibited, possibly tight-arsed and none of the dull bastards would join me in a stroll to the pub for a refreshing pot of sherbet. Still and all, after three days my part of Oliver had been studied, was happily rammed into my head, was tripping more easily on the increasingly supple tissue of my tongue and my way to the academy found me feeling light of heart and dangerously well.

---

My CLASS was rehearsing those scenes from *As You Like It* in which Oliver does not feature; as these scenes tot up to being practically the entire concert, it seemed to me that a ramble round the building would while away an amiable hour and would allow me to give the premises an educative, thorough snoop. Past experiences had demonstrated to me that fire escapes can serve purposes other than that of fleeing from flames and I had earlier noticed a cluster of the handy articles running up and down in the space between the two buildings which constituted the RADA, one with its entrance in Gower Street, the other in parallel Malet Street.

Below the base of the iron numbers zig-zagging up the backs of the buildings stood the boiler house, its stoker standing outside exchanging fumes of furnace coalfire for a gulp of rancid, autumnal London air, a draw of a cigarette to comfort his lungs, and with whom I had a chat. The hosts of builders, he explained to me, that one could see shoving wheelbarrows, carting about planks, humping sacks of cement and generally screwing and hammering and sawing on the roofs and in the approaches to the Malet Street building, were workmen employed in putting the last few months' knockings on the new theatre which had been built there. To commemorate and honour Sir Kenneth's late sisters, the actresses Irene and Violet, the theatre was to be called the Vanbrugh, a stage name by which both ladies had been known, would be on the site of the old Malet Street theatre destroyed by German bombs in the blitz of 1941, and, if all involved in the construction got a wriggle on, it was to be hoped that the theatre would be in business by the late summer of 1954.

Stoker returned to his shovel, coal and boiler while by duck-board, ladder and fire escape I took myself on a wandering tour of general inspection.

Careful carpentry had fitted and joined timbers and, though it lacked a curtain, the stage of the theatre had been almost completed; there wasn't yet a seat in place but indubitably I was gazing out on an auditorium; no mirrors in the dressing rooms, no scenery in the scene docks, no ropes and pulleys on the fly floor, no lights, no stage manager, no prompter, no actors in the wings, only me, I fancy, waiting for the chippies and the brickies and the labourers and the painters and the plasterers to give the cue that their moiling was done and the playhouse could open. Odd, do you not find, that this theatre had been newly built for a place in which the likes of me could practise and watch and learn their trade of acting and that with the making of this fine new playhouse nearly done I should at that moment stand on those bare boards who in his life had trod a stage no more than on a dozen or so nights? Well, find what you will, I found it odd, yet exhilarating, and the oddness in the exhilaration fair bounded me up the fire escape, past large vacant rooms set above the stage, feeling at once curiously proprietorial and stone bald lucky. Delighted I was to find that the final zig after the last zag of this high, iron animal I had climbed spilled out onto the flat and spacious roof protecting the Malet Street end of the RADA's habitation. Untroubled, lively and alone I was up there high over Bloomsbury so, after a quick squint at the Arden from the pocket of my donkey jacket, I gave the White Odeon, University College London, to the right of my viewpoint, the full benefit of my carefully studied part as Oliver in *As You Like It.* 'Neither call the giddiness of it in question, the poverty of her, the small acquaintance, my sudden wooing, nor her sudden consenting; but thay with me'. Fuck.

My trip back to the Gower Street end took me over wooden walkways, roofs, sundry minor hurdles, and found me scaling yet another fire escape. These choices of unorthodox access to the premises, you will surely understand, had been made for reasons which were both good and weighty: a temporary block would be put on my habit when walking the normal routes of having an open-mouthed drool at half the student body, while, with luck, I would be let play the burglar's part and give the establishment an unguided, unarrested, proper casing.

A fair deal of loitering regularly interrupted my ascent as rising frosted-glass window upon rising frosted-glass window allowed through reinforced meshed frames muted hoots from drama students. 'I am the very model of a modern major general, I've information vegetable, animal and mineral,' announced one window, telling me that some child was letting rip a rattle-toothed burst of Gilbert and Sullivan. Surprise which turned to a quiet chuckle touched me as from a higher window came softly sounding a voice, 'A fool, a fool! I met a fool i' the forest,    A motley fool'. It was my mob toiling through the Forest of Arden in a room between Bloomsbury and Fitzrovia and with Jaques in full cry. Tra la! Up the iron I go, up I go. Clang, clatter. On-guard. Quatre. Tierce. Clash, cut, swish, swipe. A fencing lesson. Up. 'Many many men, marching singing and ringing.' 'All together now.' 'Many many men, marching singing and ringing.' Voice production. Up. Another roof. The roof of Gower Street. Oh, I like this roof. It is a smaller, more intimate roof, comfortably flat as the other but with nooks and cosy corners to it. No, I shan't give my Oliver, not here, no, I shall sit on the roof, my back against this air vent, black, the shape of an upturned saxophone and smoke a peaceful cigarette. This is a charming roof, a present spot for privacy, selective assembly and a decent loll about.

My reflective puff over and what's this? A door. Through the door, down stone steps and I'm in the canteen! I have reconnected myself to the ordinary ways of going up down round and about the academy, nor shall I linger long in this canteen. It is a canteen like all the other canteens in which from the war years on I have sat and chewed my Spam and snoek and reconstituted egg. The grub here is all right, I've tried it, it's edible, served in ample quantity, not expensive, the company is cheerful but the sight of the serviceable linoleum floor on which sit the bare synthetic tables and the spindly plastic chairs is redolent of the rule of austerity and puritanism which throughout these post-war years has had hard grips on us in England, and from whose soft-palmed, hard-boned holy clench we here in 1953 are beginning to prise ourselves free.

Away, then, from what during the war had been called Utility furniture, down the warmly light-coloured stone stair, past the wooden doors of Sir Kenneth's private elevator, on to the black and white chequered stone tiles of the landing and the three blunt corridors jutting from it, leading to impressive, stout-timbered classroom doors with brass knobs to them. Yes, a whiff of the institutional is here, but one made sweet by light flowing through the twenty-four white frames of bright glass which compose a large and lovely Georgian sash window. See, as down we go, from another great rectangle of a window, light gives a deep glow to the oakwood doors and handrail on the slim black iron struts of the descending banister, cream-painted walls and, always, the warm hard stone. See the flourish of bright rails and stairs leading to the Lady Stirling Room as down we go to where the walls of the corridors and the stairways and the landings sport paintings, drawings, photographs, sculptures. See, now, the railings run to curve, the windows are bowed, and the rooms roam elegantly away in trefoils from the landing.

Gilded and geometrical, fleurs-de-lis point proudly from within thin twists of shining black iron rails but, see, there, dashing George Alexander as the Count of Monte Cristo, Faith Celli as the Dream Daughter, the bust of John Hare as Goldfinch. See on her photograph the strong sad face of young Meggie Albanesi, remark that the majority of men in the academy wear suits, that the few who don't, such as I, rather prefer their tailors to cut them the neat match of jacket and flannels, regard the women, yes, regard the rakes of lovely women, they are all well dressed, at their best and set fair to present themselves as attractively as they are able. Down the stairs we go, down we go, past glowing oak doors holding diction classes, the Forbes Robertson Room, movement classes, lectures, the Herbert Tree Room, dancing classes, rehearsal rooms, staff rooms, the library, cloakrooms, all with gleaming brass knobs on them and here's George Bernard Shaw's room. My lot are in here giving Shakespeare a walloping. Wouldn't you know? The GBS room. Right from the off the wicked old bugger has been keeping a wonderful eye on me. Right from the off. Bong jour, mademoiselle! Commong? Hélas, je suis nouveau ici aussi, baby, si consequencemong je ne sais pas où vous pouvez trouver Professor Froeschlen, mais je sais une très belle petite spot en haut, commong dit ong roof en français? Oui, oui, certainmong, ma chère angel knickers, autre fois, oui, oui, au revoir à vous too.

Hello, here is where this quite grand central staircase branches down to the front hall. No one, neither teacher nor student, is permitted to walk either up or down these few branching stairs, why not nobody knows but for practically fifty years an unwritten law has declared them to be sacrosanct and this law is invariably respected. Time, for a while, to linger by Rainbow Corner, to see my little blue slab slotted in its spot among the greens the pinks the yellows and the reds, to look, under O, if there is any post for me, no, to listen, for a further while, to the sound of little noise at all being made by students as they move along the staircases, corridors and landings on the five storeys of the academy. To hear, certainly, tinkle of talk, quiet laughter, soft treads and shuffles, but no din, no clamour, no yahoo yells. No. Rather, I fancy, one hears a gently restrained alternative to silence as young men and women gather and group and chat and gossip and singly or severally go their ways about the place. The atmosphere of the RADA, sensed when first I had stuck an investigative nostril through the door those months ago, and whose mood and tone I still sense now these forty years on. Not, perhaps, as Ned Kean's great mate Sheridan Knowles had it in his play *Virginius*, 'a sound so fine, there's nothing lives 'twixt it and silence' but something of that nature, a something more human and young and bustling, a mood unique to my old drama school. Beyond the doors of the rehearsal and the classrooms there was, of course, as much row, jabber, sound and fury, blood-letting, shrieking, weeping, leaping and howling as one could hope to witness from dozens upon dozens of multinational young mummers as they tore their passions to tatters and made all split, but without the doors there always were these memorable, quietly tensile scuffs and murmurings.

So, my lingering done, it's a little matter of trickling down one of these here side stairs which spill out on to the hall floor and I find myself facing Sergeant's guardroom on the right of the entrance under Thalia and Melpomene. To my left is Nana Brown's room and the office of Mary P., the principal's secretary, behind me Greenwhiskers is quizzically studying my conduct, while to my right are the two rooms in which work my darling Patsy B. and the lady bursar. The she who keeps the pennies polished. Facing them is Sir Kenneth's study. But who is this chap lying on the floor, sleepy and contentedly scratching himself? It's Masher, that's who it is, a browny, blacky, floppy-eared mongrel pooch and loyal companion to his master. It's Masher, Sir Kenneth Barnes' old dog. A quiet chat with Masher, possibly of bones and the cocking of a leg in the RADA fashion, a rub of his belly and before me are a few steps leading down to a basement.

Down I go to find myself wandering through the wonders of the wardrobe. Peggy the wardrobe mistress makes me welcome and, yes, those are Elizabethan costumes, aren't they quite magnificent and in beautiful repair?, in those sliding cupboards hang Jacobean, Carolean and Georgian costumes, would you like a cup of tea?, I could murder one, many of the outfits were given to us by old actors and actresses and quite a number came from rather grand private benefactors dating back to Tree's time in 1906, yes, of course we have twentieth-century clothes. This was the coal cellar, you know, in the eighteenth and nineteenth centuries, see the arches leading right under the street?, well, on the rails fitted up there hang every conceivable type of costume: togas, crinolines, military, harlequin, rustic, courtly, those huge hampers are full of quite splendid assortments and periods, over there is what we call the Middle Ages, we'll be leaving here shortly and moving most of the costumes to our more modern and spacious premises in the new Vanbrugh theatre, I shall miss this old place, I'm sure, but it will still be used for the Little Theatre.

Now, I hadn't heard of the Little Theatre but immediately after my visit to Peggy's crisply glamorous wardrobe in the coal cellar, I hopped up, turned left, right, hopped down and entered the daunting little darling.

Darkened auditorium, small proscenium stage, lighted, unoccupied. Pert rows of stalls, a few customers only, silent, eyes on the stage. Find a seat, sit, look around. A little balcony, the stage, the stalls where I sit, at the back a box with Sir Kenneth in it, a small light focused on papers propped on an angled wooden rest before him, pencil in hand, eyes on the stage. My eyes fix on the stage. Silence. Enter a man wearing a huge ringleted curly wig, dressed in dazzling foppery, all sparkling ribbons and sashes and jewels and lace, soppy great orange garters on the hose below his puce silk breeches, and he speaks as he struts to the centre of the stage, his face a plaster of powdered makeup, rouge and made proud with a beauty spot: 'My life, madam, is a perpetual stream of pleasure, that glides through such a variety of entertainments, I believe the wisest of our ancestors never had the least conception of any of 'em. I rise, madam, about ten a-clack. I don't rise sooner, because 'tis the worst thing in the world for the complexion; nat that I pretend to be a beau; but a man must endeavour to look wholesome, lest he make so nauseous a figure in the side bax, the ladies should be compelled to turn their eyes upon the play.' Who the actor was perhaps I will never know but, as I would learn, he was performing a speech in the person of Sir Novelty Fashion, the newly created Lord Foppington, a character in John Vanbrugh's play, yes, Vanbrugh, Jung terms such happenstances 'synchronic-ity', or so I'm told, Vanbrugh's play, *The Relapse*. 'I take a turn in the chocolate-house: where, as you walk, madam, you have the prettiest prospect in the world; you have looking-glasses all raund you.' The young actor was stiff, far from at ease, certainly not blazingly confident, but will you blame the poor sod? Alone up there, dressed in togs of amazing frippery, a dirty great beauty spot, no before, no after, coming on cold, no one to talk to, no one to listen, a few only of us as audience in this hundred-seater theatre, Sir Kenneth scratching notes, providing grunts, sitting in obvious judgement, the atmosphere hardly packed, breathless, expectant. No, you will surely not blame the young man, you will rather understand the poor sod's seeming lack of ease or gusto. His voice was clearly pitched, the words were funny, an occasional gurgle of amusement came from one of the few souls who were his audience, and after his final words, 'Thus, ladies, you see my life is an eternal raund of delights', with head held rigid and uncomfortably high, awkward Lord Foppington took his beauty spot and bravely careered off into the wings. Someone mustered a handclap, subdued mutters were exchanged by two or three, the stage remained lighted, empty, bare, the theatre stilled again into solemn silence, lit by his lamp Sir Kenneth brooded hugely, and Oliver, eldest of the three sons of Sir Rowland de Boys, a character in *As You Like It*, a play by William Shakespeare, 1564–1616, in the person of his mortal representative, Mr Peter O'Toole b. 1932, realizing that up among the chimneys and the birdshit had been a fancy place indeed in which to dream, carefully moved away from the auditorium of that little theatre yearning for a cuddle and a pint.

---

IT'S SIR KENNETH, I fancy. Students, in the novel *Daniel Deronda*, George Eliot has her character, the musician Klesmer, say in reply to the request for his advice by the aspiring actress Gwendolen, that she should first unlearn 'mistaken admirations'. Growl. Sound words, students, sound advice. Grunt. It may well be that your colleagues in the Skelton Thespian Society at the Ipswich Polytechnical Institute considered that as an actor among their number you were peerless. Many of you students arrive here cherishing the memory of such excitements but beware. Snarl. Praise from parents, relatives, friends and the audiences who saw your performances as Romeo or Juliet or Antony or Cleopatra, at the various schools, colleges and dramatic societies for whom you acted, must be understood only as a recognition of possible natural talent. A talent in you, moreover, that was perhaps unexpected and therefore, in their view, all the more worthy of unqualified praise. Down, Masher, be silent. You will find that for a considerable time here at the RADA such sympathetic accolades may well be withheld from you. Natural talent is viewed here as an indispensable prerequisite in a student who wishes to make the stage his or her profession. You will find here at the RADA, or you may never find it anywhere, that in the hope of learning how to play an ancient and confoundedly difficult instrument you may in the future be equipped to earn your living; and all of mankind'singenuity has produced no artefact more laborious to master than that instrument which you have chosen: a playhouse. Down, Masher, down I say, dog, and stop slobbering. Mary Pilgrim! Miss Pilgrim, attend on me, please, immediately. To pitch your voice so as to be heard in a theatre, merely to stand or move on a stage, these basics are an art which demands disciplined dedication and practice. Here at the RADA, at first you will be accepted only on trial. Once a month, after the first term, you will be required to perform in the Little Theatre, wearing makeup and costume, a piece either of our or of your own choosing. Your blunders may be large or small but none will go unnoticed. Whatever you have learned in the classrooms, bring to your arena in the Little Theatre, for you will be assessed on the footing of skill and always subject to tests. What is it, Miss Pilgrim, for God's sake, woman, what is it? Quite. One moment. We will end, students, with some few more words on art and artists by Eliot's musician Klesmer, his imperative musts: 'I must know this exactly. I must understand this exactly. I must do this exactly. You must know what you have to strive for and you must subdue your mind to unbroken discipline, shaping the organs to a finer and finer certainty of effect. Your muscles – your whole frame – must go like a watch, true, true, true, to a hair.' Time to take Masher for his walk, Miss Pilgrim, he wishes, I believe, to do number twos.

———————

STERN CONSIDERATIONS, do you not find, offered us by our redoubtable old Principal and in that way of his, severe, precise, surprising, spilling over with mulled erudition, ever shot through with an often hilarious ordinary humanity, articulate as one could wish, brusque in expression yet a man whose voice was possessed of a barnyard repertory so that often when one waited on a word one found oneself auditor to an expiring whinny, a deeply felt moo, yet your familiar rumblingly savage grunt. His smile, too, was a rare enough event but when one showed up the fixture of his scowl was played in brightness.

With whom, you might ask, could one share a view or two on these sudden batterings by notion, talk awhile on the thud of events which had so rapidly altered the shape of one's circumstances, listen awhile to a version of the whirl of these days as received by another, sit awhile and transmogrify in outward show from deep sea bell-bottomed protector of codfish to grass-green drama student and actor aspirant decked out in a donkey jacket? Bob the reliable, as was his wont, had rapidly split the scene and so he was out. With Finney, A.? Had we not found ourselves both to be sons of bookies and hadn't we both enjoyed playing at cricket and rugby? Much between us there, much shared

experience, much discipline, labour, danger, fun and risk. With
Michael B.? Languid, the man, unfazed, collected, amused, given
to fluently uttered reflections, one with whom one might wander
into myth, watch, appalled, the pair of us, at, say, the unending
labours of Sisyphus with his burdens and wonder out loud at what
we had both let ourselves in for. No better two than those, surely,
to while away an unforgiving minute or sixty in quaint discussion
and froth?

She said she was a Hopi Indian but she wasn't, she was a
Hebrew from the windy city of Chicago. She said that on the
campus of the university in the United States from which she had
just graduated, when she was sunburnt in the summertime and
had swept her hair from a wide centre parting to tie it at the back
in a twist of braids, many on that campus had believed her to be a
Hopi not a Hebrew. I said that when she tied her tumble of black
hair into a ribboned knot at the back she looked even less like a
Hopi Indian and much more like a Hebrew from the windy city
of Chicago. As I believe up to that time I had known neither
Indian nor Chicagoan that was doubtless presumptuous but she
forgave me; a merriness came in her dark eyes to tell me so, and
the mischief of her bold grin absolved young sinful me. True it is,
too, that though she was little there was quite a lot of her and
Providence had arranged her young abundance into a symmetry
of select, scrumptious proportions. What is perhaps just as true is
that the outline of her silhouette ran in a run of such dainty
curves to taper gracefully and swell delightfully, animated all by
her vivid femininity, which made matters of origin or colour or
sophistication or savagery seem to me to be such piffle that if,
instead of arriving at the academy well groomed civilized and by
bus, my darling had worn a feather, a deerskin shift and had
galloped down Gower Street bareback on a mustang, I could
think of no one that day whom I could more willingly invite to
share with me a saucer of tea and a lie-down. However, alas, on
that Little Theatre day, Pocahontas chose not to wrap me round

in a comforting cuddle but jumped on the number 134 bronco going to Muswell Hill and left me on the Tottenham Court Road alone with my remainder longing of that day: a noted, creamy pint.

---

FOOTLOOSE, now, free from thoughts of study and unhindered by women, I knew that behind me lay a Bloomsbury no more alive with that literary and philosophical set whose lives and doings and art had titillated or infuriated and enriched a generation; that before me was Fitzrovia, that giddy northern limit to the crooked mile of Soho, a jumble of dives and drums and joints which from the thirties, throughout the war, right to the fading moment of my standing there, had in its cafés and coffee houses, its lodgings, shebeens, clubs, pubs, and knocking shops, before, during and after the bombings and the fires, given rough and tumbling refuge to my own days' troupe of poets, painters, writers, actors, musicians and had shown to them, and their companions in waywardness, a supreme tolerance and a handy knack of catering for their various needs and lusts and deep dry thirsts. The rackets were held in hands of pedigree; the Lilies of the Law toiled not a lot neither did they spin a great deal. Two rules only, it seems, obtained in that ramshackle community: whatever you are doing, do not be found out, and wherever you are, do not bore.

Gone, now, most of the men and women of those days. Gone to the peacetime sun, some, to roast their bones and compose in the shade. Gone in no uniform, others, to dales and peaks and coasts. Gone the bodies of some, killed by war, gone the promise and purpose of others, killed by war; gone to other places, other cities, other arms, the poets, painters, writers, all the feckless brood who rambled through Fitzrovia; a few, it was reported, could still be spotted in the area, none of whom had yet been killed by anything. Fitzrovia, then, Dylan Thomas my first choice but Louis MacNeice would more than do, or George Barker, Francis Bacon, who knows, Thomas Stearns Eliot to be found poking in a midden with a rolled umbrella looking for the fag ends of culture.

Olivelli's in Store Street, two or so hours later, spirits all rosy from whiskey and beer, body padded by a plate of grub, it is only fair to tell you that my scrutiny of Fitzrovia had yielded little of pith and less of moment. As I rambled out down Charlotte Street it had been gladdening to see that as food rationing ended so the lives of cafés were again beginning. Greek, Cypriot, French, even Italian and German. Schmidt's where the waiters wore long white aprons, the White Tower where the bills wore long black digits, their companion caffs, greasy spoons, nosh bars, open once again to feed the faces of the ones with pennies in their pockets. Alas and alack, I must tell you that no Louis MacNeice had been spotted slowly crumbling down to that appropriate point where pavement meets roadway and he softly singing, 'Lying in Calcutta gutter leading very happy life'. No, nor a sight of Colquhoun and MacBryde at the playing of pitch and toss. Not even in the Duke of York, the Wheatsheaf nor the Marquis of Granby had bloodied noses been seen, allotted or received, on the poetical hooters of a Sydney Graham or a Dylan Thomas. No. There had been colour, though, and cheer, qualities rare enough in this dinge of post-war England, and the ramble had had its moments. I had moved on to a pub where, on the best authority obtainable, O'Liver had given me to understand that the mighty men of ink and paint did meet and chunter and sup their ale. The first thing I'd noticed was the quaint slimness of the brass footrest at the bar and as I ordered my drink I'd realized that the pub was less ebullient than the others, altogether quieter, more restrained, the chat less rudely open but, indeed, hushed, conspiratorial even. What of that? I'd thought, We have the beer, the whiskey, and chances are that at any moment a bard will enter and his words and wants will ignite the place. 'Haven't seen you before, dearie,' said a soft crisp voice. 'Might you be looking for somebody?' There was that about my new friend which I had seen and known before. 'You must be a very saucy boy, indeed,' went on the man who so quietly had found me at the bar, 'to bring your pretty self all alone in here.' You are to understand that homosexuality was then a serious criminal offence, would for a further fourteen years remain a serious criminal offence, that meeting places for those whose amorous propensities went the other way were few, discreet, furtive, vigilant and that I had chosen to drink and bustle and blather in the bar, as I would learn, at Headquarters for Brown Hatters of the area. 'Homosexual is the right word, Joxer,' as Captain Jack nearly says in O'Casey's *Juno and the Paycock*, 'but brown hatter is what the sailors said.' 'O, it's a darlin' word, Captain,' says Joxer, 'a darlin' word.' Perhaps sensing that my solicitous enquirer might be dismayed to be told that I was rather hoping to come across Lucian Freud dancing a rhumba with Edith Sitwell, I prattled of nothing at all, swilled back my drink, bade all farewell and set off to find food. My way to Olivelli's had been made interesting by my discovery that not only was my heart light but so was my head and the pathways had give in them. So here you find me, hunger blunted by a dish of pasta, at one with the world and humankind, merry, elevated, charmed to find that a study of my map and my guide-book has prompted in me a wish to walk in as straight a line as I am able from Store Street to the river Thames by alley, lane, court and yard, thus avoiding all but two main roads.

Here we go, then, and a right and a right has set us on our road. Lit from a street, see the great shapes of trees stretching their arms in a London square as we leave them to walk through a slim cobbled lane to find bulking up hugely on our left the British Museum. We are progressing well. Time for a drink. Impressive, this pub, wooden pillars, upholstered seatings, brass footrail thick and shining, nicotine's umber patina on the delicately plastered ceiling, cheerful drinkers lit by large fancy lamps, yes, we're on course. There is a lane immediately to our left; this should spill us right into the vicinity of what once was Rat's Castle, in the eighteenth and nineteenth centuries a wretched shambles of an area. Dickens had used to alarm the odd acquaintance by conducting them on tours of the manor. Your lower class of criminal thug had bedded down in the reek here, where gin shops had advertised 'Drunk for a penny. Dead drunk for twopence. Straw free'. Let's pop in here for the one. Wonderfully scruffy little boozer. Rowdy and crammed. Excellent. Now, there's a cobbled court and then a yard which should lead into Seven Dials, and so it does, Seven Dials, for centuries the homeland of an altogether higher class of criminal, and whose hideaways squatted down among the printing houses which produced the scrofulous ballad and broadsheets popular up to the twentieth century. We'll have just the one. Barrels rolled up behind a horseshoe-shaped bar, double purchase provided by brass foot and hand rails; stained glass to colour snug little nooks; etchings of men wearing top hats; spiffing little pub, one in which, if we didn't have a journey still to go, a man might sit and contentedly suck his juice.

Which way now? No trouble. Jink from cobbled yard to cobbled court, side-step into the alley, dart down the half gap of the lane and hand off the approaching lamp post. Where are we? Repeat the manoeuvre. Done. Here is a fair thread of ginnel, through we go, wind along and to my happy surprise find that we are approaching Covent Garden. Mission in sight of accomplishment. There's St Paul's, the actors' church, built by Inigo Jones in the seventeenth century and whose pillared frontage serves as the setting for the first scene of Bernard Shaw's *Pygmalion*. Of course. You won't let me out of your sight, GBS, will you? You're now shoving the scenery from your plays in my path. It is to be doubted, though, whether this choice of liquor as my companion on the zigzagging navigation from Gower Street to the river will have met with your unqualified approval. And yet I don't know. You, too, were once young and fecund and you had the curiosity.

On we go. Down the street and across the wide Strand. Here's a pub. It's the Coal Hole. It was Edmund Kean's local. It stands at the head of a stepped and a narrow alley. We shall walk down the steps through the narrowness to find at their end the embankment of old river Thames. Mission accomplished. There she flows. Nippy. Back up through the narrows of the alley and here's a door which leads down to the cellarage and into Edmund Kean's Coal Hole. It is a large whitewashed brick cavern crammed with customers and large barrels. Is this how I had imagined it to be? Difficult to say, but then by now saying anything is proving to be difficult. Swaying is quite easy and I have obviously been articulate enough to muster up beer and whiskey for they are even now sliding down my exploring throat but there isn't anywhere to sit or to lean and the standing lacks purchase. Better by far, surely, to keep moving, to blunder in the direction of St Martin's Lane and, although there no longer lives the Little St Martin's Lane in which Kean spent the first three or four years of his life, there are many small courts in the manor, eighteenth century, their dark cobbles lit by lamp posts.

Here's one such. Who, I fancy, is that child crouched desolate and shivering in the dark doorway? The child is a ragged boy and he is spidering towards me on legs so maimed and crooked that they bend into a flattened triangle under the little body moving towards me; and he walks forward on his ankles, bare feet twisted sideways, twisting inwards. See his face, though, see the fine haunting beauty of the child's face under grime and toss of black curls. His eyes, mind you, look at the eyes of the child, large they are and wide, lustrous, impenetrable, deep and bright and black as ink. It's Edmund Carey Kean the whoreson bastard of Old Drury and the year is early 1793. Do you miss your daddy, Ned, do you? You can scarce miss Nance your mum for she had it away on her toes days only after you were new dropped. One-legged Uncle Moses Kean do you miss, sweet Ned, Moses the entertainer? In your neglect and malnutrition he at least tried to mind you as

you battled to survive among the violence and despair of the
drunken poor who existed in the stews and cellars of this parish.
Moses was dying, though, wasn't he, Edmund, and the entertainment he had offered in his show *The Evening Lounge* had been a
long time not to the popular taste.

Then there was poor Daddy. Bright promise as a young
architect, apprenticed to a fashionable surveyor and all, but the
drink and what the books call his disordered intellect put a heavy
block on that and he wound up as a copy clerk. That disorder of
his intellect showed itself in a glacial melancholia, which found
him expressionless, mute and with only a seemingly mechanical
response to his surroundings. Were you there, Ned my love, were
you there a few months ago when Daddy clambered on to the
roof of number nine Little St Martin's Lane to pitch himself head
first off and break his face and his body on the cobblestones
below? Were you there or were you not, you most certainly had
the luck in being born of Irish stock, a race which long time since
had appreciated that work was for horses and in consequence,
where you were, had lived below the bread line and so avoided
being weighed and numbered in parish registers or poorhouses
or workhouses. Lucky you were, you bandy-legged little bastard.
Why, a few years earlier, hadn't the workhouses of London
admitted into their care two thousand three hundred and thirty-
nine children, and of that number, five years later, hadn't only
one hundred and sixty-eight of those children remained alive?
Deadly times for the poor and the destitute in the England of
your day, Edmund; deadly times as ever. Do you fancy, Ned, that
over the workhouse door the Irish had seen a painted sign which
said 'Work Makes Free' and had chosen not to believe it? What
was Daddy's age? Twenty-two, twenty-three? What age are you?
Three, four? Try not to grieve too long a time, my bright shiner,
not too long a time must you grieve. Aunt Tid will come along
soon and will love you all your days.

A woman indeed, Aunt Tid, the lady had been a mistress of the

Duke of Norfolk. A beauty and educated, when Tid and Jockey went their ways, Jockey arranged for Tid to have permanent employment as walk-on with the odd word to say in the company at the Theatre Royal, Drury Lane. Just around the corner, Sunshine, Old Drury, Aunt Tid soon will be here to mind you. You'll find that her loving will at first mean agony for you. You will be taken to a hospital where you will be starved of food and drink for two days and nights. On the third day you will be given all the milk that you can gulp and the milk will have been heavily laced with gin. The surgeons do it to anaesthetize you. When you are practically senseless, the surgeons will grip the young bones of your bent legs and will stretch and shove and pound and twist at those crooked limbs until they are straight. Thick iron rods with hinges and joints forming them into long splints and heavier than your body now is will then be clamped on your legs, from thigh to ankle. When the surgeons are satisfied with the alignments of both limb and splint, the heavy iron rods will be hard screwed into firm place. Night and day for five years you will wear leg irons, Ned, and at first your suffering will be much. However, in time, you'll find them just bearable; in time, they will hardly hinder you from a prank; in time, you will for good and all be rid of them and at that time when you will be nine or so, you will for the first time know a miraculous sense of freedom such as few of us on earth can ever know. Yes, King Bloody Dick, you'll become such a frisky little prat that Aunt Tid will wrap a brass dog collar round your neck saying, 'This boy belongs to 12 Tavistock Row. Please bring him home', and sometimes you'll go home and other times you won't and at all times you'll be chatting and tumbling and singing and dancing and scrapping and thieving and reciting and boxing and fencing, laughing, cursing, tight-rope walking and saying why not. Come here to me now, sweet boy, give me your hand. There. No harm and across we go to number nine. In you go, now, wrap up warm, Aunt Tid will soon come, all will be well. Byron will, in time, say to you in verse, 'Thou art the sun's bright child'. So you are, great Edmund Kean, so you are. Now get in out of that, you little bastard, and leave me get on with this engaging business of getting pissed as a handcart. The Lyceum must be right over there in the approximate direction of that way, surely, generally there or thereabouts.

We are legless at the Lyceum. Nor are we there because that for thirty years Henry Irving held dominion over the theatre. Ordinarily, we might have been but, do you see, on the smally few occasions when we salt-water mariners had been let spend an evening at liberty in the Smoke, as was our quaint name for London, we would be dressed in our sailor suits, bearing our buckets and spades, primly sitting in our carriage on the train, perhaps flushed by the anticipation of the delights to be savoured on a trip far away from the fucking seaside and would eventually arrive at Waterloo station with choices. Having safely stowed our buckets, our spades at the Church of Turkey, two of the possibly more fruitful choices would immediately present themselves to me and my mates what hadn't had no bastard shore leave since Noah was a sickbay tiffy. To our left, under the railway arches, past the square where the spunkers in residence downed their methylated spirits, stood the Old Vic. A splendid institution, one where the finest actors and actresses of the English-speaking world took on the great parts of the English classical theatre, and one where they played to large discerning enthusiastic audiences. To our right, across the wide Waterloo bridge over the Thames, stood the Lyceum; for these long years no more a theatre but very presently a rocking, shocking big-band dance-hall, one where Glenn Miller, Louis Armstrong, Lionel Hampton had played and one where Joe Loss was now wagging his knitting needle at a dirty great swinging orchestra, Lita Rosa was his thrush and the parish was flowing with women and drink. What it had invariably boiled down to, after we seamen had given these considerations a thorough thrashing, was a two-pronged nub. Were we able to walk the few minutes across the bridge to the Lyceum, or should we take a bus?

No surprise then, you may admit, that my speculative ramble round the city should have eventually pitched me into the immediate vicinity of the Lyceum, nor that you should now find me at the bar of the pub most adjacent, stocius and with scarce a leg to put under me. Merry, though, right full of high humour and the blather tumbling out of me, buying and being bought drinks by like souls, discussing, say, the recent suspension of the constitution in British Guiana, flatteringly finding myself subject to the attentions of two somewhat older women, attractive, groomed and dressed in high bright style, chucklers the pair of them, their prattle at whiles suggestively ribald, and two to whose presences over the last half-hour or so I had ever increasingly become adhered.

Call my ladies Rose and Lily, 'The bailey beareth the bell away The lily, the rose, the rose I lay'. Sisters, Lily was a young widow woman, while the younger of the brace, Rose, was celebrating her recent divorce, a rare enough event in the times that were in it then. My amused neurons will muster only a faded dream of how we three informed each other of the roles which society had allotted to us but my mind reveals to me that moment when Rose or Lily had suggested to me that I escort them both into the stomping hop raving away in the Lyceum. Lily or Rose had a friend who was an under-manager or a senior functionary of some or other sort in the establishment, a man of substance anyway, and he was eagerly expecting them both, right now, to present their handsome selves to the agreed spot in the foyer where, wearing his dickie bow of office, he would be happily waiting in attendance. So much is clear. What followed is a confusion to me, one to which it is difficult to give shape, sequence, detail or precise definition. The sound of horns and music, certainly; drumbeats rolling up a blare from the big brassy band; beams and spotlights roaming round a deep red grandeur and on to the fling and whirl of a mass of giving jitterbuggers; heat of bodies and high heat in my heart, pulse and head. We are in a room, a comfy private room, the drink is free, the party we have joined is easy, friendly, spiritedly on the razzle and Rose and I are discovering much in each other that merits our devoted attention. Dancing, I remember, wild dancing, great spins and flinging feet and pulls and shoves and breathless great hugs in sweat and laughter. Dancing slowly, I remember, rammed against each other, dreamy and drunken, Rose and I, swerving through the press, slow, unsteady, and carnal. In the room again and drinking, I recall, and talk and jokes and smoke and melody and Rose but that is all I can recall from that evening when I strode the straight way from Gower Street to the river.

The following morning, though. Ah well! The following morning. Did you ever pop into your local bar in Paris for a beer and wake up in Corsica? A dozen more years would come and go before one dozed asnore on that magic carpet but a bar or two of the overture played to suchlike hilarious and mystifying events had already sounded in my hard young head. Scandinavia, then, that time of prohibition there when, to give you a twist of the tune, one had discovered oneself of a fine summer's morning to be nine miles away from the spot where one had stood sipping the illicit horse lineament available there and discussing, perhaps, President Truman's vetoing as discriminatory of the McCarran-Walter bill on immigration quotas with Jock the Cock, one's friend and opposite number, a hairy-arsed, swaying, three-badged, able-bodied seaman, some fifteen years a salt-water sailor. Battle of the Atlantic, coastal defences, mine laying, mine sweeping, my tutor in sailoring ways afloat or ashore, one seldom seen mustering for the liberty boat without his golf clubs. Yes. What is a sailor, I ask you, without his niblick, putter and mashie? Nine miles.

Watch gone, money gone, shoes gone, even tunic and collar gone. How one got there, you may find, becomes less important than how one will get back, and in one's stockinged feet.

Corsica, though, did you ever find yourself after having done the like? At the very least it's a car or a train and a plane and a boat job, Corsica. Ye bugs!

No Mediterranean sun for me on this day, no, nor a northern midnight sun neither to shine so strangely out on this morning, for we are awake and have found ourself sprawled out under a fur coat on a sofa in a sitting room at Cockfosters, a suburb of London, the furthermost point that can be reached by the underground railway, last stop on the Piccadilly line, where outside the rain is pissing down. There is no blood, no broken glass or splintered timber, no moans of agony or anger, no vomit. My watch is there, my money, my shoes are off but are there on the carpet; on a chair, my jacket, shirt and tie flutter; on another chair, my donkey jacket stretches comfortably over the back rest, its pockets, as I will learn, retaining their guide book, map, and Arden edition of Shakespeare's *As You Like It.* My mouth has felt more honey sweet, but that's about the size of it, and the time is seven a.m. Not much bustle about the house but after lighting up a necessary fag I have put on my shoes and shirt, remarking the while the wet day through the window, and down from above come the voices of a child and a woman. Footsteps are padding down the stairs, and though one is wondering where the fuck one might be, there is yet the hope that wherever the fuck one might be, one might still be welcome there and is anyone brewing up a mess-tin of tea?

My opening of the sitting room door coincided with Lily's arrival down the stairs. Lily. Reassurance, to be sure, for one had strayed but had strayed with one whom one recalls having been with when one was conscious. Lily. Washed and dressed in sweater and skirt. Hair loose, face handsome, a shade severe, eyes blood-shot, beady. 'Good morning, Lily. Is there ever a cup of tea for I could murder one. It's pissing down. How's Rose?' Precisely what the lady quietly said to me eludes me now but its general drift wafted in the direction of the immediate lowering of my voice, my immediate return to the sitting room, the immediate completion of my dressing, to be followed hard upon by my immediate departure from the house. Rose was asleep, the child must not see or hear me, there would be no tea, my opening and closing of the front door was to be quietly made, as was my walk through the garden, my handling of the gate, while my walk away from the house was to be straight across and right down to the far corner where anyone could tell me where was the tube station. 'Give us a glass of water and you're on, sweetheart, my mouth is like a vulture's crutch.' Lily moved quickly through the door and returned in a minute with a large glass of cool milk. 'Where are we?' I whispered from the door. 'Cockfosters,' returned Lily. 'What's the tube station called?' asked I. 'Cockfosters,' replied she. 'Cockfosters,' said I, 'give my love to Rose,' and stepped out carefully into the hard pissing rain. 'The bailey beareth the bell away    The lily, the rose, the rose I lay.'

---

WASHED AND SHAVED and dry, wearing a new shirt, new underclothes, new socks, my discards from the previous evening's frolic stowed in a pull-string canvas bag, a razor and toothbrush with their companion blades and paste wrapped in a face flannel resting on the crumpled heap, I boarded the underground rattler which would bump me the couple of stops to Goodge Street station and the RADA. Other than a leap off at King's Cross railway station for a wash and brush up and the blessed suck of a cup of tea, another scamper up the escalator at Leicester Square to buy my shimmy, smallclothes, toiletry gadgets, followed by a quick scrape, scrub, change and polish in a gentlemen's lavatory hard by, I had been for two and more hours practically living on the heaving great subterranean animal. The journey from that far suburb had seemed interminable but the time had not been squandered. Each many minute spent among the sullen morning passengers staring unhappily at their newspapers had been employed in inducing the moisture clamming my person and my clothing to evaporate into the dry and smoky air of the bucking, swaying carriage, there to mingle with the breath of all who that day had travelled from Cockfosters. Of my trousers, what can be said? Whatever they had been up or down to during the night, they had been left in a sad state of stained corrugation and, in my view, their best chance lay in my being able to persuade Peggy of the wardrobe to give them a hefty dart of the smoothing iron before classes kicked off at ten a.m. My other purchases had turned the trick neatly for me and here I was, once again back on board the rattler, heading for the academy, and the time was nine thirty. Opposite me, above patent leather shoes, sits a dinner jacket, its turned-up silk lapels failing to hide an unknotted black bow tie and a starched collar gone completely astray from its mooring stud. The incongruity of formal evening dress, found pressed between punters clad in more morning and vernacular fashion, offered me an interested and an appraising eyeful. An inspection of the occupant of these fancy duds did then so fill my eyes with surprised and laughing tears that I had to shut them from the sheer delightful pain of it.

The wearer of this rumpled dress suit was good old Reliable Bob. More. Reliable Bob was unwashed, unshaven, uncombed, and unable quite to restrain hoarse hoots of laughter tumbling from his gob as I opened my eyes to see the lack of absolute focus in the glaze and glitter of his sleepless peepers seeking to bring me to their smiling attention; but I sensed in that wonky look, as he sensed in mine, that London Public Transport had bumped together two fellow spirits, fine specimens both.

Coffee is what Bob needs, quick, round the corner from the tube, two jugs of it, don't dawdle, look at the time, twenty minutes to the off, he is not far from being sober but in his view yet far enough for at ten a.m. he will be giving in the Bernard Shaw Room his nimble-witted, nimble-tongued, nimble-footed Touchstone to the class there assembled all under the sharp, ethereal eye of Nell Carter. Fuck. He has a cashmere cardigan in the cloakroom, his dress trousers and patent leather shoes will do, he needs only a wash, a shave, and a shirt. In this here pull-string canvas bag. We are marching to the academy, razor, toothbrush, paste in his trouser pockets, dinner jacket, boiled shirt in my hands, he marches down the street in his vest shaking the rammed crumples from my Cockfoster shirt, it is one mess of an article, he tells me, as on the hoof he puts it on and buttons it, and it smells of women and whiskey, nevertheless it is a shirt, it will serve, once under the cashmere cardigan, no one will know it has been out all night, lost in a far suburb, here, put on my donkey jacket, stuff those in the canvas bag, right, Good morning, Sergeant, straight to the wardrobe me, straight to the cloakroom he, Peggy not here?, I wonder, sweetheart, could you do me a kindness, yes, aren't they, what?, that's very nice of you, really, very thoughtful, thank you, this rail?, these will do a treat, really, may I change here, thank you, yes, a bit baggy, stripey and made for braces but the old belt will hold them up, this is very kind of you, here you are, really, no hurry, of course, thank you, to the cloakroom, all right?, can't shave no fucking soap, use the toothpaste, right, five minutes top, go and fascinate everybody I'll be there, certainly, Good morning, Nell, morning all, Albie, Michael, Pocahontas, Randolph Turpin took a fierce hammering from Carl Olsen so that's the middleweight title gone back to America, I see by my Arden that we are singing the Furness MS version of 'It Was a Lover and His Lass', which changes the Folio order of the verses, the second becoming the fourth, but this change has been adopted by most editors from Johnson onwards, we are to be thankful that it is no longer pissing down, enter briskly a gleaming Bob, half a yard of toilet paper stuck to his kisser, staunching blood from a gash self-inflicted when shaving, hands not steady, Morning, Nell, nicked myself, morning, all, right, 'God 'ild you, sir; I desire you of the like. I press in here, sir, amongst the rest of the country copulatives, to swear and to forswear, according as marriage binds and blood breaks: a poor virgin, sir, an ill-favour'd thing, sir, but mine own', hang on, I'm in this bit, Oliver, when Jaques says, 'You to your land, and love, and great allies', I'm supposed to nod, if my eye catches Bob's eye again we may both fall helpless on the floor, much better to stare at my stripey trousers and think of bacon and eggs, 'You to your land, and love,' that's me, 'and great allies', nod, nod, that's my part played.

> O! Wash me in the water
> That you washed the colonel's daughter in
> And I shall be whiter
> Than the whitewash on the wall.

---

THERE EXIST in my heart and mind a couple of nooks in which good old Reliable Bob lives still in both warm affection and clear image. We had met during the troublesome times of our auditions for the RADA, we had passed hours of uncertainty together, he had expertly marked my card on the Higher Education sweepstakes, gone nap on a dark horse among the bureaucratic bloodlines, given me a leg up, and I had ridden home on a winner. There had been little of the student about him, less of the actor and altogether more of the man about town. We were close for a long stretch but he was ever his own man, with his own social agenda, and, though he was my companion, his companions were not my companions, though I knew a few and did easily nod and mutter of this that and t'other with them. Arcane matters such as insurance policies, rentals and overdrafts were held as familiars to his competent grasp and dealt with as day-to-day details to be sorted by an appropriate scratch of a letter or a pertinent telephone call. Acting was a topic left undisturbed in our discussions, giving way to motor-racing, literature and women, but I well remember his telling me that Shakespeare and the classical authors of dramatic literature were not of vital interest to his emotional and physical welfare and that the prospect of poncing about in doublet and hose held less charm for him than did the lounging suits of modern comedy and drama. The closest to a declaration of a view on his life in art came when Bob told me that what had attracted him most about the theatre as a profession was the notion of turning up of an evening to a playhouse, strutting his contemporary stuff, and then bowling away with a doxy on his arm for a champagne supper and a gentle knees-up.

Closer in age to thirty than twenty, Bob was a man of mild mystery. Little concerning his life and times before these his student days came my way from his lips. However, tit-bits filtered through to me allowing me, as I would learn, to construct a fairly accurate, if patchy, outline of this modestly singular man. Straight from school in 1943 he had been conscripted into the armed forces. Demobilized in 1945, he had donned business suit, had studied and practised the skills of administration and salesmanship necessary to the efficient running of an estate agency, and for eight years in a small town in the midlands of England, assiduously had practised these skills. The eighth year of that long decade had found him fed to the teeth and staring out from his desk at a desperately limited horizon. The war had taken away incalculable lives, and had taken away childhood from many children and much youth from the young. Bob had found a great void in his life and had determined that before it was too late he would fill that abhorrent vacuum. Amateur dramatics had trailed him a lure, the line had led to his being accepted at the RADA, his pockets had been filled enough to afford the fees, and so he had tossed his bowler over the windmill and joined the students dancing around west central London. Rare, such a one, you will perhaps allow, a rare one to·have done this for there are many, I fancy, who did not but who wish that they had.

Time ticked along and within months Bob had realized that he was no actor but that he was enjoying the life, the disciplines, the company, the friendship and, of course, those visits to an unidentified society which insisted that he wear a dinner jacket and stay up all night. Bold he was and deserved luck came to him. He had managed to survive into the second year of studies but his funds had just about trickled all away and, I believe, he knew that he had had his fun and that it was over. Now, at that time I had no fixed abode, was, indeed, keen to find a loving spot where I could lay my vagrant head, rest and be cherished through nights before vigorous days and to that end my eye and hand were softly resting on the frame of a tall, long-haired and languid little cracker, a newcomer to the academy. Snag. The fair moll was not keen on a cuddle. Not keen at all. Remark the night, at her pretty little flat where she lived all alone, when enjoying together a demure yet seemingly yielding embrace, I had made a slight adjustment to the going rate of the mechanism which impels degree in human intercourse, perhaps murmuring the while, only to find her arms making a savage cross cut before her and her mouth exploding a 'no' of such vehemence that I hear it yet. Let Lydia roast, I said to myself as I tucked up to sleep on someone's floor, let Lydia Languish roast, a fair wind and a few days and we'll have another crack, but that 'no' had a strange yelp to it. Let her roast awhile and then we'll find out whether or not. If not, what of that, Michael has a vacant corridor in his digs, so that's the accommodation and then we'll have another roll of the dice. What I did not expect, over the next few days, was that I would win the chocolate watch. Lydia Languish, shortly, refused my invitation to share with me a cup of hot coffee, preferring rather to serve me with an iced 'Please. I don't want to see or talk to you again.' Have a banana. Not for the first time, I had won the chocolate watch. Out. Dumped. You know the feeling. Some months later, to both my surprise and a humour born in the comical carriage of an underground railway, I listened over a couple of large whiskey to mischievous, smiling-eyed Reliable Bob, dealing to me straight details of how he and Lydia Languish had become engaged, and, of his realizing that the gig was up, that the times told him it were better that he return to the work he knew, that the year had given him much, more than he had hoped, and that he would return to old ways with a beautiful young wife whom he plainly loved.

Reliable Bob is dead. He died recently. Indirectly, I learned that he had prospered and that his marriage had been successful, right to the end.

---

HUMPHREY was his name. Yellow-painted, named in red both sides of his wee bonnet, Humphrey was a tiny Baby Austin motor car; elderly, infirm, asthmatic, Humphrey was a clapped-out little banger, and an extraordinarily small one. A cheerful little sod he was though, and when Touchstone and Oliver were saved by the bell at lunchtime, Bob scooted off on the tube to bathe and change and to fetch Humphrey to meet me. Our class would that afternoon be rehearsing scenes which did not involve Bob's Touchstone nor my Oliver, and before he went off for a wash and his vehicle, Bob had carefully placed in my ear an interesting proposition. We had agreed to meet in a couple of hours at Momma Fischer's boozer and I whiled away the minutes by walking to the Tottenham Court Road, buying a bunch of roses, returning to the wardrobe where, in exchange for the posy, a kiss and my stripey numbers, Peggy's assistant handed me my trousers, pressed and dabbed and nifty as one could wish.

A healthy mess of grub at Olivelli's filled me with well-being, a thorough read of a newspaper satisfied my mind and I walked across the road to drink a beer with Momma Fischer who, and I suspect she well knew it, was already in the process of adopting a clutch of us. Humphrey arrived bearing Bob and with a shudder of relief halted outside the door of the pub. Humphrey batted not a broken headlight at my amazed scrutiny, let me scrunch myself into a bony knot on his passenger seat, suffered the indignity of Bob poking a starting handle into his innards to give it a few hefty yanks and then wheezed into a reluctant life. Bob fitted himself behind the wobbling wheel, did fine things with chokes and gears and double declutchings, stepped on the juice and away we lurched at a prudent rate of knots.

Our immediate target was my neat and tidy, regulated boarding house and once on the move, particularly on the flat, Humphrey proved quite keen to show us his gaudy, ancient paces. Bob had acquired Humphrey from a dodgy second-hand car dealer at Warren Street in part exchange for his posh saloon, the other part being a handful of readies that would see him through the first term or so, and when we arrived at the boarding house the old boy slumped at the kerbside in grateful, motionless exhaustion. A couple of minutes only and Bob and I had scooped up my goods and my gear, walked down the stairs and at the door I said goodbye to good living, prim companions, a month's payment in advance, and all the rules there written on their pieces of paper. Humphrey baulked, appalled, at Chalk Farm where the road rose steeply up to Hampstead, he had tried it before and had found that even with only the one person aboard, and he at the steering wheel, the steep, steep bank had banjaxed entirely his frail constitution. We parked him in his place at the side of the tiled tube station and then the pair of us strolled up the couple of hundred yards to the house in which Bob had rented a room, one, he had proposed, whose cost and comfort I might choose to share with him. The room was large, airy, held two substantial beds, had cupboards, a wardrobe, two solid armchairs, their companion sofa, a gas fire in the fireplace, a gas ring in a cubby hole, a sink and water taps handy, and large windows giving a fair sight of leafy trees standing guard to the garden close which stood off a quiet street. Yes, Bob, this will do, it's passing fair, why, from such a calm and cosy base we will be better and better equipped to bear all hardship, rigour and the mayhem anticipated in our being students at London.

----

WINSTON CHURCHILL said, Let there be light; and a lamp post was lit and there was light. It is September the seventeenth, nineteen-forty-four, the blackout is ended, five years of darkness has ended, I am twelve years old and light shines in the streets at night, just as it did when I was seven. Then, as usual, I flicked through Daddy's newspaper, singing the while, as usual, the odd snatch of a popular song.

27th August 1944. Evidence has been uncovered in Poland of what previously was only appalling rumour. Advancing Russian troops have found what may be the ultimate German atrocity. Their political commissars invited the press and the newsreel cameras into the 670-acre Maideneck concentration camp. Floodlights picked out the electrified barbed-wire fences topped with fourteen machine-gun posts. Parallel lines of trim green huts surrounded cremation ovens and gas chambers. Cattle trucks were used to transport an estimated one million five hundred thousand victims who, with clinically detached ruthlessness, were methodically gassed and cremated. Their ashes were used to fertilize German crops.

Mairzy doats and dozy doats and little lamzzitivy.

20th July 1944. In the Wolf's Lair, Hitler's headquarters in East Prussia, Colonel Graf Klaus von Stauffenberg put a suitcase holding a bomb under the table in a room where the Führer was conferring with his staff on the deteriorating military situation on the Russian front. Von Stauffenberg left the room and minutes later he looked on as with a massive flash and with a violent explosion the conference room was completely devastated. Many were injured and the men standing next to the Führer were killed outright. Hitler escaped with only minor burns and cuts. Von Stauffenberg and many other officers suspected of being conspirators in the attempted assassination have been arrested and executed, suffering strangulation by piano wire strung from meat hooks.

A kiddellitivy too, wouldn't you?

July 1944. A million children have been evacuated from the south of England between June and July 1944, removed to safety from the dangers of Germany's secret weapon, the V1, the Doodlebug, the flying bombs let loose over south-east England on June the fourteenth. Powered by petrol and compressed air, the jet-propelled, pilotless aircraft are gyroscopically steered and carry one ton of high explosives. The Doodlebug is terrifyingly planned to drop from the skies and explode randomly on England when it runs out of fuel. A total of 2,754 bombs have landed causing 2,752 deaths and 8,000 casualties. Many of the attacks are during daylight when the flying bombs are clearly visible. The Doodlebug brings terror by day when its engine stops, by night when its orange-yellow trail of fire disappears.

We are in love with you, my heart and I.

6th June 1944. D-Day. Allied forces land in Normandy.

Lightning, Thunderbolt and Mustang fighter planes have been in the air above Normandy since before dawn, bombing and strafing.

Midnight to five thirty a.m.: troops land by glider and parachute behind German lines.

RAF night bombers batter Hitler's coastal defences.

Daybreak: 1300 US Eighth Air Force heavy 'Flying Fortress' bombers take over.

Five a.m: Allied seaborne forces begin landing along the French coast while battleships pound the German installations. Engineers went ahead of the fighting troops to destroy the Wehrmacht's beach defences – clearing paths for tanks, armoured cars and self-propelling artillery. Eisenhower's UK-based HQ broadcast the news the world had long wanted to hear, the second front had begun at last and the invasion of Europe was on: 'Allied naval forces, supported by strong air forces, began landing Allied armies this morning on the northern coast of France.' Prime Minister Mr Winston Churchill told Parliament: 'The operation is proceeding in a thoroughly satisfactory manner. Many dangers and difficulties which appeared extremely formidable are now behind us.'

D-Day plus 3. Utah is the name given to the beachhead fought for by the US 7th Corps. The US 5th Corps are fighting on the beachhead called Omaha. Gold, Juno and Sword are the names of the beachheads established by the Canadian and British forces fighting for the British 30th and 1st Corps.

D-Day plus 6. Sword, Juno, Gold, Omaha, Utah have linked up to form a continuous front.

D-Day plus 21. With audacious bravery American forces expertly attacked and seized the great port of Cherbourg. Bayeux, Norman home of the tapestry, has been taken by British and Canadian troops. General de Gaulle, leader of the Free French, landed there today.

Greeted by Field Marshal Montgomery, George VI, King of England, visited the Allied beachhead in Normandy.

And we'll be always true, my heart and I.

24th March 1944. General Orde Wingate, leader of the heterodox British jungle fighters known as the Chindits, has been killed in an aircraft crash in Burma. Wingate developed his unconventional strategies of warfare during his campaign with the Jewish 'Night Squads', whose surprise tactics devastated the Arabs in Palestine.

Five nights ago, in Burma, the Allies pulled off in absolute secrecy the most bold and dazzling operation of the campaign. Silently over the 7,000-foot-high Chan Hills, gliders flew a modern army below a brilliant moon and landed 200 miles behind Japanese lines. They have achieved a strategic position for a fighting force fully equipped with arms, fighting vehicles, bulldozers – even mules.

You'll never know just how much I love you.

20th–29th February 1944. Americans open Pacific campaign. Under 'Operation Brewer', they invade the Admiralty and the Marshall Islands. Abandoning the slow landing crafts commonly used in beach operations troops stormed the island of Los Negros from swift destroyers. No matter what the sacrifice, the beachhead will be held.

22nd January 1944. Italy has been invaded. In another brilliant surprise operation Allied forces blasted ashore at Anzio, only thirty miles south of Rome.

18th January 1944. The terrible agony of Leningrad, besieged by the Germans for two years, is over. Smashing a twenty-mile gap in the German siege lines the Russian army relieved the starving citizens who poured out of the stricken city to hug their Red Army victors and saviours.

Hitler has ordered the mobilization of all children over the age of ten.

Sing it. Wail it. Fats Waller the jazzman is dead.

You'll never know just how much I care.

1st January 1944. The enigma of genes – the hereditary elements made from deoxyribonucleic acid (DNA) – is solved by Oswald T. Avery and his team of scientists at New York's Rockefeller Institute. DNA codes the genetic information for the transmission of inherited traits in all living things. It is the solution to the profoundest mystery of biology.

26th December 1943. The Royal Navy sinks the mighty battleship *Scharnhorst* in the Arctic Sea off northern Norway. The German Navy has thus lost its last great warship.

28th November 1943. Winston Churchill, Franklin D. Roosevelt and Joseph Stalin – the Big Three – have for the first time met together. In Teheran the leaders of the Allies intend to come up with the final plan to destroy Germany and win the war. They also debate the signing of a proclamation promising that the world will be free of tyranny after the war.

We'll meet again, don't know where, don't know when.

25th November 1943. 'The Battle of Berlin progresses,' declared Sir Arthur Harris, chief of RAF Bomber Command, today, following a series of crushing assaults by Lancaster and Halifax flying bombers. 'Berlin will be bombed until the heart of Nazi Germany ceases to beat,' he said, as, day after day, the capital city was battered into heaps of burning debris.

24th October 1943. Penicillin, a new and potent drug which has been proved to be effective in the treatment of infected wounds, is now being used on the injured of those fighting in the Mediterranean.

13th October 1943. Italy, which five weeks ago unconditionally surrendered to the Allied Forces, today, 13th Oct. 1943, declared war on Germany, her former ally.

September 1943. At night RAF bombers raid Hamburg. By day the US Air Force takes over. With a greater tonnage of bombs than was dropped on England during the whole of the 1940–41 blitz seven square miles of Germany's second city have been removed from the face of the earth. New phosphorous incendiary bombs are being used, producing fierce heat. Civilian casualties are extremely heavy and a Danish source in Hamburg estimates there have been two hundred thousand deaths, with 'burning asphalt turning the streets into rivers of fire'.

Jean Max Moulin, the French resistance leader, has been captured and tortured to death by the Gestapo. He was 44.

But I know we'll meet again some sunny day.

July 1943. A wave of anger is sweeping Britain and America at reports of Japanese atrocities on Allied prisoners-of-war. Thousands of prisoners allegedly have been tortured, starved to death and murdered.

13th July 1943. On the great stretches of cornfields surrounding Kursk, south of Moscow, Hitler today ordered a ceasefire following the mightiest tank battle history has known. The German army has been routed. In his order of the day, captured by the Russians,

Hitler had said, 'This is an offensive of such importance that the whole future of the war may depend on its outcome. More than anything else, your victory will show the world that resistance to the German Army is hopeless. Your victory will shine like a beacon around the world.' The Germans had their latest Panther and Tiger tanks. They had their crack battalions of the Wehrmacht and the Waffen SS. These were hurled at the Russian line, east of Orel and Kharkhov, at Kursk. But the Russians were ready – not only with fresh men from Siberia, but with awesome new equipment such as the 'Conquering Beast', a 50-ton assault gun with a nine-mile range. The Germans also had no answer to the devastating anti-tank Stormovik aircraft. The blue summer skies above Kursk are eclipsed with the smoke of battle and countless destroyed tanks and aircraft scar the cornfields. 'Bleed the enemy white' was the Russian order for their counter-attack. The victorious Red Army left the field of battle awash with blood.

June 1943. Leslie Howard, the actor, famous for his Professor Higgins in the film of Bernard Shaw's *Pygmalion*, was killed when German aircraft shot down over the Bay of Biscay the civil aircraft in which he was a passenger.

6th June 1943. Eight weeks ago, seized with a desperate courage and somehow getting hold of a few guns, the Jews of the Warsaw ghetto launched an amazingly brave uprising against their German oppressors. Today, though, German troops riding armoured cars and armed with machine guns, grenade launchers, mortars and flame throwers have almost crushed the rebellion. As the Germans advance through the collapsing buildings, killing and dynamiting, the few remaining Jews, men and women, have retreated into the sewers still fighting.

> Keep smiling through just like you used to do,
> Till the bright clouds drive the dark clouds far away.

31st January 1943. Stalingrad, the city whose defence has obsessed Hitler, was today captured by the Russians. Two months ago, Russian troops smashed through the German and Romanian lines, and by moonlight relief columns reached the Don river, effectively tying a noose around a quarter of a million German troops trapped in Stalingrad, their backs to the ice floes on the Volga river. Field Marshal Von Paulus, commander-in-chief of the German Sixth Army, surrendered to a young Russian lieutenant. The Germans had lost two hundred thousand troops – killed in battle or dead from starvation and frostbite. The Russian casualties are unknown.

> I'm dreaming of a white Christmas,
> Just like the ones I used to know.

November 1942. Golden, the rising full moon shone down on the North African desert where a Black Watch piper stood. 'The nut brown maiden' skirled from the drones and chanter of his pipes and from General Montgomery's Eighth Army one thousand artillery guns burst into action and shattered the sky. Led by the 'Ladies from Hell', as the Germans in the '14–'18 war called the Scots, the Eighth Army infantry advanced on two fronts. Britons, Australians, New Zealanders, Indians, Frenchmen and Greeks, rank after steel-helmeted rank, advanced resolutely under the thundering artillery, rifles primed and bayonets fixed. Today, 4th November 1942, Rommel's Afrika Korps is in full retreat from El Alamein. General Montgomery has achieved the first great Allied victory of the war.

> Where the treetops glisten and children listen
> To hear sleighbells in the snow.

There. A backward glance at the newspaper stories I had read throughout my twelfth year and a couple of months of my eleventh, sprinkled all with ditties we had sung at the time, but, tell that to all the world and then say softly to me: 'Inchgoole, boys, many men of the Connacht Rifles, fed to the teeth waiting for that renowned git, Adolph, to stick his gob with the little tash over it into the sights of our musketry, and knowing well that should he as much as lay a boot on our Rocks of Bawn, Sergeant Kelly would have been round here ringing the bell on his bike to give us the tip, many, I say, of us Connacht riflemen had gone on leave to our homes: we had onions to weed.' They might have heard at Inchgoole the deep drone of an aeroplane flying from the north and heading south-west. Do you see, St Patrick's day, 17th March 1943, and from the holy land of Ireland, a Very Long Range Liberator Bomber took off, determined to give the lie to the Cabinet secretary, Lord Maurice Hankey, who was putting it about that the anti-U.Boat campaign was our greatest failure. Now, the Liberator was not only loaded with the latest deadly weaponry but also with the astonishingly sophisticated instruments known as Sonar and Asdic, devices which could both detect and pinpoint the positions of U.Boats in the Atlantic, no matter their distance, depth or formation. More. The codebreakers at Bletchley Park had so successfully deciphered the German codes that the pilots and navigators of that VLR Liberator Bomber knew not merely the estimated or approximate time of the U.Boats' attacks and manoeuvres, but they were able to know the actual time of these operations. The German High Command had calculated in 1941 that, if up to 800,000 tons of Allied shipping could be sunk each month, then the war against the Axis would be doomed. And they could well have been right. No matter how many men we had this side of the Atlantic, without materials, equipment and food they would be powerless, and Britain would starve. Throughout 1941 and 1942 the lethal shoals of German submarines had sunk an average of almost 650,000 tons of shipping each month. The Liberator's flight that had passed above Inchgoole, out and over the broad Atlantic, had proved a success. Allied shipping would be alerted to immediate danger while aeroplanes, destroy-

ers and frigates would hunt and destroy the U.Boats. In March
1943 627,000 tons of Allied shipping had been sunk in the
Atlantic. In April, 245,000 tons. In May, 18,000 tons had been lost,
with 17 U.Boats sunk. For the first time the balance favoured the
Allies and perhaps the most critical point in the battle of Western
Europe had been safely passed.

---

'NOW, THIS IS what I call a composition.' We didn't write
essays, not at St Anne's Catholic School, we wrote compositions
and our teacher, Mrs Carrie, has just entered the jam-packed
classroom bearing the heap of copy books in which on the
previous day we boys had collectively scratched down our inky
creations. Authoritatively expecting and getting silence, Mrs C.
talks as she walks to her seat of power at the desk before the
chalky blackboard, facing the assembled throng of toerags risen
and shuffling before her. 'Sit.' With the usual clatter of boots and
timber and bony young arses, we do sit. 'Peter O'Toole, please
come here.' Avoiding the legs thrust out to trap and trip the
unwary, I pick my way to her desk. 'You will see that I've marked
your composition "Excellent" and I've also given you a double
bonus. Well done!'

This is a turn-up for the book. This is a notable first. This, I
believe, is the first time I've ever been praised at any school for
anything I've ever done, ever. Not that I am without esteem from
my peers at St Anne's. Certainly not. Popularly elected Commander-in-Chief of research into the dirty bits in the Bible,
possessor and generous distributor of dog-ends and whole cigarettes acquired from a wide acquaintance of adults, supplier of
copies of *Picturegoer* whose covers provide inspiration for mastur-
bators in the air-raid shelters, altar boy, considered a bit of a whizz
at playground cricket, youngest member of the school swimming
team and seldom out of the frame at high pissing, it still came as

81

a bit of a tick tock, shock, to be singled out for such a verbal laurel leaf. 'Thank you, Miss,' say I as I collect my work and stare at the faces of my mates, Luciano, Pongo and Big Hamish, just to make sure that the magnitude of my achievement has been clocked up on their ugly mugs, and am met with three faces composed in solemn wonder yet adorned with crossed eyes which, you see, is what the four of us ritually do when occasions of moment and gravity are upon us. Bugger them. Carefully back over the booby-traps of stuck-out limbs go I, back to my desk, thinking the while that that's one up the nose of that git, the swot Knickers, who sits at the front behind his spectacles. Pious Pillock. Arrive at my station at the back, make sure the seat is down and not up, which is the usual practice in this class for it allows the sitter to plonk his bottom on a seat which is not there, drop through the gap to sit with a bump on the dogshelf, bash his chin on the splintered slope of the unyielding wooden desk, and, for causing a disturbance in the classroom, cop a fierce bollocking from the teacher. Sit. To sit at the back, to think, to savour the flavoursome wee bit sweet of glory, to don an exterior nonchalance, to know that even if the next subject is maths and with it the consequent return to the reality of my dufferdom, it would hardly wipe the shine off my smile. To reflect that in spite of everything else this year is not turning out too badly for me at all. Not at all.

Consider. Last summer I daren't try swim a stroke, not a splash. As an infant, as a child, I'd been able enough, able and happy gurgling about in the bubbles, diving and floating and swimming in the shallows and the deeps. Mummy had dunked my sister and me in swimming pools before we were competent to toddle about unaided but for some reason I had grown afraid of the water. Common enough, I know, but it had irked me, made me feel ashamed and so I had turned to Tommy. Friends since infancy, Thomas and I, my companion on daring escapades riding tricycles and one with whom some seven and more years since I had swished about at the swimming. Senior to me by a year and a couple of inches, lean, spare, laconic, Tom had twigged within seconds that my confidence was shot and that I had no wish to mend it before familiar eyes. 'Otley,' was all he said. Now, as O'Liver would in time despairingly jab out to me, all men and women of the north country who know and like well their painters and paintings, who know and like well the wolds and dales and peaks and fells and broadacres of Yorkshire, also know that if the Hannibal of Joseph Mallord William Turner RA's great daubing *Hannibal Crossing the Alps* had not paused at the upper part of the painting but had continued crossing the canvas and had stepped out over the bottom left-hand corner of the frame as you look at it, Hannibal would have arrived at Otley. A market town in wide green Wharfedale valley, its borders stand at the foot of the nobly wooded slopes dropping down from Jenny's Hill and The Chevin, while through the valley and the town runs the smooth treachery of the wimpling river Wharfe. To Otley, then, Thomas and me, riding the ten miles by bus, for a large open-air swimming pool was there, as was the maypole. A wondrous huge great article, the maypole, painted green, thick as you might wish and even though prudes had abbreviated the great length of it by some dozens of feet, when let it still stretched up a good seventy-odd footer. Mostly it lay unemployed on its side, the grand Otley maypole, but came May and up he would rise proudly erect before the town. Ancient as Robin Hood and beyond, they say, these maying poles of England, and few maids these days, I fancy, to fling their legs and skirts around it, to openly adore the rampant fertile thrust and hymn its harvests.

> Hit befell on Whitsontide
> Early in a May mornyng,
> The sonne up faire can shyne,
> And the briddis merry can syng.
> 'This is a merry mornyng,' said Littule Johne,

'Be hym that dyed on tre;
A more merry man than I am one
Lyves not in Christiante.'

Ah well! To the swimming pool, then, Thomas and I, and when in the water, 'My hands will be under your spine. Take a deep breath, hold it, lie on the water and look up at the sky, high as you can.' This, with a splutter, I did. And then again. And again and again. Then one hand only under my back. And then again and again and again. Then no hands on my back, but held about a foot under me in case I felt like to drown, which I promptly did. So, dry and dress, back on the bus and home. We kept this up, Thomas and I, two or three days a week for a month. I provided the bus fare and the price of the splash, Thomas his patience, his skill and his friendship. Came the day of the great unaided plunge. A breadth at the shallow end of the pool with little mortal assistance from Thomas, only a cautionary, 'You're not allowed to drink all the water in the pool.' Away I battered till I reached the other shore. Triumph. And then a breadth of the five foot deep. The ten feet of the vasty deep end next. Done it! Mission accomplished. Or so I thought, but taciturn Thomas had dare and devil in him. When next we rolled out on the bus, Thomas had me and himself jumping off a mile or so before our usual stop in the town.

Where are we going? Through meadowlands dipping down green and lush to the ferny banks of the river Wharfe, that's where we are going, all under the glower of the battlement nature made that we call Almscliffe Cragg. Really, I fancy one wondered, is this a spiffingly solid notion, St Thomas of the Deep End? That we who have braved and won the battle of remaining afloat in the waters of the blue tiled open-air swimming pool at Otley should, if one has accurately assessed your thoughts, hazard now our body and sinking soul to the whirls whims and perils of a real running river? 'Yes, Tooley, get your kit off and do as I tell.' Jesus.

Through the ferns and the flowers lay a curved bank with stepped ledges from it leading down into the river, while beyond, some twenty or so yards to our right, a squat boulder jutted out over the flow. 'Listen and watch. I shall hop from that rock and land in the water on my backside. As I hit I shall kick and shove to my right. You'll see. The current will fetch me to right under where you're standing.' Doing as I was bid, I unpeeled my kit, the while gazing at the living river. She seemed to have a skin, that river as she ran, stretching out there silver and grey, seemingly unperturbed and still but, yet, the roaming brute under the smooth sheen broke here and there through that sinister surface to chuckle and suck in deadly little circling swills. Lord love us and preserve us with heavenly water-wings.

In went Tom bottom first, seemed barely to break the water, easily shunting and lazily kicking, he arrived at the ledges below me, nor was his hair very wet. 'Right then,' says he, 'your turn. Drop in flat as you can, close to the bank, keep your head up, just shove and kick this way. I'll be here if you need me.' He'll be here if I need him will he be, that's choice, thought I, as, too scared to admit that I was very scared indeed, I plodded to the boulder as one might who had resolved to pitch himself into a wet eternity. Here if I need the mad bastard, that's tasty. Would that we were neither here nor should I ever need again the raving pillock, for I surely will die. Didn't I gently poke a testing trotter into the slithering dip to find the cold nip in it had seemed to have the foot bit off me? Here if I need him, as I stand on the boulder, hardly pausing at all above this wide and dangerous ribbon of wetness moving below, I need my mother and my father, God and his angels, the mercy of sweet crucified Jesus, a rubdown with *Sporting Life* and an efficient disappearing act as here we fucking well go to heave ourself into this frightful mess of sorrows. Thump. Hard and cold the welcome of this hit of water as sinking, desperation, floating, panic, my manically raving limbs pound and thrash up a fine frenzy to swirl and to flounder and my foot has found a crinkle on the hard shelf of a ledge at the river bank, Thomas has grabbed the flail of my arms and seconds later the pair of us are sitting up to our necks in the river, hands grabbing the stony shelving as silently the current tugs and urges us to drift away downstream.

'Well done, Peter, that's the best bit done. It's just hard work now.' Tutored by Thomas, without moving away from the safety of raked ledges, I learnt to swim a few feet up against the river's current and then to let the waters roll me back to where I had started. By late afternoon I was with confidence swimming upstream to our diving rock and, with a little guidance, letting the drift bring me back to the bank. At summer's end, that year, Thomas and I, puckers intact, would be swimming hard against the pull of the river some thirty or so yards from the rim of the big weir at Poole, in Wharfedale, conscious of the hurtle in the cascade should we fail against the water's tug but strong enough both to know that we held the edge over the risk.

Now I'm second off in the school's relay team at the galas, and by more than two years I'm the youngest member. Thank you, Thomas, and again I thank you, may your heaven stream with bright rivers and may you tumble into every one of them. But swim, boy, swim.

> Wharfe is clear and the Aire lithe,
> Where Aire kills one, Wharfe kills five.

Yes, Mrs C., I lied, of course I've heard of Keats. Certainly. Put your old feet up, honey, rest yourself. Your severe, kind, womanly self. Light up a fag, lay your silver head on the cushion, blow your beak of a bugle on that itsy-bitsy lace hanky, take off your specs, give us a gaze of your wise big blue eyes, that's the way. You'll find that, really, you could have chosen no better man to pick a poem to chunter from the works of this here geezer Kates, than your obedient pupil, Peter O. Of course it's pronounced Keets. Same as Yeets. Exactly. I agree with you, Miss, one could easily be confused.

'Mummy, do you know any Keats?'

'Thou wast not born for death, immortal bird!
No hungry generations tread thee down;
The voice I hear this passing night was heard
In ancient days by emperor and clown.'

That's smashing, Mummy, really lovely. Didn't know Keats was a Jock. Och, no' a Jock, just the way you pronounce your Rs, is it? That's all right, then. Hoots. You see, Mrs Carrie wants me to choose a poem by Keats from this book and learn it by heart. Prob'ly wants me to recite it to the class. Yes, she gave me an 'excellent' for my composition about Obadiah. Here's the one, Mummy. 'Robin Hood'. Why should it be a wee bit difficult for me? I know billions about Robin Hood. Yes, I see. 'Where lone Echo give the half to some wight'. What's a wight? Really. Which one? 'Meg Merrilies'? 'Old Meg she was a gypsy; and lived upon the moors'. Smashing. That's the one. I'll learn it. Thank you. No. My pockets are my private property. What's in them is. They're only conkers. It's a bottle opener. No, I know I don't but it's a very fine bottle opener. Might be silver. Silver-plated? It's only a bloody carrot, Mummy. Sorry. 'And 'stead of supper she would stare full hard against the moon'.

There you are, my beautiful old girl, easy does it, Mrs Carrie, stretch yourself and click your gnashers, you do niff lovely, fragrant, we thought we might give 'Meg Merrilies' an airing. Good. Right. Here we go. Cop an earload of this. Yes? Thought you might fancy it and you do dress trim and dandy, old sweetheart. The buzz in the urinal has it that Grunter Tarpey's old feller knew you when you were a lass and he says that you were a right bobby dazzler. What? Not really is it, my old flowerpot? Well if Mr PeeJay wants to hear me recite my poem, and to read aloud to him my composition, that stuffs a complexion on matters that may not be wholly to my advantage. He's a character from an entirely different opera, Mr PeeJay, a horse of a completely different overcoat, and just when for the first time ever I've got my nose in front, I could come seriously unstuck. Blimey.

A formidable figure, Mr PeeJay, a man I well remember. In every way a big man: big of body, big of heart, big of brain. In my mind he strolls easily, carefully, watchfully, the way in which he did when I had first encountered him in the new year of 1943, shepherding the usual rag tag and bob-tailed crocodile of snot-nosed ruffian schoolboys, whose body included me, prankily tripping along to Benediction at our Cathedral of St Anne's. This association with the city's cathedral had been, throughout the nineteenth century and up to nineteen thirty-nine of the twentieth, an important factor in the school's constitution, transforming what was an ordinary elementary institution into a preparatory school for the brighter sparks to alight on the better seats of Catholic learning throughout the north country, a happy situation which had ended, never to return, when the war began. In nineteen forty-two, when English schools reopened, the old place had been compelled into a less exclusive scrutiny of candidates for entrance, and toads of all sorts had hopped in from every point on the compass. Progressive education, thrust on the school by the ideologues holding political power, completed the work, and when I went to visit the place some score or so years ago I found, with an unexpected but deep sense of loss, that my old rough-house had been bulldozed into the clay.

Mr PeeJay, though, half a century away: jaunty and huge in russet tweed, his hat at a rake, facing the oncoming traffic as he walked the road to patrol his flock of charges, skipping and fighting and chattering on the footpath. Khaki lorries filled with khaki soldiers singing khaki songs would rapidly approach. Mr PeeJay would halt, turn with outstretched arms to us and announce, 'Stop, boys. Stay still. O'Toole, or Pongo or Luciano or Big Hamish, cease instantly that crude nonsense or I will hurl you under the wheels of war and you will lie crushed and no longer a burden either to me or your poor parents.' When his tilted hat was off, in his classroom or the corridors at school, one could see that he was totally bald. The story was that one evening before the war he had unwittingly dived into the deep end of an unfilled swimming pool. The injuries he suffered were terrible, both bone and brain had been smashed, but he had endured a protracted and uncertain period of mending and healing, survived, and with his wife and children had gone into a quiet and contented retirement on the outskirts of the city. Came the war with its emergencies and, of course, he had rolled up in his motor car to what had been his old school and taken on the job of instructing the likes of me in our letters and numbers. Whatever was the truth about his accident, the pate on him certainly had been hairless as an egg, with an aura and appearance of fragility to it that was at odds with the burliness of his frame. There was that about his movements, too, I reflect, that had seemed deliberate and considered. A much-travelled, highly educated man who for years had lived in America, it was natural that such a rare bird should hold a glamour for us schoolboys but there was something else. Many of us were Irish stock and Mr PeeJay was related to one of the executed leaders of the Irish rebellion in Easter week of 1916. We held him in awe.

The handbell tolled at four p.m. to tell that school was out. With my mask and personality of Hunsbeck hard chaw firmly fitted over my features bone and skin, my copy book bearing the red badge of 'excellent' on a composition, the book of poems containing the Keats in my hand, my thumping heart sticking in my gob, I knocked as instructed on the door of Mr PeeJay's classroom. 'Come in.' In went I and there was he, not sitting as I had expected on his raised desk before the blackboard, but, huge and stern and bald, he was lolling with a leg perched over one of the classroom desks at the front and reading a newspaper. 'Mrs Carrie gave me your composition on "A Sound of Revelry" to read,' I fancy Mr PeeJay said. 'I found it unusual and lively but your presentation was so sloppy and untidy that parts of it were incomprehensible to me. You will please stand with your back to the window, read it out loud to me in your best playground voice, but clearly and carefully, and you will, perhaps, cast light on its more obscure passages.' Sloppy and untidy, thought I, clumping to the window, fumbling for the page and dropping the poetry book, you try being tidy and unsloppy with Pongo shoving your elbow with his foot as you are carefully penning a loop to your handwriting, the loop becomes a squiggle and a blot, you turn round to whisper threats and cop an eyeful of blotting-paper pellet soaked in ink fired by Big Hamish with his ruler, you rise to step and remonstrate only to find, too late, that Luciano has tied your shoelaces to a leg of the desk, you pitch flat on your kisser, bust your pen nib and your nose on the floor and, for causing a disturbance in the classroom, cop an unmerciful bollocking from the teacher. I am before the window, the poetry book has been retrieved, is being used as prop for my copy book, which is turned to the appropriate page, my throat has been cleared, a big breath taken, and off we jolly well go. 'Well done,' says Mr PeeJay when it is over. 'Very good indeed. Thank you for translating the passages you had written in Egyptian hieroglyphics. Perhaps, to help me, you will in future write in plain English.'

'Yes, sir.'

'Splendid. Now, I understand you are going to read a poem to me. Fire away.'

Chunter, chunter. Playground voice. Carefully, clearly, 'God rest her aged bones somewhere; she died full long agone!'

'Come here, O'Toole. Put your books down and prop yourself on this desk near me.' I did so and looked in his eyes. They were light-coloured, clear, friendly and twinkly. 'Did you choose that poem,' he asked, 'or did someone suggest it to you?'

'My mother picked it, sir, but I agreed with her.'

'I see,' he said. 'I've met your mother. She is a lovely woman. What does your father do?'

'Until a few months ago, sir, he was working as a civilian for the Royal Navy.'

'War work?'

'Yes, sir.'

'I see.' He nodded. 'Do you have a favourite poem?'

'Yes, sir.'

'Recite it for me.'

'Then out spoke brave Horatius, the captain of the gate,
To every man upon this earth death cometh soon or late.
And how can man die better than facing fearful odds,
For the ashes of his father and the temple of his Gods?'

Mr PeeJay held up his hand for me to stop. His eyes were closed, a smile on his face and, with his head tilting back, he was quietly chuckling. 'That's a grand poem. I like that one too. Tell me, do you read much?'

'Yes, sir.'

'What are you reading at present?'

Oh dear, can't tell him that even this afternoon playtime I had been gasping my way through *Health and Efficiency*, ogling the bumps on the women in their swimwear, so I wound back the clock a few months and told him, 'My mother and I took it in turns and we read all of *A Christmas Carol* by Dickens.'

'Really,' said Mr PeeJay. 'And did you enjoy it?'

'A lot of it was very sad, sir, but the ending was cheery enough.'

'That's right,' he said, 'and do you remember the names of the children that the Spirit shows to old Scrooge?'

'Ignorance and er, ummm.'

'Want,' supplied Mr PeeJay.

'That's right, sir, Ignorance and Want.'

'Yes,' said my doughty teacher, gazing full of faraway thought at the window. '"Are there no prisons? Are there no work-houses?"'

'Those are Scrooge's words, sir, that the ghost stuffs back in Scrooge's teeth.'

'So are they,' said Mr PeeJay. 'Tell me, Peter, is there one writer that you've read who writes as though he was writing just for you?'

Even though you've called me Peter, big bald Buddha and relative of a noble Irish rebel, which has made me feel special indeed, I am reluctant to tell you of my writer. He means the world to me. Sometimes I find him difficult to understand and have to ask my mother what certain words and passages mean, but many shames I had I find he celebrates. Fear, for one. It seems as though he has read my heart, knows what I dread and wants to help me overcome all terrors. Confusions I had, my being Irish with a Scots mother, travelling around when a child and now being reared in England. These facts he knows and loves and many of his men and women are in those respects similar to me. Whiskey, too, he has a good word for. Women, as well: though he often says that the devil should sweep them, he delights in their company and has an eye for a fair figure. History, too, and fishing and swimming and singing and poaching and swearing and scrapping and nonsense. All these and much more, written in such a way that often I want to speak his words out loud. Songs and dreams and tears of sadness, he says, are in the book of God. He is the best writer in the world bar none and by a street and if you gainsay him, Humpty Dumpty, then you and I will be at serious odds and will find it unlikely, ever again, to share common ground. He is my pal and my big brother, I love him to death, he is my secret guide to all that is good and bold, a bit naughty, sometimes very, funny and daring, he is blood of my blood and I share him only with one man and my mother. I don't care to tell you who it is in case you are thick enough not to have heard of him, or that you might disapprove, but be damned! I will proudly tell you:

'Yes, sir, I do have. His name is Maurice Walsh.'

It seemed a light lit up in Mr PeeJay's eyes. And did tears, too, spring in those light eyes? Perhaps. Not enough, though, to quench that light.

'Maurice Walsh,' he repeated, gazing first at me and then at the window with that faraway look on him. 'By God!' he boomed. 'You could read a good deal worse. By God, so you could!' He then let rip a deep great laugh and smashed a clenched fist into the open palm of his other hand. 'Maurice Walsh. And who put you on to him?'

'Donal MacBruin, sir.'

'The piper?'

'Yes, sir.'

Again he laughed a deep rolling laugh, nimbly hopped off his perch, rummaged in his desk, produced a book of poems, flipped through, found one and came chuckling back to me. 'Here's a poem by W. E. Aytoun. Listen.' He read with dramatic emphasis the first few lines. 'Learn it all. You will recite it in the verse-speaking competition. Learn it. Picture it. Feel it. Speak it with great clarity. Off you go, boy. Keep up the good work.' As I was leaving the classroom I heard him chucklingly muttering, 'Maurice Walsh. Donal MacBruin. Of course, who else?' And again that heartfelt rumble of laughter.

On the heights of Killiecrankie
Yestermorn our army lay.
Slowly rose the mist in columns
From the river's broken way.
Harshly roared the swollen torrent
And the pass was wrapped in gloom.
When the clansmen rose together
From their lair amidst the broom.

This is the stuff. This beats old Meg on the moors wearing a chip hat, whatever a chip hat is. This is proper meaty gear.

Then we belted on our tartans.
And our bonnets down we drew.
And we felt our broadswords' edges
And we proved them to be true.

We had seen him often, of course, the small dark man himself, Donal MacBruin, lithely and lightly stepping in and out of our cathedral, clad in his swaying kilt and his neck frills, his cuffs and his small neat silver-buttoned jacket. We had been particularly impressed by the black-hilted dagger that he wore tucked down the top of the stocking on his right leg. The haft of it had an oval dark yellow stone on its butt. We coveted that knife and would have very much liked the ownership of one. We being Pongo and me and Big Hamish, when he turned up. We were altar boys, you see, Hamish, when he turned up, Pongo and me. We would have liked Luciano to don cassock and surplice with us but Luciano wasn't interested, couldn't be bothered, didn't give a toss. He preferred going to the pictures and the swimming pool and smoking and running with the wild lads and sniffing round the girls' school and the general joys of aimlessly buggering about. So, too, did we but having once joined up as acolytes, having become used to wearing the long black or purple cassock, the cracklingly starched laced white surplice, having got over the stuttering diffidence and the stumbles of the early days, it had proved well worth getting up at sparrow fart to play our parts in the gorgeous ceremonies and display which were on the menu practically every day at our cathedral. My cathedral, really, I suppose, for after, say, a mass or a baptism or a wedding, Hamish, if he'd turned up, and Pongo would be out of their robes in seconds and be off to tumble in whatever hurly-burly was going on in the Institute at the back, or loosely to potter about up to no good at all around the city, at the railway station or in the covered market. Not I. It was my delight to explore every holy crack and nook in my cathedral, and only then would I join my scabby-kneed mates at the smoking and the sniffing and the tumbling and the splashing and the tear-arsed romping on the roofs. Proprietorial, I fancy, was the way I had felt as I wandered through the choir to the high altar, up into the pulpit, down past the confessionals in the north or the south transepts, viewing as I passed the poor sods queuing up to unburden themselves of steaming sin. Down the aisles hung with harrowing stations of the cross or, having genuflected, down the nave to the narthex where for coppers you could buy a holy candle or a life of a saint or bung a penny in the box for black babies. The presbytery where the priests lived; the sacristy where clergy and acolyte enrobed and derobed and where the sacristan regularly got pissed on North African altar wine. The steps behind the altar which led to the Tabernacle. The side chapel with its secret door that let me up among the bells in the belfry and the fine view of the city from its topmost height. Loveliest of all, though, behind the miraculous picture of the Virgin, south of the high altar: the dainty Lady Chapel. Here was my refuge and my quiet sanctuary when at whiles I wished to be on my own and to ponder on this or that or t'other. Here for three years I would serve mass, often at seven thirty a.m. before school, and here I would learn in Latin the liturgy of the mass, the pronouncements of the priests and the responses of the acolytes. It was here, too, in my Lady Chapel, that one day when school had broken early and I had sloped in for a quiet sit-down and a brood, who should I spy sitting at the back with a pipe in his gob but Donal MacBruin. I was enchanted. Never before had I ever seen anyone smoking in church. True, the pipe was unlit, one could soon tell that by the lack of fumes and glow and sharp savour, by matches not being struck, by no implement being used to prod and dig at dottle and plug. Nevertheless, the pipe was filled with baccy and was clenched between his teeth. What price would you give me against, over the centuries of both pipe-smoking and church-going, the law givers of the One Apostolic Church not having knitted up a canon to contain such coincident practices? In the sin stakes, I'd say, it's odds on a venial and odds against a mortal. Whatever, the sight of Donal at the church with a dudeen in his face delighted me. My amused eyes found his eyes, which stared at me for a moment until they, too, spotted this cause of my happiness. He removed it, gave me a quirky grin, and together we left the chapel. Unusually enough, he was not wearing the kilt but was dressed in thick cord breeches, a tweed jacket, and a dark shirt and tie. No bonnet on his head showed me his thick thatch of tight black curls. His face was angular, deeply lined and his eyes were dark and bright. Only a little taller than I, he stood with me on the steps outside the south porch of the cathedral. The pipe was soon in his mouth and just as soon again he struck a match and lighted up.

'I wish you had done that in the chapel,' I said.

'It wouldn't have troubled God, I don't think,' he answered, 'I hardly think He would mind if I prayed while I smoked.'

He let me munch well on that thought for a while and then he said, 'Can you dance, young son, can you dance at all?'

Excluding a skip around the table with my mother and my sister and a sashay down the pitch to knock the ball back over a spinner's head at cricket, the proper answer to that question was

'No'. Which is what I said. That question, however, was loaded. That question, put to me so unexpectedly, would in time lead me to leap and puff my way down paths on which, for all my day-dreaming, I had never imagined I would put a foot.

A speaker of the Gaelic, Irish and Scots, Donal spoke some Welsh, a little Cornish and amused himself with Breton phrases. You see, as now I see, Donal was at worst extravagantly eccentric and at best a man who brought richness and colour and adventure to our lives. The exigencies of the twentieth century had caused him to run a small business manufacturing brushes in England, but MacBruin rather preferred to inhabit the world of Gaeldom. A precariously realized world this, the world of the Gael, it had existed in parts of England before the invasions of the Romans and the Angles and the Saxons, lives on long and deep in Wales, was, until the eighteenth century, the tongue and the leaven of northern Scotland, thrives still in her western Isles, and, before the sixteenth and seventeenth centuries, had been the national life of Ireland. Donal had chosen as his mode of living a particular and personal interpretation of the Gaelic way of life. He knew and loved well the poetry and sagas of ancient Ireland and, if requested, would tell the great yarns of Finn of the Fianna and Cuchulain of Ulster, of Deirdre of the Sorrows and Maeve of Connacht. The language of the Borders, too, Burns or Dunbar he was equally and happily familiar with and, when squeezed, would give a squirt of, say, 'Tam O'Linn' or the 'Lament for the Makers'. Nor was MacBruin in the business of proselytizing his somewhat dotty enthusiasms. He would 'gang his ain way' and if one fancied taking a step or two with him on that way, one would be welcomed, could join him on a journey and, at the end of the road, could take one's leave with ears not thickened by any preaching from him on the virtues of the trudge. When the mood was on him, he could and would live off the land. His knowledge of the ways of the countryside was deep and keen. Wearing sturdy clothing, humping a waterproof, a tin can and a few oats, armed only with a stretch of string, a box of matches and a knife, he did for days and nights live out in the fields among woods and streams. With branches and clods and grass he would build a shelter among the roots at the foot of a tree, light a fire in an arrangement of stones or logs, snare a rabbit or tickle a trout, root about for edible berries, herbs, shoots, and tubers, fill his can with water from a beck and, thus encamped and supplied, would skin and cook his catch, eat his concoctions and tuck up to snore among the ents and whispers of the forest. Only, I repeat, when the mood was on him. No worshipper of discomfort, Donal Mac also had a delightfully cosy caravan parked out in the dales, and he and his amused, tolerant wife would cycle out to it there on weekends. One time he invited me to spend a day out with them. I was pleased to go and wheeled out there on my fancy drop-handlebarred, three-speed bicycle. It was early morning and as I arrived I spotted a goat tethered a space away from the caravan with Donal tugging at its teats to milk it. New spuds were boiling in a fanny over a fire outside and I popped into the van for a blather with Ban MacBruin, Donal's wife. Through a window we watched the small dark man, the milking over and clearly productive, place a covered pot in the shade and then set off through the trees to forage wild comestibles. Mrs Mac fetched in the boiled new potatoes and spooned them into three bowls. Donal returned with his sporran stuffed with fine pickings, washed them, caught up the pot of goat's milk and came into the caravan. We sat down over the steam of the spuds in their dishes, MacBruin poured the goat juice on to our portions and then sprinkled them over from his crop of raw dainties. I spooned up a fair dollop of the mix, braced myself, shovelled the load into my mouth, and then let my molars loose on a vigorous chewing. The taste was only hideous. Nor did I pretend it to be otherwise. Nor did it faze or offend Mr or Mrs MacBruin. My reaction seemed to have been anticipated, an anticipation perhaps honed by regular occurrence, anticipated and, moreover, catered for. Mrs MacB. removed my bowl, gave me a glass of water, reached into a locker, brought out for me a Spam sandwich wrapped in silver paper, picked up her spoon and with her husband returned contented to this feed of dandelions, nettles, spuds, toadstools, goat's milk, truffles and wild hedge-rose berries.

A piper of renown, too, Donal MacBruin: Irish warpipes, Scottish bagpipes. Not suited to the ear of all, the pipes, they can have a raw thrill for the hearts of many but 'others', as Shylock says in Shakespeare's *Merchant of Venice*, 'when the bagpipe sings i' the nose, cannot contain their urine'. Anywhere out of doors can be a marginally less alarming place in which to encounter a shock of their drone and shrill. For Gaelic warriors in the long ago it is claimed that the voice of the pipes cried out, 'Come to me, you sons of dogs, and I will give you meat.' Certainly, when expertly played, they can truly stir me. Yet another of Donal Mac's many accomplishments was dancing. Sword dance, step dance, jig, reel, fling, hornpipe he gracefully hurled and whirled his hard-muscled legs and sturdy body into the complex disciplines of these leaping dances. Point, toe, heel, check, step, cross, skip, turn and up he'd leap and howl, his arms flung high and bowed, the fingers light in touch, or down his sides the arms would stretch, body aloof, still, while the legs the knees the feet intricately flicked and flourished. Superb. After a set with the pipes the pumps or the shoes, he would call for and be given his two fingers of malt whisky in a tumbler. This he would sniff and sip and savour. And be done.

'No, Mr MacBruin, I can't dance.'

'Perhaps you can't, O'Toole, you namely boy, perhaps you can't. Perhaps you may wish to learn.'

That was how it began. You see, before the war Donal had run an outfit of pipers and dancers called Lord Kilmorey's Own Hibernians. Yes. The war had seen them disbanded, the wee stocky fellow with the curly dark hair had it in mind to revive them. To that end he had listened to counsel from teacher and priest, had put an appraising eye on the young lads kicking or batting a ball about in the playgrounds near the cathedral, and had most particularly watched the show-offs who enjoyed serving as altar boys.

Well, if Pongo and Big Hamish were game, I was game. Hamish was game if I and Pongo were game, and Pongo was game if Hamish and I were game. Over puffs from a communal dog-end in the school air-raid shelter, which, as always, included the bitterly competed sport of deciding which of us had mustered the mightiest drag, inhaled the most smoke, held it deep down in the lungs for the longest time and, decisive factor, exhaled the fewest fumes, we agreed that the three of us all were game. Thus it was that Lord Kilmorey scooped into his Own Hibernians we three bright shiners. Tall, raw-boned, fair-haired Hamish; red-headed, meaty Pongo; and the lanky Hunsbeck kid himself: me. For many months under the tutelage of Donal Mac we laboured two nights a week in the big hall of St Mary's on the Mount at the desperately difficult business of learning to play the pipes.

We found the dancing much easier. To records played on the old crank-handled gramophone, we skipped away at the reels and learned the basic steps of the jig. The reels gave us the most pleasure. Not only could one leap to land with one's full weight on the skimpily shod trotter of a pal, but when linking arms as one kipper-stepped up the line, the right purchase, the unexpected shift in the disposition of the body, the gleeful tug, and one's pal would find himself heaved head first into a bleeding heap against an unyielding wall. Donal both enjoyed and encouraged this horseplay, occasionally added his brawn and cunning, and then the three of us would in turn find ourselves being hurled about the dogshelf.

How does one practise playing the pipes at home? This is a reasonable question and fairly put. Thank you. One does not, mercy, use a full set of pipes. Of course not. To blow on such a beast under one's own roof would inflict terrible suffering on one's kin and household pets. Yes, quite right, the neighbours too. Maddened by the agony of it, they would batter down one's door with a telegraph pole, cut one's throat with a hacksaw, with large sharp axes they would chop and chop and chop the three-droned brute into matchsticks, scraps and silence, heave vats of kerosene into the building, toss in a roaring flambeau and, when ashes only remained of a building, its occupants gone thoroughly to raging blazes, the neighbours, equanimity restored, would then return to their houses, close their doors, and live in peace. No. One does not need bagpipes on which to practise. One uses a charming little article called a chanter. Very like a smaller version of the instrument used by snake charmers over their basket of cobras, your chanter. It charms no snakes, few humans and produces but small sounds. Strained, I recall, and seemingly distressed small sounds, putting me now in mind, I fancy, of the fundamental notes so originally expressed by the late great Monsieur Joseph Pujal the Petomane who, for his adoring audiences, which included a weeping divine Sarah Bernhardt, through the special aperture fashioned at the rear of his leotard, would melancholically fart the 'Marseillaise'.

The first tune we learned to finger on our chanters was 'The Wearing of the Green'. The second, 'The Skye Boat Song'. Third, yes, Lord love you, 'The Truetodeedle Song'. And the fourth was 'The Rakes of Mallow'.

You may be pleased to hear that these days, having neither the puff nor the lip, no longer can I satisfactorily play the pipes. However, give me a week's practice and I could reel you off on the chanter a 'Rakes of Mallow'. It is the only tune from my piping days that I can remember how to play.

Came the day, eventually, when for Lord Kilmorey's Own Pongo, Hamish and me, there arrived from Scotland three big and hefty oblong black wooden cases. We snapped open the metal catches, lifted the handled lids, and there resting on the padded interiors of the cases were our own sets of brand new, hand-made pipes, the mahogany wood of the instruments polished, gleaming.

Came another day, shortly after, when, having been measured and fitted and told of the mystery of how ten to twenty yards of cloth would be needed for the proper folds and tucks and the stitches and the pleats which alone could fit them with the right hang and swing, we were given our kilts. Donal, when in Scots Gaelic mood, wore by familial entitlement either the restrained Lamond tartan or the more gaudy MacMillan but, as we were Irish pipers and dancers in the service of Lord Kilmorey, he had chosen as our single colour not the familiar saffron nor, as we three had been surprised to learn, the true national colour of Ireland, which is blue, the dark blue of St Patrick at that, and we found ourselves strutting ever so self-consciously about the big hall of St Mary's on the Mount clad all in kilts of a deep dark green. There was further joy for us, too, measureless joy: Donal presented each of us with our own *sgian dubh*, the small knife with the black hilt that fitted into the top of the stocking. He had himself hand-carved the hilts to our short keen blades; at the butt of the haft of each, fixed in an oval of steel, he had set a chip of dark yellow Cairngorm stone. Yes, I know, too bloody well I know, knives are dangerous weapons which these days are so often, so randomly and so terribly used by all manner of grievous thug. But. Did you ever know a little boy who didn't long to own one? Well, we were young boys; with these princely gifts Donal Mac-Bruin answered our longing.

Once safely back into short-trousered mufti, Pongo, Hamish and I, our proud new possessions in our hands, of course we shot off home to show them to our families. Home for me was Hunsbeck. The school, the cathedral, the verse, Lord Kilmorey and all, indeed, a good deal of my emotional and physical and cultural life was being lived on the altogether more grand northern slopes of the city. St Anne's stood by colleges of commerce and art, civic and town halls, medical school, hospitals, the university, the civic theatre. South of the turd brown river slithering along under its bridges in a long slow motion, and some three miles away, squatted Hunsbeck. Here, in its reek of slag and soot and waste, among its factories, chimneys, mills and furnaces, beside the railway sidings, lanes, warehouses and mazy ginnels, along the black-cobbled narrow streets where the ceaselessly scrubbed small houses hunched, was where another good deal of my emotional, physical, and cultural life was being lived.

Not too grand at all, do you see, our industrial flatland south of the river, the absence of great centres of sanctity and learning went largely unremarked, being considered not indispensable to the various cultural pursuits of *Homo hunsbeckian*. What, I ask you, could possibly be more sacred than the crowd's throaty howl of our gathering cry, 'We've swept the seas before, boys,' as our rugby team cantered onto the park in their green, white and gold strip? Where but outside the Beulah pub, could one learn and forever memorize the haunting lyric, 'Old man Brown, upside down,     Mopping up the whisky from the floor'? Who, in the entire city, was possessed with more ice to his nerve, skill to his eye and hand and a calm courage than the he who in the Golden Cross billiard hall stood poised with no chalk on his cue, the six remaining colours yet to be potted and so to cop or blue the fifty-shilling wager? Was there ever a group of more enthusiastic cineasts than those of us who on Saturday mornings bayed in our hundreds as the doors opened and the threepenny rush at the Crescent cinema was on?

Cricket. Yes, we had no green field, no pavilion, no rolled square, no stumps, whites or coloured caps. No. But wasn't there a perfectly good lamp post as a wicket, a carved chunk of plank in shape of a bat, corrugated cardboard tied on with string for pads, no gloves at all, a communal tin box and a roundish stone as the ball? As for swimming, well, it was all right as daft activities go but few if any paid much mind to the lark, there being little call for it in the gasworks, the engine company, or down the pit. Roly and Willis and Hooky, however, perhaps intrigued by my understated account of fighting for one's life in the white water swirling above a cataract in Wharfedale, began exaggeratedly to feign a complete indifference to this swimming. That gave me an opening, wide as one could wish in Hunsbeck, to bust their collective flush.

'Thaz not frit, art tha, Roly?' You're not frightened, are you, Roly?

'Frit? Am frit a nowt.' Frightened? I am frightened of nothing.

'Reet. Then thaz dared. Swim.'

You will understand, I feel sure, that what I had done was dare Roly to swim. A someone in Hunsbeck, dared to attempt a something, if that something were deemed possible, life or liberty threatened but in the grip of the one dared, then that someone's standing and esteem in the community rested wholly on a readiness to dare all on a something. In Roly's case it was to take a dip. There being no swimming pool adjacent, the upshot was that a couple of days later found the four of us stripped to our knickers and floundering about in the thick slimy water of a rancid old canal. My job was animated lifebuoy to the other three as we thrashed and spluttered and kicked our way through the few yards of sludge oozing in the breadth of the canal.

And a very good lifebuoy I made too. Witness Roly, whom I had do die dared, he, with my assistance, made it across. As did Hooky, dare die do'd to it by Roly. So, too, Willis, not do die dared by any of us, unprompted, manfully, one great beating flounder and he was safely across the slime. Victorious, the four of us sought the community water tap by the old man's shelter on the moor, there to wash off the clinging stink and ponder well where it were a better place in which to continue these larky aquatics. Miggy Woods, in the flooded quarry there, won the vote.

\*

You may wonder why we chose no swimming pool for our sport. The answer is that, excepting the persons and families such as mine who had become adoptive citizens of the area, few men or women, lads or lassies, for generations born and bred to lives of unskilled labour in the workplaces of Hunsbeck, would consider as a likelihood the thought of having any truck with anything so institutional as a municipal swimming pool. There were exceptions, of course. Why, on the fringes of the parish there lurked a highly regarded secondary school. Some brainy buggers had even been scraped up from the cobbles and sent to it for their eddication. One or two of its former pupils, not, however, handsome, haunted W. Hall, bard of the barony, have seen fit to jot down their thoughts on the ways and modes, habits and customs of the district's population. Very tidy jottings they are too, and readable, but one seriously wonders if the authors ever ate knuckle sandwiches at the back of Pint's warehouse, played pitch and toss for a week's wages outside Ida the moneylender's or settled in the railroad ginnel to a game of milk-bottle cricket. Essential activities to have taken part in, surely, for those who would go chronicling.

True it is, too, that in my time most of the inhabitants of Hunsbeck seldom felt moved to journey farther than its boundaries, finding within them all that they could wish to stomach. If not more. Miggy Woods, though, now they were an allowable exception. A lung and a jungle and a grove of bosky copulation, these trees sprouted up some three or so miles south of Uncle's pawnshop. A few minutes only, you might think, and one could reach them by bus or by tram. But not so. Not, certainly, among my lot. Use of public transport was held by us to be the way of the cissy, of the prat fit only to play skipping rope with tarts. Clinging to the back bumpers of the bucking tram car, that was deemed honourable, worthy. Stowed away on the supposedly unloaded grit lorry returning to its base was dandy. Best of all, in our view, that day we rode out to take our dip in the flooded quarry in Miggy Woods, was sitting at our ease on the scraps and tatters and jumble as we made up the load of the rag-and-bone man's horse and cart.

Deep and clear and cold the water in the quarry, I splashed about in the middle, quietly enjoying myself while at the rim Hooky and Roly and Willis shoved each other in and hauled each other out, playing drown the bastard. After, well, a wrestle and a rub of a shirt and we were dry enough to play Tarzan in the trees, swinging from branches, shimmying up, tumbling down, howling and beating our expanded bony little chests.

Rowdy boys, innocent as nettles, liberated a while from chimney stacks and soot, you may be amused at a perplexity which the four of us had shared. Drooping from a considerable number of branches were what to us might have been a dangle of hugely elongated mistletoe, or stalactites, or a forest fungus. No. This strange fruit proved to be used french letters, contraceptives, loaded and, perhaps as trophies, tied up by lovers to the sheltering twigs.

> The way to hump a cows
> Is not to elevate your tool,
> But put a penny in the slot
> And bellow like a bool.
> O! Some like it shot,
> And some like it hung,
> And some like it in the twot
> Nine months young.

Came a time shortly, the cricket season ending and the rugby season on, Hook and Roll and I sat crouched in our cranny on the wasteground 'twixt the railroad and the mills, watching Will riffle his flicker cards of the Don playing the pull shot. On the same principle as the motion picture, I suppose, your flicker cards. You hold them as you would a pack of playing cards but upright, resting on the palm and supported by the fingers of your right hand. With the fingers of your left hand held from above to support the back of the pack, you impress your left thumb on the head of the pack and, in time, when you have the knack of it, a slight pressure causes the cards to ripple towards you and to display, one after another, the images printed on the cards. The pictures on Will's flicker cards were of the great Australian batsman Donald Bradman going through each stage of his famed and mighty pull shot. The cards were Will's most prized possession, respected as such, and every now and again we would ask him to give us a shufti of the Don whacking the knacker, for Will, naturally, was a whizz at the manipulation. The ball flies at the Don's teeth, back he steps, round and down comes his bat in a horizontal swing and, crack!, the pill is crashed front of square through the on-side, its bullet rapidity, we had been told, being such that no fielder had time to move before the ball screeched over the rope. Mighty stuff, your flicker cards.

A couple of sort of familiar heads approached the four of us, one on a large burly figure, one on a smaller stringier number. Burly spoke:

'Which on yeez Tooler?' Which of you is O'Toole?

'Me.'

'Reet. Thaz lakeing wi uz Sunda. Sparrer. Two sharp.' Right. You're playing with us on Sunday at the Sparrow Park. Please be there at two p.m. precisely.

'Reet.'

'Spunk tod uz thaz windy but sharp.' Mr Spunk has told us that you are not desperately keen on the mortal combat involved in playing rugby but that you are a very quick runner.

'Reet.'

'S'long.' Ta-ta, see you soon.

I'd been picked. Burly was the spokesman but Stringy was the skipper. The team was composed of thirteen lads chosen from an area of ten or so streets in the manor; our opponents, lads chosen from ten or so other streets in the manor. Our ball was a huge affair, almost as big as some of the player's bodies, made of strips of stitched leather approximately forming an oval. When we had a bladder to inflate inside the ball, that bladder was a poem of bicycle tyre repair patches. Without a bladder, newspaper proved the better stuffing; flock or straw or rags made the ball too heavy. When we had no ball, some poor sod spectated wearing but the one clog. Kicks at goal were taken out of hand on the full from an angle on the twenty-five-yard line. Kicks of the clog were ill-advised. The recreational parks and moors we used for pitches were, in fact, patches of cinders. Two or three matches between teams from various clusters of streets were played simultaneously. One sometimes found oneself straying into others' matches. Goalposts were a premium. If the pair had been already snatched, often a player's younger brother, 'our kid', would find himself elected as a post. Kit was irrelevant. A familiar figure with the ball, you supported him; an unfamiliar, you downed the bastard. At the age of twelve my feet were large, two sizes smaller than Daddy's; he had a pair of light half-boots a size too small for him; thick socks and a strip of cotton wool, the cobbler banged in little rings of leather into the outer soles, I was elected. Our spectators were old men, children and aspirants to the teams roaring on their sides to victory. The matches were always vigorous, often chaotic, sometimes brilliantly skilful and always played in deadly earnest. Our side played together irregularly but cheerfully for two seasons. In my first match I didn't score but coming inside I made some good breaks, which put both Burly and Stringy over the line for points on the board, and I didn't miss a tackle. Sometimes I was picked, sometimes dropped, at all times I was there or thereabouts. The teams had grand names. Chip Shop Wanderers, from the streets around the fish and chip shop; the

Silly Army, from nearby the lunatic asylum; we were the Raggy-arsed Rovers. The times were glorious.

You are to imagine, if you will, that you are, say, Burly or Stringy and that you are loafing around the wasteground up to not a lot of good nor harm with either Hooky or Roly or Willis. From the ginnel bridging the railway lines comes a young fellow, tall for his age, striding towards the tram stop under Uncle's three brass balls. The young chap is well known to you but what you might find remarkable is that you see he is carrying a big, oblong, black wooden case and is wearing a green kilt. Yes. 'Tooler, thaz picked. Sunda. Moor. Two sharp. I' that fucking skirt if tha durst.'

---

PERHAPS AT closing time one night in that year before the war's end, a moon had shone down bright above the Madhouse. Perhaps. If it had ever had another name, the Madhouse, that pub behind the markets in the Golden City, I never knew that name. Should, however, you have fancied your chances as a streetfighter, well, you really could have chosen no better arena for your art than the cobbles provided outside those licensed premises. Sights and sounds of knuckles and boots mashing flesh and bone were a nightly feature in the alley by the pub, as were the head butt to the nose, the knee in the balls, the boot to the face of the fallen combatant, and the roars and the blood of the spectators and participants. Even as 'Time, gentlemen, please' was being hollered by the landlord that night, before the usual frolic had begun, a small van backed up the alley, its rear doors were flung open from inside, a man was pitched out to fall face down and moaning among the muck, the piss, the vomit and the cabbage stalks, and as its doors were being closed, the van clattered away into the concealing night.

Captain Pat O'Toole it was, that man tossed from the van, my father, my beloved old Pop, and though he was alive, he was barely conscious, and when he hit the cobbles he didn't bounce. Nearby was an accident hospital, which regularly received a supply of customers from the precincts of the Madhouse; an ambulance delivering yet another battered body was more or less a common-place; the choice of dump for Daddy had been judiciously made. Big Bluey turned up at the hospital in the early hours, Educated Evans was there before daybreak, by early morning the patient had taken his own discharge, by noon he had been motored away to a safe sanctuary, and there he would undergo extensive repairs and a refit. In the words of my father's chosen playmates he had been 'duffed up'. Duffed up professionally and skilfully too, barely a scrap of him not having been given rigorous attention. Particular care had been taken of his right hand. Each knuckle and finger had been scrupulously broken. The thumb had remained more or less intact, but not for want of trying. Who had done the duffing up and on whose instructions, I shall never know. Daddy may have known, or may have thought he knew; Bluey, too, may have had informed notions; neither, whatever the sum of their knowledge, could have offered potent protest. Daddy was almost nearer sixty than fifty, Bluey was older. They were spent forces. The Australian Mob with whom they had racketed and galloped throughout the twenties and thirties was a lusty memory only; in many places not a popular one. Bluey wanted, and was to have, a peaceful old age; Captain Pat's day was done. Suspicions as to the 'who' of his undoing still flit about as bats do at twilight. Daddy never offered an opinion to me. His crippled right hand when it clutched a glass or a cigarette may have prompted in him a great brooding, but that's as far as it went.

At the time, I was told that Daddy had been hurt in a motor accident but that he was all right and shortly would be home. Indeed, it would be a number of years before all the scraps and fragments which came my way assembled themselves into a clear picture of that night outside the Madhouse. The 'why' of it was, to a degree, obvious to me at the time. Daddy had enjoyed splendid doings while working with the Royal Navy at its inland base on the river. He had been an industrious and efficient governor of his own department, earned solid wages, had made a book for the service and the shipwrights on events of all manner of sort, and his poker school had been both lively and popular. When the fortunes of war shifted in favour of the Allies, this work ended. Another job was found for him, one closer to home which allowed him to commute, and, for a while, the four of us, my mother father sister and me, were closer and more happy than we had been at any time since the beginning of the war. It became all too easy for us, when we talked of where we would go and what we would do when the war was over, not to realize that Daddy was incorrigibly Daddy, that the shady world in which he'd walked had its own conformities, its codes of accounts and conduct, and that Daddy's offences against them were many and warmly remembered.

Jim the Waiter, hero of Dunkirk, with Pop my rescuer from evacuation, now demobilized from the Army, called in at the house more and more often. His intake of whiskey was modest enough, his chat smooth, but there was a menace about him which troubled me and his little eyes were stones. From time to time, too, Paddy called in to see us. Big, bulky, clumping Paddy; Irish, humourless, silent, a stranger to us and one made entirely of heavy-footed muscle. Could it be long before Daddy roamed out team-handed to former haunts in which he was neither solvent nor popular? No. Not long. His roaming ended at the Madhouse. Paddy, I never saw again.

Five or so years later, out on the moors with O'Liver, we fetched up in a pub and standing at the bar was Jim. We drank a beer together and he told me he was working as a market gardener at a convent nearby. Fancy that. No better man than Jim the Waiter, surely, to dig up for the brides of Christ their turnips, spuds and carrots. My old fellow, of course, made a comeback, a modest one, the first leg of which I loathed. On the racetracks of England, and by arrangements of interesting complexity, generally there are three main areas for a bookie to stake out his pitch: Tattersalls, the Silver Ring, and the Rails. There is another arena where business may be done, one whose name may tell you much; it is called the Jungle.

Daddy in the Jungle, under the name of Albert Marre, loyal old wonderful Archie Woodbine clerking. Daddy in the Jungle, no hat on his head, his eyes frantic, voice chalky, shouting the odds. Frail, ineffective, defiant, in my mind I see my old daddy, the last time he stood by a chalk board at a racetrack, hoarsely shouting the odds in the Jungle. Captain Pat had bidden him a fond goodbye and he in turn soon bade good riddance to Albert Marre, whom I despised.

At Hunsbeck, Pop formed a sensible association with the former copper from around the corner, an unobtrusive agreement with the chubby bookie at the far square, and with discreet presence of our honorary kinsman Podge the ganger being never far away, he began to turn over an unpretentious tinkle of business at the back of the shack. You may imagine, though, that if times had been hard for us at the beginning of the war, after Daddy hit the floor towards the war's end, they became desperate. We were destitute.

Constance Jane Eliot Ferguson? Well, as the dainty wee lady, our mother, my sister's and mine, knew only too well, 'The state of man does change and vary,   Now sound, now sick, now blyth, now sary'. Little enough had been either blithe or sound for her these last half a dozen of years and now were sick and sorry indeed. Now. In repose or in her few moments of quiet reflection, Mummy's beauty seemed wraithed by an ineffable sadness quite at variance with her manner and quality which were both joyous and generous and fused by acuity and authority. At some point in her young life, or so it appeared to us, our mother had determined that whatever she did she would do thoroughly, and having done a deed she would make sure the deed remained done. The bad times that were in it left her little time for repose, less for reflection, as with no trace of sadness but purposively and with an energy which I now see had been wholly invigorating, pretty Connie Jane set to keeping the listing, crippled SS *O'Toole* buoyantly afloat. Never one for walking when she could run, sitting when she could stand, sleeping when she could wake, my little mum fair tore into troublesome tasks and made them seem glad duties. Ever ready Magilligan, who throughout the war was running a general goods shop in the city, volunteered to keep an eye on my little sister's safety and the filling of my stomach. This gave Mummy the breath needed to dash out to where Father was and promptly to return with the good news that nothing was wrong that couldn't be fixed. Reassured, I could run my wilful ways while my mother sought and found work. Work of all sorts, washing windows, scrubbing floors, dusting, ironing, sweeping, lifting, shoving, making, mending. On a handcart borrowed from the corner warehouse, my mother and I loaded up whatever bits and bobs of any value we could lift from home, rattled the cart into the city and hawked the goods at market. The ship once stable and under the tug, Mummy found a job running a newsagent's shop. One day the delivery boy didn't turn up. Mummy wrapped that ridiculously heavy bag round herself and delivered the newspapers. The next day, I was the delivery boy. So for weeks and months we bustled on. Eventually, with Daddy back in the house, in bed, hurt, patched, brooding, my old mum took it upon herself to answer an advertisement in one of the news-papers she had been selling. A somewhat grand house in the environs of our enchanted Roundelay Park had put a call in the situations vacant column for a general help. Constance Jane answered the call and found that it had been made by a woman who in earlier years had educated, encouraged and, indeed, inspired the young Emlyn Williams. The situation was offered to Mummy, she took it, enjoyed it, and in time became fast friends with her employer. The good ship *O'Toole* put safely into harbour. All would yet be well.

---

GREEN AND DARK the flesh and sheen on the leaves of your red rhododendrons, Ned Kean, and though it was in the fall of the year when I saw them, therefore with no blood red bloom to them, the sight was only gorgeous. Your copper beeches too, and that's a lovely tree, rustle and murmur as they sway between your house and the lake. However, these one hundred and seventy years on, what I think would have had you and your friend Reid the gardener reaching for the whisky bottle, both to restore the fabric of your tissues and to drink further health to their prodigious might, would be the sight of your Douglas firs. What height would they have been, Ned, the last time you saw them that Christmas of eighteen thirty? Seven or eight or nine feet tall? A hundred feet and more, now, rotund, thick, with great outreaching branches and they are the pride of that lonesome, beautiful isle, that island of Bute off the western coast of Scotland, which you chose as your refuge and where you built your modest house. It will, I hope, amuse you, King Bloody Dick, that to your choice of sanctuary, chance and the imperative majesty of King George the Sixth had me between 1951 and '52, when not crashing about the Atlantic and the black Scandinavian seas, regularly tying up at anchor at the port of Rothesay on that same isle of Bute. Sorry to report that your favourite pub, the Bute Arms, was burnt to ashes some years back. It had been one of my pubs, too. One day, attending on a senior officer, we were scooting about the island in a little motor car and pulled up at the gates to your house. 'That's where Edmund Kean lived,' said His Nibs. Mustering what I hoped was an appreciative grunt, I took a squint at the four busts set on pillars at the lodge-gate. From left to right we had Massinger, Shakespeare, Kean, Garrick. Shakespeare, yes, knew of him. Garrick? Perhaps. Massinger? Kean? Sorry, sweet Sir Pisspot, neither you nor he at all chimed in my recollections. But I had no notion of becoming an actor then, Ned, not a flicker. Indeed, my performance as salt-water sailor would have been at best described as adequate. Different from you who, from the age of five, leg irons and all, instructed by Aunt Tid, dreamed of becoming an actor and worked at becoming an actor with a singleness of mind and an intensity of purpose which, salted and peppered by your being the merriest of little scoundrels, lives unique amongst anything I've known or read or heard about actors and their beginnings. The timing of your determination and ambition, too, E. Kean Esq.! Spot on coincident with an era when theatre, and the art of acting in particular, was held in so high a regard as to be without parallel before or since and would today be incomprehensible. Lord love us, Edmund, we know about you and your contemporary actors and actresses from the pens of some of the finest writers that this or any other country has produced: Byron, Keats, Hazlitt, Coleridge, Leigh Hunt, Shelley, Macaulay, and they are only the front runners. The Theatres Royal, Drury Lane and Covent Garden, from the middle of the eighteenth century to the end of the first third of the nineteenth, were patronized by highly intelligent audiences whose enthusiasm for us actors and actresses and whose knowledge of what we are attempting to do might possibly be matched today only by those who follow the opera or pugilism. Wits and high intellects busied themselves with our merits, considering that we unquestionably diffused more pleasure among all classes of society than any other body of people whatsoever and that we materially influenced the progress of civilization. That we who perform the drama generate it into the public heart and though it show itself upon the boards in painted face and costume, the drama is itself essentially natural, being wrought out and compounded of the passions and actions and characters of men, thus being a grand and terrible instructor whose influence might be extended beyond any point that has ever been attained in this country. Yes, Ned, you will understand that my tone and polemic have been borrowed from some of the more optimistic commentators of your day but I fancy that they are fairly representative. Well, weren't you a bold little bastard from out the stews down by the river to have wished not only to enter but to lead our profession at that time. What? Of course we envy you, you whoreson gimp, and of course we wish that we'd been with you, I, Uncle Ron, Griffith, Bletchley and Mr Jim. Why, we could all have taken our ease down the Coal Hole in the Strand, sunk a bevvy or four, sauntered out for a ramble, and that would have wiped the shine off the smile of a considerable section of respectable London.

It would also, I fancy, have given me a deal of delight to have seen your first performance at Drury Lane. Seventeen ninety-six when you were seven or so, still in your iron splints, manacled and chained to a group of similarly encumbered infants, circling around and solemnly trudging in a representation of the Children of the Damned, an interpolation into the cauldron scene in Act Four Scene One, of Shakespeare's tragedy of *Macbeth*, introduced by Mr Kemble and termed by him to have been the 'finest commentary on and illustration of Shakespeare ever attempted on the stage'. No doubt, but, having died the death in that part and having had the agonies of that death loudly and gleefully shrieked out by every newspaper in the land, thus promoting what was a mere botch into one of the hottest Shakespearian tickets of the century, I was given for six cheerful old months as much opportunity as any actor might wish to be involved and to watch at desperately close quarters the mechanism and operation of the play which for theatre folk is the synonym of ill luck. The piece is short, with rapid energy one after another the scenes and acts swiftly tumble on, much of the play is set at night, anything that can go wrong will go wrong and thus invariably does so in the dark. The speed of the action insists that the detritus of disasters great or small in any scene remains to litter up quite the one ensuing.

Picture then John Philip Kemble, tragedian, striding on to the stage at Drury Lane, Act Four, Scene One, A dark cave, In the middle, a cauldron boiling, Three witches. The scene adorned by this commentary on and illustration of Shakespeare, an assembly of shackled children chained together and circling the stage in a moaning shuffle, among their number Master E. Kean, hindered by leg irons but encumbered further yet by property fetters. 'How now, you secret, black, and midnight hags!' says John Philip Macbeth Kemble. 'What is't you do?' 'A deed without a name,' chant the three witches and accidentally down goes the iron-bound and unfortunate Master E. Kean to topple into the fearfully restricted child in front of him and to whom he is chained and who in turn topples over and knocks down the trussed infant before him who in his turn needs must crash into and fell the poor baby blundering about in physical connection to his fellow and so on until the stage is heaving with chained unfortunate damned children who, when one should attempt to rise will promptly be tugged down by others attempting to rise. And there still are acres of text to get through, aren't there, Master Kean, and apparitions to appear: an Armed Head, a Bloody Child, a Child Crowned, with a tree in his hand, a Show of eight Kings, the last king with a glass in his hand, and Banquo. The witches vanish and then in the next scene Lady Macduff and her son have to be murdered, while all around John Philip Macbeth Kemble and the stage at Drury Lane, trussed and shackled little children crash about weeping and baying for their mothers.

If mine be a true experience of playing Macbeth in a production where matters go seriously awry, then by that point the auditorium at the Theatre Royal, Drury Lane, would have fair sounded with cheers and the laughing hymns of happiness.

We are told, Ned, that as wages for your part in this fiasco

Kemble gave you a hearty clip on the earhole, did not sack you, let you shuffle on in the crowd scenes or as a page in other productions, expunged from his repertoire this commentary on and illustration of Shakespeare and that for the long eighteen years that followed to the time when you would topple him as the first actor in England, you held Black Jack Kemble always in admiration and respect.

---

SOON THOSE wretched leg irons would come off, Kean, you would find yourself miraculously to be straight-limbed, sound, driven by a boundless energy and deep into the study of movement and speech, the basic disciplines that we who act for a living must master. D'Eggville to teach you dance, Angelo swordsmanship, and Incledon speech and singing. Incledon lives merrily on in many books about your period and he seems to have been a man whose skills as a teacher and performer meant much to you and whose friendship you cherished. Even as you lay dying you summoned up for the old mates around you your celebrated impersonation of that time when Incledon attempted to sing a sweet solo to the lone and ripe accompaniment of a fruity bassoon. It is to be hoped that it pleases you to hear that a generation of us who studied voice under Mr Clifford Turner at the Royal Academy of Dramatic Art do often when we meet find ourselves lending voice to our memories of that lovely man. Why, just the other day, on a boat moored in southern England, I and an old pupil of his found ourselves to be giving out unbidden our separate versions of Clifford.

I fancy, 'Sugar Bush, I love you so. Sugar Bush, sugar bush, sugar bush. That's it, that's it, that's it. / Apeneck Sweeney spreads his knees, Letting his arms hang down to laugh. / Ha ha ha ha! In the beginning there was the breath. Yes, and breathe in through the nose as though you were having a deep and a satisfactory smell. A deep and a satisfactory smell. Smell, smell, smell, a satisfactory smell. In for three or four or five and slowly out through the mouth for three or four or five and never hold in your breath but keep a rhythmical flow with no block and breathe in and out as though on a wheel not up and down as though on a lift. That's it, that's it, that's it. Why through the nose, you ask? Have you read my book? *Say Shibboleth?* Say Shibboleth, say Shibboleth, say Shibboleth. It has a good title but is a very boring book. A very boring book, boring book, boring book. A very very boring book. It will answer most of your pertinent inquiries while at the same time your buying it will provide the Clifford Turner Benevolent Fund with shillings. With shillings, with shillings with shillings! We breathe in through the nose because it makes anatomical sense. We fill our skull with air and directly connect to the gut below our diaphragm. We speak from the gut. From the gut, from the gut, from the gut. We warm the face, the skull, the lungs, the body, the gut with oxygen and air and we give ourselves support. Support, support, support. Breathe in for three or four or five and then out for three or four or five. Rhythmically, flowing, wheeling in and back and round and out and never push, never hold, never be tense, flow, flow, flow, flow. Fill the lungs, the diaphragm goes down. Empty the lungs, the diaphragm comes up. Remember, the voice is already big, we are just learning how to release that bigness. Release that bigness, that bigness, that bigness. Nimminy. Nimminy. Nimminy. Many men, many men, many men. Sniff in from the one whose odour you fancy most is my advice. And read my book. Sugar Bush, I love you so. Sugar bush, sugar bush, sugar bush. / Rachel *née* Rabinovitch/Tears at the grapes with murderous paws. / That's it, that's it, that's it!'

Clifford, I fancy.

---

YES, AND AFTER my second audition at the RADA, spent and uncertain and wandering down the staircase to the front hall, it was Mr C. Turner himself who had followed me down, halted me at a turn on the stair, repetitively told me that the job had gone well, asked if he had heard a slight lisp and sent me off with a bright beam of hope to warm away my doubting. Dearest of men, I picture him now, tall, a fine head, frank eyes, spare powerful frame, fluently beautiful vibrant voice, chortlingly wicked humour. Stylish in dress and manner, a self-mocking man, a dedicated and extraordinarily effective teacher.

Clifford had soon pointed me in the direction of a Miss Scott, the academy's remedial speech teacher, a brisk and cheerful little woman whose rapidity and clarity of speech came chirruping from her in a sprinkle around the room. The lady took a proper interest in my explanation of how a boot in the gob had provoked my gnashers into taking a bite out of my own tongue, inspected the offended article, trilled of a tongue's muscularity, protrusibility, moveability, suggested that I say to her a few sibilant words, which I did. 'Lazy tongue,' she pronounced at last, 'nothing serious and easily remedied. Please write this down. "Amidst the mists and coldest frosts, With barest wrists and stoutest boasts, He thrusts his fists against the posts, And still insists he sees the ghosts." As any muscle does, your tongue simply needs regular exercise. Say that silly verse ten times before you sleep and ten times when you wake and by the end of term you will not have the slightest trace of a lisp. Sad about Dylan.' A memory of evacuation days with my elocution teacher and her litany of ghosts and posts and cloths and clothes had bobbed up in my mind as I was scratching down the hissing nonsense prescribed as remedy for my lisp by Miss Scott, and I had thought to tell her of those times but her flat and unexpected statement wiped that away: 'Sad about Dylan.'

'Yes, Miss Scott, it is sad. Thank you, good morning.'

Dylan Thomas was dead. After a ferocious whiskey binge at the

White Lion bar in Greenwich Village, New York, Dylan Thomas
had collapsed into coma and later died of what his doctors
described as 'an alcoholic insult to the brain'. There will therefore
be no longer any point in my sticking my face into the pubs near
the BBC, or in Fitzrovia or down St Martin's Lane, clutching a
fiver and the hope of buying you a drink, Dylan, for it seems that
you've drunk quite enough, nor can I be of any use to you. 'Ten
adjectives a penny, the Rimbaud of Cumdonkin Drive', you called
yourself and it is true that when O'Liver first threw a bucket of
you over me much of your poetry bewildered me, but also it is
true that most of your poetry has now stormed into my mind to
sound and sing and to whisper there and this news of your death
is a shock and I'm sad. So sad, really, that what I chiefly need is a
sympathetic Red Indian Jewess who will with sorrow hear of the
death of a thirty-nine-year-old Welsh bard, and there sits Pocahontas sipping coffee in Olivelli's, with a newspaper before her, but
the darkling little plum seems abstracted. What troubles her she
tells me but she tells it warily, slowly, carefully, not wishing, it
seems, to share with me what may be unwanted. She has just read
in the paper that Dylan Thomas has died in New York, she likes
his poetry and she wonders if I do, too. Very much. That helps
her, she tells me, because her sense of loss is goddamned
ridiculous, it's too much, really, the news has hit her like a truck,
which is absurd, but, she goes on, at least I share her joy in his
words, in his wild images, for right now she's feeling crazy, what
reason has she to feel grief?, it's so unexpected. Had I ever heard
him speak verse, ever met him? No, sweet baby, no. Just a few
months ago, Peter, she tells me, at the Young Men's Hebrew
Association in New York, funny, yes? go on, you can laugh, at the
YMHA, why, there she had heard Dylan Thomas give the first
reading of *Under Milk Wood*. There'd been other readers, too, she
says, but Dylan had read First Voice and the Rev. Eli Jenkins and
his voice was like an organ, like a trumpet, like an angel, really,
Peter, and he had seemed so fine, she tells me, and well, and

strong, the play had tickled her, and moved her, the audience had been with it, every word, at the end there'd been such applause, such a buzz, there'd been no obscurity, the play and the characters had come over with such clarity, such humanity, such richness. Jesus, she tells me, what a damned shame! Jesus, she tells me, what a damned waste!

'Amidst the mists and coldest frosts'. Bollocks.

---

THEN THERE had been Madame Fletcher's ballet class. It sounded quaint enough, quaint as the suggested but not compulsory leotard and ballet shoes which one could wear for this fancy hoofing. Nor had the idea of squandering my pennies from heaven on such fripperies so much as pressed a reaching hand into my pocket. Not, that is, until Jilly and Jenny had come smiling by me, linked their arms into mine, bowled me away to the Charing Cross Road, waltzed me into an establishment there, an outfitters for practitioners of the art of the ballet, and seen to it that the place promptly set to kitting me out with appropriate togs.

Jilly and Jenny were a delightful pair, typical of a sort of young woman for whom the academy served well as a finishing school; educated, confident, middle-class girls who had no intention of becoming actresses, every intention of enjoying for a few terms, before stepping on the marriage-go-round, full lives as students and fortunate enough to own daddies who could afford the fees. Knock it if you will, it was surely knocked in my day, but the Jillies and the Jennies whole-heartedly pitched into everything that was going; with their relaxed manner they brought charm and gaiety into all the daily doings; were warm and encouraging to their peers, and gave the old place much style and attractiveness. Thus it was that Jilly and Jenny saw to it that in no way would I be let to show up to Madame Fletcher's ballet class wearing shorts and plimsolls but would arrive properly clad in leotard and ballet shoes.

Came the day of the race, Bob and I set out from our spaciously comfy diggings to walk the few steps downhill to where Bob's ancient, gaudy, chronically disabled and tiny Humphrey was parked. To stuff ourselves into Humphrey's confines, to crank a handle, to wrench and grab and shove at levers gears and knobs, to hear life reluctantly wheezing in his venerable mechanism, to start the poor old bugger, to feel him judder away in arthritic canter, to enjoy for a mile or so his merry old groaning progress, to hear his enfeebled faculties grunt, complain and shudder into paralytic immobility, to shove him into a grateful peace at a kerbside, to hop on to the underground rattler for the rest of the trip.

As is the way of matters, we students of Miss Carter had drifted into a number of small groups, groups by no means exclusive cliques, just groups of young men and women at ease with each other, happy to enjoy together a blather or a drink or a flirt or a visit to the theatre or cinema. Slim Mac, Albert Finney, Mikey B., Bob and I, the male ingredients of our mix, Pocahontas, Jilly, Jenny, Sal and Jeannie the female. Jilly and Jenny, cultured, friendly, attractive; Sal, a 22-carat golden honey, leggy, pretty, shapely, a lass to lust after right enough, a lass who knew it, was charmed and amused by it, didn't flaunt it overmuch, and who was a cheerful chatty companion; Jeannie, a beautiful girl, graceful, slender, shy, long black hair and wide light eyes, not difficult to draw into our laughter and tumbling old talk, but a girl who did so easily draw apart from us and over whom there regularly fell a strange and disturbingly dark shade; Pocahontas was my fancy, my Hopi Hebrew, that is all you need to know.

Into the room in which Madame Fletcher conducted her ballet classes, then, this troupe of students rehearsing Nell Carter's production of *As You Like It*, all variously and in fine assortment clad, the more diligent among us sporting the proper attire of leotard and ballet shoe. Bare the room bar one large mirrored wall; at the opposite end stern Madame Fletcher stands, watchful and impassive; along the length of the long side walls barres jut out, some four feet up from the dogshelf, rib height, sturdily made and strongly fixed into their moorings. Sternly, Madame Fletcher suggests that we take up separate positions at these barres on both sides of the room. Shuffle, shuffle, jockey, jockey, we are standing at our barres, facing Madame Fletcher, before me is Finney, A., behind me Reliable Bob. More sternly, Madame Fletcher advises that we clutch the barre with our right hand and then, in perfect copy of her demonstration, we are to assume what she terms the First Position. With flowing ease Madame Fletcher's hand lightly rests on a barre and then deftly her heels come together while her feet point out at absolute right angles. 'First Position,' says Madame Fletcher in a sharp voice. 'And one, two, three.' Placing one's trotters at an unaccustomed quarter to three, as it were, is not an easy manoeuvre. However, grab the barre, plonk down one foot in disjointed fashion, pointing sideways from the body, add the heel of one's other foot to the heel of the plonked foot, stick it out in a similarly unnatural way, and there you have it, the First Position. Well, I do. Albie does. From behind Bob is mouthing quite a lot of quiet, fruity dialogue but one imagines, surely, that he's managed it. From my position of inverted letter T, my gaze around the room shows me that a fair number of customers, mostly women, are dab hands at this ballet lark and, really, thus far everything is going fairly smoothly. 'Stand up straight,' slices Madame Fletcher's voice. This we do. There is a slight ache in the knee, the calves, a few curses are being wrung from Bob, that's to be expected, young Finney is in no trouble at all, relaxed and poker straight with feet akimbo. True, that from in front of him a harmony of small whimpers issue out of Slim Mac and Mikey B., but what of that? All the class seem to be doing well and it's only a matter, surely, of rendering the limbs the ligaments the muscles lithe supple and pliant. 'Turn round,' scythes Miss Fletcher. 'Left hand on the barre. First Position.' It's obvious from my new angle that the most Bob can muster is an arrangement of his feet into an irresolute ten minutes to two, nor does he even attempt to stand up straight, his head is bowed, he seems to be peering in astonishment at the behaviour of his feet, that they should have chosen to stick out from his body completely in the wrong direction. Second Position next. In this exercise one contorts and distorts the poor feet in like manner to the First Position, but the trotters are screwed round to the right, to the left, with one placed apart from the other and twelve inches of space between each twisted heel. Turn round. Right hand on barre. Second Position. Stand up straight. Aches in the limbs constantly gnaw away now; the odd pang, the odd twinge shoots hot into unexpected parts of one's person; oaths float about the room, from Slim Mac certainly, from Mikey B. of course; I'm all right, Albie's all right but Bob behind me is spouting a soliloquy on the doubtful benefits of splayfooted deformity. Positions Three and Four, razored by Miss Fletcher, when they come, turn out almost to be a strange relief. True it is that one needs must wrench one's sorry rear trotter into a right-angled deformity, with consequent spurts of gyp shooting up the twisting limb, but the one in front is encouraged to flick itself out in unrestrained freedom for a breath of air and a shake, its task, then, merely to return from this giddy liberty and to touch with its heel the instep of the one behind, rooted as it is complaining and askew. Turn round. Left hand on the barre. Away we go. I've survived, Albie's survived, there is comparative calm from the direction of Mikey B. and Slim Mac and with both elbows Bob is leaning on the barre giving in turn both his feet a little shake, mayhap to promote circulation of the blood, mayhap to reassure himself that both of them are still attached. 'Fifth Position,' slashes Madame Fletcher. No, no, no, Madame Fletcher, really, a joke's a joke but fuck a pantomime. We are to do what? Both our feet are to be warped into these bizarre and suffering right angles to the body but with the heel of the front foot pressing against the toes of the back foot and the toes of the back foot pressing against the heel of the front foot? This, Madame Fletcher, is to put ourselves on to a grievous rack. This cannot be, when our Maker built them, what He had intended as right positions for our feet. He set them, surely, to point ahead of us, set and ready for the lope, the trot, the easy amble, not thrusting out to the east, to the west, not jammed together in parallel and hideous distortion. Grinding and straining I torment my feet into an approximation of the contortion demanded by the Fifth Position. Stand up straight. Oh, oh, I do, I do my best to stand up straight but the calves, the knees, the ankles are in knots and screaming. Turn round. Left hand on barre. Bob has gone. Has pissed off. Out of the room, away from this misery, hobbling, no doubt, in the direction of the nearest pint of beer, while behind me Finney grunts, curses, and beyond him Slim Mac and Mikey B. are gibbering in hysteria. 'Plié,' stabs Madame Fletcher. That means bends. Bends, I tell you, bends. Your Demi-Plié, your Full Plié. One's feet remain in a cruel and squashed swastika but, with back erect and head poised, one grabs the barre and sets to bending the crooked, twisted, misshapen knees, and as the ligaments, tendons, muscles burn and split, one lowers one's bottom towards the ground, heels on the floor for the Demi, heels raised for the Full. As the suffering class press their racked bodies into this gruesome labour, the rifle shots of cracking bones ping from all directions and bullet through the howls of agony.

'Grand Battement.' Leave it out, you mad woman, leave it out. We are young men and women of flesh and bone and sinew not puppets of rubber, string and pipe cleaners. How can one possibly, with feet remaining mangled and grotesquely ill-directed in this Fifth Position throw one leg ninety degrees to the side, insist that one's entire body is straight, throw one leg ninety degrees to the front, again insisting that one's entire body is straight, throw one leg ninety degrees behind, yet again insisting that one's entire body is straight? This would be to maim oneself, madam, to inflict on oneself dislocations, grief, ruptures. To be sure, I will have a crack at this cruel insanity, sure as I am that so will Finney, A., and it is obvious that a number of your female charges can with skill execute these perverse manoeuvres, but can it be doubted that since infancy they will have attended these torture chambers of ballet classes and by doing so deformed bones and brain when they were yet young and pig ignorant? Oh, Lord have mercy on all bar Madame Fletcher, here we jolly well go. Dear me, that's over, pain grinds through each inch of me and I have grave worries concerning the whereabouts of my testicles. Yes. Turn round. Left hand on barre. That, more or less, by and large, give or take, is over. What? What is it you say? What? You are a woman gone barking mad, Fletcher the Stretcher, one that is foaming with sadism. Grand Rond de Jambe. From the Fifth Position and at ninety degrees the leg is thrown in the air to the front, in the air to the side, in the air to the back and all in one grand round sweep! Look at the faces of your charges. Haggard with agony gouged deeply into their young features. Bob is undone quite and has retired hurt. Albie and I have played much at the ball, are fit, strong, yet look at us. We both are crocked. Mikey B. and Slim Mac are scholarly men, bookish, game for a romp on stage but not your likely candidates for medals at field and track events. Observe, do, the state they are in, the pair of them. Rictus grins on suffering kissers, their breaths the shallow gulps of the near dead. Grand Rond de Jambe, here we come. Grand Rond de Jambe, there you go.

Ruined; ballet class over; muscles, tendons, general bits of me, parts, perhaps, never in twenty-one years' existence ever having been employed before, whine out complaints at being pressed into such unexpected crude service, as I sit with my back against the wall under the tormenting barre and puff my necessary cigarette. Jilly and Jenny join me, to sit one on either side of me, to share my smoke, the three of us dressed in leotards and ballet shoes.

'Did you enjoy that?' says Jilly. 'You certainly looked the part.' I am not able to croak a word.

'You'll find,' says Jenny, 'that your feet shouldn't be too blistered. That's why your shoemaker spent so much time on measurements and fitting. Your thighs and knees and calves shouldn't be chafed raw, either, the leotard helps stop that. Pity about the osteoporosis.'

'The what?' wheeze I.

'Brittleness of bone,' says Jilly. 'Many ballet dancers, particularly if they began dancing young, lack density in their bones. This may lead to the bones becoming brittle. Osteoporosis.'

'Just imagine,' says Jenny, 'all our legs and arms snapping like old dead dry twigs for art's sake. Too droll.' What is there to do but only laugh? So we do that. We laugh and we laugh and we laugh. Osteoporosis, here we come.

---

WE HAD BEEN GIVEN our instructions, Bob and I. Our duties as relief party entailed that at four p.m. precisely we would report to the queue for tickets in the gallery at the Old Vic, where we would relieve the doughty souls who had braved a brisk November afternoon patiently to stand in the van of dozens of souls waiting for the opening of the box office and the good chance of scooping up a clutch of some of the most prized theatre tickets to be had in London. The twenty-eight-year-old Richard Burton was said to be blazing up the stage and certainly the town was trooping to the Vic and the old place was alive and packed with the press of customers. These our orders had been given us by my Hopi, my Hebrew from stormy, husky, brawling Chicago, for Pocahontas was daily revealing herself to be not only a knowledgeable, deeply interested student of the theatre and its plays and players, one resolute in her determination to witness its modern and innovatory manifestations, a true lover of its history and traditions, but also one with skill for organization and an effortless bossiness. Now, my part had been merely to mention that this here Burton bloke who had made it big and wide in a film called *The Robe*, bigger yet and wider than any other new twinkler on the cinema scene, not only by the scale and breadth of his talent but also on account of the film being made and shown in a new process dubbed 'Cinemascope', a form which was to vie with our received black and white square silver screen and to replace it with a huge oblong yardage of colour, and that this magnified polychromatic Hollywood film star, Burton, was at present on the boards at the Old Vic having a crack at some of the big parts in Shakespeare. 'Ought to be worth a look,' or such like, I'd said to my Hopi. '*King John*,' she'd replied. '*The Life and Death of King John*, a new production of it has just opened, with Burton playing Faulconbridge the Bastard. One of Shakespeare's histories that's not often done. Not much action but there are some sharp scenes, terrific language and the characters, men and women, are subtle and gutsy, Constance of Bretagne is a furnace while Burton looks born to rip into that ballsy Bastard, d'you agree?'

'There can be no doubt,' or somesuch, I'd said, knowing only at that time that Shakespeare had probably written a play called *King John* because I seemed to remember seeing the name included among the titles listed in my *Collected Works*, 'no doubt at all. We must make shift to see it, mustn't we, Bob.' Pocahontas had pointed out that tickets were almost impossible to get but that she and her flatmates and a friend were going to work a rota system for gallery seats at the weekend and that if Bob and I wished we could join them and that she would rearrange matters and see to it that we both occupied a designated shift in the queue. Well, freezing our bollocks off on a winter's day down the Waterloo Road while shuffling along in the hope of being sold tickets for comfortless seats which gave one a view from half a mile away of the tops of the players' heads had not been an option which had loomed large in either Bob's brain or mine. Still and all, there was a crackle in the air about the company playing at the Old Vic, staff and students of the RADA were going there in bunches, there was increasingly sweet pleasure in her company, that Chicagoan, Bob was game for practically any lark, and so we had said we would join the dance.

Once again I invested in an Arden and boned up on the play. The text and the footnotes delighted me, while the scholarly introduction had me plodding so that Bob was amazed to find me actually staying in our digs for two whole evenings, breaking my concentration only for a couple of brief visits to the pub, there to rinse my teeth with refreshing light ale. Within a couple of days or so, I think I had the drift. In the context of Elizabethan Tudor England, Shakespeare's play *King John* must have been excitingly, even dangerously, topical. It seems that Shakespeare may have taken some shakily rewritten history and the bold lad had made it even more shaky by implicitly commentating on the accepted histories of disputed successions to the throne and the cynical methods of dynasties. By thrusting these daring manipulations of historical fact with the floating knowledge of the age, W. Shakespeare has a thirteenth-century Plantagenet, John, utter great echoes of the recently dead sixteenth-century Henry Tudor's Reformation. The Pope is called an 'Italian Priest'; civil war, the great dread of Elizabethan England, is a feature of scene after scene; it is played out that neither the youth of children nor disparity of age or character is a bar in the case of dynastic marriage, so long as Church and State come to terms; in the fictitious form of Faulconbridge, Shakespeare puts on stage for the audience's delight a bastard son of Richard I, a reincarnation of legendary Lionheart himself; but, there again, Elizabeth was childless, there was much gossip and more high and serious talk about legitimate succession. Tudor? Stuart? Usurpation? Rich, speculative, provocative matter this, especially in the context of a late sixteenth-century playhouse and its audience. Thus armed with painlessly swotted knowledge, I felt much better able to encounter my savage Hopi.

Gallery queue replacement day arrived, Bob and I agreed it would be more prudent, more compassionate to let old Humphrey rest on in undisturbed slumber and so we hopped on the rattler to ride along and to spill off at Waterloo station. Nearly four p.m, dim, and the shrill November nip baffled out by my warm and roomy donkey jacket, an overcoated Reliable Bob and I approached the considerable queue of punters lined up at the side of the Old Vic.

My darksome little lass was already there, flask of hot coffee in hand, patrolling the queue, quick eyes on the lookout for the arrival of the relief party. 'Hi,' says she, 'you have choices. A slug of hot black sweet coffee or no hot black sweet coffee. Come and meet your new friends.' Towards the head of the queue, sitting on the little canvas stools which in those days had been kindly provided by the management of the Vic for patient prospective customers of the gods to park their waiting bottoms on, was a handsome young chap of my age, with bright light eyes and a friendly grin, perching next to two of the prettiest girls you could ever wish to see.

Call the bloke Cotton-eyed Joe, call the birds Nina Von and Nina Van. Prior to this relieved party going off for a shake and a stamp of cramped cold limbs, a belt of warmth from inside somewhere, and over welcome gulps of coffee prepared exactly to our several tastes, we all had a quick sort-out of the who and the where and the what and the when of each other's lot, leaving the why of our being drama students properly in its imperfect state. Joe was a recently demobilized young English Army officer, he told me, who had turned up to his RADA auditions wearing a three-piece suit and a bowler hat. He had been accepted as a student but left with the burden of paying his own fees and living expenses. This totted up to a considerable chunk of change, with which chunk he was providing himself by working as an usher and ice-cream vendor at a cinema near the academy. To date, he told me with a bemused cheerfulness, he had seen the film *Houdini* seventeen times. Nina Von was a tall and an attractive scattily funny buxom Californian with a great tumble of dark hair who had, said she, comically batting long black eyelashes, vamped her way through the New York auditions for the RADA and whose parents were well off enough and happy enough to pay her fees and to give her wedges of folding lettuce for lodgings and living. In the intuitive way which one learns to trust only much later, it was clear to me, and in time would become much clearer, that Nina Van had gained her place at the academy on merit. A merit, moreover, buoyed up by having pennies enough to preclude anxieties over fees or scholarships, and a merit which lived in charming diffidence and an exquisitely featured yellow-haired blue-eyed tall and lovely Canadian frame. Mercy.

We six huffed and puffed, came and went, chatted and prattled, until at last the lid was lifted at the box office. The precious gallery seats safely bought, we galloped up the stairs, claimed six of the best pews at the front, took it in turns either to guard our claims or nip off to the boozer for a livener, then settled down warm and ready for the play. The red plush of the Vic was jammed to the rafters, the hubbub of the packed house contained but crackling. Though it is probably true that no audience goes to a theatre expecting to see a poor performance, the anticipatory excitement one sensed that night will ever remain a rarity.

One matter alone irked me: a pattern of protuberances decked out four square about an unlovely extrusion jutting from what surely should have been simply a stage. My programme, I believe, told me that it was a façade designed to provide a permanent setting in which the entire canon of W. Shakespeare's plays could be contained. Fancy. The same, I thought then and firmly think now, could have been said of the little stage in the attic theatre at my old Arts Centre, and without so much as displacing a plank. Over the years my poor ears have been cauliflowered by bore after bore after crucifying bore, each with his or her particular shriek on the form of the Elizabethan Playhouse; with the further shriek that the content of Elizabethan or Jacobean plays can only fully be realized in his or her preferred form. As there exists no reliable contemporary representation of an Elizabethan theatre, one truly wonders what drives these fidgets of form to such clenched emphasis. A copy drawing done from memory of a sketch made by a Dutchman when visiting London of what may have been his idea of what the Swan Theatre looked like, is to be found in many a thick book and often is used as hard evidence of the pattern of all sixteenth-century playhouses. A contemporary engraving of the shady area outside the jurisdiction of the City of London where Shakespeare had his Curtain Theatre was often waved at one as proof positive of the exterior shape of this theatre. However, in the sixties the American scholar Schöenbaum suggested that if you took your eyes away from the round building with the flag on top in the middle of the engraving and slid them down to the bottom right-hand corner, you would find a polygonal building with a flag on its top which was much more likely to be a playhouse, one to which the name Curtain would not be inappropriate. There also is a document which tells us that the Fortune Theatre was an eighty-foot-square timber building which had two galleries. A while back, after an archaeological excavation had uncovered the Rose Theatre, contemporaneous with Shakespeare and on the south bank of the river Thames, I had a word with the archaeologist who was attempting to make an architectural reconstruction of the theatre in model form. Much of the theatre's shape would have to be a matter of educated speculation, he told me, but the stage was in dimension, situation, material and setting almost exactly the same as the stage of the present-day Apollo Theatre on Shaftesbury Avenue. Well, of course it was. Building regulations and safety precautions have insisted that, for fear of collapse, circles and galleries no longer should jut out over the stalls, thus removing those sitting in them further from the stage, and that playhouses no longer should shove as many customers as possible into one great squeezing heap inside them but, give or take a little comfort and precaution, over millennia our vernacular playhouse has evolved into a fair and pretty shape which makes busybodied tampering a howling bore. An auditorium seating about a thousand in more or less shape of a horseshoe, with the stage set facing in from the blunt end of the shoe. The stage should rake down, the seating areas rake up. When the stage is lit, this arrangement allows an audience a fair sight of any production and, more importantly, gives a focus of concentration to both the audience and the actors and allows an author's work to be seen and heard in the ordinary context of a playhouse. Painters have long known of this focus of concentration. True, you have your triptych, your diptych and even J. M. W. Turner painted a couple of roundy jobs but most painters are content to see their daubings wrapped safely in rectangular frames. The frames, of course, are irrelevant; the subject within them, and their reciprocity with their viewers, being the whole of the point. So too it is with playhouses. As the violin has, so to a certain shape have theatres evolved. Yes, I'm aware of implications from within a text. Yes, the inn, the courtyard, the upstairs and downstairs. Yes, stick the stage out a little into the auditorium if you really must, but for God's sake don't make it a religion.

In the middle of this century, my dislike of fidgetry was as keen as it is now that the bloody thing shunts into its terminus. In 1953, though, as Nina Van and Nina Von, Reliable Bob, Cotton-eyed Joe, my Hopi and I sat on our seats at the front of the gallery in the Old Vic, it proved only to be a temporary distraction, clumsy but of no importance as the house lights dimmed and the warmth of our companionship melded with the individuals and the partners, the strangers and familiars, the men and women in the auditorium of the playhouse, united all in the body of that wonderful and eager animal, an audience. 'Now, say, Chatillon,' spoke King John, 'what would France with us?' The play had begun. That apprentice actor I was that night, consciously sensed, and perhaps for the first time, that rich communion in the trinity of author, actor and audience. A wholeness of purpose flowing in connection and consent from the stage to the house, from the house to the stage, from the author to the actors, from the actors to the audience, from the audience to the play, from the play to the players, from the players to the playhouse. A co-operation of will and imagination that for its two or so hours' traffic becomes our chosen actuality. One often hears parroted that dreadful phrase 'suspension of disbelief'. It reminds me always of cowpokes being compelled to hang up their six-shooters before being let into the saloon. Are the parrots aware, one wonders not too earnestly, that those three often iterated words were plucked by a penny-a-line journalist in the early nineteenth century from one florid twist in a conversational curlicue uttered by Coleridge as set down in his *Table Talk*? After sinking a pail of opium Coleridge's drift on any subject must have been a rare old ramble round the houses, no doubt interesting if riddlesome to his listeners, but one quaint dropping from his tongue on the subject of the metaphysical composition of an audience's mind should in my view be looked on with kindness but no great seriousness. Our game, actors', authors', is old as speech. It is story-telling. It is tacit participation in a fiction which in theatre mode is made by audiences and actors. An audience trusts that we actors will deliver the goods in the shape of a fine play well acted; to that end they will travel to a playhouse, pay for a seat and give themselves over heart and mind to what they see and hear. When we at the business end take our wages and keep faith with that trust, the work of a playhouse can be deeply satisfying both to act in and to witness. Break that faith by serving up rubbish either in play or performance, a disappointed audience might sound out a boo or two but they can and will do worse and the actors and the author will find that they are playing their entertainment to what for centuries has been known in the theatre as Mr and Mrs Wood: empty seats.

Mr and Mrs Wood were not present that night at the Old Vic when a crowded house lived every moment of Michael Hordern's serpent-subtle King John. Now smoothly, now jerkily, always regally, he smiled and blustered and soothed a virtuoso politician's way through Shakespeare's five acts, finding as he went the price of all men, including his own, on a royal progress made at the cost of his life. Poisoned by a monk, the king sits on a chair in an orchard, slowly, agonizingly dying as the corrosive venom unhurriedly burns away his vitals. How Michael Hordern brought dignity and ironic humour to this tormented end, his body convulsed, scalded, his mind detached, able to witness and to comment on his awful suffering, is a question which only the finest actors can answer. When Richard Burton strutted his Bastard on to the stage, he fetched with him a virility and poetry which neither before nor since have I seen matched in any playhouse. Power he brought, and insouciance; laughter, energy, danger; a rapidity of action and mental agility which throbbed; a relaxation and stillness which magnetized; an eye and a presence which commanded, and a glorious voice which rang and hushed and boomed and stung into every sounding inch of the auditorium. Much of what the Bastard says is a compound of slang, eloquence and yokel speech. Such was Richard's understanding of the very nature of the Bastard, and the skill he brought to the weight, nuance and balance of each word and phrase, that this mix blended into a singular essence which defined and made whole Shakespeare's reincarnated Lionheart. Patriotic rhetoric he sang out with stirring vigour, while his candid soliloquies revealed a man who with no change of manner yet showed a quality of supreme contempt for the ways of the world, the follies of kings and a determination to get with relish anything of worth that he could grab. Fay Compton, known to me only from films and from having read that she had played Ophelia to John Barrymore's Hamlet, scorched her way around the stage as Constance, her cry in Act Three Scene One of 'War! War! no peace! peace is to me a war', searing into the audience with a force that was astonishing.

Nell Carter had quietly impressed on the students of her class that the blank verse in which Shakespeare wrote held ten syllables in each line and if we had the will mechanically to make sure that the tenfold sounds were pronounced clearly, then very shortly the sense and rhythm would conjoin into a distinct and inseparable harmony. 'Human speech as an art form', is what she had said and though at first it is difficult for novice actors and actresses, whose concerns rightly are with feeling and meaning, to accept this crafted fact, the entire cast of *King John* at the Old Vic that night spoke with an energy and a clarity and a music that was thrilling and made me long to have a crack at the lovely stuff.

The final words of the last act had been spoken. The play was done. A thousand pairs of arms hammered hands together in a great clatter of admiring approval for the cast and the play, and as the house lights came on that extraordinary creature, an audience, divided itself into its hundreds of groups and individuals who then went their variously separate ways from the theatre.

Nina Von made it clear that the rest of us could do as we wished but that she was going to the stage door in the hope of having a sumptuous ogle of Richard Burton, whom she considered to be a cute hunk of real man. No demur came from the heap and so round to the stage door we trooped where, pretty prospect, I saw that right next to it stood a welcoming pub. Mentioning, I fancy, that from where I had sat the spouting out of reams of blank verse had looked desperately thirsty work, that after their labours some of the players might feel moved to wet their dehydrated whistles, that what with the pub being so adjacent and all it could well be the very spot in which tired mummers from the Vic might choose to reinvigorate and to lubricate themselves, that, any road, my throat was dry as a loofah, it croaked for moisture so why didn't we pop into the pub, that I would buy a round of drinks, and from this hospitable base Nina Von could shuttle to and fro in hope of copping a squint of her cute hunk of real man. Done. Into the pub we went, there was a cluster of unoccupied seats at a table near the bar, these we claimed, drinks we bought, Nina Von Nina Van and the Hopi at whiles wandered in and out of the boozer, Joe and Bob sucked their drinks and chatted and I arranged myself for a smoke and a sip and a ponder. Yes, no doubt my reading of a scholarly introduction to the play *King John* had been interesting and instructive. No doubt. Yes, the expert juggling by Shakespeare of received history had empha-sized similarities in the reigns of John and Elizabeth. An English sovereign, rumoured to be a usurper, possibly a bastard, defies the Pope, becomes Supreme Head, suffers excommunication, imprisons a rival; the Pope promises to canonize his murderer, invites another king to invade England; the English sovereign hints to a loyal subject that he should kill a rival pretender to the throne; with the help of disaffected Englishmen a foreign invasion is attempted and the invaders intend to kill their helpers, their navy is providentially wrecked off the English coast and English unity is finally achieved through the failure of this invasion. These considerations had been informative and germane to the matter of the play, no doubt. But. I had seen and heard the words of a play that I had read transubstantiated into the bodies and blood of men and women on a stage. I had seen actors and actresses who had incorporated into their beings the words of that play and by making life from those words had created such a living link with us men and women in the audience that we had lived with them every phrase and action made by the characters of the play. A little miracle I think, scholars, and though I thank you for your work and will in the future always read your commentaries on the classics, I know that it is from the example and instruction of first-class professional players and from somewhere deep inside myself that I will learn how to act in these plays.

Hello. It is less than half an hour since the play ended, the Hopi, the Ninas sit with Bob Joe and me and into the pub pushes what appears to be the entire cast of *King John*. The King of France has bought drinks and is passing them to Cardinal Pandulph, the Dauphin has his head dipped into a foam of Guinness and here comes Burton calling for a pint. They are a cheerful bunch, sparky, voluble, dry as one expected and the ale goes around and down. Here is Constance of Bretagne. Stern yet mischievous, handsome, and giving what appears to be a ribbing to a donnish and perplexed King John. Burton has lifted his pint with an ease and sure-handedness that tells of diligent practice; parched ancestors from the coal pits of Wales live on in his sturdy body as the glass pint pot is applied to his mouth, and no miner up from the shaft after a double-header at the black coal face could have managed better his deep first sweet suck. Well played, Richard Burton! Laugh your easy laugh, light a fag, swig your ale, lean against the bar and look about you. Here sit six drama students, lately up in the gods, now come down to earth, sitting in a pub and looking at members of the Old Vic Company who this evening have so thoroughly entertained us when performing in a play. What my friends are thinking, I can't know. Me? The sight and sound of the chatter and the laughter made by you and your companions, and the ease with which you are all spreading yourselves about the pub, the warmth and vitality engendered, why, it delights me but though I can see and hear all this, I cannot yet touch it, am excluded, for you are professionals and I am not. Not at all, not even an experienced amateur. Not, in fact, an actor. And yet. Do I sense a tie of kinship? A tie which I have already sensed with my teachers at the RADA, professionals all? Perhaps. We will see. Meanwhile, though I am in a true sense excluded from it, I shall be happy on the fringe of your company.

Hello. Burton, R., is having a deep greeny-blue eyeful of Ninas

Von and Van and the choice Pocahontas. Can you blame him? These three bonny babes would fill a gladdened eye on any man and what price but the fluttering and batting eyelashes of Nina Von are quite disturbing the smoky air? Not half. Yellow-haired Nina Van and the blue sparkles of her eyes, though, seem at present to be keeping him from his beer but, yes, there goes his look right into the hithering welcome so shamelessly and hilariously being put out by Nina Von and when he gets round to the savage he will find her to be deeply interested in the theatre programme. Now, did you ever meet a young man who with complacency could watch while the women in his company were being given a thorough scrutiny by another young man in a pub? A stranger at that? An actor? A bloody film star? It was while I was adjusting my ears to their pinned-back position and mustering up one of my better grim scowls, that Richard took his gaze away from the women, glanced at Joe, at Bob, and then looked straight at me. A grin as big as it was friendly and as warm as it was wide spread over his face. His eyes sent a merry message which said that, on the whole, I could be in much worse company. He raised his glass to me, to my friends, we raised our glasses to him, and then with the grin still on him he ambled away to sit with Lewis and Philip of France at a table on the other side of the bar.

Six young drama students went happily home that night and Bob and I drank bottles of beer and talked until dawn.

---

A HINT OF VICAR hovered around Denys Blakelock. Attach a straw hat, bicycle clips and a dog collar to him, let him judge a marrow, solemnize a marriage, raise funds for a steeple and there you'd have him, your perfect platitude of vicarhood. Nor did he mind my mentioning these fancies. Not at all. Roses bloomed on his clerical cheeks, he laughed his clerical laugh, wiped his clerical spectacles, and before going off on his clerical way, he told me that a couple of years previously he had played the Vicar in *The White Sheep of the Family* at the Piccadilly Theatre, that one of his favourite parts had been the Dean in *Dandy Dick* and that he was the son of the Reverend Martin Ogle Blakelock, an Anglican vicar.

A distinguished actor, Denys was our teacher of diction at the academy and it was only after months of my being one of his pupils that I would cough up about the role I had ordained for him. Rich months they were, months during which I learned much and not only on the subject of diction, although what Denys taught us on that matter remains with me now and is indispensably valid, but also he was a thoughtful, bookish, friendly man, one who had no thought of condescension as he looked on us his students for the young green colleagues he believed we were. A richly experienced man of the theatre, his professional life had been long and deep and varied. After leaving the RADA in 1920, a play by the Indian philosopher Rabindranath Tagore had given him his first job; after that he was continuously in work. Mostly in London, occasionally in a classical revival, usually in new plays, he had acted dozens of parts the range of which was remarkable. Characters different as the silky aristocratic assassin of Rasputin, Prince Felix Yussoupov, to the raw, dissipated Branwell Brontë, he had acted with success. Throughout the war, Denys worked at the Arts Theatre, acting in plays by Shaw, Shakespeare, Odets, Pinero, Sheridan. At the war's end he played Cecil Graham in Oscar Wilde's *Lady Windermere's Fan* but in 1948 came *Dandy Dick* and his performance of the Very Rev. Augustin Jedd, DD. A performance which, surely, had sparked off in him parsonical mutations and had blessed him with that whiff of vicar which I was to encounter some five years later. This wealth of experience, diverse and solid, had allowed Denys Blakelock to bank up many notions and considerations about actors and acting, none of which were dogmatic, all of which, if one wished, he could precisely express, and the whole of which began, departed, returned and ended on one simple theme: clarity.

Quietly, conversationally, the pitch of his voice effortless, his diction limpid, the Rev. Blakelock strolled among his flock of students and in ways which were relaxed and unusual, ministered to us on the subject of articulate speech. His reputation in the theatre for speaking clearly, he said, had probably been a factor in Sir Kenneth Barnes' decision to offer him the post as teacher of diction at the RADA. However, having accepted the job, he had thought it wise to read a number of books on the subject and to discuss with colleagues technical points. What he had heard and read, he confessed, had at times quite astonished him. For example: many of us may be aware, but he had been completely unaware, that it was only when pronouncing the consonants B, M, P, Y and W that the middle of our lips should touch each other. This had been a complete surprise, had led him into making mouths in a looking glass, the better to perform an experiment, and the mirror and his mouth had shown him concrete proof that the assertion was correct. The pronunciation of B, M, P, W and Y, but no other letter in our alphabet, requires the centre of our lips to connect. Surely, he said he had thought, the consonants F and V were candidates for involving the lips in the lightest of connections. Alas, no. Another bout of grimacing and sputtering at a looking glass had revealed to him that a properly pronounced F or V demanded the lower lip briefly to press against the upper teeth but that the sole function of the top lip was to keep out of the way.

Further astonishment was his lot, he said, on first hearing and reading about vowel sounds. Oh. Ay. Ee. Ah. Oo. It was rather the tongue, he discovered, not the mouth whose function it was to modulate these sounds made by the voice into their rounds, sharps and flats. The mouth has a part: it should have a lively tension which will assist in the release of the vowel sound but the mouth should not form the shape of that vowel sound. Once again, he said, he had presented himself to the mirror, opened his mouth but only slightly, gone carefully, quietly through the vowel repertoire and to his surprise found that by experimentally moulding with his tongue the sounds he was summoning from his vocal cords, the while moving his mouth hardly at all, he was able successfully to produce Ohs, Ays, Ees, Ahs and Oos. So much, said the Rev. Blakelock, for any photographer who might in the future ask him to say 'cheese'. It had then been suggested to him by a phonetician that he clench between his teeth a rubber eraser, pucker his lips relaxedly but firmly, and then recite the first line of Hamlet's advice to the players. 'Speak the speech, I pray you, as I pronounc'd it to you, trippingly on the tongue; but if you mouth it, as many of our players do, I had as lief the town-crier spoke my lines.' This, at comical intervals, he had practised for a week; at the end of which week, he told us, he had discovered several new and refreshing facts about speaking. One was that thus encumbered and with only minor stifles and strangulations he could clearly enunciate the line from Hamlet. Another was that, despite his reputation for clear speaking, he had overworked his mouth but under-employed his tongue. Yet another was that, though there was still too much movement of his upper lip, he quite enjoyed munching his rubber eraser for five minutes each day, and was confident that his tongue was enjoying its new nimbleness. The single most refreshing discovery he had made, though, he said, was that his friend the phonetician had not arbitrarily chosen for use as an exercise the first sentence of Hamlet's advice to the players. Not at all. The sentence had been chosen because it exactly expressed the physical fact that it was control of the tongue which enabled all speech properly to be pronounced, while the mouth, if employed at all, were better left to mouthing town-criers.

Until this recent discovery, he went on as he wandered round the room, addressing his remarks now to this student, now to the next, he had always taken his diction for granted. He was from an educated middle-class family, both his parents had spoken clearly and his sole standard regarding correctness of speech had been in the custom and common usage of the community in which he lived. When he became an actor, the largest adjustment to his speech that he made had been a huge increase in volume. How many of us, he wondered, came from similar backgrounds to his, where clarity of utterance had been practised from birth? How many had been raised to speak sloppily and indistinctly? How many had strong regional accents which nailed them to precise geographical locations? For that matter, how many cleaved to these accents in the belief that any disciplined adjustments to them would lead to the erosion of their identities? To these last, if any, he would suggest that they make sure they were not merely mimicking slovenly speech, while to all of us he would suggest a specific consideration. All actors and actresses dealt largely in a common currency: the spoken word. What we call speech. Speech allows us to make our thoughts known to others. Articulate speech allows us to make our thoughts known clearly to others. Over the next two years we would do well to decide if articulate speech was to be our preferred means of communication, or if articulate speech should be reserved only for special occasions, such as when playing Hamlet. Please remember, he said clearly, that it is my happy task to help you if you so wish, and also please remember that communication must be understood or it is a nonsense. Now, there is much to be done; mouthing to be discontinued, tongues encouraged to function trippingly and a warning note to be sounded. In 1928, Bernard Shaw gave an address to the RADA. There was one sentence from it which he quite enjoyed repeating. 'The way in which the stage will find out every single weakness that you have got, every folly that you have got, every vanity that you have got, every little slip in self-control that you are subject to, is really very terrible.'

———

As vehicles for expressive plasticity of the body go, being a bubble is not without its snags. The very insubstantiality of the article insists that to survive at all one must be always on the bobble, the float, the drift, the bounce; never to be at rest, ever in dread of the immolatory pop. Better by far, I reckon, to be a cloud. To scud at whiles, to hover at times, to lower, to loom, to waft, to be still. Right. I have burst my bubble self and am become a white and fleecy cloud, one that will gently roam its vaporous ways, nor hop nor dart nor leap nor shoot as must a bubble. We have been invited, do you see, by our movement teacher, Miss Boalth, no longer to be mere creatures of the earth but imaginatively to become more elemental entities; its winds, say, its waters, its vegetation. Scope, Miss Boalth had implied, for improvisation, for free expressionistic movement. Reason, I'd thought, to blow me into a bright bubble, bowl about the room and with a bob here a bob there put a bright eye on the inventive doings of my fellow sods and soddesses. Fair enough, you may admit, as a wheeze but one, you should know, not easy very long to sustain. The restlessness of a bubble's life can be tiresome, while the fragility of its nature leaves one exposed to sharp criticism. 'Bubbles', said Jilly or Jenny, who were petals softly falling from a flower, 'don't lean against walls and smoke.' Neither do they, but who can tell as it wanders by what a cloud may conceal? Here comes Finney, A., slowly spinning by me. 'A leaf,' he tells me he is, 'blown where I know not but only as the wind wills.' Balls. Only feet away from where I hover there sways a shapely daffodil, the golden Sal, set to face the winds of March with beauty and, unless I am very much mistaken, about to acquire on her slender stem a substantial copper-knobbed leaf. There. As neat a bit of grafting as one is like to see. The Hopi. Motionless. Her arms are being gently raised now, her fingers given a wee wag. 'The still surface of a lake is what I am, honey, but every once in a while I give myself a quick ripple. Don't you love action?' I pass on, past a Jeannie hot with energy and an undulating frame. She is waves in a sea. Mikey B. stands there. His arms spread out, his body slowly swaying. 'I'm a tree,' he tells me. 'I've read a couple of pieces in newspapers which somewhat contemptuously wrote of drama students always spending time being trees, so I thought I'd keep the blighters honest and give it a go. It's good fun and rather relaxing.' On I float. Slim Mac droops before me and wobbles. His nature? 'Seaweed,' his response, 'boring seaweed. Seaweed, moreover, that sits down.' Which it does. I drift by and loom over a Reliable Bob who is lying down. 'I was a perfectly good, upright tree,' he tells me, 'but Mike hogged the part so I had myself chopped down. I am now a felled tree.' Stirring music sounds from Miss Boalth's sweet crone at the piano. We are to renounce vegetation and the elements, return to the fold of humankind, discover in ourselves ferocity, hatred, anger, and freely to express these emotions in impoverished dance. Rock on, Bessie Boalth, this lark puts Rackmaster Fletcher out of the game.

---

BEYOND THE BOURNE of a theatre curtain lies a world that we call 'Backstage'. To explore and to understand the complexities of the topography, customs and language of this world and, to learn how to become inhabitants, the RADA had thought it wise to provide us students with two experienced guides. One, Mr Hayes, gritty, practical, commonsensical, a man whose business it was to instruct us in the basics of stage management; the other, Mr Howard Williams, patrician, elegant, sophisticated, a man who, as we would learn, felt it his duty to give animation and a soul to what at first seemed disconcertedly rigid technicalities. Mr Hayes made it plain that, as a stage manager was responsible for the overall management of everything connected with the stage and backstage, the first action a novice stage manager must take would be to go backstage and on stage and learn something about all of the things over which he would have the responsibility of management. The scene dock, the paint dock, the prop room, the wardrobe, the dressing rooms, the wings, the fly floor, the prompt corner, the opposite prompt corner, the flats, the stage braces, the pulleys, the grids, the battens, the spot bars, the perch platforms, the box sets, the screens, the ground-rows, the built stuff, the spotlights, the 2Ks, the footlights, the jells, the switchboard, the back cloth, the stage cloth, the scrim, the tormentors, the teasers, the curtain, the apron, the proscenium, the false proscenium, the thunder sheet, the wind machine, the rain drum, the panatrope, the wardrobe mistress, the electricians, the carpenters, the fly man, the stage hands, the painters, the prop man, the call boy, the assistant stage managers, the dressers, and, of course, the actors and actresses. The stage itself; on to which one enters and off which one exits and which has sixteen zones. Right centre back, centre back, left centre back; upstage right, upstage centre, upstage left; upstage right centre, upstage left centre; centre stage right, centre stage, centre stage left; downstage right centre, downstage left centre; downstage right, downstage centre, downstage left. When one was familiar with the functions of these rooms and docks and areas; when one could with confidence handle and operate the various pieces of equipment; when one knew the precise role of each member of the stage staff; when one could both set up and strike the scenery; when one knows that, for instance, H crosses B throne from USR to DSL, LX20, is a stage direction meaning that from the upper stage right Hamlet will move down across the stage, passing in front of the throne, and that when he arrives down stage left a light will focus on him; when, in short, one has grasped a fundamental understanding of stage technicalities, codification and conduct, then one may be ready to Make a Prompt Book and know how Properly to Mark It. It was exactly at that point that I heartily wanted to punch Mr Hayes in the gob and generally break his face. Throughout the sorrowfully long length of his entire litany of person place and apparatus, a half-dozen or so items only were matters with which I had acquaintance, an acquaintance yet uncertain, diffident, in all cases bar one: making a prompt book. I know how to make a bloody prompt book! You buy a hard-cover loose-leaf blank paper file and two paperback copies of the same play. The plays will have been printed with their pages one and two, three and four, five and six, and so on occupying both sides of the leaves of paper in the copy; a prompt book demands that every time you turn a leaf only one page of the play will be there, hence the need for two copies of the bloody play. With scissors you then dismember both copies, thus supplying single pages of the play and in numerical order. Having dabbed, one at a time, a little gum, a little glue on to the back of each separate page, you then gently, carefully, laboriously, one at a time, press the bastards on to the right-hand blank paper in the loose-leaf file, leaving the left-hand blank, ready to receive what annotations you may consider necess-ary during the course of the subsequent rehearsals. That, Mr Hayes, whom I hope will cop the mange, is How one Makes a Prompt Book. True, the left-hand side of my book bore no fine markings such as 'H crosses B throne from USR to DSL, LX20', and did contain such stuff as 'Jack walks to where Harry is sitting, pulls out gun and shoots him. Shove in the plug'. But, still and all, a proper prompt book it had been.

My gaze wanders around the stage of the Little Theatre, littered quite by the persons of my classmates, as they loll, as they sit, as they lean, as they lie down. Several pairs of eyes wear an opaque glaze of incomprehension; others, indifferent, perhaps, to what they have just witnessed, seem to dream of future professional lives which will include no humping of heavy scenery, no distrib-

uting of props, no tabulating effects of sound or light or choreo-
graphed movement, lives to be lived that let other souls manage
stages on which they, the dreamers, will be content simply to act.
A few eager bodies continue to scribble down notes on pads,
others, including myself, discontinued this practice minutes only
after the beginning of Mr Hayes' barrage, mayhap believing, as is
the case with me, it were better to buy a book on the subject or,
better yet, determining that my hands will get grips on these
tangibles. The Chicago gangster's moll sits cross-legged and easy
on the floor, arms propped on knees, hands relaxed, head tilted,
eyes attentive. Can there be any doubt but that all Mr Hayes said
has been absorbed, is being mulled, compared with knowledge
already received on the matter expressed, found wanting, or
instructive, or at one with previous studies? For she is a clever
cow, as gangster's molls go, a very clever cow indeed. Nor can the
darling any further maintain this absurd subterfuge concerning
her bloodlines. Why, only this morning didn't Bob and I hear her
own sweet lips give the lie? A verse from *Kiss Me Kate* she was
quietly singing, quietly, that is, until warbling the lines, 'Where is
Fedora, the wild Virago?    It's lucky I missed her gangster sister
from Chicago'. Her voice slightly increased its volume, true, which
was a clue, but it had been that purr of gleeful ownership in her
tone which for Bob and me clinched the business. Hopi Indian,
Hebrew, my pale foot. More Valentine's Day massacre, I reckon,
more mob, more Cosa Nostra, more tommy gun, more Black
Hand, more bootlegger, more Scarface, more racketeer. Well,
think of it, as Bob and I have thought of it: eyes nothing like the
sun, colouring probably Mediterranean, compulsion to organize,
to boss, ease of execution, self-confessedly from Chicago and all.
Can there be doubt? Hardly. Where's Bob? In the wings having a
snore. Mr Hayes is trying to ameliorate the shocking effect that
his catalogue of stage management tasks has had on us by quietly
suggesting that we take and examine each item one at a time, that
we have two years in which to do this, that the door to his office is

ever receptive to the enquiring knock and that he or a member of his staff will always be of assistance at our student productions. Not a bad old stick, really, one is supposing even as the courtly Howard Williams steps lightly on to the stage to suggest that we repair to his room where he proposes to deliver a lecture.

---

OUR CARCASSES comfortably parked in his well-appointed, rather snazzy book-lined large room, Howard Williams perches his immaculately suited self on the edge of a small table before the window and begins. The subject he has chosen to talk to us about, says he, is to be called 'Snaggery'. His dissertation will be brief but he hopes to give two or three examples of things that during the performance of a play in the theatre may go wrong. Snags. It is also his hope to offer for our consideration ways, rooted in example, by which we may, or may not, depending on our personalities, our temperaments, choose to wriggle out of these snags. For example, imagine, he continues, blithe and composed, that you are exiting a room, you grab the doorknob, pull, and the door refuses to open, it is jammed, you pull somewhat more firmly and the doorknob comes off in your hand, the door remaining tightly jammed. What to do? You can murmur to your colleagues onstage, if there are any, if not you can soliloquize, a short sentence to the effect that this has happened before, that you have telephoned the carpenter and that, really, it is a nuisance. During this short speech you will be listening for reassuring noises offstage which, you hope, mean that the stage management is at hand and that the door is being eased open. Should no noise be heard, should the door stay desperately jammed, why, there still are options open for you. You can toss the knob from one hand to the other, nonchalantly stroll down to the prompt corner, turn your back to the audience and out of the corner of your mouth hiss, 'For Christ's sake go to blackout so I

can squeeze myself round this flat and get off the bloody stage.'
That is one way, said Howard Williams, the conservative way, he
added not disapprovingly. There are others. There usually is a
window. You must realize that by this time the audience will have
twigged that the door is stuck and that you, so to speak, are in a
jam. They will be behind you in everything that you do. Stride
boldly to the window. Tell, or soliloquize, of your eccentricity in
this regard. How you don't mind entering a room through the
door but, when leaving it, that you much prefer going through
the window. Snag. The window may not be practical. May not
respond to tugging, shoving, heaving. May not, in brief, open.
What to do? There often is a fireplace. Head for it. You need no
lines about, say, what Father Christmas can do you can do. The
audience will be shouting you on. Be careful of the red cellophane
and the light bulbs pretending to be a fire. Electrocution is an
altogether too radical way of removing yourself from this predicament. Insert your body up the flue, the stage management may
have mustered to give you a helping lift. As your legs are seen
ascending the chimney, you may be quite sure that the audience
will be on its feet and cheering. You may also be reasonably sure,
such being the nature of snaggery, that at this point, of its own
accord, the door will slowly open.

Willy, as in time we would learn to call him, by his humour, his
irreverance, that morning tickled our young souls while at once
giving us and our business a sense of proportion and a perspective
different to a degree from the glum and careworn views carted
about by some of our number. The more gloomy among us, the
more introspectively troubled of mien, never altered, becoming
even glummer and raddled with care. Most dropped out of the
game, some stayed on and by doing so walked into lives of misery.
One can only perversely hope that they enjoyed themselves. From
Willy, that morning long ago, we who were ready for it were
beginning to learn that acting is too serious a business ever to
take too seriously.

Howard Williams ended his formal lecture on Snaggery by illustrating for us a number of ways by which we might wriggle out of the snags caused when persons had to be killed and one's sword had broken or the gun failed to go off. After describing a number of increasingly whimsical ruses, he concluded his dissertation by telling of a John Barrymore, on stage, a man to kill, no dagger or gun or sword or garrotte to hand. 'Jack Barrymore', said Willy, 'slowly walked towards his man, moved up behind him, kicked him up the arse, turned to the audience and said, "The toe of my boot is poisoned".'

---

MUTILATE, DISFIGURE, maim and kill, can it, this here sabre that I've grabbed and am at present wagging about, Professor Froeschlen, de l'Academie d'Armes Internationale, my old sweetheart? Well, the view from behind this meshed steel veil on my fencing mask tells me that, judging by the dirty great trench you sport dug down deep from the ear to the mouth on the left cheek of your face, I could hardly hope to be instructed by a fencing master who in his slashing time has been in a better position to know. Absolutely. Nor can there be any doubt that quick thinking, muscular control, poise, balance, intricate accurate footwork, speed, finesse and skill with the blade will quite overcome brute strength. But. This is a formidable old poker you have thrust in my hand, Professor, and though it is no Excalibur, no Toledo blade, no Andrea Ferrara, it is yet a rare chunk of V-shaped pig iron running about three and a half feet long from its dinky curved handle and guard, weighing well over a pound and one would surely have to search hard, sweetheart, to find a better instrument than this job with which to give a man a frightful crack on the nut. There's a great, murderous feel to it. Right. Salute. On-guard. Prime. Seconde. Tierce. Quatre. Quinte. Sixte. Parries all and, yes, governor, I'm getting the knack of them, including the low Tierce, hand level with hip, blade almost vertical, and I realize well that cuts carry considerable force and that the forte of my blade must firmly oppose the foible of my attacker's, but what I would dearly love is to be let loose for a while to have a swipe and a whack at some bastard's head. Under conditions of absolute control, of course, and while remaining on the piste. Tell me do, Professor, what truth is there to what I read or heard somewhere, sometime, that one should grasp the handle of a sword as though it were a live bird, not too firmly lest one crushes its breast, not too easily lest the bird may be let fly away? Rot, is it? Right. It is a sabre and one holds it as a sabre. The first finger, thumb and the little finger are called the Manipulators, are they, and they impart movement to the blade either by pulling or pushing or rolling the handle between them, do they, while the remaining fingers are called Aides? Well, so be it, Froeschlen my old flower pot, and goodbye to all that bollocks about the grasping in the hand of a flightsome dickie bird. Of course I'm ready; and of course I will try to use my thumb and fingers as both manipulators and aides. Here we go. Salute. On-guard. Prime. Seconde. Tierce low. Tierce. Quatre. Quinte. Sixte. How was that? Not fluent, still jerky. Well, the truth is, petal, that though there can be no doubt that the art of sabre-fighting finds its deep base in the ability firmly, smoothly and reflexively to present these seven parries and so prevent the attacker's blade from finding the valid target of trunk, arms and head, it is precisely, in my view, my ungranted wish to have a grand lunge, to give great hacks at the flank, the head, which is inhibiting me in my resolve properly to assimilate these defensive positions. Let me but once loose on the giving end, maestro, and then I will better know, honest, how to cope with what is increasingly becoming this boring receiving end. Let me give the Balestra a crack, the short jump forward and the thrusting lunge or, better yet, that running attack at great speed, the Flèche. Go bail on it, sweetheart, go bail. Good man, yourself. Full length of the room as the piste. Better and better.

Right. Salute. On-guard. Have some of that, and this, and that, and this, and that again, and this, and this, and a great thwack of that. There. You are an astonishingly nifty cove, indeed, my dear old Professor, and not once on your gliding person did I so much as manage to lay a belt of the toasting iron, but I feel happy; released from frustration and ready to recommence, resolutely, the practice of these seven basic and necessary parries. And you are pleased with my footwork? Well, now, there, then, Lord love you, sweetheart, let me tell you. Albie Finney, who is much taken with this lark, and I had a serious discussion about the trickiness involved in your fencing footwork. Advancing or retiring on the piste, gaining or breaking ground. We have both determined that it is not wholly unlike boxing southpaw, sunshine, or, more pertinent yet, batting left-handed while playing at cricket, stepping right on to the back foot or going down the track when attacking the spinners. Yes. Cricket. It doesn't matter. My turn? Certainly. You will attack me along the full length of the piste. Your attacks will be strictly in sequence, going from the first to the seventh position of my parries. This should allow me to anticipate and to defend myself against your cuts and thrusts. Got it. Ready, chuckles, when you are. Salute. On-guard. Here we go. Blimey. There we went. The mercy is in the padded jacket, glove and mask or I would have been made butcher's bits of, I didn't see one of your cuts and thrusts let alone parry one, you are quick, sir, you are mustard, you are bloody deadly. Absolutely, Professor Froeschlen. Of course. No question. Salute. On-guard. Prime. Seconde. Tierce low. Tierce. Quatre. Quinte. Sixte.

---

RELIEF, THOUGH, to be able to walk the few steps from the RADA, through streets that were still a London of the late seventeen hundreds, plonk one's bottom down and enjoy a cup of coffee in Olivelli's, a shish kebab in Joe's Greek Cypriot greasy spoon, your noted creamy pint in Momma Fischer's boozer. Few of us at the academy were Londoners, most were from different parts, many had come to study there from a score or so of foreign countries, and lots of us, from time to hollow time, knew loneliness, displacement, absence from kin, loves, friends, familiar places. Even seasoned sods such as I, away from my family for three or so years, and who had fetched up in ports and cities all over Europe, knew the emptiness in the minutes of the times of great solitude in this great city of London. However, as Emerson, R.W., would have it, cities give us collision, and London and New York knock the nonsense out of a man. This may be true, true as what is often said in Ireland: that it's for the sake of the company that dogs go to church. So, then, to a church, Olivelli's, for coffee. Nor do you find me on my way there for the sake of the company: at my side is my little dark dote, and, as in half an hour's time there is an important class to be attended, it is to be hoped that I shall avoid any serious collision. It is all right, as we suck on our coffee, we are once again in a humming harmony with each other, I have apologized for mistakenly confusing her with a gangster's moll. A crude error. Molls are indolent blondes, slinky in satin, the bosses' baggage, a liability in the hideout, sharp or honey-tongued according to mood, sometimes querulous, fit only to be stuffed in the moosh with a grapefruit. Not so is it with my companion. Bold, luscious, vigorous, independent, a burden to no man, one with brains and through whose heart, surely, the deep dark blood of an ancient and a deadly family pumps. Yes. You have it. Kin must she be to a Capo di Tutti Capi di Mafiosi. No moll, she, no leech, no moody dummy; rather the proud representative of generations of bloodstained hoodlumdom. When told of my latest grasp on the true nature of her identity, her glance to heaven told me much; the patient, slow, shut-eyed shake of her head told me more, and the brazen mischief in her peepers when she looked at me to smile a smile sweet as a razor perhaps told me much much more.

Oilily handsome, this finger in a slick suit, a senior student known as the 'king of the film extras', a young man who, for a slice of the wages, can fix one up with work for a day or two milling about in crowd scenes for films, and who knows everything but everything about everybody associated in any way with the RADA, is coming to our table. 'Do you see', says he confidentially to me, 'that chap in the tweed jacket over there?' His eyes slide in the direction of a red-haired young man with sensitively battered features who is standing in an easily erect posture, quietly gabbing to a wonderfully languid, tall and slim youth who looks as though a particularly wayward mistress of Charles the Second had pupped him. 'Well,' goes on Oily, 'he is still technically a student but already he has been Donald Wolfit's dresser, and played parts, he was understudy to Cecil Parker in Noël Coward's *Apple Cart*, has just played at the Glasgow Citizens and in a couple of weeks he will be joining the Old Vic Company.'

Impressive. 'Impressive,' say I. Languid is looking at his fob watch and, I believe, suggesting to red-headed tweed that it's time to go to the pub. They are both aiming for the door. Slick suit suggests that I should meet this busiest of actors. I hop up.

'Hello,' says Ronald Fraser to me.

'How do you do?' says his long mate. 'Villiers is my name, lovey, James Villiers.'

We have collided. Inextricably collided.

'You're a remarkably pretty girl,' says the Open Razor to my dote. 'I'm sure a kiss from you would be a benediction. Are you Italian?'

'Sicilian,' say I.

'Sicily! Ah, Etna smoking, Corvo Salaparuta, sun, golden ruins, olives, bandits, bloodshed.'

'Oh, do shut up, Ronnie,' says Jimbo. 'Forgive him, my dears, he opens that cuckoo's arse of a mouth and out pour streams of quite rancid rubbish. We're popping across the street for the one. Care to join us?'

Another time, Ronald and James, another time. And another and another and another. Time, gentlemen, time, gentlemen, time. We have a technique class to attend.

---

'WHAT'S TECHNIQUE?' I said to her as we rambled towards the RADA.

'You have barrels of it,' she said to me and we rambled on.

Before we entered the classroom, again I asked, 'This stuff you say I have barrels of, technique, what is it?'

She looked at me, thought for a moment, and then said, 'Know How.'

John Gabriel, our teacher, a small man with classically fine features, eyes lit with intelligence, fluently, confidently articulate, began by saying, in effect, that some are born with a feel for stage technique, others slowly, often arduously, acquire stage technique, quite a few never get a true grasp of it, and that stage technique was difficult accurately to define. That was my cue. 'Minnehaha here says that technique is know how.'

'Minnehaha? That can't be your name. My dear, what is your name?'

'Pocahontas.'

'Pocahontas. I see. It certainly suits you and is a charming name.'

'Beats the shit out of Alice Capone.'

'Quite. Know how, you say. Know how. Well, acting is a talent that one is born with, or not, it is a gift which cannot be learned. However, this gift of talent can be taught how to discipline itself, can learn to know exactly what it is doing. Know how. Do you know, I believe that "know how" is the most succinct definition of acting and stage technique that I've ever come across. Thank you. Pocahontas.'

'You're welcome, Mr Gabriel, sir.'

And then John Gabriel was, with enthusiasm, off. He told of the late Gerald du Maurier, of how, throughout his long and successful professional life, this distinguished actor's complete naturalness of manner when performing had been much remarked on by both the public and the profession. How it had been said of Gerald du Maurier that when he walked on to a stage it seemed not at all like an actor making an entrance, more like someone who had accidentally strolled into the scene on his way to the club. Take, said John Gabriel, I fancy, for example, this short scene from *Old Rope* by F. J. Monnoyer. Lionel walks into his brother Timothy's chambers in The Albany saying, 'This may amuse you. It was clear to me weeks ago that marrying Claire would be disastrous for both of us, so I decided not to go through with it. Trouble was that actually telling Claire of this decision was something I kept putting off doing. Until an hour ago, that is. Next month, and the damned wedding with it, was hard upon us, so I stiffened the sinews and rang her. Wretched line was engaged. I put the phone down and went through my lines again: "Claire. Listen, darling. We've always been candid with each other," and then the phone rang. It was Claire. She said: "Lionel, darling, we've always been candid with each other, I don't want to go through with it. Don't say anything. I shan't change my mind. Try not to be angry. Goodbye." I've been jilted, Timmy, the lady has left me in the lurch. I propose to accept her decision calmly, as a gentleman should, and put a brave face on it. Cheero!' During this speech, du Maurier would take off his hat, coat and scarf, hang them up, help himself to a Scotch and soda, take out a cigarette case, put a cigarette in his mouth, light it from a pocket lighter, and then, talking the while, sit in an armchair. Du Maurier's voice, which seemed effortless and musically conversational, had, in fact, been honed and trained for seven years under the tutelage and management of Sir Herbert Beerbohm Tree, a kind man, a *bon viveur*, a disciplinarian, the first Professor

Higgins in Bernard Shaw's *Pygmalion* and the founder of the
establishment in which we are at present working, the Royal
Academy of Dramatic Art. Having studied and learned the part in
the library of his home in Hampstead, du Maurier would grab a
hat-and-coat stand, kit himself up with the necessary props and
carefully and mechanically he would go over his entrance speech
and business dozens of times. More or less like this, said John
Gabriel, more or less like this. He would walk towards the coat-
stand, simultaneously speaking his first line and taking off his
overcoat. 'This may amuse you,' he would say. Start taking off
coat. 'It was clear to me weeks ago that marrying Claire would be
disastrous for both of us.' Coat off. 'So I decided not to go
through with it.' Hang up coat. Start sliding off scarf. Address line
to Timothy. 'Trouble was that actually telling Claire of this
decision was something I kept putting off doing.' Hang up scarf.
Say line away from Timothy. Reach for hat. 'Until an hour ago,
that is.' Hang up hat. Walk to drinks and pick up bottle of Scotch
while saying next line. 'Next month, and the damned wedding
with it, was hard upon us, so I stiffened the sinews and rang her.
Wretched line was engaged.' Pour whisky. Put down whisky bottle
and pick up soda siphon during following line. 'I put the phone
down and went through my lines again:'. Squirt soda. Put down
siphon and produce cigarette case and lighter from pocket
during next line. '"Claire. Listen, darling. We've always been
candid with each other."' Put cigarette in mouth. 'And then the
phone rang. It was Claire.' Light cigarette. Put in pockets cigarette case and lighter. 'She said:'. Puff cigarette and take it from
mouth. '"Lionel, darling, we've always been candid with each
other, I don't want to go through with it."' Pick up whisky and
walk to chair while saying the next line. '"Don't say anything.
I shan't change my mind. Try not to be angry. Goodbye."' Sit
in chair. 'I've been jilted, Timmy, the lady has left me in the
lurch.' Lean back in chair and cross legs while saying next line. 'I

propose to accept her decision calmly, as a gentleman should, and put a brave face on it.' Lift glass in a toast and then drink. 'Cheero.'

In this way, said John Gabriel, by providing himself with a tight physical mechanism, by artifice, du Maurier liberated himself from fumbles and uncertainties and was able, by a precise technique, freely to walk, talk, sit, stand, drink, smoke and, above all, act on a stage in ways that seemed to be unrehearsed and completely spontaneous. Be assured, though, he did not so much as adjust his tie, hesitate before a word, emphasize a word, or shut a door without knowing exactly what he was doing and how he proposed to do it. Know how. Yes, I like that. Minnehaha.

Much later, in the deep evening of that same day, you could have seen a slightly sozzled Bob and me going through our paces back at the digs. Bob had given himself the roles of audience, judge and commentator; I was equipped with my donkey jacket, coat; a tea cosy, hat; a towel, scarf; a packet of Capstan Full Strength and a box of matches, cigarette case and lighter; two bottles of beer, whisky and siphon; and a glass, taking off, hanging up, lighting up, pouring and sitting at precise moments while smoothly reciting the Lord's Prayer, which was the only speech that I was confident of speaking without having to think about what I was saying. Jesus.

———

YOU'RE MAD, Stretcher Fletcher, you're a woman gone mad, you're mad as a fucking meat axe. The likely consequences of these stretching exercises you propose we rack our bodies at in order, as you insanely put it, to render them supple, trim and limber, are as gruesome as they are grotesque. To place one of my poor feet on the barre, which is at rib height, recall, rib bleeding height, means, because there is more than two yards of me, that I needs must for the sake of sweet purchase plant my other forlorn trotter a considerable distance away from its fellow foot. This would involve me not only in doing the splits, a deed I never before have attempted, but also in doing the splits diagonally. The diagonal splits, you cruel and mad woman, the diagonal splits? Yet more: place both my hands on the agonized foot on the rib-high barre and lower my forehead down to press against the splitted knee. You are aware, are you not, that from the base of the buttocks to the root of the lower belly is but a short stretch of territory? In my imagination, madam, there exists from my groin to my throat a dotted line. Should I be successful in my attempt at this hideous manoeuvre, why then, surely, the instant my brow so much as touches my knee then all must give. Slowly but with certainty the tearing will begin, up the dotted line my trunk will tear and tear until it is entirely torn apart, leaving on the floor of your ballet class merely the two halves of me and a howling head. Here we go. Almighty God have mercy on us. Pocahontas?

Herself. 'Yes, dear.'

Me. 'Marlon Brando. Do you reckon him?'

Herself. 'He's the business.'


You may or may not be aware, or surprised, or even delighted, to learn that we have both a soft palate and a hard palate. Most of the soft palate stretches about at the rear of our mouths and is, so I've been given to understand, helpful to us when sucking or swallowing. Quite. However, we also have a sliver of soft palate wrapped around a ridge at the front of our mouths. What my dentist tells me is termed the 'incisive capilla'. Sounds so precise, you might agree, and it is precisely this slice of oral tissue that is pertinent to our immediate purposes and to which I shall be referring when I talk of the soft palate. This roll of soft palate is located immediately behind the row of upper front teeth, while the hard palate, what we commonly call the roof of the mouth, is immediately behind and above this bulge of soft palate. Now, I've noticed that what I'm going to ask you to do next often elicits coy giggles from some of my students. Can't think why. I would like you to use your tongues to feel inside your mouths for both the soft and the hard palates. Perhaps I should be more specific and say feel inside your own mouths with your tongues but all I really wish is that you all be satisfied that you all possess both soft and hard palates and can feel them with your tongues. You see what I mean? The more adventurous among you may care to thrust your tongues back to the hindermost section of the soft palate, above the tunnel of the throat, just for the nonce, for this is the section we shan't be using. That's it. Thought so. Pull yourselves together. Say the consonants G, S, W, X, Z, and flick with your tongues the rear of the soft palate. Say the consonants C, D, H, J, L, N, R, T, and tap with your tongues the hard palate. You may find this less disconcerting when you practise it in private. Try to control yourselves.

Me. 'Two of his films are playing in London right now, *Viva Zapata* and *Julius Caesar*.'

Herself. 'Three. *Streetcar Named Desire* is on re release.'


I've got a lovely bunch of coconuts. A lovely bunch of coconuts. Coconuts, coconuts, coconuts. A lovely bunch of coconuts. That's it, that's it, that's it. / Polyphiloprogenitive / The sapient sutlers of the Lord. / The body is the vowel. Ee, Ay, Ah, Oh, Oo. Not at the front of the face to get a mouthful of gum. A mouthful of gum. Gum, gum, gum. Out of the back and up and round the face, the throat is open, out of the back and up and round the face. That's it, that's it, that's it. The body is the vowel, the mouth is the percussion. Percussion, percussion, percussion. The tongue taps consonants, the vowel flies up from them and becomes colour. Get rid of self. Become the body rhythmical. The tuned body. Have you read my book? Become the body rhythmical, body rhythmical, body rhythmical. Breathe. Breathe. Breathe. Along the garden wall the bees      With hairy bellies pass between      The staminate and pistillate. That's it, that's it, that's it. The staminate and pistillate. Pistillate, pistillate, pistillate. I've got a lovely bunch of coconuts. A lovely bunch of coconuts. Sugar bush, I love you so.

Me. 'Fancy seeing one of Brando's films? Or even two?'

Herself. 'All three if you wish.'


Being things mechanical, railway trains chug by me, ships float, aeroplanes bank and swoop, we have dodgem cars, tractors, tramcars, threshing machines. There is a clock, an egg beater, a gramophone, a printing press and, from the looks of her, what may be an ocean-going combine harvester. Bob is a traffic light, from red to amber and green he goes, and from green to amber and red. I am a lamp post.

Me. 'Do you know where the films are playing?'

Herself. I fancy. 'We can take the 987 bus to Pullem for the one p.m. show at the Rexy. From Pullem we take the 654 bus to Feckem and catch the five thirty p.m. at the Roxy. Take the 321 bus from Feckem to Clappem where there's a late showing at the Ritzy. If you're up to it.'


Back cloths are extremely useful. They give a tidy symmetry to any stage, are helpful to acoustics, can provide a cyclorama, are especially useful for light projections and, as we know we've had such projections since the early seventeenth century at least, admittedly only special trick effects by rotating the lamps on vertical poles, with our technical equipment becoming more sophisticated, I expect to see more use made both of front and back projection. Judiciously used, it could be quite interesting.

Me. 'Did you see Brando on the stage ever?'

Herself. 'Yeah. Twice.'

Me. '*Streetcar Named Desire?*'

Herself. 'Yeah. And *Truck Line Café.*'


Measure how many paces will take you to the tree. Seven. Walk them over and over again until they become natural to you. Right. Keep your eyes on the distant figure and walk to the tree. That's it. Now reach for the binoculars. No, don't look for them, know exactly where they hang, keep your eyes on the figure. Reach for them over and over again. Got it? Right. Eyes on distant object. Walk to the tree. Binoculars. Good.

Me. '*Truck Line Café?*'

Herself. 'He had a twenty-minute scene in the third act. He pulled the theatre down.'

Me. 'That good, yes?'

Herself. 'The business.'


Did you ever, Professor, see *Scaramouche* with Stewart Granger? The swordfights were mighty. Of course. Supination, fingernails up. Half supination, fingernails to the side. Pronation, fingernails down. Prime. Seconde. Tierce. Quatre. Quinte. Sixte. Seldom used.

Me. 'Could we, my dear and juicy little Hopi, stagger our visits to see Mr Brando at the cinema?'

Herself. 'Sure.'

Me. 'Take them in, say, one at a time on different evenings, thus giving ourselves opportunity for a bite or two of a macaroon and a cup of tea and a lie-down?'

Herself. 'Sure.'

Me. 'When, then, kitten, when?'

Herself. 'You know what, honey, to put ourselves in perspective, to see how we think our acting shapes up compared to Brando, how's about right after I've played Phebe and you've played Oliver in *As You Like It.* Cool, yes?'

> Brush up your Shakespeare,
> Tippity tap tap
> Start quoting him now,
> Tippity tap tippity tap tap
> Brush up your Shakespeare
> And the women you will wow,
> Tippity tap tap.
> If your girl won't respond when you flatter 'er
> Tell her what Tony told Cleopatterer
> Tippity tap tap
> Brush up your Shakespeare
> And they'll all kow-tow,
> I trow.

---

'But these are all lies: men have died from time to time and worms have eaten them, but not for love.'

Came the day of the race, why even old Humphrey played his part unaccustomedly well, rolling us to within trotting distance of Gower Street and the academy before shuddering into exhausted and senile immobility. Well done, that ridiculous matchbox on wheels, well done. Bob and I had come to what we decided was a sensible little arrangement with Shakespeare. Over the weeks, while watching and listening at our rehearsals of *As You Like It,* the play had wrapped me in its enchantments, ripped layer upon layer of dull and cosy thought out of my mind, shone its keen and naked light on much of humankind's darker conduct, and had left me finding Oliver to be a part difficult sympathetically to inhabit, agreeing with the commentator Mr Swinburne who considered certain of Oliver's scenes to be 'the one unlucky slip of the brush.' Bob had found Touchstone or Jaques or, for that matter, Shakespeare to be not quite his meat, not quite the writer of plays whose characters he could cheerfully act, so he had handed over his burdens to others more worthy, and he and I had agreed to split the part of Oliver. I would play the beginning and the end of him, Bob would fill out the bit in the middle.

Olivers both, we walked into the George Bernard Shaw Room; here, this morning, our class would perform *As You Like It* before Sir Kenneth Barnes and members of his staff. Nell Carter, whom all these weeks I had never seen anywhere other than in this room, no, not along a corridor, on a stair, in a street, yes, nowhere bar this room had I laid a peeper on her, had materialized mayhap from out the inkwell on her desk, certainly the frail kind tough old girl was top to toe dressed in blues various, and was gently flitting hither and yon among her charges sprinkling encouragement, counselling calm and, with the bluest of all her adornments that day, her wise eyes telling us to be strong. Tensile strands of excitement, nervousness, anticipation stretched along the length and through the width of the room, threading an unusual restraint into the speech and comportment of even the more boisterous and gigglesome of my fellow students. Dressed as we were in our best clothes and behaviour, I recall now a group of attractive young men and women glancing at the glare thrown by the strong lamps set in the room's corners brightly to light the acting area. Young men and women mustering up concentration, a soul here muttering a line or two from the piece, a soul there murmuring of good mornings and good luck, Jilly and Jenny arranging the chairs which would serve as scenery, Albie pacing by the windows, eager for the off, Slim Mac, Mikey B. breaking off from their gazes at infinity to nod greetings, the honey Sal, the lovely Jeannie drifting in the shadows examining the floor, and the bold Pocahontas who, with a jiggle and a bound, clasped my head in her hands, pressed a warm and smacking kiss on my mouth, stepped an inch or two away and sexily with her fingers wiped away lipstick transferred from her lips to mine saying the while that maybe she should have left on a trace, in hope of starting rumours. Half a dozen chairs had been set in front of the wall facing our makeshift stage and at precisely ten a.m. Sir Kenneth came clanking through the door grunting rumbling scowling and with several colleagues following behind him treading in his turbulence. A clatter and a shuffle of chairs, Sir Kenneth stabs at a clipboard with his pencil, beams at Nell Carter, and Nell says clearly that the curtain is going up and then that the curtain is up.

---

'As I remember, Adam, it was upon this fashion'. The first words of the play spoken by Peter Needham, a stocky young chap with a sulkily romantic face and a fine ringing voice. Old Adam is being given by Slim Mac and a more stooped and ditheringly antique portrait of oldest age you surely couldn't wish to see. Oh Lord love us bless us and save us, it's my turn. 'Now, sir! what make you here?' The top half of me is controlled and steady right enough, but below there both my legs are shaking and shuddering so it seems as though I am supporting myself on a brace of pneumatic drills. Chunter, chunter, growl, snarl, grab, shove, exit Orlando and the oldest man on earth, bellow, here comes Charles the wrestler, Finney, A., our eyes engage, lock, and at once I am free from wobble and perturbation. Actor's eyes, you see, eyes, as I would in time learn, that can focus on their partner's in truth, concentration and character and yet be aware of all that is around and before them, players and audience; eyes that know what they are doing, why they are doing it and with whom it is being done. Actor's eyes, immediately recognizable only to other actors who hold the touchstone of shared experience and common memory but of great reassurance to the customers who intuitively know that those eyes tell them that the fiction they will witness shall be credible and alive. More good chunter, more relaxedly spoken, more confident my manner, exit Albie, brief soliloquy, 'nothing remains but that I kindle the boy thither; which now I'll go about'. That's me done for an hour and a half and so I'll sit against the wall, light up a fag with my shaking hands, inhale deeply down to my parked bottom, and settle myself to soak in the sounds and sights of the play.

SCHOLARS TELL US that *As You Like It* is a comedy of Shakespeare's middle period, one that shows the complete balance of his powers and that it is the perfection of his handling of lighter comedy. So, indeed, is it. And yet. Sitting against the wall with a fag in my gob, just looking and listening, I heard sweet and bitter fancies in the language, a humorous sadness in the tone of many of the speeches and the sentences; saw that the play is peopled by a good number of tyrants, killers, murderous thugs, usurpers, cynics, libertines; realized that in this his version of the pastoral plays fashionable in his time, Shakespeare's mind had wrought from iron and bleak stone phrase upon phrase which throughout the play drop and cut into scene after scene, uttered by mouth following mouth from his men and women, and that each phrase sounded out a dread bell telling of the human predicament: our consciousness that we are human, all too bloody human, precisely being the predicament. Within minutes of the play's beginning a brutal fratricide is plotted, minutes after this Rosalind the heroine and Celia her cousin and friend are heard prattling of love; this leads to the two women word-spinning generalities about their own gender and to Celia saying of Fortune and her own sex that 'those that she makes fair, she scarce makes honest, and those that she makes honest, she makes very ill favouredly'. An assessment with which the lovely Rosalind concurs, quibbling only that it is not Fortune but Nature that so shapes the female kind. By the second act we hear, through Jaques, of the Fool Touchstone's less than rosy view of time and life: '"It is ten o'clock: Thus we may see," quoth he, "how the world wags: 'Tis but an hour ago since it was nine; and after one hour more 'twill be eleven; and so, from hour to hour, we ripe and ripe and then from hour to hour, we rot and rot; and thereby hangs a tale."' Cheerful stuff, this, for a lighter comedy, made more prankish yet when we consider that in Elizabethan times a tale, and therefore in Touchstone's meaning, our life, is at best only idle blather, mischievous gossip and very probably merely a rank falsehood. A couple of pages on and we hear Jaques giving his famous disquisition on the seven ages of man, a party piece for generations upon generations of numberless verse speakers. One wonders how many of the boys who pipe it at their school concerts, or the proud parents who wince throughout the piping, know that for Shakespeare's contemporaries the name Jaques owned lavatorial associations, or fully realize what bleak and godless assertions round off the ditty: 'Last scene of all,      That ends this strange eventful history,      Is second childishness and mere oblivion,      Sans teeth, sans eyes, sans taste, sans everything.' Samuel Beckett, how are you? Amiens, the sweet singer of this lighter comedy, then gives pert punctuation to Jaques' ruminations on the ages of man by warbling 'Heigh-ho! sing, heigh-ho! unto the green holly:      Most friendship is feigning, most loving mere folly.'

Lolling there in that large room, watching and listening as my classmates, green at the game, without costume, without makeup, on no stage and in no theatre, valiantly played their parts as they acted the scenes and the acts, my eyes found Sir Kenneth. Seventy-six years old, most of his long life spent serving the interests of young men and women who wished to become professional actors and actresses, a friend to all that was fine in the drama throughout the twentieth century, who year after year after year must have sat through hundreds of performances of Shakespeare's plays when acted by stumbling novices in big bare rooms, and there was the lovely old bugger, perched on his seat, alert, engrossed, his brooding scowl at whiles dissolving away to be replaced by pink beams of pure delight. At times he dabbed down a quick pencilled note on to his clipboard pad, at times he closed his eyes, tilted back his head and let the sublime sense in the characters and language of William Shakespeare, gent, actor and playmaker, sing their melodies into his ears, while at other times he crouched forward in his chair, still, rigid, eyes fixed and appraising, it seemed, on some young soul who may have given original nuance or phrasing or timing or twist to a familiar passage in the piece. Throughout, of course, the production was decorated with Sir Kenneth's by now indispensably choric snarls, gurgles, growls and deeply felt gruntings.

Act Three and we find ourselves looking at Rosalind and Celia deep in the Forest of Arden. Or do I mean goggling. If the parts are played by fine actresses, if those fine actresses are fair of form and feature, then, by God, goggling is what I do mean. Remark: Rosalind is disguised as a youth, wears doublet and hose and calls herself Ganymede, Celia has dabbled walnut juice on her face, wears a scanty shift, and is pretending to be Ganymede's sister, a shepherdess called Aliena. The effect on an audience when the roles are judiciously inhabited is altogether splendid. Liberated from formal court dress, prim little Celia is translated into a tousle-haired nut-brown maid, a lass with whom, flimsy smock and all, one on the instant immediately fancies a tumble. As for Rosalind, well, with masculine hose on her legs, a shirt and doublet over her breasts, the swagger of a male to her manner, the effect is of an umpteen-fold increase in her sensuousness and femininity. A fact to which those of us who in the sixties saw Vanessa Redgrave wantonly roaming around the stage when playing Rosalind will vigorously attest. There was scarce a man or liberally inclined woman in the house who did not feel urged to clamber up on to the stage and simply leap on her. Yes, Big Van, for all your sincerely held and serious-minded political views, that was the sort of performance that gets actresses a saucy name. Rejoice! Orlando is wandering about the twigs too, his lust for Rosalind as hot as hers for him, he goes crashing about the place nailing up his pomes to her and carving her name on practically all the woodwork in the forest. Eventually, to be sure, the panting lovers meet but, true to the convention of the play, Orlando does not see through the guise of Ganymede, accepting her as the saucy youth she is feigning to be and so he, Orlando, is lured into a deliciously bawdy chat with her, Ganymede, concerning his love for her, Rosalind. In short, we have him who is her talking to him about her and he who does not realize that she is not him but is, in fact, her, telling her that she, Rosalind, is the finest she that he, Ganymede, could hope to see should it be in him to have the luck to encounter her. The scene then becomes quite complicated. We see Rosalind as Ganymede thanking God that he has not made her a woman, therefore freeing her from all the giddy offences with which the entire sex is taxed, and telling Orlando that if he will think of her not as the male Ganymede but as his fancy woman, Rosalind, and come every day in sport to woo her, he, Ganymede, will soon cure him of this wretched love sickness for Rosalind. The scene ends with Orlando agreeing to this and saying, 'With all my heart, good youth.' To which Rosalind as Ganymede replies, 'Nay, you must call me Rosalind.' Take what you will and have it as you like it, one thing alone is clear: Rosalind has Orlando by the short and curlies.

Immediately after this romp of gender juggling, Touchstone enters and speaks a line which to this day sounds in my mind with as much emphasis as it had when first I heard it. Talking of the effect suffered when neither a man's verses nor his wit can be understood, Touchstone says that 'it strikes a man more dead than a great reckoning in a little room'. The effect of these words on me is visceral, and it seems I hear below me reverberations after a great iron door has been rammed shut into a stone wall.

Yes, true it is that most scholars and commentators believe the line refers to the dreadful and sinister death of Christopher Marlowe, stabbed to death through the eye with a twelve-penny dagger at the age of twenty-nine in a little room at an inn in Deptford, according to the coroner's report, after a quarrel over the reckoning, the bill of fare. True it is, too, that Mikey B., Slim Mac and I had made much mouth music on the theme of Marlowe's probable work as an agent in Walsingham's secret service, Elizabethan London having been infested with informers and government spies. Also it is true that in *As You Like It* we have the one and only play in Shakespeare's entire canon in which the good William both quotes and acknowledges a contemporary fellow playmaker, one Christopher Marlowe. In a whimsically wicked spin on the play's convention, the shepherdess Phebe, having met and immediately fallen in love with, yes, Rosalind disguised as Ganymede, believing the youth's doublet and hose to contain a he not as we know a she, which pops Rosy into a pickle, considerably ripens up matters and leaves Phebe to exclaim, 'Dead shepherd, now I find thy saw of might, "Who ever loved, that loved not at first sight?"' The quotation is from *Hero and Leander*, written by the dead shepherd Marlowe. Why 'dead shepherd', I had wondered. Shepherd, yes, poets, I learned, in classical pastoral poetry are conventionally 'shepherds'. Six years killed when Shakespeare wrote this play, Kit Marlowe was still anathema to the Elizabethan authorities who proclaimed him atheist and blasphemer, so 'good shepherd' was hardly a starter and anyway the title had properly been bestowed on another outlaw. Fair shepherd? Fair to middling shepherd? No, not really. One thing only was certain about Marlowe; he was no longer alive. Therefore, I had reasoned, Shakespeare had chosen the spare the bleak and the bare and had called him 'dead shepherd'.

There is an eloquent and adventurous book, *The Reckoning*, by Charles Nicholl which carefully examines the life and death of Marlowe. Persuasively, Mr Nicholl suggests for our consideration that a number of phrases in this play refer not only to Marlowe but also to the raw and violently dangerous circumstances in which during the Elizabethan era our poets and playmakers worked and lived. A beautiful poem there is, too, one written by Louis MacNeice in 1951, a couple of years before we students stumbled through our ramshackle production of *As You Like It* in the George Bernard Shaw Room. This poem on the page fair smokes with the energy, treachery and brute vitality living in the age of Spenser, Raleigh, Sidney, Kit and Will, and urges the players and poets of these our modern times to assess the heritage we have been handed by those inordinately brave, even desperate men. The poem is called 'Suite for Recorders', scarce a stanza in it but which calls on scenes and lines from *As You Like It* and whose sub-title is, 'It strikes a man more dead than a great reckoning in a little room.'

Hello, it's Bob's turn now. Act Four and Bob is to give us his Oliver, Oliver's middle bit, the bit eagerly anticipated most certainly by the heavy firm in this here class of Nell Carter's, Mac and Mikey, Jilly, Jenny, Jeannie, Finney, Sal, the Hopi, me. And not merely to give us scope for odorous comparisons of his chewing of the sandwich we both have made of this, one of Shakespeare's lousiest parts, with my juddering rendings of the top and the bottom bits, but because he will essay the role opposite the Celia of Ingelrica Bloodaxemansdotter, or somesuch, a seriously myopic Icelandic maiden who has taken off her spectacles for this great occasion, and who speaks no English at all. To be sure, over the weeks the lady has mustered up a 'Goot Mornink' and a 'Goot Buys' but it had proved impossible for me to communicate to her that only a short time ago I had been locked in deadly sea battle against her countrymen, resolute that no longer would they be let blast through the waters in their longboats to go nicking the Queen's Codfish. Admirably brave it is, too, that Miss Bloodaxemansdotter should be party to our frolic, if inexplicable, but also it is, alas, cruelly comical. Here we go. It is that famed 'slip of the brush' scene, the one in which Oliver, converted to decent bloke after witnessing his brother's bravery when saving him from being savaged by a lion, and, under the transforming magic of the forest's bosky spell, falls instantly, on the spot and irretrievably in love with nut-brown Celia. What a load of bollocks. Nevertheless, Celia as Aliena, is being played by Ingelrica, and Bob, who has made it plain that he understands very little of the yards of text he is about to spout, cares less, and would very much prefer to be in a decent play, one in which he could sip a martini, chunter a few words, puff a cheroot, all of which deeds he could do while sitting down, is giving his Oliver. Now. In this scene Celia has nine very short lines and one line not very short. It runs: 'West of this place, down in the neighbour bottom:     The rank of osiers by the murmuring stream     Left on your right hand, brings you to the place.     But at this hour the house doth keep itself;     There's none within.' By parroting and with perhaps a mug-up from an Icelandic translation of the work, our game and Nordic girl had throughout rehearsals coughed out a rough approximation of the sense and sounds of her nine shorter lines, but this long job had proved to be a bugger for the maiden. Somehow, however, someone somewhere had succeeded in pointing out to her that the words about a house keeping itself, there being none within, were supposed to be an extravagantly funny joke. We knew this because if and when the lady arrived safely at the end of her travels through the verse, her head would fling itself back, her hands clap themselves, her feet give a little stamp, a little kick, the while roaring out a loud and hollow shrieking laugh.

Nerves have struck Iceland. Yes, nerves and blindness. Nor does Ingelrica Bloodaxemansdotter seem to know in which portion of the room the performance is being held. Rosalind and Silvius are playing their scene in the allotted area but our brave blind girl is waving her arms about, shuddering and staring sightlessly at

174

nothing at all but about an inch from the nose of Sir Kenneth who seems to be on the point of giving her a belt of the clipboard. Here, though, comes Bob, no better man, surely, than him to bring to these proceedings order and calm. 'Good morrow, fair ones: pray you, if you know,    Where in the purlieus of this forest stands    A sheep-cote fenc'd about with olive trees?' Bob looks and sounds as though he's asking for a match but, Tra La!, Bloodaxemansdotter has recognized her cue, round she whirls away from a barking Sir Kenneth, blunders in the direction from which the sound came and she's off: 'Vest off these pliers,' I shall spare you, 'Ronk off hosiers' etc., 'Zee horse dooth kip its elf.' Ha, Ha, Ha, Clap, Clap, Stamp, Stamp, 'Zares noon wheeze in!' Stamp, Ha, Clap, Clap, Ha, Stamp, Ha, Clap.

Throughout the rest of the scene, the long descriptive passage concerning his trials in the forest and the noble actions of his brother notwithstanding, Bob found that the shine on his shoes was of a particular interest to him, that and a slice of the floor just ahead of where these polished brogues had been set. True it is that there was a shake to his shoulders during this gazing. Emotion, surely. True is it, too, that there was one vigorous moment when, grabbing out the flourish of handkerchief from his breast pocket, with eyes tight shut he flung back his head to face in the general direction of the ceiling; that, quivering in an agony of passion, he stood there racked, beseeching, before opening his eyes, dabbing them with his hanky, violently blowing his nose and then returned to his inspection of the effect of polish on shoes. Came the end of this bubbling scene, and though Shakespeare strongly suggests that his three characters exit in companionable harmony, our players chose to effect a perhaps more exciting but certainly different ending. Rosalind shot towards the door, Oliver ambled straight from the middle of the acting area to a seat on the floor against the wall and Celia, flailing and honking, lurched to where bright light spilled in from the windows.

Patches there are of this play which for my poke are plainly erotic. Take the scene at the beginning of the fourth act between Orlando and Rosalind. Once again we see him believing her to be a male but with the juicy twist that she has persuaded him to pretend that she is not the youth Ganymede but is the maid with whom Orlando is in love, Rosalind. More. They then go through a mock marriage, over which Celia as Aliena presides. After this dainty charade in which Rosalind, who is believed by Orlando to be he, Ganymede, feigning in sport to be she, Rosalind, are wedded, Rosalind as Ganymede being Rosalind makes herself clear on how she will behave towards her husband. 'I will be more jealous of thee than a Barbary cock-pigeon over his hen,' says she, 'more clamorous than a parrot against rain, more new-fangled than an ape, more giddy in my desires than a monkey.' This is explicit, racy stuff and it provokes Orlando into the interested enquiry: 'But will my Rosalind do so?' 'By my life,' says Rosalind, 'she will do as I do.' A few seconds later Orlando exits the scene leaving the two women pretending to be nothing other than women, and we hear Celia chiding Rosalind's behaviour, suggesting that it has been perhaps a scandalous representation of their sex. Rosalind, unfazed, raves on saying of Cupid: 'that same wicked bastard of Venus, that was begot of thought, conceived of spleen and born of madness, that blind rascally boy that abuses every one's eyes because his own are out, let him be judge how deep I am in love.' The bitch is on heat, say I, in this one of Shakespeare's lighter comedies, on heat and like to be foaming at the crutch.

The epilogue was spoken, our play came to its end. Welcome and generous applause came clapping from the four or five men and women who had been our audience and then, rumblingly led by Sir Kenneth, they clattered out of the room. Weeks in the toils of technical difficulty, study, the demands made by the work on nervous and physical energy, the sheer neck needed to get on one's hind legs and put down a best effort had been spent, it seemed, for little enough return and many of us in Nell Carter's class found ourselves in that George Bernard Shaw Room feeling in the aftermath of the performance a flat purposelessness and a worrisome uncertainty over what we had achieved. Self-conscious, empty, most of us sat on chairs which minutes ago had been trees, stones and the banks of brooks in the Forest of Arden. Some stood on the spots where they had had their moments, perhaps to wonder over what had gone wrong, or right, indifferently, hope-lessly, better than expected, worse than they could have imagined or, maybe, in vain to wish they could be let do it all again. Feelings which those of us who stayed in the game would meet and know for the rest of our professional lives. However, as Nell with reassuring words flitted from student to student, one thing was clear: we had all given performances for the first time in a play at the RADA and it was now lunchtime.

———————

IT IS DIFFICULT for me precisely to remember who had played what parts in which scenes when forty years ago we had done the play. To give everyone a slice of pie, the leading parts had been carved up into portions to be chewed by different actors and actresses in scene after scene as act followed act, and even the lesser roles had been placed in the teeth of more than one master or mistress. Take jolly Oliver, a morsel not to the taste of either Bob or myself, one which we had both coughed up, spat out, and whose savour neither of us wished again to visit our palates. Charles the Wrestler had been in the sole charge of Albie Finney; by a distance not the finest role to have dropped off Shakespeare's pen, yet one to which Albie had given vigour, menace and a rollicking display of athleticism. Pocahontas had swayed about the place as Phebe, giving the gamesome shepherdess a sophistication which, though possibly at odds with the manner of a rustic lass, was bold and alive and did nothing to deflect me from my view that the little dark dumpling was fair edible. Slim Mac, I believe I remember, had been let cast out all old Adam and Mikey B. had been first on as one of the several Jaques, and a beautifully spoken exotic he had made of him too. A surprisingly demure Rosalind had been given to us by honeyed Sal but it is sweet sad Jeannie whom I best recall.

Young, virginal, inhibited, an aura of solitariness circled about her, and although, as I have said earlier, it was a simple enough matter to lead her out of this circle and have her join the dance, when the bottles were empty and the sparks were all out, back to this solitariness she always would return. Uncomprehending quite the raw sexuality throbbing in the very nature of the play, when Nell pointed out to her the salty meanings of some of her lines Jeannie would then attack them with an energy and sincerity which showed gleams of that pure gold which glows ever in the work of gifted actors and actresses, but which was far far away from the piping hot yearnings of Rosalind and nearer, I fancy, to a Gloria in Excelsis Deo passionately mouthed by a nun from an enclosed order. Time would see to that, one thought, time and trouble and luck of all sorts. Consider, one time when we the heavy firm had our faces in bowls of spaghetti, Jeannie asked if any one of us knew the significance of Hymen's appearance at the end of the play; that, and who or what was Hymen? Bob immediately told her that he, Slim Mac and Albert Finney, all three, similarly had been perplexed by this matter but that I, from the great heap of my knowledge, had sorted them out, marked their cards and that they were now, all three, sanguine about their knowledge of the spiritual and physical implications of the whole affair. Mac and Albie bellowed their hearty affirmation of this untruth, emphasizing to Jeannie that what O'Toole didn't know and could not tell of hymen, or for that matter hymens, would scarcely be worth hearing, adding that Jeannie could find no better man than Peter to fill in this gap for her.

Nineteen fifty-three, a time when sniggering ribaldry was about as far down the dalliance road as many young men and women went. Yes, a couple or so years on and with the promulgation and enthusiastic adoption of female contraception, our modes of that time would both startlingly and cheerfully change but in those early fifties casual coupling was far from being a commonplace. Indeed, though the academy was heaving with the available, the toothsome and the unattached, sex was a pleasure more talked of than practised and what little copulation thrived invariably was the hobby of couples for whom babies and rings and wedding cakes were happy thoughts, rash couples for whom the consequences of pregnancy were to be dreaded, or couples among whom the bloke would dutifully strap on his member the numbing rubber goods indispensable to quiet minds getting down to the deed of darkness. Bitterly odd, do you not find, in these grim days of the Aids pestilence, that sex should bring to us not fear of life but dread of death and that use of the french letter be described as 'gossamer protection' not, as in my young days, compared to having a bath with one's socks on?

Whatever, convent-educated Jeannie, who in that first term attended the RADA from her base at a Catholic hostel for girls, although inexperienced and a young girl uneducated in country matters, owned an intelligent, enquiring and a determined mind, had sensed the smut hovering over the spaghetti and as we walked back to the academy she drew me aside and insisted that I tell her all about this hymen business. Three years on and off a salt-water sailor, a long-time novice on a three-edition daily newspaper, and from a racy old background, I had a crude working knowledge of the doings but was far less experienced than I let my outward show allow others to believe. Still and all, there stood Jeannie, beautiful and insistent, there stood I, lustily young, a sensitively intimate chat with a darling being called for at her command and equipped, technically, to provide her with these details on demand. Deflowered was a word which had come my way, one that I was fond of, and so for openers I put that poetically plucked verbal petal to her. Not enough, she said. Don't fob her off. Be explicit. Be honest. All right, sweetheart, here we go. Provoked thus, I do believe that it was with considerable relish that I told her of what happens to a woman the first time she makes love. Of a membrane we term a hymen going pop, of the ensuing gyp, of how after the grief the lovers can rub bacons together to their genitals' content and poke happily ever after or until one or the other or both hollers 'nuff. Of a tradition that I'd read about, I told her, in southern Italy and Sicily, one which on the morning after a wedding night requires the bridegroom to stick his head out of a window in the nuptial digs, wave a bloodied sheet at the representatives of his and the wife's family mustered for the purpose on the cobbles down below, and so prove to them that he had indeed bagged a virgin for a bride.

Quietly, Jeannie had listened to me, and when I stopped my chunter it was only then that I truly saw the expression on her face. God be good to the pair of us, I see it still. Impassive, her face, the steel in the blue of her wide round eyes showed hot and hostile as unblinkingly Jeannie stared at me. No one had ever looked at me in that way before. Or so it seemed to me then. Minutes later we were with the others back at the shop, merrily prattling of this and that, setting ourselves to whatever business was at hand and Jeannie was herself again: now smiling, good-humoured, now earnest, hard-working, now slipping away to her strange solitariness. The ways of the academy saw to it that after the next two terms we were separated and that we both attended different classes but we stayed warm and friendly, each to each, and when at times we met and larked about we were glad together and untroubled.

A year would pass and you could have found us both living at George the Greek's gaff in Notting Hill Gate, where I had vacant possession of a busted sofa. One time I hopped in there with an injured leg. Now, George and his woman and Jeannie were solicitous, helpful and kind but, came a few minutes when Jeannie and I were left alone, my concern was my limb, the state it was in and perhaps I was trying to mend it with foul curses. Jeannie was sitting with me on my sofa; I looked at her and there on her still face was that expression. Motionless she sat but it seemed to me that in the stillness of her body hot anger roamed and shot out of her eyes in that startlingly implacable gaze. That, any road, is how it had seemed. 'Leave it out, sweetheart,' I fancy one had croaked, 'leave it out. I know that people sometimes get cross with people who have for whatever reason taken a tumble, but right at the moment I'm feeling very humpty dumpty one and what I would by far prefer is a cup of tea, a Marmite sandwich and a lie-down. For fuck's sake, lovey, leave it out.'

Towards the end of our training at the RADA, Jeannie and I were sitting with two or three other students listening as a senior teacher talked of the profession and what it might hold for us. He told of how, because of the density and the difficulty in the language and the characters of *As You Like It*, the play was often chosen as a dish for beginners to gobble on. The reason for the choice being that Sir Kenneth and his staff had hoped to gauge from their performances of it which of the novices had battled best with its complexities of tone. Had, with a player's intelligence and auditory imagination, understood the compound of its humour, its lewdness, its melancholy, its robustness. To hear who was equipped to speak with truth the richness of the verse and the prose. Jeannie, he said, had surprised her auditors, had delighted them with her determination and vivacity, rare in one so young, immature and inexperienced. He went on further, saying that over the two years she had slowly but always surely deepened and improved her work, and that what he heartily would recommend to her now was that she get herself a job in a provincial repertory company. Play part after part after part, everything and anything, charwomen, queens, whores. Fling herself into the rough and tumble of the business, be catapulted through weekly or even twice nightly rep, rehearse all day and play eight shows a week.

There were, he implied, dainty spots which needed to be knocked off her.

Jeannie, of course, paid his advice no mind. Simultaneously, she was taken up by the intellectuals who needed a princess as patron to their theories and enthusiasms and by the commercial laddies who suggested to her that it was to their mutual benefit that she immediately exploit her youth and beauty while she still had it. A couple of years later and one fine day found me rambling into a small café in what was the decrepitude to be found in the warrens off the Tottenham Court Road. Having gasped out my urgent need for a large slug of coffee, I spotted Jeannie sitting at a table with her then lover. Lovely, too, she looked and so I joined them, soon to find myself in a lively conversation with her man about a painter whom, it turned out, we both admired. Her bloke was an interesting man, the jaw was good, the coffee too and we both gave our tongues a fling. Eventually, there was a pause. I was lighting a cigarette in that pause when Jeannie quite unexpectedly said, 'Are you still sleeping on sofas?' It may be no surprise to you to learn that I was. But that wasn't it. There was that in her voice that I didn't want to hear; nor did I want to look at her; but I did look at her. There it was. That expression. The third time over the years that it had been fixed on me.

Unquiet, Jeannie, you were, and for all your stillness.

What, I wondered, was this time in the steel and the heat and the unblinking blue stare of her eyes? Resentment, did I sense? If so, why? What could she find to resent in a penniless young actor friend, up from the provinces for a few days in town, kipping where he dropped and, if lucky, landing on some kind bastard's sofa? Disturbing it was, uncomfortable I felt, and so I pissed off to Joe Henneky's boozer where I sank a pint on tick. A year or so came and went during which Jeannie appeared in a couple of not supremely excellent films. Her parts were ropy, she made nothing of them and her appearance on the screen was stiff as a doll. Another year chugged by, I heard word that Jeannie had married, borne a child, given up the lark and that she and her husband were living in the countryside, cosily, happy and contentedly.

One morning Jeannie walked out into a woodland glade, put up a little tent, a bivouac, smoothed a tartan blanket over its grassy floor, lay down inside the tent, placed at her side a bottle of mineral water, a plastic beaker, a bottle of sleeping pills. There, away from the house and the watching eyes, neat and tidy, planned and prepared, making no fuss, lovely young Jeannie killed herself. Yes, I wept then as I weep now but what troubles my mind is this wondering, when she laid herself down, what was the expression on her still face.

> And you, a would-be player too,
> Will give those angry ghosts their due
> Who threw their voices far as doom
> Greatly in a little room.

BAR THE VEXSOME business of underwear, life was turning out to be not too bad at all for Bob and me, perched as we were in our leafy nook off a northbound hill in London. Socks were easy enough. One just simply fitted them over the droop of the hot tap in the sink, secured them with your knotted piece of string, your elastic band, the grip of your fist, turned on the tap, let the water flow and filter through the sock, watched the accumulation of debris gurgle down the plug-hole, turned off the tap, released the sock, squeezed it, gave it a couple of belts on the sink, hung it on the towel rail, repeated the process with a partner sock, and in reasonably short order one had two or three pairs of socks all fresh and ready to encase the slim white trotters. Soap was to be avoided. On a couple of occasions my mind had lifted up to fine hygienic realms and I had found myself giving the socks a dab with a bar of the stuff only later to find, and when wearing them, that, impervious to the rinsing or the slapping, a sud or two had remained jammed in the material. This led, after an hour or so of trudge or cavort, to an induction of sludge and bubbles in the shoe. Disagreeable. Soap was to be avoided. Undershirts, your singlet, your vest, also proved not to be difficult to maintain. One wore none. It was the underpants that proved to be sods of jobs, the smallclothes, the knickers. To be sure, efforts were made to render them purely white and wholesome. A bucket, one time I recall, was pressed into service. Two-thirds filled with hottish water and shitty knickers, we stood it on the bottom of the bath, added a dash of boiling water from our kettle, sprinkled a flake or two of some fancy powder into the mix, battered and stirred the whole with a long shoe horn, let it brew for a while, fished out the contents, flopped them in the bath, poured the remainder juice in the bucket down the sink, shoved in the bath plug, turned on both bath taps until there was a decent degree of water and floating knickers, stripped off our clothes, stepped into the tub and began firmly to trudge up and down, down and up, treating by our treading these knickers as though they had been vineyard grape. Our plodding done, Bob set to a doughty squeezing and rinsing of our trodden underwear in the water from the flowing taps and I set to erecting a clothes line over the bath. Two belts, a tie, and a cord from his pyjamas served very well indeed. Lacking clothes pegs, we agreed that a simple fold of the knickers on the line should turn the trick nicely for us and so, our long labours done, we dressed, went to the pub for a deserved, relaxing drink or two, returned to the digs, undressed and then we dossed down for a solid snore.

Came the morning and through the blear Bob's voice foghorned at me telling me of bathrooms and sights to be seen.

Creaking out of bed, I wrapped a blanket round me and tottered the few steps down the corridor to our bathroom. Using the pan as a seat, Bob sprawled smoking a cigarette and chuckling. Little wonder. Clinging to my delicately strung clothes line were a couple of pairs of knickers, the rest had slithered from their perch and lay where they had dropped but in scrunched blobs. More. Not only did they seem to be more sodden than when in hope we had hung them up to flutter and to dry, but also that their colour had been translated from a smallclothes white to a battleship grey, and a greater pity, surely, was that the knickers yet remained shitty.

Of course there was a laundry round the corner and of course that's where eventually we wound up, both bearing pillow cases stuffed with dirty linen, but laundries were fierce expensive places, that I'd discovered. On request, my old mum had parcelled up two of my poshest shirts and had posted them to me. White they both were and made of silk poplin. When they became grubby I took them to a laundry where I was told that they didn't accept silk, that silk shirts were the province of either hand laundries or, less expensively, dry cleaners. So, to the dry cleaners, handed over the shirts, was given my ticket, returned a few days later for the goods, was about to tuck the crisp packet under my arm when the woman at the till shook me by announcing the cost of the operation. It was a considerable bite out of the wages. Wages, moreover, which I had intended to spend on matters fitting and proper to my present needs: theatres, cinemas, whiskey, beer, cigarettes, women, grub; not good money to be squandered on the upkeep of one's threads. Yet it was so. Indeed, ever had been so, for not once in my life had I successfully washed a single article of clothing. There had been one hilarious week during the earlier months of my naval training when I did a Housewifery course, pronounced Hussifry. I recall buggering about with a mangle, failing to darn a sock, dunking gear in bubbling vats, and one whole morning spent clashing together a pair of knitting needles, with a ball of wool attached to one or the other or to both, and at the end of four hours I had constructed a small woollen dark blue moustache.

Even on board ship at sea where, technically, it was compulsory for a sailor to do his own washing, there invariably had rolled about one or two or more dirty great hairy-arsed salts known as 'dobie bosuns'. A rocky head weathered by all manner of storms would coyly peep round the mess deck door; its mouth would set itself into a prim smile, its eyes drift heavenwards, and then, as softly and girlishly as the horrid thing could grunt, it would sing, 'Dobie, dobie, never go ashore. Never have to muster outside the sickbay door.' 'Dobie' being sailoring slang for washing, this was the cracked but fluted cue for those of us incapable or unwilling to do our own laundry to load up the singing dobie bosun's steaming bag with our dirty gear which, in return for consider-ations of rum or tobacco, he would dobie, press and return by the following forenoon. Handy. And, compared with the cost of laundries or dry cleaners in London, inexpensive.

Eventually, Bob and I were dealt a lucky hand; the wife of the landlord of our regular local boozer had taken a shine to us and the plumply motherly darling volunteered to take in our washing, silk poplin shirts and all. These latter, she explained to me as I bought a round and feigned deep interest, needed to have their fancy and fragile fabrics lightly dipped in cool or lukewarm water, that or they would perish. 'Heaven forfend,' quoth I, 'do have another milk stout.' Elected we were, you may think, but not so. There yet remained the mystery of the multiplying shitty knickers. What with the dancing and the fencing and the leaping and the rehearsing and the general vigorousness on the menu at the RADA, if one wished to go out of an evening, and one went out practically every evening, it were often wise, after a soak in the tub, and for the sake of both comfort and fragrance, to change one's knickers. Now. Indolence, incompetence, an initial lack in numbers of the wretched articles, added to a reluctance to wander out bare-arsed under the tickling woollen strides, had led one perforce into shelling out shillings to buy yet more pairs of knickers. An economy as false as the growth in quantity of bloomers was true. Remark. Drop a pair on the armchair before tumbling into snore, let Bob do likewise and while we both slumbered I swear that the little bastards would breed. My word, come the morning and though the knickers discarded the previous night lay chaste and shitty where they had been put, a discovering eye would soon discern an offspring shamefully squeezed under a cushion on the sofa. By the week's end, such being the potent attraction of shitty knickers, there would be throughout the room a proliferation of the sods. And no designated pillowcase for them. Certainly not. Stuffed under the bed, draped over the clock, wrapped round the handle of the kettle, here a book marker, there a window wiper. Everywhere and anywhere these children of knickers would sprawl, brazen or concealed, pleading for a turn with the dobie bosun.

Our landlady was your archetypal crone, never seen other than when collecting the rent. Either by her own hands or those of some skivvy she kept parked in the coal cellar, once a week the top sheet of our beds would take the place of the bottom sheet and the bottom sheet take the place of the top. Every two weeks we would get fresh sheets. A couple of times each week she or her slavey would flick a broom about the room, give the hole a general dusting, a tidy, and, of course, gouge out absconding knickers from their hiding places. Such as they were, and tacit at that, the rules of the house seemed to be: No dreadful rackets after midnight. Don't set the house on fire. Obey these command-ments, be regular with the readies, and that's about the size of it. Suited us, Bob and me, much as it seemed to suit another guest at the digs, Carleton, a middle-aged Brown Hatter who had for himself an entire flat at the top of the shack, and who, in younger years, had, he told us, been a performer in musicals and, as he enunciated it, 'light-hearted entertainments', but who was now a mover and shaker in the world of fashionable clothing for ladies. Expensively dressed, he would nod greetings on the stairs, at the door, or in the pub where he, too, was a regular. Acquaintance grew with the chat, the chat with acquaintance and I found Carleton to be affable enough, somewhat precious in manner, generous and ever so faintly sinister.

Between Belsize Park and Chalk Farm was where we lived, in one of the myriad villages whose clusters constitute London and bottle parties were the style. I and a young chap hoping to become a portrait photographer had chummed up. Nor would I sit for him; this didn't faze him; through him I met an aspirant writer, scraping a crust by scratching down advertising copy; at his place one night were two nurses; yes, nurses; one of whom was called Gloria. Think of it. The days when nursecake was starched and crisp, silken-hosed and sinfully wholesome. Such was Glorious; and when she was on duty she wore a little clock turned upside down ticking on her tit. She told me, in so many words. The cry would go out. 'Party at Harry's, Emily's, Gunther's, Marjory's.' The plonk shop would be peeled of its red stock, of its white; my game was a half-bottle of whiskey which, queerly, few but I fancied. Round to Betty's or to Bert's we would clatter. The days of the crank-handled gramophone were just gone, the days of the dinkily disced 45s had just arrived. That or the wireless and we had glad music. Timeless these ceremonies in which we hopped a measure, bellowed endearments, heard and mouthed the clash and fell of mighty opposites in argument, in philosophy, in disputes over cricket and the price of turnips; sorrows were soothed, noses punched, neighbours were aggrieved, songs sung, and the fucking among the buckets in the broom cupboard made a fine din.

These loud days, as the year two thousand comes blaring in our direction, to our young men and women the plucked guitar is common as acne. Not so had it been in the England of the early nineteen fifties. To be sure, we who then had been young shared our quota of acne but no one that I knew owned or played a guitar. Yes, at the pictures we'd seen cowboys humming, strumming; on the wireless we'd heard Reinhart, Ledbetter, Crummet; but Bream, say, and Segovia, who would play this child of the lute and raise its tones into the greater consciousness of humankind, were yet to come; as were, Lord knows, the amplified electrical twangling Jacks who break their banjos even as they thrash and beat the buggers. Anyhow, one nippy night, after sharing a chew with us in a café by the tube station, Cotton-eyed Joe came back to our digs behind the trees, carrying with him his guitar in its case. We kept among the knickers in the wardrobe a crate of bottled beer, and as Bob beheaded the bottles Joe told of how he had forsworn all ushering and vendoring of ice-creams at the cinema and of his modest hope that he might be invited to turn a copper or two by playing his guitar and singing at a shebeen off Charlotte Street. Splendid, unexpected news and would he please, when he'd seen off his pig's ear, beer, give us a taste of his talent? Certainly. There is a lovely mingling, do you not find, of the feminine and the masculine in the structure and form of a guitar and Joe's machine was a daisy. Hand-made for him in Spain, he had blown much wedge on the darling, and he cherished it, and he played it excellently well, and he was a sweet singer, and his songs ranged from the ripe and salty, the popular balladry, ditties from musicals, lyrical Elizabethan, roamed they did all the way home to his version of Flanagan and Allen's 'Underneath the Arches' and far, far away to a minuet by Dowland.

Tap tap tap tap tap came sounding from a gentle knocking at the door. Complaints? Rubbish. Our music-making in our dirty little spot has been gently melodious, our warbling subdued, not at all raucous and it's barely nine o'clock. Open door. Three figures are there. The middle one is Carleton and he is flanked, flanked mind you, by the considerable haunches of two tall and handsome, terrifically well-dressed women. 'We've been naughty,' says Carleton, I fancy. 'We've been eavesdropping. It was simply irresistible. The sound of that guitar so exquisitely played had us quite glued to your keyhole, may we trot in for a tick?' Do, Carleton, do, and pray lug in with you this brace of strapping lasses. Such a personal instrument, the guitar, might you agree? It has a voice, it's almost conversational, speaks to you rather than plays at you.' I'll buy that, Carleton, I'll buy that. This here geezer is Joseph, our visiting harpist. Who, old sausage, are these fine females squirming about inside their elegantly cut two-piece suitings? And, bye the bye, you look particularly dapper tonight, Carleton. 'May I introduce Florence and Adelene? This is my dear Adelene, this is my lovely Florence, and here, my dearies, are the handsome men I've been telling you about. My young friend Peter, my young friend Robert, and their gifted friend Joseph whom I'm having the pleasure of meeting for the very first time. Told you, didn't I, Florrie, didn't I, Adie, that Uncle C. has lots of surprises squirrelled away about his premises?' Uncle C.? Squirrelled about his premises? You're fairly pissed, Uncle C., that's clear to Bob and Joe and me. Pissed enough, in the hope that he, too, is a Brown Hatter, to beam roguishly at Joe; pissed enough, and sinisterly charming enough, to play the pander between the women Bob and me. That's all right, I'm sure, for Bob and me, Uncle C., you really couldn't have chosen a better firm, but in Joe's case I fancy you've put your money on the wrong squirrel.

Under thick paint, Florrie and Adie have both glued haughty expressions onto their faces, but which regularly come unstuck as from time to time chuckles burble out of their bright red gobs, and the betting is that they've been at the gargle too. Hello, Uncle C.'s off again. 'Such soldiers they've been for me these last two days, my dear and lovely girls, such soldiers they've been. We've just finished a two-day shoot on the Heath, do you see, and though the weather's been kind to us and, thank you God, beautifully bright, it's really been most bitterly cold. Brrr! My photographer and my assistant and I were chilled through and through but not a syllable of complaint from my lovelies. Well, Florrie did have a little whimper when her botty got wet down at Highgate Ponds, but, then, who wouldn't have? Soon over, though, and then she went straight back to work like the proper professional she is. They've been perched on the branches of evergreens, up on Kite Hill, posing in front of Kenwood, all over the Heath. And in spring clothing! Can you imagine? I'm quite exhausted but the girls are fresh as fresh could be. They know that I'm very, very pleased with them. They have it in them to become first-rate mannequins. They're divinely photogenic, disciplined and thoroughly good sports, both of them. We were talking as we finished our business over drinky-poos in my flat; I told them of my two young Royal Academy friends who lived below, how I was convinced, but convinced, that the days of the man mannequin, if you'll pardon the wordplay, would shortly be with us, and was just going to drive Florence and Adelene to their hotel round the corner, when we heard that heavenly guitar music coming from your room, so we crept up close and had a sneaky listen. Please, please will you play and sing one more song for us, please? And then I'll take us all to the pub, drinks on me.'

Carleton, my old flower pot, we've got the drift. The particular branch of the rag trade you work for needed to have their Spring Collection photographed with bodies inside it. To that end you've been harrying this pair of dollies all over Hampstead Heath in deep winter and taking snaps of them dressed in skimpy threads. Your peroration has reiterated to your employees, and demonstrated to Bob, Joe and me, that your powers are magisterial, prophetic, and that if we all play our cards right you could be of indispensable assistance to us in the rosy future. Silly old queen. How do we lose him? Adie has caught my eye; behind all that mascara I spot large tawny peepers with a twinkle to them. Florrie is staring at Bob and no wonder; straight-faced, he is literally tugging his forelock and saying, 'Thank you, Carleton governor, most kind I'm sure, sir. The ladies are a credit to you.' Dramatically, Joe strums a chord on the banjo and announces in a husky voice that I've not heard before, 'It will be a pleasure to sing for you, Carleton, a pure pleasure.' Then, without once taking those bright chips of blue ice that serve him as eyes off the wretched Carleton, out of his cakehole poured a song, novel to me as the voice the wicked bugger used to sing it, in which a Brown Hatter ranch-hand laments his only having two hairs on his chest, and a fate which has ridden him into a Wild West far too butch for his unusually delicate sensibilities, which ditty was called 'I'm Only a Lavender Cowboy.'

A comical enough cod ballad, clearly a forces favourite, the circumstances in which it was sung had Bob, me and the birds baying with laughter and Carleton almost coming his cocoa in gleeful rapture. Abruptly as he had begun the number, having looked at his wristwatch, Joe jumped up, fitted his Spanish banjo back in its case, and using the same husky tones firmly announced, 'Right, that's me off.'

'Off?' said Carleton. 'Off where?'

'Have an engagement at ten sharp. Must get a wriggle on. Take the tube.'

'Aren't you coming with us?'

'No.'

'Just for one quick drink? The pub's only across the way.'

'Don't have time for quick drinks. Have an engagement. Ta ta.'

'Where are you going, Joseph?'

'Charlotte Street way. Oxford Street end. Ten sharp.'

'I was going down West. After I'd dropped the girls off. May I give you a lift in my car?'

'Yes.'

A bundle of bodies clattered down the stairs. Bob and I and Adie and Florrie watched as Uncle C. tucked himself behind the wheel of his large Austin Princess, and, with Joe and his machine comfortably settled on the back seat, we waved them goodbye as the car rolled out of the Gardens heading down for Soho. Then we scooped up the chunky beauties and wheeled them into the boozer.

Adie wanted a gin and it, so did Florrie, I wanted to know what it was that was in the it, Adie told me it was Italian vermouth, Florrie said they both wanted sweet it, Bob and I thought we'd try it, so we all had gin and its, sweet, I liked the gin but not the it, so did Bob, I remembered drinking my skipper's pink gin, that's gin with Angostura bitters in it, Bob knew of it, liked it, so we had pink gins while our fleshly mannequins drank gin and its, Adie was warm and Scots and tactile, Florrie feigned elegant sophistication and was from the Midlands, they had more gin and its, we had more pink gin, it seemed wiser to buy a bottle of gin and a bottle of it and a bottle of bitters, landlord's amused roly-poly missus heaved the three bottles out of the off-licence, warned me that such women were only interested in us for our wealth, chalked the cost of the gin, bitters and it on the slate, where it joined the sum of what we owed her for laundering shitty knickers, then clutching the bottles and each other, a zig and zag and a blunder up the apples took us into the drum, with the lights out and the gas fire on, we cracked the bottles of it and bitters and gin, had more pink gins and gins and it, it became tricky to tell if the drink one was sucking had in it it or bitters or gin or it and it or bitters and it, nor could we remember many of the words of 'Lavender Cowboy', though boozily we crooned what few we knew, all then became a confusion to me: waltzes resolutely rasped through a comb and paper by Bob, I and a Clydeside chemist's daughter dancing to their strains, gin and it and pink gas firelight glowing on the it and the faces and the smoke and the haunches, high kicks hoofed out by sophisticated Florrie who had learned her trade in pantomime chorus lines, 'How do you do, everyone, how do you,      How do you do-de-oo-do,      Are we here to entertain you, Yes well rather,      Hope you're feeling in the pink and, How's your father,' sang and kicked the shoeless four of us, determined shushings and hopeless failures with light switches in corridor or bathroom which anyway is occupied by blind Bob who has missed the bowl and pissed on his feet, tweed and whispers and sweat and buttons and musk and slaps and squeaks and anger and lurches and doors and steps and cold and dark and figures and trees and stumbles and the bang on the head and the stairs and the crawling and the room and the heat and the fire and the quiet and my hair being pulled and pulled hard, lip stuck sucking and breasts and elastic and buttocks and when I woke up I found myself naked in Bob's bed and my bed was full of a deeply asleep Midland Sophistication. This was a surprise to me. Bonnie Scotland and Bob were not there and where they were I did not know. Nor were there any coins left for the meter in the saucer by the gone-out fire. On went my donkey jacket, I wandered through the dead or dying bottles of gin and bitters and it with my sponge bag under my arm, went to the bathroom, bathed, shaved, returned to our room and dressed. How Do You Do Everyone had covered herself with the eiderdown; she lay face down, one knew that from her legs which were sticking out from the cover, meaty and shapely over the bed's end and with their feet pointing down. I scribbled a note on my lined pad, put it on her handbag and went off to the RADA. The note said, 'Gone to school. Peter. X'.

Outside Goodge Street station was a café which I went in for coffee and a doughnut. In the café, eating a doughnut and drinking a coffee, sat a rumpled cheerful Bob. He'd had occasion, he told me, to spend the night with Annie Laurie in the room that the women had been sharing at their hotel. Later in the forenoon, he telephoned the hotel and left a message for Adie, suggesting that she and Florrie should meet me and him at seven p.m. in a restaurant in Belsize Park near the hotel. At our digs in the early evening, the beds remained unmade but the bottles had been stacked neatly by the gas ring and propped up against the clock face was a note for me. Written on a page torn from a small diary, it said: 'Good boy. Florrie. X'.

Bob looked at me, I looked at Bob, we both had a large pink gin, arranged ourselves, went to the restaurant early wondering if Adie and Florrie would turn up, they did, none of us was displeased. To the contrary. The four of us had two or three nights of that and whatever else was going on, which included my first sight of Revue, at the Royal Court; lovely, funny, witty tuneful stuff. Sober, Florrie turned out to be a bit of an affected bore; nevertheless, she was a fine chunk of a lass. Adie was a delight; outspoken, warm, kind. Also, she was a lass with fine chunks to her. That winter's Spring Collection was dispersed, we went our own ways; but Bob wrote regularly to Adie and Adie to Bob.

Before stepping out of the Austin Princess with a brusque thank-you and goodnight, Joe had told Carleton that if anything turned up that he thought might be of use or interest to us, he could be contacted either through me or Bob. From time to time in the boozer our Lavender Cowboy came up with the odd pink gin, but that was about the size of it.

> Where do you come from, where do you go?
> Where do you come from, Cotton-eyed Joe?
> Well I come for to tell you and I come for to sing,
> And I come for to show you my diamond ring.

NEVER LESS ALONE than when alone, a rich state discovered in my childhood and regularly visited throughout my life, had found expression in solitary ambles round the manor and its purlieus. Counterweight perhaps to the joys, bumps, sensations felt among companions, the choice of being on my own rests high on my pile of pleasures, and in those long years ago I would go out of the Gardens, a right and a right and an immediate left took me on a long rambling widdershins down the arc of a peaceful tree-lined road; sharp left, a jerk down the dogleg and, by God, there was I, staring at the fountain Mrs Crump had had built for Cousin

Warburton in 1887. Why she did I do not know but there it was, high, arched, monumental; gothically dotty, a shrine whose masons had chosen entirely to build, surely, with petrified potted meat. A slug for the nonce from its gurgling play and there, yards only ahead of me, was Hampstead Heath railway station. Rural, it had seemed, not of the city and there beyond swayed high and mighty trees. The Heath. Behind the fountain, a small cinema; to its right, a bus stop; further on, before and up a little ginnel after the station, two fine rub-a-dubs, pubs. On the fountain's left, a row of shops in what is Hampstead village. Step away from the fountain, there was a café given over to quiet chat, chess, newspaper reading and White Russian refugees. Bowl along the few steps to the Heath, clamber up through the tough tussocks on the mound and there before me was a royal proliferation of great elms, oaks, willows; tangles of thick and ragged grass running wildly green through ferns and bracken and brambles, up hills, down a down down the steepy hollows and all along the pitching stretches of this heathland.

London's highest point, eight hundred primitive and uncultured acres yet remain, timelessly the commonland on these islands of ours off the far north-western seaboard of Europe. Paths, of course, tracks and ways had been over the centuries scratched down on the Heath; from here to there, that side to the other, across and through or around, but the more interesting caper, you should know, is to navigate your own stride through the untamed hillocks and thickets on the heath. To be sure, thorn torn and nettle stung, lost and up to your arse in shite, you may find yourself floundering about miles from where you had wanted to be, but what of that? A rub of a dock leaf on the rash, a scrape of the shoes, a shake of the trousers and a brisk tumble down the slope with luck might lead you to the pub at the end of Keats the poet's lovely grove. After a soothing pint there, why it's only a few steps to my willows. To the wooden bench there under my willows. My willows under which, shit or shine, I sat and spoke my lines.

With privacy for study a scarcity, the roof of the academy and those willow trees at Hampstead heard from me a deal of Shaw and Shakespeare, Gilbert and Sullivan, too, those early months at the RADA. On top of the parts in plays we had to study, each week, each fortnight, each month we students were set pieces of prose or verse to learn, bone up and utter before distinguished members of the acting profession who, in rooms, would sit and assess the merits or demerits of our diction or tone or breath control or appraise the conviction we brought to this utterance. My first crack at it was in front of Sybil Thorndike, Bernard Shaw's own Saint Joan. 'Oh, what a rogue and peasant slave am I', Hamlet, was the piece which I had to offer that great lady and when my turn came, I marched into the room, stood on the spot provided, was about to burst into full honk, when Sybil said, 'Come here, you young rascal. Let's have a good squint at you.' I approached the presence. 'Mm. Good face, good physique, are you eating enough? No, don't answer, you're probably as bad a fibber as I am. Does he eat enough, Clifford? He seems quite sturdy, does he eat anything at all?' 'From time to time, I think Peter must do, Dame Sybil, he must do, must do, must do, from time to time to time. Yes, Peter must do, from time to time.'

Having, it seemed, satisfied herself that I was not malnourished, Sybil asked me what I was going to speak for her. When I told her, a soft smile beamed out from her strong face and, rising from her seat, she put an arm round my shoulders, walked me round the room and asked me if I found the speech to be as complex and difficult as it had seemed to her. Did I find in it many of the variances of Hamlet's personality? His vacillation, his determination, his self-disgust, his humour; the numbing grief over his father's death, the anger, the introspection, the passion, the dangerous instability? Why, yes, of course, Dame Sybil. Good. Now try to overcome having to act it in a room before two old owls like Clifford and me, just shake up all that you have thought about and practised on the speech and come out punching. A ripple of what I hoped was clear speech and phrasing, a rip, a roar, a bitter chuckle, an idea, an enthusiasm, 'The play's the thing, wherein I'll catch the conscience of the king!' and it was done.

'Excellent,' said Sybil, clapping.

'Very good, very good, very good.'

'Needs to work on his breath, consonants and the stretch of his vowels, Clifford, doesn't he?'

'He does, he does, he does.'

'Truthful and intelligent though, Peter, I'm going to give you colossally high marks. Probably seven out of ten. Tell me, when you cried "vengeance" do you think you strained your voice?'

'Perhaps a bit, Dame Sybil.'

'Thought so. Tell me, when you rehearsed it, did you ever feel it deeply?'

'Yes, Dame Sybil.'

'Strain your voice then?'

'No. Not at all.'

'Of course you didn't. No tension in the throat, you see, that's why you must learn all about breath and relaxation and the technical placing of the voice. Can't expect to feel deeply eight times a week, you know, with matinées on Wednesday and Saturday.' At this point Sybil suddenly let fly a screaming strangling blood-sodden yell that rattled the windows. 'Did that in *Medea*, Peter. Woke up Dame Lilian Braithwaite who was snoozing in the box, let me tell you,' chuckled the splendid old girl. 'All technique, Peter, all technique. Just remember how it came out when you felt it deeply and do your best to reproduce the effect. Heard of those old Greek orators and actors, have you, who on the seashore bunged pebbles in their mouths and roared out over the boom and rush of waves?'

'Yes, Dame Sybil, Clifford told us.'

'Well, I'm sure that's an admirable exercise but we don't have very much wild coastline in Gower Street and so listen to me.'

Sybil then, in a remarkably resonant whisper, said to me: 'Whispering puts more strain on the voice than any hollering or bellowing or shrieking. Try to whisper that speech, or any speech, to someone who is ten yards away from you. Whisper, mind, none of your quiet speaking, real whispering, and see if they can hear every word you whisper. You'll find you need great lungfuls of breath and great care not to strain the voice.'

'Right you be, Dame Sybil, right you be.'

Resuming her normal rich and bitingly articulate voice, Sybil then said, 'Thank you. Work hard. See if next time you can wangle eight out of ten from me. And be sure that you eat.'

On my wooden bench on the Heath you could have found me, whispering to my willows, talking to them, reciting, watching the mournful, majestic sweep of them; listening to their rustling voices and the whispers they spoke to me in return. You would have found me on my bench under my willows during the next thirty years of my life.

---

AGAIN AND OFTEN, when the solitary mood was on me, a favourite ramble was the straight run at the river I had successfully and luckily staggered over that one potty evening at the beginning of my time at the Academy. Invariably at night, fine adjustments were made to my course, direction and speed but the stroll essentially remained the same. A couple of pubs became favoured for the necessary, thoughtful and refreshing pause, the blessed hot sausage sandwich with the mug of strong sweet tea at the stall in Covent Garden, an indispensable. What I had loved most, though, was to potter down the streets named after the actors of old time about whom I enjoyed hearing and reading. Garrick, Betterton, Kemble Street, tucked away from the lighted din of the

West End. The columns running to the stage door at Drury Lane, to which, when he hadn't ridden the beast up the stairs to his dressing room, Kean had tethered his black stallion, Shylock. Which of the doors at the back or at the side of the Lyceum had been for thirty years Irving's private entrance and exit to and from his theatre? The modest job in Burleigh Street had been the door I plumped for, and years later I was pleased to learn that indeed it had been the very one through which the tough old lanky governor had rolled his rocky gait. Down, then, to the embankment; to lean on the wall and to gaze at the wide dark streaming river, to sit on a bench by the memorial to Gilbert and Sullivan, to smoke a fag, to dream, to ponder, to rise and wander for the one at the Coal Hole, to hop on the rattler at Charing Cross station, to shake and judder all the way home, to fall into bed, to endure the missiles and complaints hurled by Bob as I rattled out my lisp-removing exercises, to chatter of this and t'other, to drift into cheep, deep snore.

Soho, the ancient hunting cry by which the district is known and named, soon regularly featured as a fine place for my footfalls. Out of the RADA, on one's way to Shaftesbury Avenue's theatre-land, a left, a trafficky longish right, a dish of grub, your sharp left, one in the Burglar's Rest, a wander along down Charlotte Street, wriggle a little, straight on, plod over Oxford Street and there one was, right in the Crooked Mile itself. However, at first, was one on a run ashore in Nyhavn, along the Reeperbahn, up The Gut, where red lights also twinkled and lurching sailors tucked their ends away? No. Rackety, rickety, glamorous and seedy, old as sin and streaming with novelties, uniquely itself sprawled the lanes, yards, alleys, courts, passages, streets, the mazy old voluptuous body of these parts that West Central London lets squeeze right up to Shaftesbury Avenue, fair buggering the backsides of those posh theatres standing there.

There's St Anne's church tower with the hands of her clock stopped at twenty minutes past nine, the time in 1940 when she had been wounded by one of the first bombs Germany dropped on London. Here's Van Damm's Windmill, the joint in which, when the Blitz sundered the city, the girls still wriggled and kicked and stripped, their memorial writ in the brazen lights which tell me, 'We Never Closed.' The Blue Posts, yes, this must be the French, there are the Greyhounds and the Coach. Do I hear jazz?

It took a while to crack into private nooks behind above and below the public glare. Protective and exclusive, do you see, those dens and dives who wanted on their premises no toerags, but eventually, they let me in. In the Nuthouse, into the Gargoyle, the Mandrake and Ronnie's, and into Muriel's. And yet I live. Mercy.

True, the more consistently welcome encounters this young student had made in the days, in the nights, in those first few months of living in the metropolis, had been the greetings given him by the warmth in the air wafting up from the tunnels when he had entered an underground railway station. Warm and welcome to his chilled frame in its donkey jacket as the whiff of new-baked bread to a receiving nostril. True it is, too, that from the Hopi creature, whom he fancied something horrible, there had streamed a warm affection, an open friendliness and a sensitive encouragement for his work, which was slowly banishing uncertainty, nourishing confidence and making him feel more fitted for this business of learning how to become an actor than he had felt at any other time. And yet. Pocahontas contrived it so that seldom was she alone with me. To be sure, we were together at rehearsals, at classes, in cafés, among groups at the theatre, the cinema, the chatter in the pub; inches only apart but which, with others there or thereabouts, might well have been miles. That gap closed one time, and comically too, on an afternoon when I lugged her away from our companions and took her to the pictures. Now, in a cinema, as in a theatre or at a boxing match, as near the front as possible is where I prefer to sit and so, presenting myself at the box office, I asked for two tickets for the two and ninepenny seats.

'I'm not sitting in the two and nines,' said she.

'One two and nine,' said I.

No, she didn't pout or get huffy or flounce off. Her eyes at first showed disbelief but then they closed and she sighed and then she smiled and then she laughed. 'Tell you what we'll do.' She chuckled. 'The five and sixes is where I'm going to sit, right?'

'Right.'

'If I give you five and sixpence you could add it to the money you were prepared to shell out. That's enough to buy two tickets for comfortable seats. Join me, then I can truly say you took me to the movies.'

Generous this, you may admit, muddled, point missed and all that, but generous. Gap perhaps decreasing, explanations to be deferred, her money stayed put as I forked out eleven shillings, bought us both tickets for the posh seats, sat there in comfort with my dusky daisy, and from far away and up so high watched and heard figures and voices flicker on the distant screen. Selfless behaviour, I call it, and who can deny that as we walked to her stop, as we waited for her bus, as we prattled of the film that she had seen and at which I had peered, we felt between us both, man and woman, that unmistakable strong sweet tug. Yet she wasn't having any. Not in private. In public, yes, hugs, banter, good cheer. The few times we were alone together, though, subtle but certain, guarded she became, excluding me from her person and her thoughts.

Compensations, however, were at hand. That night, for example, when Jenny and I were driving around Hampstead Heath in thick fog, Jenny at the wheel, I navigating. Top of the Heath, at Whitestone Pond, in which ducks do paddle, children sail their ships, and whose further purpose is to serve as huge water trough for the cavalry, there are any number of roads that one might take, choices galore, though the one we had hoped to spot was a little number which, according to Jenny, would lead us to the top of the very hill at which through the dense murk we were aiming. Staring wide-eyed and alert through the windshield at the fog-lighted area ahead of us, there I spotted it, there it was. 'We've cracked it, Jenny, pedal down, away we go.' And away we jolly well went, straight down the track provided for thirsty nags, into the pond at a fair old rate of knots and wound up door handle deep in the stilly dark hoggin wash. Why of course I played the man. Didn't I splash round to Jenny's door, heave it open, grasp up into my arms the considerableness of the dear young woman? Didn't I, with a light laugh, resolutely wade me and my bundle through fog and water in the possible direction of the indiscernible bank, trip over a sunken object, mayhap a horse or boat or duck or child, and then pitch the pair of us head first into the chilly dip? Of the aftermath, why, there is little worth recalling. A shuddering, dripping trot over a sightless mile or so to Jenny's house. Unreasonable grumpiness, surely, from father and mother, strangers to me both, many many questions about the bloody car, the way to a bathroom shown to me, the loan of a bathrobe, yet more questions about the car, the whereabouts of the spare room, a cup of hot beef essence handed to me without enthusiasm, and even as I tucked up warm in the bed, wondering where the whiskey was kept, Father could be heard still banging on about the car. Odd parents Jenny had picked for herself. Daughter safe. Me safe. Safe enough, surely, the car. Only having a bit of a soak. Nothing that a tow away in the morning and a visit to the dry cleaners wouldn't fix. Why the fuss? Grumpiness is charmless, don't you find?

---

HUMPHREY, TOO, had his hour. Late one Friday afternoon an uncommonly smug Bob had entered the digs and suggested that I should look through the window. This I did. There, in the shade of the trees, squatted old and custard-coloured Humphrey. By a series of deft manoeuvrings, Bob had coaxed the ancient old geezer up the series of less harsh gradients which crissed and crossed at the back of the Gardens, and with quiet triumph had steered him up to this eminence where not once before had he been able to set a wheel. A modest jaunt was on the cards, Camden Town our aim. Into the little antiquity we squashed ourselves, Bob made very fine fiddles with levers knobs and pedals, and, perhaps invigorated by his successful ascent, probably light-headed in the high altitude, Humphrey made no complaint, no groan, no grunt of agony, just a cheerful hawk and a spit before wheeling out of the Gardens to chug along the lane leading to the long road sloping down to Camden Town. We three no doubt were young that day, Bob and I, of course, and Humphrey positively scampish as down and away we bowled past the Round-house, past Camden Lock, under the railway bridge, effortlessly up the wee rise in the road and then freely wheeling down again with Camden Town in our sights. A multifarious citizenry, in those days, bunked down at Camden Town. Representatives from isles and countries of the Aegean, the Mediterranean bulked up large among the populace and threaded their Eastern ways round and about and in and out the throngs of thousands of hard-handed Paddies from the Holy Land of Ireland, pick shovel and ten-pound hammer artists labouring on the lump, dossing down a dozen to a room and known among themselves as McAlpine's Fusiliers. In those early fifties there had been few enough cars on the roads, but as we neared the town, skittering along at a fair lick, more and more cars appeared, more and more pedestrians too, and so, with the probability of a congestion of people and vehicles forming ahead of us, it seemed to me a good idea that Humphrey be slowed down. It had seemed to Bob, too, a good idea that Humphrey be slowed down; better yet, it had seemed to Bob a good idea that Humphrey should stop. Humphrey, how-ever, couldn't stop. Nor would the stamping on footbrakes, the

wrenching on of handbrakes, the imprecations or the howling of
prayers hinder the mad old sod. The events of the day clearly had
unbalanced ancient Humphrey and with that terrible strength of
the wholly insane he had plunged into a wild, careering hurtle. A
glance behind from Bob, clear; a glance for'ard, objects approaching but not immediately; a dextrous grind of old gears in their
box and a loud, completely unnecessary yell to me of 'Hold tight!'
Now, had you in the hope of scraping a crust come to Camden
Town at London from perhaps Famagusta or maybe Ballinasloe,
and had you walked out at late-ish of a December afternoon to
view the High Street and to take the air, for your delight a dainty
sight might have entertained your eye. Hideously yellow and of
great age, crammed stiff with a brace of raving drama students,
an inordinately dinky motor vehicle roared plunging and bucket-
ing down the hill, abruptly shot to its right, and to its right again,
and then again, pirouetted in a blur of horrid ochre stage centre
of the highway, came out of this giddy spin, calmed down and
then proceeded backwards up the hill down which it so unexpectedly had sprung. We inside the little brute, doughty driver Bob,
aghast passenger I, had, alas, not been able to witness this reckless
display of motor-car cavorting and had, as occupants and joint
authors of the novelty number, merely known a whirling and a
clattering, a dread of being killed or of killing, a giddily swift
panorama of this stripe of north-western London, a pitch, a lurch,
and, now, here we were, facing in the same direction we had
been taking when Humphrey lost his senses, but on the wrong
side of the road and with our objective, Camden Town, slowly
receding from us. Happily for all, Humphrey loathed the uphill.
Loathed it. The uphill backwards may have been a new sensation
for him but yet he loathed it. One knew this by the great rusty
sigh he heaved out, the spume of anger steaming from his spout
and the bilious rattling in his abdomen before, once more, he
subsided into mute, boiling paralysis. As usual, we shoved him a
short distance, yanked him down a side-street and parked the

gaudy crock by the kerb. Bob, in shock, I'm sure, I think, began to flourish pliers and wires and screwdrivers, but I had had enough of all that, enough and more, and so I firmly wobbled my way to Camden Town, walked into an eatery, wolfed down a pile of baked beans on toast, a mug of hot and strong sweet tea and found myself shaking like a Sheffield dog shitting penknives.

Composure restored, it was into a pub with me, a fine pub, the Mother Redcap, a Friday night and surely filling up with brickies and navvies, mixers and diggers, the building site labouring-men, recruits all of Ireland's own McAlpine's Fusiliers, wages in their pockets, having a pint or two before washing, changing into dark suits, open-necked white shirts and heading in the general direction of the likes of the Blarney Dance Hall in the Tottenham Court Road and its neighbour gargle houses. A pleasing and a peaceful hour or so I passed, sipping porter and blathering with a ganger, the he who hires and fires and runs the job on the scattered sites, when from back of the bar rumbled out a loud and a deeply vexed voice: 'Who are you calling an Irishman, you mangy git? I'm not a shagging Irishman. I'm a shagging Galway man!' Heedful of my father's advice that, when taking a drink, should one hear voices raised, glass breaking or timber splintering, it were best to head away with all convenient speed, I knocked back my froth, ambled through the door, into the chill dark and stepped the few strides which would lead me to another pub, a pub I knew well, one I liked well, the Mother Black Cap. To reach the famously unwarlike roomy and tolerant nook at the back of the boozer, one must walk down a long length of alley wide enough only for one at a time or your heap in single file. This done, I entered the bar room, which already was more than half filled with quietly chatting men wearing dark suits with white shirts open at the collar, many of whom also had on cloth caps, scooped up a pint of plain, found a quiet seat and settled myself down for an untroubled, ruminative sip and a smoke.

An hour or so passed, a pint or two had slipped down, the room was fair full but the extreme of noise came only from rich laughter, when through the door walked a small man in a long overcoat, the peak of his cap pulled over a lean, grave face, and who under his arm carried a substantial parcel made from newspapers. He stood at the bar, his packet under his arm, and, taking his time, drank a couple of whiskeys, a couple of half pints of beer, picked up another dram of whiskey, walked to a table at a corner, and with his back to the room he placed down the glass and the bundle on the table. His face set away from us, he began slowly and carefully, sheet after sheet, to unwrap his newspaper parcel. Again he took his time, had a sip of his drink, smoothed out each sheet as he peeled away the wrappings of his parcel, and when he was done, there on its cushion of newspapers lay a fiddle and a bow. Another sip of whiskey but this one, after setting down the glass, he rolled and savoured with his tongue. He then lifted up the fiddle, tucked it under his chin, gently put the bow to the strings, and as he adjusted the tuning the laughing chatter in the bar room quietly stilled. The long overcoat on him, the cap over the grave face now turned to the wall, his back to the room, he began to play. Firm, assured and simple he stroked out the tormentingly beautiful melody of 'Boolavogue' and when that was done he then played the air to the lonely and disturbing, lovely song, 'Banks of Primroses'. Turning to the room, he placed his fiddle and bow on the newspaper, carefully, meticulously, wrapping and pressing the sheets around them until once again he had his parcel. A small smile lit up the gravity of his lean face as he nodded to a few voices quietly saying, 'Thank you, Jonjo.' A polite shake of refusal to the softly spoken offer of a drink, he downed his whiskey, put his bundle under his arm and walked away through the door.

> Come all you pincher laddies and you long distance men,
> Don't ever work for McAlpine, for Wimpey or Jack Laing;
> For you'll grind behind the mixer till your skin is turned to
>     tan,
> And they'll say, 'Good on you, Paddy,' with your boat fare in
>     your hand.
> Oh Mother dear, I'm over here
> And I'm never coming back.
> What keeps me here are the rakes of beer,
> The women; and the crack.

––––––––––

HE WAS LOOKING at me again today, that Welsh fellow, the film star, actor, that Burton bloke, Richard. Determined to see him play Hamlet from a seat near as possible to the front, determined to be alone when I watch his performance, against the possible event of an opinion offered before I'd made up my mind for myself, knowing well that if it takes my fancy I'd be happy to come again with any of my friends: Albie, Jenny, Slim, Jeannie, Mikey, Jilly, Bob, Sal; why, a stripe or two laid out for posh seats might even corrupt Alice Capone and lure her away from her body-guards, if not, well, 'How do you do, everyone, how do you'. I had taken the rattler down to Waterloo, walked to the Old Vic and bought myself a ticket in advance for a seat slap in the middle of the front row. Mission accomplished, ticket safely tucked in the sky rocket, pocket, on my way back to the station, there was he, looking at me, Burton. Claire Bloom by his side, he had been strolling back to the Vic at the head of a very cheerful heap indeed, composed, I remember thinking, of at least half the cast of *Twelfth Night*, the production then in rehearsal and in which he was to give his Toby Belch. He was on the pavement coming one way, I was on the same pavement going the other way. It was two-ish. There was a glow about his group which may have been inspired by the effects of a thoroughly nutritious lunch. Whatever, hadn't he stopped, and wasn't he looking at me. That Burton bloke, Richard, the actor. Not, it should be said, in the way he had done when Pocahontas and the Ninas Van and Von had been with me but God knows that's hardly surprising. More quizzical, the look, a crackle of humour to it. It seemed to me right that I too should stop and return look for look with him. So I stopped, but as I was doing so it popped into my mind that it might be sport to give Taffy a run at his own game and so I looked not at the film-star chap, that Richard, the actor, Burton, but rather at his leading lady, Miss Bloom, a gracefully lovely young woman and one at whom I pitched what I hoped would be a comprehensively appraising ogle. It is altogether possible that Claire Bloom's remembrances of that day, forty and more years ago when on a busy road down by Waterloo station for a couple of seconds her eyes had been shamelessly peered into by a long young stranger wearing a donkey jacket, perhaps lack the bright clarity of my remembrances. Who knows? It doesn't matter anyway but at the time I fancy it turned the trick nicely for me because Miss Bloom soon slipped her gaze away from mine and planked it on Burton, R. Now's the time to look at the bugger, I thought, did so, and wasn't there a big grin stuck on his kisser. Heigh Ho! *Twelfth Night* went their way, I went mine. Twenty yards on, say, something prompted me to stop and look back over my shoulder. At a distance, Richard, too, had stopped and was looking back over his shoulder. Then we moved on.

———

TOAST THE MARSHMALLOWS. All right. Here's the electric fire. Provided by Nina Von, who has swayed herself away to spruce up, plugged into its socket on the wall. Here's the toasting fork.

Curious-looking animal. Two sharp prongs, long shaft, wooden handle. Bit devilish. Here are the marshmallows. Great load of them on a large plate. Another large plate beside them. The marshmallows when toasted are to be put on that plate. The entire issue is then to be bunged into the oven and kept warm for the party. Not by me it isn't. Kitchens terrify me. Toast the marshmallows. All right. Uncertain whether or not I've ever before seen a marshmallow. Round fat little white jobs. Never eaten one, that's certain. Hang on. Maybe before the war. It's possible. Yes, perhaps fourteen years ago I did. Or was that Turkish Delight? Doesn't matter. Never toasted a marshmallow. Definitely not. Never toasted anything. Not a slice of bread. That's what normally is toasted, surely. Bread. Toast the marshmallows. All right. Try one neat. Dissolving rubber. Sweet. Sticky. There are better things in the world, are there not, Lord love you, to chew, than a marshmallow.

However, matters have their brighter sides. That Hopi Hebrew invited me to these diggings she shares with Nina Von and Nina Van. At last, and not before bleeding time, the lady has taken up some of the running. And what diggings! These three bonny beauties have blagged for themselves the whole top half of a hefty Edwardian house. Acres to the place with rooms of all sorts scattered over two floors. Living rooms, bedrooms, bathrooms, spare rooms, a kitchen, an attic, and whatever else I do not yet know, not having had, thus far, opportunity to give the chambers a proper casing. Shove one little bugger on one prong another little bugger on the other prong. Hold steadily before the hot red element. A shindig's on the cards for tonight. As the women are in three different classes at the RADA, an elect few from those classes have been invited to attend the knees-up. Bob's gone to the Gardens for a sluice but I jumped on the bus with the birds and came early. Perhaps make myself useful. Quite. Toast the fucking marshmallows. Pocahontas and the Ninas are about somewhere. Titivating, curling, dressing, generally getting all lovely, I suppose. Quite right too. They are three extraordinarily pretty girls. Hot, smoking, sickening pong. Consider yourselves toasted. Get on that plate. Emprong a further two. Hold steadily before hot red elements. Have mercy on me please, will you please have mercy on this sinner. Nina Van, whom God only can love for herself alone and not her yellow hair, is come slowly walking through the room, the long form of her curving and moving under a white silk robe. Jesus! Jesus! Jesus! I've stuck the fucking fork into the fucking element. It's true what's said. I can't let go. It's punching driving ramming battering through my hand up my arm into my body brains head being! Jesus!

The Son of Man heeded my sincere entreaties. He made arrangements for me to disconnect myself from the dread power of the voltage thudding into me through the media of electrical fire, marshmallow and pronged toasting iron by encouraging me to launch myself into a spectacular, high arching back-somersault whose terminus was reached when the top of my head landed into a tidy right-angle made for me by a skirting board and the dogshelf. The rest of me, of course, followed hard upon; the display ended when I lay sprawling and concussed on the carpet in the corner of this sitting room in which diligently I had squatted at my task. The Daughters of Woman were around me when consciousness returned. Concerned young women, lovely girls, and, no, a doctor won't be necessary, yes, please, a brandy would slip down a treat, what?, an ice pack on the nut, certainly, thank you, from the refrigerator?, I'd like to see that, seen a few in stores and shops but never before in the kitchen of a house, yes, we're a bit behind here in domestic gadgetry, hand is fine, not burnt, bit of gyp, ice on that?, certainly, another brandy, I'm sure, would work wonders, does look pretty, doesn't it, sparks and marshmallows and buckled prongs, yes, a minute or two on a bed would turn the trick nicely for me, thank you, yes of course I can walk, whoops a daisy! groggy, that's all, come here to me, then, I'll wrap my arms around you, support away, my beauties, support away, this is great, through here?, right, thank you, here we go, you're very nice girls, you're very kind, this will do a treat, I'll be right as ninepence, again, thank you, see you shortly.

Comfy bed, pretty room, quiet, aching head on the pillow, ice wrapped in a dishcloth packed on the bump, held in position by a tea towel wrapped around my nut and tied under my chin. Comical, really. Hand and arm still shooting gyp, that will fade but, holy hour, that had been alarming. My eyes are closed, my thoughts are of the distraction caused so readily in me by the sight of a fine woman, the pillockdom one feels after stupidity and the perils of cooking. Three remarkable young women, I reflect. No fuss, no jabber, just cool, practical action, that rare quality we call common sense, their good humour and the separate and singular attractiveness owned by all three of them. Someone is in the room and asking may she put the bedside light on. It's my Hopi and of course she may. There she is and bearing herbal tea with sugar in it which she assures me will be much better for me than brandy. Thank you very much, say I, yes I'll sip that. No, not another ice pack, this one's done its job, my old head feels numb and the ice has turned dribbly. Give it to me, says she, and she dumps it in the sink. On the edge of the bed she sits, her hand on my forehead. Do you reckon you'll live, Buster, the lady wants to know in her gangster voice from Chicago. There's every chance, I tell her, and she smiles. Well, she wants me to know, you gave us all one hell of a shock. Laughter there is from her sweet wide mouth, laughter, too, in her merry dark eyes, laughter from me which hurts not at all, laughter because she is audacious and funny and clever and tough and pretty and she has on a lovely dress and her hair has been done differently and has twiddly bits I've not seen before. We both are silent now. Pocahontas is thoughtfully gazing at the lamp. Of what or of whom she is thinking I don't know but I am quite sure that her thoughts don't directly refer to me. A sigh from her. Looking at me now, she is, candour, warmth, humour in her eyes. She tells me that I'm special and that she thinks I ought to know that. That electrocuting myself when toasting marshmallows would have been a particularly bizarre way for a gifted actor to go. Would I please just stay quiet till she's said her say? You're gifted, she says to me, gifted as anyone she's come across, with a real urge to bring organization and precision to the work, which for an artist is how it should be, for it's sweat as much as talent that does it, I should know, right? I'm saying nothing. She tells me that she can tell that I enjoy being with her but that I am to tell her that I enjoy being with her. This I do. OK, says she, then just take it easy. It will be all right. A gentle kiss on my forehead from her, a chuckle, a wisecrack about shocking behaviour, and she leaves the room.

The party was only a riot. Cotton-eyed Joe had warmed things up with a rattle on his banjo, Albie had the place in a roar with his wonderfully lewd versions of Christopher Robin. There was grub galore, booze galore, the gramophone rarely flagged. The heavy firm were there, students from other classes whom we'd only nodded to in corridors or cafés were there, faintly anaesthetized with liquor I was more or less there. And there was leaping and shrieking and shouting and talking and dancing and singing and smooching and drinking and laughing and howling and hooting and jigging and flinging and tumbling and stumbling and shoving and loving and fighting and biting and twirling and whirling and falling and crawling and growling and howling and weeping and sleeping and waking and aching and saying why not and why so and that was my first visit to the house of the bonny lasses at Muswell Hill. Well worth another visit or two, though, surely, wouldn't you think?

---

THE NEXT TIME you are sitting at night on the right-hand side of the upper deck of the bus going north which passes by

Mornington Crescent underground railway station, have a dekko through the window at the stone statue of Ernest standing up there on his plinth. Note, do, the erect but easy stance: weight on left leg, right leg languidly thrust forward, left arm up to his breast and holding a script or a scroll or a cigar, right arm extended palm upwards in one of his easily eloquent gestures, and his head, as ever, slightly tilted back, hair flowing down to the collar of his long jacket. A workmanlike job, its stone is not inhabited by the fantastic, the danger, the comic, the quick intelligence which roamed through and in and around and out of the living Ernest, nor should you expect to find such rare sparks flying from that grubby white sculpture, so the brief view of him through the window, which your seat on the bus at night affords you, will be quite enough; you will be given a hint of the man, no more. Be warned, to seek further, by the light of day, on foot, as all those years ago Bob and I did, will yield surprise or even drear disappointment. The statue is not of Ernest at all, but of Cobden, one instrumental in the repeal of the Corn Laws in 1846, and which was erected by public subscription to which Napoleon III was principal contributor. The chiselled inscription on the base tells this. And yet. There is a touch of Ernest to that figure. Perhaps not as much as when Bob and I first spotted him from the top of a bus and we both yelled, 'It's Ernest.' Enough, though, for me always to think of Mr Cobden as being Ernest. Enough, indeed, so that a short while only ago you could have found me slowly driving in my car past Mornington Crescent underground railway station, head stuck out of the window, chuckling not a little and fondly gazing up at Ernest standing there on his plinth.

It is said by some, and it was surely true of Ernest Milton, that having made him, his maker then broke the mould. An original in person in mind in manner, his personality will live with me for ever. News that he had joined the teaching staff of the academy and that we of our class were to be his first pupils went rocketing about the building, and the gab was fierce. True though probably it will be that most of you never will have heard of him, know then only that during the first third of this twentieth century Ernest Milton had shaken the English theatrical world by acting with a startlingly original brilliance of performance a whole series of different characters. Parts in plays by playwrights ancient and modern, Shakespeare, Shaw, Sheridan, Ibsen, Pinero, Pirandello, Granville-Barker, Ansky, Hamilton, Housman, Kaufman, Woollcott, de Musset, all and more including a play of his own, *Paganini*, had been given a taste of Ernest's talent. Practically all our teachers had seen him act, most students knew of his reputation, and as theatre books bearing his photograph were handed about through the hubbub over the mince in the RADA canteen, a consensus seemed to emerge on which parts he rightly had been judged to be most famous: Hamlet, which he had played twice at the Old Vic, the Emperor in Pirandello's Henry IV and Rupert Cadell in Patrick Hamilton's *Rope*. Indeed, there is a description of the poet Cadell, provided by Mr Hamilton in the printed version of his play *Rope*, which makes me wonder, when he wrote it, just who first saw whom a-coming through the rye. Cadell or Milton? It goes: 'He is a little foppish in dress and appearance. He is enormously affected in speech and carriage. He brings his words out not only as though he is infinitely weary of all things, but also as though articulation is causing him some definite physical pain which he is trying to circumvent by keeping his head and body perfectly still.' You could sing that if you had an air to it, Patrick Hamilton, couldn't he, Ernest? For he has you there, bang to rights. With deference to you both, I shall add: Ernest entered the room moving in a wise somewhat between a soft-shoe strut and a saraband for dead actors. His lustrous grey eyes, aching the while for spectacles to aid them in their task but knowing their owner at the age of sixty-four would deny that their powers no longer were quite up to snuff and who anyway would loathe having a pair dangling over his beautifully Semitic features, slowly and deliberately inspected the assembled students. Of medium height and slimly built, Ernest reached the centre of the room, stopped, tilted back his head, closed his eyes, raised his hands in a seeming supplication and then groaned out, 'Why anyone should call a room Johnston Forbes-Robertson quite bewilders me. Calling a man Johnston Forbes-Robertson seems a little excessive but a room! Sweeties! Nonetheless, *chacun à son goût*, here we are and it is to be hoped that you have all studied your parts and are dead letter perfect. Who is on the book?'

Albert Finney and I were on the book; I and Albert Finney also were the stage managers. The stage we were managing was situate at the far end of a room called Johnston Forbes-Robertson; the book we were on was a play by Bernard Shaw called *You Never Can Tell.* You see what I had been up against? True though it was that at the age of ninety-four and three years prior to my joining up at the RADA, the right reverend sinner George B. Greenwhiskers literally had shuffled off this mortal coil, but also it was true that the devilish old git had yet arranged for his brazen head to be stuck up under the branching stairway in the shop, not, as was generally supposed, to bring fine ornament to his surroundings but specifically, you will agree, to cast a bronze and beady eye on me, his adoring disciple, and to goad perplex and torment me into inchoate adherence to the lettered spirit of his preachments. For example: his choice that I should act the leading part of Valentine in his play *You Never Can Tell.* That, coupled with the responsibility of stage managing the concert, under the tutelage of the amazing Ernest Milton, all on the strength, one supposes, of my successfully lurching through two thirds of the role of jolly Oliver in *As You Like It,* had come to me as something of a delightful shock.

Now, tell me do, from under the stairs, Bernard Shaw, of your Jack Tanner in *Man and Superman*, your Higgins of *Pygmalion*, your Undershaft from *Major Barbara*, you really couldn't have picked a better man to have a crack at them for, since the age of sixteen, haven't I been reading aloud to myself every wise and comical, choice and cracking syllable of the plays? But what's this here *You Never Can Tell* number? Never have I read this fellow aloud, not ever. Never have I read it silently, either, because, not even knowing that it was in the canon, never have I read it at all. Ah well, GBS, you always were one for a right prank and now you have me skinned. Let's have a see. It's an attempt to comply with the many requests you'd had by theatrical managements in search of a fashionable comedy for a West End theatre, is it? Requests with which you'd had no difficulty in complying as you had always cast your plays in the ordinary practical comedy form in use at all the theatres. Sounds ominous. Oh, and far from taking an unsympathetic view of the popular preference for fun, fashionable dresses, a little music, and an exhibition of eating and drinking by people with an expensive air, attended by an if-possible comic waiter, you had been more than willing, had you, to show that the drama could humanize things as easily as they, in the wrong hands, could dehumanize the drama? So far, so dangerously good. Now, the piece and the part. This is good, Greenwhiskers, this is good; this is bold and human and achingly funny. Variously described throughout the play as an 'ivory snatcher', a 'gum architect', our man Valentine in fact is a dentist. A dentist. Yes, that agrees with the popular preference for fun, I see that. Go on. His dental surgery is in the cheerful sitting room of his lodgings in a house on the sea front of a fashionable spa on the West Coast of England. He doesn't have a penny, not a tosser in his pocket, he's broke. He's been in practice for six weeks, has not had a single customer, the furniture belongs to his landlord, he's not paid the rent, is eating and drinking on credit, and the dentist's chair's on hire. More. Under the professional manner of a newly set-up dentist in search of patients lies a thoughtless pleasantry which betrays the young man and shows him to be still unsettled, fond of a beer and in search of amusing adventures.

You have me, Bernard Shaw, you have me. Surely as you have Valentine in the root of your heart when you hand him the huge adventure with which the poor sod has to cope. Love. And you tell us that you took a chair in Regent's Park and sat there in the public eye writing this play? It hardly surprises me, truly, though I'll bet green wages that the theatrical management in search of a fashionable comedy were a mite surprised by the first few seconds of the play's opening scene. His first customer still seated in the hired dentist's chair, immediately after having had a tooth extracted, we find our Valentine, the pulled gnasher clenched in the pliers he has in his hand, with a degree of satisfaction telling his victim, 'That was my first tooth.' Yes, George, I realize the pliers are implicit but that is the instrument employed by a fang farrier when he goes about his plucking business, and that's what my Valentine will wave about. What's more, Ernest will encourage it; he'd have Valentine kneeling on the patient's chest and tugging, he's wonderful. You then involve Valentine in a family reunion; and what a fine family you've created.

Your first patient of Valentine, Dolly, turns out to be the eighteen-year-old female half of a set of twins. The male complement to the pair, Philip, arrives in the van of other members of their family who are coming to the dentist's to comfort Dolly after her ordeal, dust her down, as it were, and then whisk her off to their seaside hotel for a soothing luncheon. Decorum is a word with whose meaning the twins are perfectly familiar, this allows them swiftly and continuously to bombard the poor dentist with deeply personal questions and statements about themselves and him which are probing and frank but which cannot be thought of as impertinent because the twins' manners are so exquisitely good. Also, by the time Valentine has been let utter the few words he has which are not merely responses to keen interrogation, but which include, after some prevarication, an acceptance of the twins' invitation to lunch with the family, an offer he takes up not from good manners but because he hasn't eaten for days, the taxingly difficult business of exposition is well under way, GBS, and by your dramatist's cunning the setting forth of the plot of the play has emerged from character and action, making the laboriousness of this task seem effortless. Admirable, Greenwhiskers, for the who, why, where, what and when of a play stumps most authors and many plays just stop so that these necessary points may be chucked at an audience.

What's next? Mother, that's what's next. Sensibly dressed, brisk and businesslike Mrs Clandon. A veteran of the Old Guard of the Women's Rights movement which has had for its bible John Stewart Mill's treatise on *The Subjection of Woman*. A militant agnostic, Mrs C., one who insists on a married woman's right to her own separate property; to champion Darwin's view of the origin of species and Mill's *Essay on Liberty*; to read Huxley, Tyndall and George Eliot; and to demand university degrees, the opening of the professions and the parliamentary franchise for women as well as men. Now there's a dainty dish to set before an audience in a play cast in the ordinary practical comedy form in use at all the theatres.

Better yet, though, is that you have redoubtable Mrs C. enter with beautiful, beautiful twenty-year-old daughter Gloria, unconventionally dressed in saffron skirt and jacket and a blouse of sea-green silk. Gloria has been educated by Mother to take up her work when she must leave it, which is why the family, who have been exiled in Madeira for eighteen years, have returned to England; to propel Gloria into carrying on mother's vital mission and to confront the father from whom they have all these years been estranged, a man the children have never known. Mum shows great fondness for her children and is passionately humanitarian. Gloria shows high-mindedness, haughtiness and is all passion. This is a dangerous young woman. Valentine falls drop down dead in love with her on the spot. Gloria falls just as hard for Valentine. Valentine's fall is obvious to all. Gloria, in a certain wise, manages not overtly to reveal her tumble. You have the pair of them, Bernard Shaw, in the grip of what you call the 'Life Force'. Others, as you put it, piously do term this phenomenon

'Providence'; but you won't have that; no, for you it is the 'Life Force'. You may call it the Divine Spark or a Rub of the Relic, GBS, but it's chance that brings together the man and the woman through whose beings this nameable power floods, you must know, mere fortune; a roll of the dice.

Whatever, after this happenstance matters really begin to roll and what you said of your essential self to students of the RADA years ago truly is let rip. You confessed that time that for yourself you found the comically absurd to be a desperate and an irresistible temptation. For my money, as I am discovering, *You Never Can Tell* is a play in which your yielding to that temptation is made sublime. The contrived coincidences which form the structure of numberless comedies, and whose manufacture authors often try carefully to conceal, for you become occasions in which your writing exults. You're on wheels! When at the end of the act you provide Valentine with a second customer, his dogmatic old curmudgeon of a landlord, who is allowing this penniless dentist of a tenant to extract a tooth he has broken on a nut in lieu of paying the rent, you have laid enough groundwork for me to anticipate that this tough customer might well be the husband and father with whom Mrs C. and her children will be reunited. As you shift your scene to the terrace of the Marine Hotel and the grumpy landlord turns out to be just what you have made me think he might be, an old man who unexpectedly finds himself meeting the wife and children he has not seen or heard of for eighteen years, to be sure your scene is deeply funny, but also it is touching and packed with human feeling. That, however, is what you, Bernard Shaw, have said your business is about: to move us to laughter. Yes, you have an evident relish for horseplay but you will not tickle an audience's ribs, believing as you do that any fool can make an audience laugh, you want to see how many in that audience, laughing or grave, are in the melting mood. 'One whose subdued eyes, albeit unused to the melting mood, drop tears.' *Othello*, V.ii, Shakespeare. Blimey. This result you tell us, and already I am sweating, cannot be achieved, even by actors who thoroughly understand your purpose, except through an artistic beauty of execution unattainable without long and arduous practice, and an intellectual effort which your plays probably do not seem serious enough to call forth.

Bollocks. That is deliberately provocative, you greenwhiskered old demon, that is what was known in Hunsbeck as a dare. You're on. The luncheon party may prove to be a cracker, though. Your incomparable William the waiter, well, not only do you have him being mild and melodious, fluent and philosophical in manner mood and speech, but also you have him dishing up and serving wine, soup, fish, poultry, salad, pudding and cheese to seven of us, with a cigarette for Dolly, while expressing all of these fine qualities. That would tax the techniques of the most experienced actors. Slim Mac is giving us his William. There's every chance we'll all wind up covered in stage grub booze cutlery and crockery. Nor, should we be able to contrive such wreckage, would it matter a toss to our Valentine. Heedless of either circumstance or consequence, you have him fair tearing away now, don't you? Lovestruck a couple of hours ago, blundering and blithering after his first sight of Gloria, mute and aching throughout the lunch during which he sat next to this beauty, he has been translated into a very engine of wildly articulate speech and passionate energy. Alone with Gloria for the first time, he squanders two whole minutes on discussing with her the nature of the dread forces they feel flowing between them, one to another, before abandoning talk and, in a demonstration of how these inexplicable urgencies need fusion in order to thrive, he wraps his arms around the lovely bundle of her, presses his mouth to her mouth, and slides a yard of tongue down her throat. Yes, I know that you specify only that he kisses her with impetuous strength but that means that he is violent, fast and strong, so be bold and stop quibbling. Gloria finds the tongue sangwidge given her by Valentine to be very much to her taste and, after he has cheerfully bowled away, properly feels ashamed of herself. This can only mean future deep woe for the dentist.

Last scene, the sitting room of the expensive apartment on the ground floor of the hotel in which the Clandon family are staying. The french windows are open, it is night, and strings of Chinese lanterns are glowing among the trees of the garden outside. Stars glitter in the sky and a band is playing dance music at the fancy-dress ball which is being held in the grounds of the hotel. This will be the little music, fun and fashionable dresses with which you have sympathy, will it, Bernard Shaw, as promised to managements? Scarcely before time, because thus far an audience hardly will have witnessed a spiffing frolic. Yes, laughter there has been, and flying off practically every page, but it will have been laughter of the deeply felt sort, the only laughter you care for from your plays and on which your characters and situations insist.

Daddy has turned out to be a bad-mannered, tactless, graceless old sod with an abominable temper. He longs for affection and respect from his children, for civilized conciliation with the wife from whom for long years he has been separated but has only been able to show himself to be a hard, gruff man who expects these graces to be given to him by right and seems incapable of understanding that, even in relationships determined by law and consanguinity, respectful and affectionate responses must be earned. Dolly and Philip are coping well enough; with deadly politeness they are treating him as an eccentric stranger they somehow picked up at a dentist's. Not so, though, Mrs C. and Gloria. You have them making it plain to the old man that they will suffer his society with an implacable coldness and that he is to expect nothing more. True to your principle that drama is conflict, GBS, this behaviour has driven Daddy into a re-examination of the deed of separation, hoping to find in it a clause that will let him ease his hurts by hurting his long-lost family. That an unsuitable marriage is as fortuitous as our birth seems to be your theme in this here fashionable comedy, a theme you underscore by having Gloria put the nutcrackers on Valentine and having her lead our poor chap about to a point where the light-hearted lover boy is raving.

Having been persuaded by the family solicitor to attend an informal, neutral meeting, and to hear counsel's opinion on where legally they stand, you have the participants in your drama mustered all in Mrs C.'s apartment at the hotel. William the waiter serves drinks, the band outside is playing, members of the group wander in and out the window, going to and coming from the fancy-dress ball, not, of course, Valentine, he doesn't have the price of a ticket, but where is this counsel? Who is the counsel? What? In town for a few days, to sniff the sea breezes and to visit a relative, is a most eminent barrister. He's been good enough to say that he will come and help the parties with his opinion, on the chance of arranging a quiet friendly family adjustment. This should be good. Come on, Bernard Shaw, you've primed the charge now press the plunger. Here we go. Wearing a cape, a false nose and goggles, a majestic stranger has appeared through the window. William the waiter's not having this. Oh no, sir, this is a private apartment, sir, if you will allow me, sir, I'll show the way to the American bar and the supper rooms, sir, this way, sir, but the majestic figure takes no notice. He takes off the false nose, cape and goggles and you present us with a tall stout man whose bearing is sufficiently imposing and disquieting but when he speaks his powerful, menacing voice, impressively articulated speech, strong, inexorable manner, and a terrifying power of intensely critical listening raise the impression produced by him to absolute tremendousness. That he is the eminent barrister for whom we've been waiting, come to give counsel's opinion on the human dilemma you've presented for our entertainment, is one thing; that, as we learn, he also is William the waiter's son, is indeed quite another. It's an outrageous daisy. Splendid.

Albie Finney's playing him, GBS, you won't be displeased. Albert has guts and power and humour and he's on to you. He knows that you would show men and women as they are but talking much better than they do and that an actor must play on the line not between the lines and must do most of his acting with his voice. You'll see. You'll hear. Auditorium. The place of hearing. Yes. Right. Slowly, slowly the way of it is coming to me. The ironical Irish compliment you pay Mr Du Cann in response to his article 'Shaw the Shakespeare thief?' likes me well: 'You would guess eggs if you saw the shells.' You play the old game in the old way, you say, on the old chessboard with the old pieces just as Shakespeare did, and that you have entered into a great inheritance: the Athenians, Shakespeare, Molière, Goethe. It is by blind instinct alone, you say, that an artist keeps on building. That he cannot explain it, he can only show it to you as a vision in the magic glass of his art work, so that you may catch his presentiment and make what you can of it. And that this is the function that raises dramatic art above imposture and pleasure hunting.

Harlequin and Columbine come spinning through the window and into the room where your Mr Bohn, pronounced Boon, the barrister, the facts of the matter assessed and most of the persons involved appraised, has begun to assert his considered views. That the whirling pair in fact are Dolly and Philip come hot from the fancy-dress ball, aids Mr Bohn to a more complete picture of his task. In tones infused with logic, perception and an authority which brooks no counter, he voices to the parties their actual positions in regard to their claims on each other, makes clear that these positions may be in conflict with their desires, and then presents them with not necessarily welcome alternatives to their current schemes of conduct. This vigorous dose of sane reason has a calming and a joyful effect on me, old Playwright of the Western World, and when your Bohn has clapped the false nose on to his face, allowed his father to assist him into his cloak, scooped up Dolly and waltzed her out through the window, a similar feeling seems to affect all your characters. Notions of kindness, of being amiable, steal into almost each separate one of them, why, they even begin to dance. Little is left to do but only for Gloria to grind our Valentine into bits and then to insist publicly that he tell her mother they have agreed to marry one another. You end your play with a terrified dentist being cheered up by the waiter who assures him that as the outcome of human affairs is difficult to predict, his marriage to the masterful young lady may turn out not too badly for him at all, you never can tell. Off we go. You'll find me at rehearsal or on the roof, or under my willows, I'll be there.

———

'ERNEST.'

'Who speaks?'

'It's Peter, Peter O'Toole.'

'Of course it is.'

'Should I go to a dentist, do you think?'

'From the cradle to the grave!'

'How many?'

'From the cradle to the grave. We came toothless hither and we shall go toothless hence. Between all is teething and toothache and fillings and extractions and gruesome dentures. Haste you away but bid the dentist, if pull one out he must, to contrive to leave you a stump so that a slab of pottery may be hammered into the gap and then you won't look so hideous.'

'There's nothing wrong with my teeth, Ernest, I just thought that it might be an idea to watch how a dentist puts himself about.'

'Quaint idea. Variation on train-spotting, is it?'

'No, Ernest, just thought it might be helpful. I am, after all, playing a dentist.'

'Oh, I see. Well, no, actually, I don't see. You believe dentists to be all of one kind, do you? Hath not a dentist eyes? Hath not a dentist hands, organs, dimensions, senses, affections, passions?'

'All right, Ernest, point made. Just thought it could be useful for the end of the act. When Crampton doesn't want anaesthetic and Valentine drops down the back of the dentist's chair and rams the mouthpiece from the gas machine over the old boy's gob. Thought it might be an idea to see how it's properly done.'

'It might. Might also be insufferably dull. I'd do it as if I were the Duke of Cornwall putting out Gloucester's eyes.'

And. One fancies.


'Words and character are one, sweeties, they are a unity. Fragment the lines into itsy-bitsy lumps of talk and you'll present only itsy-bitsy lumps of people unable to talk. Thus, "like sweet bells jangled, out of tune and harsh", you will bring discord to the musicality of Bernard Shaw's phrases. A shameful way to treat one of the supreme romantics of the nineteenth and twentieth centuries.'

'But Ernest,' say I and Mac and Mikey and Pocahontas and others, 'Shaw said he was against romantics and romanticism.'

'Phooey! Of course he said that but look at his life and what he did. Young Irish boy, left school at fifteen, drudged as a clerk in an estate agent's office, came to England penniless a few years later, educated himself in the Reading Room at the British Museum, wrote five novels, all unpublished, somehow wangled his way into being an art, music and theatre critic for Sunday newspapers, believed in the betterment of humankind, joined various societies who promoted such Quixotry, began writing plays, had dalliance after dalliance after dalliance with actress after actress after actress, dressed in a bizarre fashion, married an extremely wealthy woman, for fifty years wrote imaginative, fantastic, visionary plays which, at least in this country, were either banned or unsuccessful or misunderstood, won a Nobel Prize, became world famous through films and died alone at the age of ninety-four, if that wasn't the life of a supreme romantic *je me mange mon chapeau.*'

'Listen to me, pray listen: "Sex contains all, all hope, benefactions, bestowals, all the passions, loves, beauties, delights of the earth." Do you comprehend that, Sal?'

'I'm not Sal. I'm Jeannie.'

'So are you. You've done your hair differently.'

'No, I haven't.'

'Well, you should. You mustn't wander about being unrecognizable. You're a beautiful girl and you're playing a gorgeous and a desirable young woman, you must bring your sexuality on stage with you as surely as you bring on your feet. No one will lust after you if you're juiceless as a turnip. Observe, all, do, male and female. Torso and head erect, controlled, thus. Below the waist, where there's hell, there's darkness, there's the sulphurous pit, relaxed and thrusting on secure but moveable pedestals. No, no, no, don't mince and wiggle about, it looks as though you have worms. Oh dear, waterworks, here, have my hanky. Where's my stage management? Peter! Albert! How can I teach acting to virgins and semi-virgins?'

Life at rehearsal with Ernest was seldom calm, frequently hilarious, often infuriating, sometimes outrageous, occasionally frustrating, usually lively, continually surprising, always instructive, never boring and, most importantly, from start to finish it was theatrical. Which, as the musical to music, the mathematical to mathematics or the logical to logic, is the business of theatre. Earning their living off the theatre's periphery, some sad souls there are who use the word theatrical as a disparagement. Worse, though, by far, are the men and women working within the theatre who use the word theatrical as a disparagement. This may be hypocritical of them; it surely is nonsensical; above all it is a crucifying bore.

Of what T. S. Eliot has described as the ultimate sin, doing the right things for the wrong reasons, Ernest Milton was wholly guiltless. Large of scale and often bizarre in manner movement and speech, all the gristle and nerve in his body was tuned to what was fine and vivid in theatrical terms and when at last he acknowledged the wear and tear the years bring to the senses by producing and wearing, to cheers and applause from his students, a pair of spectacles, his observation proved as acute as his methods of instruction often were startling. For example. It is a habit of mine, and whence it comes no one seems to know, of crooking up my left arm to my breast and, with knuckles turned inwards, folding my left hand into an unclenched fist. The gesture is not done consciously. When lolling, say, or sleeping or reading it certainly does no harm, may, indeed, even be decorative, I have no way of knowing. What is sure is that this curious positioning of a limb hardly fits all the characters one may be called on to act and had been considered inappropriate for Shaw's amorous dentist. Ernest came back to rehearsal from lunch one day sniffing a long-stemmed yellow rose. Now, it was not Ernest's habit to sit judge-like before us as we rehearsed. No. Ernest rather preferred softly to prowl around the room. Looking at a sight line here, the angle of his staging there, sometimes to join in a scene with us, coaxing, laughing, encouraging, snarling; sometimes, I fancy, preferring to be an actor than an audience, he would mingle among us for the merry hell of it. This time, however, as I stood on stage uttering the jokes, my arm unbidden writhed into its contortion, Ernest came wandering into the scene, his bloom to his nostrils. Unfazed by this, indeed, used to Ernest's many quirks, I continued to act. Ernest chose his moment well; sauntered sniffing by me, deftly popped the yellow rose into the hole made by the encircling thumb and fingers of my hand and, saying not a word, sauntered on and away.

With a rose sticking out of one's mitt, it is difficult to be unaware of an awkward and unsightly involuntary positioning of one's arm. The yellow rose and I clung to each other for the remainder of the rehearsal, it rested overnight in a friendly milk bottle with a drop of water to it, and the following day we accompanied each other through our scenes in *You Never Can Tell*. The rose went one way, I went another, and though from time to time my arm would attempt to curl itself up, it never did so without my being aware of what it was doing. To this day, there are moments when the arm begins its old manoeuvres and if the time is meet I leave it be and let it roam. Should I be performing on a stage or before a camera though, we remember Ernest's yellow rose and my arm does as it's bid.

Came the day of the race, why, there was excitement among us, nerves too, but informing an eagerness for the off. Hour upon hour upon hour, day after day after day, I had plodded around on the roof at the RADA, muttering, chuntering and howling, occasionally bumping into Albie, howling, chuntering and muttering, and, whatever else, studying and rehearsing Valentine had proved a joyful labour to me and I was now prepared, ready and set publicly to perform him. Sir Kenneth and his flotilla came steaming in, the imaginary curtain went up and in a room called Johnston Forbes-Robertson our play began.

My memory of the show is a whirling blur merely. The Hopi, voluptuous, sensual, thoroughly enjoying being the eighteen-year-old innocent Dolly; icy and beautiful Jeannie surprising me with the fitful gusts of fire she brought to Gloria; Slim Mac, who obviously had collared the market in ancients, serenely doddering about, happily at home with Shaw's text; Finney playing a blinder, capping it with a spinning, excellently danced waltz; and me? For a year and more I had chanced my arm at the game and though scarcely a detail from that performance remains with me to remember, I recall feeling for the first time a relaxed oneness with all that was doing. Concentratedly alive both within and without the play and the character, aware of the language, the wit, the situations, watching and listening to my colleagues, catching and responding to a different nuance, an unanticipated emphasis, completely focused on the living moment yet conscious that these moments were being made for an audience, so immersed was I in the fiction and so sure that it was in my control, that paradoxically I felt liberated and detached from the part and the play; at once being both observer and participant. Good or bad, right or wrong, clumsy or adroit, skilful or inept, or none or some or all of these qualities, our performance of *You Never Can Tell* that morning long ago had a conviction and a vitality that was exhilarating.

The last words spoken, the play over, there was yet a crackle in the room and even Sir Kenneth didn't make his customary clanking lumber for the door but stayed a moment to rumble and to nod at students, the while chatting to an Ernest who had forgotten to wear his agony and fatigue and who instead had assumed a mischievous but dignified glow.

Most memorable to me from that time is an incident at the party which, on the evening after the show, Bob and I had laid on at the Gardens for Ernest and our chums from the academy. Pocahontas and Sal had been commissioned to meet and to escort Ernest to the premises, a task they both performed with efficiency and affectionate merriment, arriving beautifully dressed, arm in arm with a glad smiling old boy. Throughout the course of the fling, as drinks were drunk, songs sung, dances hoofed, yarns spun, the women deepened and enriched their commission by becoming Ernest's handmaidens and body slaves: their own words. They placed cigarettes in his mouth and lit them for him. Should his glass be empty, it was removed filled and replaced. A snack fancied, it was on the instant supplied. Indeed, a clear picture lives in my mind of Ernest lounging on the sofa, cushions under his head, Jeannie kneeling at his feet, Pocahontas and Sal sitting on either side of him, one stroking his hair, the other feeding him grapes and Ernest murmuring, 'I feel like Nero.'

The chimes at midnight long sounded, the wee small hours on us, some guests gone, the stayers warm, peaceful, tipsy, the laughter and the talk easy, quiet, when one of our number asked Ernest to recite a little Shakespeare. A sonnet, perhaps, please, Ernest, or, whatever, a favourite snatch, even, Ernest, if you will, a soliloquy. Hamlet? 'Don't see it as thought. See it as an emotional outpouring: "To be, or not to be – that is the question; Whether 'tis nobler in the mind to suffer the slings and arrows of outrageous fortune,     Or to take arms against a sea of troubles, And by opposing end them?" Imagine if you can, if you will, plainsong richly coloured, racked with heartbreak, yearning for a certainty that cannot come, and think of us young men and women years ago, listening to words familiar almost as daily prayer and hearing them spoken as though they never had been said before. None of us who heard Ernest's soliloquy that time ever will forget it. For my part, the effect of such feelings in my spine, in my hair, in my stomach, in my eyes was of such an intensity that although I did not truly realize it then, in time I would come to know, when art in any form so affected me, that this physical criterion beats out of sight any moral or metaphysical evaluation.

The first bus into town would stop at the end of our street at shortly after five a.m.; Ernest wished to catch it. His body slaves, his handmaidens devotedly linking his arms, Bob, Albert and I mazily leading the way, a group of students with their teacher cheerfully chatted along to the bus stop. For whatever reason we all sang the words that the American forces had preferred as lyrics to the tune which, during the war, had heralded on the air waves the voice of Tokyo Rose the Japanese propagandist. 'She ain't got no yo-yo,' we crooned as the bus came along and to our surprise stopped ten yards further down the road than we had anticipated. Almost immediately we discovered that it was at a lamp post we were standing not at a bus stop and that quite properly the bus had stopped at a bus stop not at a lamp post. More. Having stopped, the bus began slowly to start up again. Swift as a whippet Ernest was after it. 'Stop!' he cried as he neared the bus. 'Stop! You're killing a genius!' Niftily he hopped on board, turned to us, lifted his hat, grinned, and as the red bus rumbled away we watched him sprinting up the stairs for a smoke on the upper deck.

> Why, let the strucken deer go weep,
> The hart ungalled play;
> For some must watch, while some must sleep;
> Thus runs the world away.

DO YOU FIND ME with Christmas a-coming standing in a lamp post's light under the high medieval walls in the ancient city of York and hawking balloons? You do. Your blue balloons, your white, your yellow and your red. How I came to this pretty pass is not entirely clear to me. Up in the North Country over the Christmas vacation to see my parents, I and O'Liver and Rats had mustered in Polly's for a refreshing lunch. That much safely can be averred. That R. C. Scriven, the blind poet, better known to his friends and myriad acquaintances as 'Rats', had poured out through the lubricant hours a high loquacity, too, is a sure bet; certain as drear closing time had come to find us full of verbal fancies and parched as dry bones. These licensing laws notwithstanding, Rats had told of a spot he knew down by the markets, a place where we would be welcomed, where our discussions could continue and where our tongues and throats would be moistened. There, I know is where next we went and a merry little wobble of a journey it turned out to be. As the more direct route to the markets from Polly's takes one through a rambling warren of alleys, ginnels and arcades, through these narrow paths and passages, his white stick a tap-tap-tapping, confidently strode out the blind man Rats, tracked by O'Liver and me who, to our credit, were seldom off the pace, arriving at the shebeen in a respectable dead heat for second place behind the clear winner, Rats.

Safely installed in the cosy pisshole, our vocal mechanisms irrigated, we resumed our chuntering on subjects ranging from, say, the poesy of Thomas Campion to the odds against the five dog hitting the lid and bounding to a win at the evening's grey-hound meet. It is after this session that my mind no longer holds in sharpest shape its grip on events. That opening time came I am sure for, led by blind Rats, as freemen we ambled from boozer to boozer, taking a wet here, a noggin there. That at one point, when peering through a pub window, O'Liver suddenly howled, 'Brown Owl!' downed his pint and shot out the premises, not to come back, is an alarming fact. 'What's going on?' squeaked Rats. Looking through the same window I told what I saw: O'Liver hurtling towards a startled and a pretty girl, jumping on her, wrenching her round in a wrestler's pinfold, biting her, and then by the hair, it had seemed, dragging her away into the night. 'Must be a lass he's fond of,' Rats squeaked. 'Let's go to the Robin Hood.'

Yes, I know it's in the Hood that goods which fell off lorries may for reasonable sums be bought and right well I know it was in this place, which is not only a leery pub but also an exchange and mart to bookie's runners, associate toerags, buskers, market men and women, street traders and all, that Rats and a mate one time allegedly bought a crate of tortoises, set up stall and within hours had exchanged the brutes for the tinkle of coin on coin. This, however, in no way satisfactorily explains to me how it was that I came to be the proprietor of a job lot of balloons. A cardboard case of them, the lid of which had a cord attached to it and could be used as a tray. That we had played Spoof, the murderous little bar game in which the players guess the collective number of coins gripped in the fists of each other, the winner taking all, may be germane to the matter. Could it be that I had triumphed over a travelling salesman and, goaded by Rats into attempting to do with balloons what he had achieved with tortoises, had taken in lieu of winnings the huckster's stock? Possible, Lord love you, but not certain. Nevertheless.

Balloons, I ask you, balloons. Hundreds of the flat bulgy little buggers, blue and white and yellow and red, sprinkled with powder, crammed thick into their case and with eight 'flashes' lying on top of the crush. 'Flashes' are very large balloons. They are to be inflated by using the small pump provided with the job lot, tied to one's person or the strings of the tray, let float above one's head, thus providing an ample advertisement for what the sod below them is selling while luring customers into the belief that the wretched little articles they buy will inflate to a similarly huge size. So, not at all keen to be seen selling balloons in the streets of the city where I grew up to be a man, yet resolved somehow, somewhere to offload the rubber bladders and for cash, I had jumped on the rattler for an hour's trip to the bustling city of York, there to ply my ridiculous trade, nor wonder too deeply how on the day before had I come to be in possession of the blighters, and in the hope that, undetected, I might pouch a penny or two before again hopping on the rattler and chugging back home.

There: you now know, as much as ever I will, just how you came to find me hawking balloons in this medieval city. The why behind this indistinct progress however is altogether more clearly discernible. You also find me skint. Broke. My student days at London have proved fierce costly. The generous living allowance for each term, which my scholarship affords me, alas I had blued in the first few weeks. Since then I have lived on my own modest hoard of the green and blue crisp folding lettuce; now only a sad leaf or two is left. Still and all, after a diffident, nay, hesitant beginning under the flashes in my role as balloon pedlar to the citizenry of York, a few minor successes at the trade have encouraged me into a more confident attitude, and with a certain vigour am I exchanging my limp and rubber stock into solid silver to fill up the empty spaces in my pockets.

Not, please understand, that I grudge having spent all my wages; far from it, my pockets became empty only in proportion to my life becoming enriched. Fine acting have I seen, fine plays too, sitting in fine seats and in fine theatres. True, a couple of tickets for decent perches at a show and that's cash for a week kissed goodbye, but what of that? Such joy I've had, and all that's needed now is a tinkle of change to tide me over merry bloody Christmas and then again we'll be in funds. The fall of night and the opening of pubs seems not to be unhelpful to my trading, either. A festive mood hums from passers-by, many of whom, it would appear, perhaps unused since the war to the sight of inconsequential trifles, smile up at the dotty gaiety in the coloured rubber bubbles swaying above them. Customers, yes, customers come fairly to exchange for these bouncing fancies coins to keep me comfy, to encourage me into more persuasive patter, to discard tentative 'Balloons for sale. Buy your fine balloons', to tongue out in style, in energy, inspired as I have been in nineteen fifty-three by the plays and players I have seen: 'The final clearance of my stock of bargain balloons, ladies and gentlemen. Eighteen pence will buy you four, a florin gets you six, and for half a dollar you will be given an amazing eight. That's right. Eight balloons for only half a dollar.' Yes. *Guys and Dolls*, with Sam Levene and Vivian Blaine. Charles Goldner and Yvonne Arnaud in *Dear Charles*. Graham Greene's *The Living Room*, with Dorothy Tutin and Eric Portman. *Airs on a Shoestring*, with Max Adrian and Moyra Fraser. Rosemary Harris in *The Seven Year Itch*. 'No, ma'am, I have no pink, no green, no orange, nor no stripey numbers. Tests have shown the dyes used for such ones render perishable the rubber of these charming articles.' Yes. Jack Buchanan in Vernon Sylvaine's *As Long as They're Happy*. Trevor Howard and Wilfred Lawson in *The Devil's General*. Rodgers and Hammerstein's *The King and I*, with Herbert Lom and Valerie Hobson. Peggy Ashcroft and Michael Redgrave in *Antony and Cleopatra*. Laurence Olivier, Vivien Leigh and Richard Wattis in Rattigan's *The Sleeping Prince*. 'Inadvisable, sir, to blow up balloons in the dank night air. Take them home to room temperature, caress them in your hands till they are warm, then inflate and the results will astonish you.' Yes. Shaw's *Pygmalion*, with Kay Hammond and John Clements. *A Day by the Sea*, with John Gielgud, Ralph Richardson, Sybil Thorndike, Lewis Casson and Irene Worth. Donald Wolfit and Michael Redgrave play *Lear*. Richard Burton, Claire Bloom, Fay Compton, Michael Hordern, Robert Hardy at the Old Vic playing in *King John, Twelfth Night, The Tempest* and *Hamlet*. 'Here you are, ladies and gentlemen, just in time to buy your bright balloons from this final clearance of my limited stock. Balloons to bring colour to your homes this Christmas. Balloons to enchant your children.'

From under the broad brim of a hat a pair of green eyes are watching me. Green with red flecks and a dark rim around the iris. Singular eyes; eyes well known to me; eyes watching me in amused wonder.

'Hello, Daddy. Imagine seeing you here.'

'Hard to imagine, right enough.'

'What brings you to York, then?'

'Been at the shuffle, son. Quite heavy.'

'Do any good?'

'Has been worse. Decent hands scooped me up a couple of fair pots and at the death bluffed ace high at last face down five-card stud, the others folded and I came away chortling.'

'That's the style. Well done.'

'Went to the Oak for a wash and brush-up. Been playing gee gees over the sticks for buttons. Had a sandwich and a jar, was just going for the rattler when I saw this apparition. What brings you to York? Arrive by balloon, did you?'

'Keep this up, Pop, and I'll give you a puck in the kisser.'

'The Royal Academy of Dramatic Art. You know, my associates

Justice Wrottesley, Bob the Liar and the Flea were only the other day asking me what exactly it was that you studied there and by Jesus would you believe I scarce had the ghost of a notion what to tell them? These are Royal Academy balloons, are they? And the Dramatic Art lies in the selling of the little hoors, does it?'

'Pop. I'm skint. And I'm only trying to knock out a few shillings.'

'I'm fair flush, son.'

'Thanks, Daddy, but I don't want to be always cadging.'

'No, you wouldn't, Peter, you wouldn't. Give us a kiss. Now. Shove over. Mark them up to a dollar the eight. Your last chance, ladies and gentlemen, to buy these red white blue and yellow Royal Academy balloons! We're practically giving away these dramatic Royal Academy balloons at a mere dollar for eight. Don't miss your Royal Academy balloons!'

'Royal Academy balloons!'

'Two for a florin or a dollar will give you eight. Dramatic balloons!'

'Academic balloons!'

'Artistic balloons!'

'Royal balloons!'

---

WE ARE ON the good ship *Venus*. A big-bellied forty-footer. She is moored to the bank of a ford over a trickling tributary to the river Thames. In her young days she had fished the silver sardine but now in her creaking old age she has been translated into a houseboat. Her timbers are rotted, she is holed fore aft and midships, and in the hold where once the netted fishes shimmied and wriggled to their last quiver, I squat fuelling the pot-belly stove. Warmth I need, for me above all in this biting winter of 'fifty-four, but also in the hope of bringing a little cheer into this old girl's hulk. Oh blimey, the wood's wet, the coal's wet, even the bloody paper's wet. I'll hop ashore, root about in the piles, and try to find at least a little dry kindling.

The transition from the Gardens to the boat may be of interest to you. After the break, a van had lifted me and my trunkful of natty clothes back to London, very considerately dropping off me and my fine burden right outside the digs. Up the stairs I'd hauled the trunk, lugged it into our chamber and had discovered there no Bob but a note to me from him. He was at the hotel round the corner, the note told me, and would pop round in the morning to fill me in on the whys and the wherefores. Little need for too much of that, thought I, for if he is nae having a few nichts wi' his braw lassie from the bonnie banks of Clyde then my prick's a bloater. Letters with thistles on the stamps practically every day had come flying into the letterbox and, very much his own man, secretive as ever, he had deliberately been vague and uncertain when asked what he would be doing over Christmas and the New Year. However, it had been when I was hanging up my posh threads in the wardrobe that I realized my dilemma: elegantly draped on coat-hangers, two dresses gave me tangible evidence that Flora McDonald had indeed come down from Scotland to be with Bob for Hogmanay, but the dresses also told me that the pair of them had spent sweet hours together at the diggings and that they must have vacated them to accommodate my return. Can't be right. The digs are Bob's, I am his lodger. Why should he have gone out of his way to be out of my way when it's me who is in the way? Because we are friends, that's why, who respect each other's privacy even more than we do one another's company. It's I who should be at the hotel while Bob should be with his bird at the diggings. Can't be right.

*

Living in London for the first time, one from the other Bob and I had both drawn a greater confidence. But. Given our separate but similar propensities, this very fact had made it inevitable that our gloriously giddy days together at the Gardens were limited. Of course, as that evening I hung up my togs in the wardrobe, I didn't so articulate it; but I knew in my water that it was so. Well, now, there, then, Pocahontas, who had wafted herself to the Continent by ferry for the vacation, before the break, and with a tune to her tones that charmed as it assured, had asked me to telephone her as soon as I got back to London, herself intending to return a couple of days early to recover from the trip. To the dog and bone, phone, went I. Ring. Ring. Ring. Hi, Peter. Good to hear my voice. Had I had a crazy Christmas? She'd had a fine time. Had talked herself speechless. Had eaten herself sick. Yeah. Real food in place of that crappy mush that in England passes for chow. No. She was alone, the Ninas hadn't gotten back yet. She had a present for me. Wouldn't tell me. Would I like to come over and pick it up? Sure. She'd poke about in the freezer and fix us something for dinner. An hour? OK. See you, honey, bye. Meredith, we're in.

Rolling along to Muswell Hill in a taxi, bathed and shaved, relaxed and comfortable in my long grey overcoat, bespoke tweed jacket, well-pressed fine worsted trousers, crisp shirt, new silk tie and my feet at ease in comfortable brogues, a mood came on me that was a mingle of confidence, anticipation, curiosity and that buoyant calm which a pocketful of folding fivers can bring to one. Big Bluey's dark red dressing gown with the invisibly mended bullet holes in the shoulder, his lovely gift to me that Christmas, hung next to Bonny Scotland's frocks in the wardrobe at the Gardens, and in a pocket of that gown I'd known and loved since child-hood, stashed and tidy, waiting to be shoved into the bank along with the cheque for my term's living allowance, lay yet more of Bluey's munificence: a thick wad of readies. In funds again, by God, I'd peeled myself a roll of five spots, trousered them, the peace that pennies can bring had entered me and by the time the taxi spilled me out at the house in Muswell Hill it was flowing through me.

Lovely she looked, prettily dressed, girlish, welcoming. We hugged and chattered and wandered up the stairs to that half of a house the lassies called their apartment. It was after we had talked for a while, she'd asked me was I hungry, I'd said that I was, and she had gone into the kitchen that I realized that something was up. What exactly it was that was up I did not know, I knew only that up something perceptibly was and when she came back from the kitchen, bearing plates of mushroom soup, which daintily she plonked on the table, I could see in her face that she knew that I knew that something was up, and whatever it was that was up, I was resolved to find out. 'What's up?' said I. Now, a more graciously well-mannered savage than that Hopi creature you would have been hard pushed to discover. Fact. However. Candour was a quality she owned in abundance, a candour moreover tempered by a nice discretion, but, when put to the question, her candour found no way to spare me. Tears spurted up in her eyes. She looked down. She looked at me. She looked away. Again she looked at me. Her face twitched. Her lips quivered. 'What's up?' she choked out. 'It's those clothes, Peter. That swell topcoat. I'm used to you looking, you know, kind of relaxed, easy, Pete, you look so different, you look, Pete, so spruce, so God damned goofy!'

Jacket off, tie undone, a couple of hours later, my sweet girl gave me the present she had had sent over from the States. I undid the Christmas wrapping and what do you think I had been given? Yes. A pair of Levi Strauss jeans. Laughter bubbled up again, and hugs, and laughter and hugs and having been scolded for spending money on taxis when there was efficient public transport, I kissed my dumpling goodnight and was driven back to uncertain tenure at the Gardens and a wardrobe full of goofy clothings.

The sleet has stopped. That's a mercy anyway as on the bank, guarded against the shrill wind by my handsome donkey jacket, I truffle among the blocks and choppings for a few chips of drier kindling. Fat chance. He hadn't shown up at the Gardens, that morning, Bob, but later in the day he found me sucking down a pint at Momma Fischer's. Annie Laurie would be in town only for another three or four days, he told me, our arrangement was perfectly satisfactory, he continued, it was unconscionable that I should move into the hotel and that they would return to the digs, he protested, there was no question of him becoming seriously involved with his young woman, he added, they both knew the score, were having a holiday fling, it would soon be over, and the pair of us would then return to our old crackpot muddling ways which for months had worked so successfully. He also mentioned that my nightly exercises may well have rid me of my lisp but that somehow it had passed itself over to him and that now he'd got one. Gentleman that he was, his statements rang with such pure conviction that I hauled him out of the boozer, flagged down a taxi, we spun up to the chamber, left the taxi ticking, I jammed a toothbrush, knickers, shirts and trousers into a bag, asked and was courteously let to leave my fancy threads dangling in the wardrobe, jumped back in the flounder, flounder and dab, cab, shot back to Store Street, took a room at Olivelli's with, Tra La!, a snap of Danny Kaye hanging on the wall outside the door, moved in and, other than returning at whiles to pluck a goofy article or three from my ensemble, bade a truly fond farewell to the Gardens.

'Twas Joe who turned the trick. Cotton-eyed Joe, his banjo on his knee, turned up in Olivelli's a couple of days later to find me with my face in a dish of macaroni. Accommodation I was looking for was it, he enquired, producing a huge bottle of poisonously vicious Spanish red wine which we carted up to my room and gave a horrible thrashing to, accommodation? This is thick red ink, I told him, shudderingly bitter, you don't drink it you bite it, and it will take ten times the water and yet keep its colour, may I have another glug. It is a raw, inexpensive rustic tinto as enjoyed by generations of Andalusian paysanos, he assured me through foam and crimson teeth, I need three others and we shall have super accommodation which will tot up to costing us practically nothing, pass me the jug. Where, I asked him with a mouth all aching and bloody from the slurp, will this be then? On a houseboat. A houseboat? A houseboat.

And that is why you find me here, alone and palely loitering with intent, a bundle of sodden firewood in my arms, remembering, though, that our light at night comes from oil lamps and that there is fierce flame to be had from the juice of those. She'd been a trim old girl, I reflect, reflexively nodding to a quarter deck as with my burden I board her again, a stout old tub, but her timbers too long have been neglected and though her holes have been corked up, tarred and nailed with slats, the hoggin wash comes seeping up and I fancy she's a condemned girl with but a short while only left for her to bob at the mooring. Cosy enough, mind, especially at night with the lamplights lit, the pot-belly stove fired, growling, and my bunk is a snug pit. *Souverain* is her name but after a quart of indelible Spanish ink we called her the good ship *Venus.*

We have neighbours, too, bobbing up and down in their

houseboats and it has become our custom to ramble round with bottles, board each other's ships, Joe will thump the banjo or we'll switch on the wireless or spin a record, you get the drift, frolic about, chunter, sing, grunt, shout, whisper, 'Night, night,' and step into the fucking river. Last night, so many of us were there on board the *Venus*, the leaks spouted so, we had to man the pump at the stern and wank the bastard in dread of her sinking.

Careful, now, with this spirit you're dashing onto the tinder and coal in the stove. Remember the night at that concrete frigate of a signal school on which you served in Hampshire? Freezing in that tin Nissen hut, you were there when the lads squirted petrol into the pot-belly stove, struck a match, flung it into the stove and blew up the entire issue. Wreckage and burnt sailors? No, we don't fancy any of that, so, find a twist of paper, light it with a match, get to the side of the stove, turn your face away, peep as you gently poke the lit paper in the stove, all will be well. Paper's wet. Hang on. Tear a stretch from the lined pad. So. Kneel. Was it lamp oil in that can you squirted in the stove, or was it the fierce stuff Joe uses in that Primus job when he's cooking? Doesn't matter. Easy does it. Light when I strike you, you red-headed little git, light. Matchbox must be damp. Strike it on the iron of the stove. There you go. Light the paper now. Go on, light. Right. Steady.

It was at that moment when, brass ashtrays hanging from her ears, a blue wool dress glued to the swells and swoops of her magnificently buxom body, through the entrance to the hold stepped Rough Harriet.

Boom! Jesus, Mary and Holy Joseph I've done it again! My mind had flown from the here, I confused lighting with poking, thrust the lit taper into the belly of the stove, and the flaming animal has exploded on me! This all has to stop! Too easily does the sight of a fine woman send me into a rash distraction and if I'm not electrocuting myself in houses I'm blowing myself up on boats!

A punch to the gob, a kick in the face and to some extent one knows how hard one has been hit. It is altogether different when, with a crump and a whoosh, a blast of flame bursts from a stove and belts one in the kisser. The energy is ferocious, the instant terrifying, the heat savage, but the impact has no solidity, is as though for an instant a fiery zephyr had wafted into one, balmily roasted one's features and then immediately, gently passed on, leaving one shocked and wondering if one had a face at all. Rough Harriet was a strong young woman, as strong in mind as in physique. She unpicked the ball on the deck that I had made of myself, firmly took my wrists and prised my hands away from my face, demanded that I open my clenched eyelids, keenly peered at what I was dreading would be a cinder only, assured me in a cultured, husky drawl that she didn't think I'd done myself any serious damage, explained that the burning I could smell came only from my hair and insisted that I go up top with her for further scrutiny in the daylight. Leaving me leaning over the gunnel, calmly she hopped up into what had been the wheel-house, returning within seconds bearing a bottle of scent. She dabbed a little on my cheeks, forehead, nose, lips and neck and asked me if it smarted. It didn't. This, she said, made her feel even more sure that, although, as it were, I had been introduced to the flame, my face had not been burnt, was merely a cheerful roast red, that for a few weeks I would lack lashes around my right eye, that a little singeing to the eyebrows and the hair was in some countries considered to be beneficial, and that before going to sleep I should rub a little butter or grease into my skin. We then introduced ourselves to one another.

It transpired that the brass ashtrays I'd noticed dangling from her ears were neither made of brass nor were they ashtrays but were in fact large earrings made of copper. Moreover, they had been shaped up by Rough Harriet herself, who, skilled in the art of hammering up, shaping and welding that metal into bangles, brooches, buckles, torques, bracelets, earrings and the like had, that year, chosen as her occupation such fine manufactory and who hawked her wares from Chelsea to Soho, where, strumming his harp in a coffee house, she had a couple of nights ago encountered the cotton-eyes of Joe. Rough Harriet had been looking for a spot in which she could combine both workshop and living quarters; Joe assured her that chance had brought her to the very man to advise on this matter and signed her up as the third member of the crew of the good ship *Venus*. A woman of parts, Harriet, she also was a sculptress, a painter, an occasional poetess, a free spirit, one whom her Maker had shaped up a tall and a splendid figure for these talents to flourish and at liberty inhabit and who happily joined me in going to a scruffy little café yards only from the boat for a plate of nourishing egg and chips.

Harriet had stoked up the stove before we left and when we returned, Joe was sitting by it with the fourth member of the crew: Miss Cornflower Blue from the lone star state of Texas. The cork was out of the huge Spanish ink bottle; by the oil lamp's light its stains on the mouth and teeth of Cornflower and Joe showed an even more ghastly colour than it had done in electric or in day light; Rough H. took a swig, pronounced it filthy, took another swig, and as her mouth turned purple she gave an agonized shudder, poured herself another tumblerful, heaved the carboy over to me, and, wincing and shivering, I did my duty, forced down a deep draught, poured myself the next one, the important one, the one which when down ensured that the taste and pain would fade away quite, and then carted the great bottle to the self-possessed, dainty Cornflower.

It had been while we sprawled there indelibly stained and swigging that I thought it meet to tell my fellow crew members of my view that the ship we manned surely would sink, probably in fairly short order. Not wholly unexpectedly, this thought, mixed with thick Spanish ink, painted for us a picture that we found to be inordinately comical. Our visits to the boat being speculative, investigatory, none of us had brought much kit on board, we could abandon her in minutes; if she went down in the night and we drowned in our sleep, nobody, we hooted, could say our lives had been at one with rats, that with my evident talent as an improvising dynamitard, we might yet, we howled, go to glory in the inferno of a Viking funeral. Dangerously would we live, hysterically we agreed, and with tumblers of that crude inexpensive rustic tinto which for generations had bludgeoned Andalusian paysanos into alcoholic coma, we drank to our precarious healths and that of the good ship *Venus*.

Let's see. Eyelashless at RADA, my appearance had given my chums occasion for ripe merriment, another reason for the Hebrew Minnehaha to close her eyes and enquire of Big Chief Abraham what would become of me, myself an expression whereby the left side of my face was alert, interested, amused, the right side vacant, unhappy, fed to the teeth; and which may have, one cannot be sure, somewhat disconcerted our new teacher, Mr Edward Burnham, a small chubby bright-eyed dynamo of a man.

We are to rehearse, for performances in the Little Theatre, two productions of the same play: Arthur Wing Pinero's *Trelawny of the 'Wells'*. In the first production I am to play the leading role of one Tom Wrench and in the second the minor role of O'Dwyer. Knowing nothing about either Pinero or his play, I am looking forward to reading the piece and to studying both parts. Clifford is in fine fettle, fine fettle, fine fettle, as is Denys, and both men are urging us on to the expansion and the fine tuning of our vocal mechanisms; John Gabriel is dashing away with his smoothing iron at the rough edges to our technical methods; satisfied we have learned the fundamentals of defence, Professor Froeschlen has let us loose on the attack and the flash and clash of sabres has taken on a dangerous edge; with eloquent humour Howard Williams is demonstrating that though trousers and bodices and hats and shirts may over the centuries have changed, the people who inhabit them have remained much the same; the tortures of Madame Fletcher are just as hideous, cause grievous bodily harm to all and are hardly to be endured but I did enjoy buggering about as a bumble bee at Miss Boalth's movement class; Mr Hayes has pronounced himself to be not wholly dissatisfied with my and Mr Finney's stage management and Sir Kenneth has told us to think well on a saying of Henry Irving's: 'No audience, no art.'

We are four runners shy, our class, this year; two having fallen, two refused. This, apparently, is not uncommon. Miss Bloodaxemansdotter has floated away through the floes back to Iceland. The lady, for the wrong reasons, will be missed. The other three? Well, having hardly pasted their personalities on to the ether, the wonder is, to me at least, that they had bothered to be at a drama school at all. The heavy firm is intact and strongly cantering but Bob is altogether glum. What ails him? Could it be, softly I enquire, that his appetite for porridge and thistles is yet unblunted but that his source for these commodities has returned to where the cabers toss and the monsters play on the bonny bonny braes of Loch Ness? Worse than that, he tells me, far far worse. True though it is that he is keen on this dish, it is a dish which he finds more tasty when taken after intervals, a view not shared by the Lady Sporran who feels that the dish should be taken regularly or not at all. Would he please make up his wee mind? Soon. Aye or nay. And who, in anticipation of a prompt response, has planted herself at the Gardens. Trouble. There is an altogether more cheerful bustle over at the Vanbrugh. Although the new theatre is not due officially to be opened for some months, the rooms provided above the stage for the wardrobe and the designers and the technical staff are, under the twinkling eyes of Willy, already being staked out, filled up, and generally occupied. Great Heap the set designer and I have exchanged amiable words and it will, of course, be perfectly in order for me to keep there a toothbrush, razor, a couple of shirts and a bar of soap. This is kind. This is handy.

Let's see. As stricken vessels go, Rough Harriet and Cornflower have made the good ship *Venus* more ship-shape and cosy than any boat in such a plight possibly could hope to be. It's a fair stretch to and from the academy for Joe and me, but we return to warmth and grub, the ink when it is red, quiet, peace, study and reading when we fancied it, knockabout and good cheer when the mood was on us, but that, alas, was then. Now, Rough H. and Cornflower have gone. Harriet, as practical a woman as she is unconstrained by common ordinance, has set up shop by King's Cross station but not, however, before seeing that all was trim as could be on the *Venus* and finding in Archway a studio which she considered impractical for her needs but thinks is right for Joe's and mine, should we want it. She will carry on banging up brass ashtrays and such, we have promised to keep in touch. A singular woman, Rough Harriet, one whom I like a lot. Cornflower? For her the few days were a drawling giggle which came to a certain end. She just upped one morning and went on her way. So long, honey. And then there was Joe and me.

Lately, Joe has been talking much of thrift. Some strain is off him because his father, astonished that his son successfully had stretched over the first few fences, has been persuaded, one term at a time, to cough up the dibs for Joe's RADA fees. This leaves Joe merely to find loot enough to pay for food, roof and spending money. Spaghetti is his answer to the question of food. It is my business daily to buy, for a few pennies only, at a little Italian shop in Fitzrovia, bundles of the stiff and snappy little sticks all wrapped round in blue paper. These I hand over to Joe and he busies himself in that frightful galley, emerging after a boiling while bearing platefuls of steaming pasta covered with the fine sauces he has concocted. Remarkable. Tasty, too. So long as the boat stays afloat we have the necessary roof, and he hopes to earn spending money by industriously banging his banjo at various gigs. He also has a thrifty stratagem, one which I do not fully comprehend but one that must be, surely, lawful, whereby the cost of our journeys on the tube train drastically has been cut. It involves buying in advance a number of tickets to ride but from three different stations. One gets on the train with one ticket, rearranges one's collection, and then one presents a different ticket when getting off at one's destination. Of course, I have no idea how the system works but it is quite definitely thrifty. Alas, often I am too late for the last train, that means a taxi and so many of my attempts at thrift often go awry. Still and all, what with Bluey's money and my living allowance I am at present quite flush and the trick will be to spend less than I did last term.

Eating always in restaurants and cafés will have to stop; that has proved prohibitively costly and I will in future make much more use of the RADA canteen, spaghetti, and the fridge at Muswell Hill. Galleries at theatres, too, are rooky places in which I must learn to sit more often. Yes. After all, last year I sat in the gods for a couple of shows and it wasn't too bad. On Saturday, though, I'm taking Pocahontas to see an actor about whom we've both heard much, Paul Scofield, in a play called *A Question of Fact*. Not that I intend to go on making a habit of it but, you will understand, for that we must surely sit in the stalls. Yes. Let's see.

'I'll stay with the ship, boys, you save your lives.
I've no one to love me, you've sweethearts and wives.'

Hands to the pump! She's rapidly taking in water, she's going down, and never were sardines so enthusiastically crammed into their new tin cans as have been the ladies and gentlemen of the Royal Academy of Dramatic Art so stuffed together aboard this old sardine boat as down to doom inexorably she slipped. We are at the shank end of a sinking party. A festivity which her crew of two had mooted and agreed on when, two mornings ago, we awakened to find that overnight she had taken in a foot of water for'ard, that her plugged holes midships and aft cheerfully were seeping and bubbling and that the good ship *Venus* had but a little while only to bob upon the waters of this breathing world. The responses to our invitations to come bib and frolic on a drowning boat in late and freezing winter were heartwarmingly enthusiastic and, finding the occasion one hardly to be missed, the flower of RADA's finest have been swilling about her in strength. Joe's class provided representatives in thick number, they tugged along chums and lovers, sinners from neighbour houseboats were pulled aboard, the heavy mob from my team turned up in strength, of course, every oil-lamp-lit inch of cabin, bunk, hold, galley or wheelhouse was jammed with revelling flesh; this great burden of bodies so suddenly thrust on stricken old *Venus* proved to be insupportable and her stem is awash to the bilges. 'You swim for the shore, boys, trusting in heaven above, While I go down to the angry deep with the ship I love.' Although most of the guests sensibly are gone, yet two or three knots of folk still dance and caper in the lapping nooks and it pleases me to report that, made of stern stuff, a number of the leading players from Mr Edward Burnham's production of *Trelawny of the 'Wells'*, with adjuncts, romp on, romp on. Pocahontas, the Ninas Van and Von, to be sure; your Slim Mac, Mikey B. and Bob; Jeannie, Sal, Jilly and Jenny and Albert. 'O, a dollar a day is a Jackshites' pay, Leave 'er, boys, O leave 'er,' Mr Gary Raymond and I are aft pumping manfully, 'To pump all night and work all day, Leave 'er, boys, O leave 'er,' and the voice you hear wailing out sea shanties belongs to my long and dilapidated old mate O'Liver.

He fell into London from nowhere in particular a short while ago, intends in another short while going on to nowhere in particular and is filling in the gap by doing not a lot and dossing hither and yon. More. Having arrived at the sinking party accom-

panied by a tall and a handsome fair-haired young woman with
the most spectacular pair of breasts that I ever did see in my whole
puff, O'Liver discovered our well of rustic ink, deeply dipped
himself into it and now he sways daubed and gaudy singing on
the wheelhouse roof, while ten-gallon Lulu blunders all alone
along the splashy gangways. 'It's pump or drown, the old man
said,    Leave 'er, boys, O leave 'er.' Unfair to the dear, you might
think. 'Or else damn soon you'll all be dead,    Leave 'er, boys,
O leave 'er.' So, too, thinks a rancidly sozzled, unhappy Bob.

Pie-eyeing this unknown fair fine figure of a woman, he is
moved to effect an introduction of himself to her. This he
attempts by leering hideously, grunting a greeting and aiming a
bow in her general direction. For these courtesies he cops only
the belt of a tit in the face as, after this briefest of encounters,
Lulu wades on and Bob sways away towards laughter and guzzling.
It is clear, however, that Mr Albert Finney also is looking with
compassion on this lovely and neglected creature. Yes. Albie has,
I believe, suggested to her that together they take the air abaft of
this mortally crippled ship. Lulu has, it seems, agreed. Here they
come. Timely this for Mr Raymond and myself, thirsty and
knackered from our labours. We put it to them that they might
enjoy a turn at the pump. Splendid strapping couple that they
are, and sporting, Albert and Lulu both agree that this is a jolly
idea. Off seeking company and cuddles and ink go Raymond, G.,
and I, leaving behind us pneumatic bosoms and copper-knob
heaving and pumping in vigorous harmony at the stern. 'O, we
struck the whale and the line played out,    But the whale made
a plunder with its tail.' Through the racket and the shanties I can
hear Joe whacking his banjo and calling, 'Pass right down the
boat, ladies and gentlemen, pass right down the boat. The front is
flooded and to give a better balance and to keep the vehicle afloat
we need more customers in the middle and at the back. So, ladies
and gentlemen, will you please pass right down the boat.'

Now, I have a cup of ink, there's the stove, through the press of dancers stepping a measure to a cheery version of 'Abide With Me', two steps along here, there's my bunk, Pocahontas is on it, as, at a guess, are six or seven others, most of whom, I think, are known to me, whatever, a chirpy crush, eager to know how the sinking is going, all, it seems, thoroughly enjoying the event and with a lack of cynicism which, to me, is most refreshing. Mac? Is that you buried under everybody? Good. Will you, Mac, in five or so minutes, with, of course, a volunteer of your choice, relieve Albert at the pump, for I do believe he might be spent? That's the man. Bob? Saw him last up top having a breather, lonely, sad and pissed as a boiled owl. Forgive my kneeling on you, whoever you are, but I must have a kiss from my sweetheart for I'm raging with lust. Better. Must just wade along beyond the wheelhouse to the bows, see what is the water level. Back soon. Hello. More guests are leaving. Understandable. The water is tumbling in. Goodbye. See you soon I hope. Ta ta.

> 'Farewell and adieu to you, fair Spanish ladies;
> Farewell and adieu to you, ladies of Spain.'

What with my sense of taste being numbed to death by Joe's horrid ink and all it's difficult to be sure, but I think I've just had a swig of what could be whiskey. From a bottle handed me out from a huddle of young men and women, strangers to me I'm almost certain, who are telling me of their view that our boat is in danger of going down. Excellent, say I, you should immediately disembark. They do. Farewell and adieu to you. Brandy? 'For we've received orders to sail for old England;     And so shall we never more see you again.' Back to the Hopi. Splash. Armagnac? My bunk, so recently a stout support for a thick pile of merry bodies, is without a soul to stretch on it. Wallow round the corner. There, grouped around the hot stove, weary certainly, tipsy quite, apprehensive perhaps, stand Sir William Gower, Avonia Bunn, Rose Trelawny, James Telfer, Imogen Parrott, Augustus Colpoys,

Clara de Fœnix, other characters from Arthur Wing Pinero's play *Trelawny of the 'Wells'* and student friends from the RADA. I, Tom O'Toole Wrench, approach them. Avonia Minnehaha Bunn tells me that she thinks it's time to vamoose. Sir Albert Gower, released from pumping duty, underlines her thoughts by pointing out that the sizzling we hear from the base of the stove probably is being caused by contact with rising water. 'The rats have gone, and we the crew,    Leave 'er, boys, O leave 'er.' Little is there left to do but douse the oil lamps, switch on an electric torch; for Joe to fetch Mac and Jenny from the pump, to grab his guitar case and bag from an overhead locker; for me to sling my knapsack on my back, reach up for my hold-all, wrap an arm around Pocahontas, and for us all to start clambering off the *Venus*. 'It's time, me boy, that we went too,    Leave 'er, boys, O leave 'er.' Big Lulu had given shantyman O'Liver notice of our departure by heaving a bucket at him; he has joined us as we stand on the shore, murmuring our goodbyes to the old girl, now settling deep in the river.

Inches only were we from the tube station, the huddling bundle of some ten or so of us, hugging and trotting in warmth, in pleasure and steaming in the dark, when, of a sudden, it struck me that something was not right. But what? What was not right? Where's Bob? No Bob. A missing Bob that was what was not right. O'Liver, Joe and I sprint back to the river and the foundering *Venus*. Joe's flashlight carves great slices out of the darkness. I spot, amazingly enough, a bicycle's bullhorn handlebars, bell and all, floating in the slime below the boat's bows. Ting-a-ling. We hop aboard. Knee deep in hoggin wash we slop about searching. No Bob. Wheelhouse? No Bob. Down below we must go and waist deep on the stairs in the sludgy bubbles we are when O'Liver cries, 'He's here. He's gone bye byes in a cupboard.' Curled up in a tackle locker by the companion hatch to the hold, Bob contentedly snoozes; nor does he wish, please, for fuck's sake, to be disturbed. Come on, old son, you can't sleep on the town hall steps, Jack, better by far is it that you come along with us, that's the way, you can snore on unmolested in a seat on the tube train, beats out of sight kipping under water among the turds and the drowned kittens and the bicycle handlebars, that's the trick, grab his legs, I have his head, here we go, heave the bastard on to the shore. Done.

An hour later, if not wholly dry then certainly more warmly wet, we all sprawled in Joe Lyon's Corner House on the Strand and there took breakfast of sausages and beans and fried eggs and bacon and toast and mugs of hot strong sweet tea. No doubt, the party had been a thrilling success.

> It's windy round Cape Horn;
> Go down you blood red roses, go down.
> I wish I'd never been born;
> Go down you blood red roses, go down.
> O! You pinks and posies;
> Go down you blood red roses, go down.

---

RIGHT, A DART of solder from my electrical soldering iron on to this here chassis from a model motor car, so; bung the stiff little twist of brown-skinned wire on to the hot blob, so; a dart of solder on the brown job, so; bung the yellow wire on to the hot blob on the brown wire, so; a dart of solder on the yellow fellow, so; bung the green lad on to the hot blob on the yellow job, so; bob a final dart of solder to seal in the green yellow and brown wires now soldered on the chassis of the model motor car, so; there, that's another little bugger all wired up and done for the dozen. Time for a tumbler of crude ink and a fag. Saw Ireland take a hammering against England at Twickenham. Played well in fiery bursts, mind. Won good possession but the pill wasn't shifted about nimbly enough. Jackie Kyle not playing may have been a factor. He'd scratched, injured. Superb fly half, it's said. Perhaps, now, I'll never see him play. Still, the roaring and the howling at Twickenham was mighty. Eamon de Valera says that rugby suits well the Irish character. That will have gone down a treat with the Gaelic Athletic Association for the body firmly disapproves of Irish citizens even watching rugger or soccer or cricket. The long fellow, Dev, handled the timber and the cherry, too, when a young man. Ah well. How many soldering solderers do we have in this here soldering factory into which Joe and I have converted our large room at Archway? Eight. Including Joe and me. It's a rare old sight. The room's fair snaking with wires running out of plugs and sockets and those metal gadgets which, apparently, according to Joe, inform the electrical juices running into them from the mains how better to conduct themselves when they leave their boxes of tricks and flow up the flexes on whose ends are the soldering irons held by the solderers. It's a bafflement for me. That's right, sweetheart, first the little brown worm, and then the yellow, then the green. Fancy a squirt of Andalusian tinto? Good girl yourself. The laundry won't take my cheque so the fruitful knickers are running amok. Under the carpet they're scampering about, there's a shameless pair climbed up on that coat hook and I know they're at it in the guitar case. Back to the soldering, me. Joe's instructing me how to play four chords on the banjo; he tells that if I master them they should give me solid mileage. Come here, you little brown bastard. Tricky instrument. Lovely, though. Stay put. Now the yellow. There's noble eating in a pig's trotter. A view which Joe finds difficult to share. Pity, that, for there's a pork butcher round the corner who's giving them away; trotters. We could eat for nothing, practically. Cooking arrangements remain more or less the same. I buy the spaghetti, he cooks it and conjures up mysterious sauces. Green. A trotter would go a long way. Tasty, virtuous, thick with meat. But no. Can't eat them raw, can't cook, snookered. I'm the shover-in of the spaghetti, though, that's an advancement of sorts. Joe plonks a pan full of water on the gas ring, waits till it's very hot, stirs in a drop of olive oil, a plug of garlic, then it's my turn. Into the boiling bubbles slowly I shove my bundle of brittle wee rods; on the instant of contact with this scalding miniature maelstrom the spare stalks of spaghetti abandon their proud dignity and circle in writhing agony around the base of the pan; remorselessly down shove I till an inch or two only of slender stems remains unshoved; keenly sensitive to all horrors of fire and boiling oil, these remainder stalks I persuade in and down with a belt of the chassis of a model motorcar. The brown job. Thrift. That's what all this is about. Thrift. Into the room I wandered a couple of weeks ago to find Joe opening a pair of large cardboard crates. In one were hundreds of yellow brown and green wire squiggles. The other stuffed with what turned out to be the chassis from model motor cars. No, not toys, models. Ah. Small oblong steel plates with corners missing. So? A kind relation of Joe in the model motor car business had suggested to him a way in which in his spare time Joe might thrive. Solder three bits of coloured wire flex on to a steel plate and he would be paid a stripe for each dozen done. Joe reckoned that soldering three bits of wire onto a chassis would take five minutes. Twelve fives being sixty that would mean dabbing down twelve in an hour. One stripe. An hour before going to the academy, or when he came back, or before going to sleep, once a day for five days, that's five stripes. Five stripes, a week's wages. Thrift. Should I choose to join in we might work out a system and who knows how many stripes in a week we might knock out. Kind relation would supply solder and soldering irons. Principle sound. Yellow. Practice? After four hours of solder, soldering irons, coloured scraps of flex, toil, bungling, exasperation, exactitude, sweat and curses we had managed to attach wires in their proper sequence to but six model motor car chassis merely. Half a stripe. Hugely laborious and not thrifty. That's when we hit on the wheeze of having soldering parties. Now the green hoor. All the spaghetti you can eat, all the ink you can drink, here's a soldering iron. Merry and productive sessions they proved, too. Joe hauled in more irons and wires and electrical metal boxes, from time to busy time our shack fair hums. Another done for the dozen. Thrift. O'Liver's grave distinguished and delightful father was up in town for a few days. He took O'Liver and me to the Tate. Long flat drawers downstairs were pulled open for him. They held watercolours; landscapes, seascapes, cloudscapes painted by Constable, by Turner. Beautiful. Sections of cloud, of land, of sea were by the pair of them pointed out and examined for me. Rapid handling of paint, indistinct shapes, large rhythms, broken colour, uneven saturation, pronounced brushwork. Thus, the fathers of the impressionists, of abstract expressionism were introduced to me. Astonishing. Cost not a tosser. Bus fare. More ink. Taste coming back. Needs desensitizing. That's the trick. Yes, all around the room, crimson-toothed and cheerful, happy solderers solder on, solder on in this here sweatshop we're running up in Archway. We'll have Joe play the guitar and honk. Music while you work. He is really very good. The gigs will come; in time. Troubled at present, Joe. In love. Claire. There is familial disapproval. Heavy. They have the odd sweet hour, in the odd cheap hotel, on the odd happy evening. Joe loathes being furtive. He's bold. A brown bugger. Come here to me, you soldering iron, till I dip you in the solder. The bonny lasses at Muswell Hill see a fair deal of us. Joe and the Ninas are classmates. He's there as friend and minstrel, I'm there to play a rubber of whist with Pocahontas and to make myself useful in any way that I can. It's also true that we give the fridge a thrashing. We spend, we save much time together now, Pocahontas and I, daily the times grow more and more captivating. We're thrifty, too. A lecture on the plays of T. S. Eliot at Hampstead Town Hall cost pennies and was, to us, silently, certainly, shriekingly funny. A yellow sod. The glories going on at the Old Vic, seen and heard from the gallery, why, it costs so little to be given so much. Then there was the New Lindsay. An Irish theatre club, for buttons we saw players of true distinction, particularly Jack MacGowran and Liam Redmond, performing a masterpiece of playwriting, Sean O'Casey's *Plough and the Stars*. Afterwards, the bar stayed open till the sparrows farted. Lovely girl, that Hopi. Wields a nifty soldering iron, too. Green git. Utilitarian, dingy, the RADA canteen has turned out to be a fine eaterie. That's down to Mrs Brazier. Cook, manageress, surrogate mum, her chief joy seems to be watching hungry young students chewing down a hearty nosh. An Original Comedietta in four acts, Pinero's *Trelawny of the 'Wells'* is a vigorous and a charming piece. Bernard Shaw thought so too, I am surprised to have read. Of Arthur Wing's play he wrote, 'When he plays me the tunes of 1860, I appreciate and sympathize. Every stroke touches me: I dwell on the dainty workmanship shewn in the third and fourth acts: I rejoice in being old enough to know the world of his dreams.' Another one done for the dozen. A boilerplated romantic backstage comedy in which civilians bump into actors and actresses, I should hardly have thought it would have been to Greenwhiskers' fancy. If it's about anything at all it's about changes in the theatre of fad and fashion. Bugger this. Time to pour red rustic ink down the throats of our willing workers. Mac? There you go. Yes. Thick as treacle. Jilly. Jenny. Think of it as anaesthetic. Must have Joe learn 'Ever of Thee' from *Trelawny*. Haunting number. Pops up throughout the play. Bet that's what touched Shaw. My part. Tom Wrench. In his first scene a chuckle stuck itself on my gob. He has his landlady take a pair of scissors and trim off the frayed edges of his shirt collar. Bob Hope did that to his collar in his film *The Lemon Drop Kid*. Damon Runyon. Ace comic, Bob Hope. Top man. Ten years at the Wells, Wrench, T., aged thirty, still playing coughs and spits, no matter what manner of play he's in when he enters the gallery always greets him with a volley of ripe laughter, suggests that the poor sod is not the best of actors. That's all right. Could be interesting. Misfit in a theatre company. In love with Rose, the leading juvenile, the most he does as an expression of this passion is to wait until Rose leaves the room then pick up her shoe and kiss it. Her shoe? Foot fetishist? Oh, all right, he's diffident, shy. Sodden with self-pity. So what, I know, so is Richard the Second. 'Come down? Down, court! down, king! For night-owls shriek where mounting larks should sing.' A prig. There are more engaging qualities but one could live with it, I suppose. It's when he starts chuntering about his being a playwright that I fear for the man. 'I strive to make my people talk and behave like live people,' he says. 'To fashion heroes out of actual, dull, everyday men – the sort of men you see smoking cheroots in the club windows in St James's Street; and heroines from simple maidens in muslin frocks.' You're kissing the wrong end of the shoe entirely, Tom Wrench. A writer doesn't strive to make his people talk and behave like live people, my duck, a writer strives to create people who live. So, no reproductions of actual surfaces, please, we want a world that you have made; an artefact not a cobbled-up version of the real world. It is because it is not nature that art is art, Wrench. We want makers. People made alive and living in a world made by an artist. 1860, Tom Wrench? Christ. Shaw and Wilde and Chekov and Ibsen had been born. Makers, Wrench, creators. It gets worse. Later in the play we find him looking at doors in a drawing room. In his plays, he says, there will be, yes, 'locks on doors, *real locks*, to work; and handles – to turn!' The man's insane. Think of Peggy Ashcroft when she performed Cleopatra, in her desire for Antony truly a lass unparalleled, killing herself by pressing a real snake to her breast. The turnover in smothered Desdemonas would be prodigious; Forests of Arden in productions of *As You Like It*, there'd scarce be a twig left to twitch about in England. Wrench, my old fruit, you're attracted to the theatre but you have neither the understanding nor the mettle to be theatrical. It's real fiction we want in the theatre: real plays in real sets performed by real players wearing real makeup. You're putting a good man out of a job. You're a false pretence. You're a fraud. It's a locksmith you should be, or a doorknob maker. Thud. That's the sound in our soldering factory that we solderers heard. Thud. Sounding, it seemed, from both below and from above us; a solid weighty loud thud, then black dark with not a sizzle from our irons and a strange absence of reverberation. Silence there was as in that darkness silently we waited for a while wondering would an explosion follow, or a fire, or the ceiling fall in, or the floor collapse, or alarm bells ring or a hellish racket of some or other sort clatter down upon us. But no. Nothing. Shock in that silent dark gripped us for a clutch of waiting seconds only to be released into an excitement of whispers and no it was not I. Not I. Not this time. Not directly I. Doubtless a contributor but when that thud sounded, heavy, abrupt, above, below, the darkness, the silence, I was sitting in a chair, was I, thinking, I was, perhaps drinking, probably smoking, possibly muttering, in my hands no soldering iron, no, nor a lit taper, certainly not a toasting fork, neither was I in any way physically connected to any one holding any apparatus of any sort. So. Not I. Indirectly, of course. But go you and find others than I, say I, blame them for this calamity in Archway. Out. Everybody out. Quietly does it. Dissolve, babies, dissolve. Piss off with a degree of caution. Two flights down and you're away. That's it. Easy does it if anything does. Ta-ta. Other than the dark, what's eerie is the lack of an additional detonation. I'll strike the matches, you do the gathering up. Right. Festooned with flex and soldering irons, doing our damnedest quietly to lug down and away two hefty cardboard crates stuffed with coloured wires and the chassis of model motor cars, faint light suddenly spurted from beneath us. Joe and I heard voices below us on the stair. A stealthy peer through the banisters showed to me on the landing below two figures, one holding a candle. A red-headed woman was in vain trying to flick on a wall light, the man with her turned and I could clearly see his face. It was the young poet Adrian Mitchell, one whom I'd met a couple of times. But not in Archway. Talking quietly, the couple went into a room, the door closed and it was again dark. Joe and I with our loads reached the door of the lightless building. Into the street. All the buildings on this side of the street were dark. All the buildings on the other side of the street were dark. Burdened into the darkness Joe and I quietly stole away. Our days as winos, as solderers were done.

———

DID YOU EVER take a double bed on an underground railway? If not, well, what you do is first choose a gusty day in the early spring of 1954, a day before barriers, turnstiles, hard-eyed guards and harsh regulations featured at public transport stations in London. Then, having bought your bed at a junk shop and second-hand furniture store off the Tottenham Court Road, you have Joe grab the head of the bed, you grab its foot and you plod with all convenient speed to Goodge Street tube station. Goodge Street is highly to be recommended for this undertaking: it is one of the few underground railway stations in London in which, by trudging down the somewhat sinister twists of the spiral staircase there, you can gain direct access to its platforms without using the wheezing great elevator provided. By use of this route, by avoiding the press of passengers in the elevator and the eyes of its uniformed attendant, you can maintain a certain modesty about your intention to employ a tube train to transport your double bed.

Now, from the entrance to the station, past the vigilant ticket seller in his booth, to the mouth of the looping stairway, you will find that there is considerable yardage to be covered. Assistance at this point is in my view indispensable. Fire one. On an agreed nod, you have Nina Von sway her way to the ticket booth, practically thrust herself through the window and in a great flutter of eyelashes and shameless sensuality she will tell of being a little lost American student confounded by the complexities of the London transport system. So charmed will the official be that he will begin to gibber. Fire two. Squeezing her exotic way to the window, the Hopi will then join Nina Von, fix the gibbering man with her brilliant gaze and will ask for his help in deciding what would be more economically sensible for her to do, buy a weekly return ticket, a monthly, a season pass, is there a reduction for students? Not able to believe either his eyes or his luck, our worthy official will start distractedly to grab at books of rules, manuals of procedure, fare tariffs, the while aiming what he hopes are roguish grins at the women. Fire three. Yellow hair, eyes speedwell blue, cool and beautiful Nina Van will as a vision then appear among the forlorn sensuousness, the enquiring sexuality, will sadly smile, will murmur of her need to find a map of the London Underground railway lines, and will express her wistful hope that the kind man will be able to assist her. Broken quite, his dreary window so suddenly stuffed with darlings three deep, our shuddering man in the ticket booth will not notice the two upright young gentlemen, some seven feet apart in line astern, walking resolutely, if stiffly, towards the spiral staircase.

Once on the spiral staircase you merely take up your bed sideways and walk carefully down the steps. On the platform you lean the bed against the wall and let Joe, who is gifted at such matters, remove the headboard from the bed. This is to make the object slimmer. When Pocahontas and the Ninas join you, the headboard will be handed into the care of the Ninas, Pocahontas will be in charge of the newly purchased cover, the sheets and the tickets for the trip. As the tube train roars rattling into the station, pick up the bed sideways and upright. The train stops, its sliding doors slip open, on to the train with the bed you march. Once the train is on its merry way, place the bed in the centre of the space on to which the doors lead and which separates the carriages. Make sure the bed is resting on a beam end, upright and pointing in the direction that the train is travelling. This will allow fellow voyagers freely to get on and to get off the vehicle, while presenting an easily negotiable obstacle for those who choose to move from one compartment to another.

At Camden Town a change of trains is necessary. Among the intestines of the London underground railway you will find an endearing eccentricity. Go with the bed and your gorgeous accomplices through the door clearly marked 'No way out' and you will find that the way to the exit is only yards from you, while the platform you need for your change of trains will be signposted and will have its entrance just across the way. Safely on board the next train, no bother should come your way but complacence is not to be recommended. A loose grip, a lapse in concentration, a hefty lurch of the train could send you and Joe and the bed sprawling on the deck of the heaving rattler. Above all, ignore the hoots of laughter issuing from the headboard carters, Nina Von, Nina Van and the shoulders shuddering on Pocahontas as with eyes closed, tears tumbling down her face the savage sits there weeping in disbelief.

On arriving at your destination you will find that the back of your task practically is broken. Hump the bed off the train, allow a few moments for other disembarking passengers to scatter, pick her up, send the women on ahead and leave the platform through the space marked 'No way out'. The escalator to the exit will be immediately before you. Tickets, headboard, cover, sheets, female associates to the fore, step on the moving staircase, place bed upright lengthways on the steps, grasp firmly and have a breather as upwards you will be transported. Realizing that the ticket gatherer in his kiosk can at most say words which in effect mean 'What's all this, then?', and hardly 'You must immediately put that double bed back on the train', as the escalator reaches its summit you will hoist the bed on your shoulders, in the same position it had when being given a ride, tricky but manageable, let the young encumbered ladies gaze adoringly at the official as they hand him five tickets, let them step beyond him, and then determinedly you march past the man nor heed the puzzlement in his glare. Out of the station and into the breezy air go you with the bed. Mission accomplished. Now, what you do with your double bed is, of course, your own affair; Joe and I heaved ours up the stairs into the apartment of the Bonny Maids of Muswell Hill, and moved in with them.

––––––––

'IF WE ARE SET to scrub a floor – and we may come to that yet – let us make up our minds to scrub it legitimately, with dignity.' So says Mrs Telfer in the fourth act of *Trelawny of the 'Wells'*. A leading lady in the first act, Mrs T., in the fourth, jobless but eager to work in the theatre, we find that the old girl has taken on the position of wardrobe mistress, a demotion which both surprises and upsets our heroine, Rose Trelawny. For Rose, this is a fall from grace by her friend and colleague, a descent with which she needs must commiserate, but her attempt at this commiseration is met by those strong, simple words from the wardrobe mistress and thus resolutely demolished. Throughout all the giddy ups and the deep downs which one meets in my profession, those words of Mrs Telfer often bob unbidden into my mind, bringing with them at least a notion of balance. At that time at the academy they had been spoken by a slim, seemingly scholarly American girl, a young woman with whom I was friendly without coming to know well but whose quiet earnestness when speaking that line stays with me now, clearly as had her expression of Mrs Telfer's thoughts those many years ago aided me in my troubles playing the toad Tom Wrench.

Now, it is altogether possible, although by no means certain, that during his years as a teacher at the RADA no pupil had found more favour than I did with Mr Edward Burnham, our man responsible for the two productions we were doing of A. W. Pinero's play. Who knows? Not I. All we can be sure of is that in the report given to me by the academy at the end of my course of studies there, Mr Burnham had been kind enough to write of me that in his view I was an exceptionally talented young actor who should have no difficulty in finding work but that unless I learned to control a rashly hot temper I might have a great deal of difficulty in keeping it. A man sparking with enthusiasm and good ideas, Edward Burnham, it is true that my manner and his manner did not chime. What harm, say I, what harm? It also is not impossible that his bright-eyed bossiness had got on my tits, had prompted me into the occasional snarl or woof but not once did I ever kick the fellow in the bollocks or nuffink like that; no, sir, not never.

Perhaps these minor dissonances had been the result of a remarked difference in tenor, in tone from our studies and rehearsals with Mr Ernest Milton. With Ernie sometimes the room had been a grand pandemonium of weeping or shrieking birds, deeply beady or bellowing blokes, me barking, Ernest a wolf in snarl and howling. Moments would pass, the room would be translated into a rapt and blistering zone of concentration on the work in progress. A gauge of a rehearsal with Ernest Milton, indeed a qualitative measure of any rehearsal, would be carefully to listen to the voice and the voices and assess how many of the words spoken had been provided by the author of the play. If during rehearsal hours the voice heard is not predominantly that of the playwright you may be sure you are listening to the blatherings of a gobshite. Ernest Milton and his students chirruped and squawked at intervals, Bernard Shaw occupied the hours.

It is to be hoped that what may be a comfort for you is to know that Teddy Burnham and I essentially had been on the same side. His zeal in wanting a responsive vitality to flow between us students rehearsing *Trelawny of the 'Wells'*, his zest in promoting an urgent energy to ignite the actions, reactions, conflicts, harmonies, moods and tenses in the various and varying scenes and acts of the play were qualities I found to be wholly admirable. Most of the members of my class showed more animation and fluency of speech and movement over lunch or in the pub or on the stairs or in the street than ever they showed at rehearsal. Gone, when we went through our paces, the breath of humankind; arrived, stiff, robotic dummies, wind mutedly breaking from tight lips. Burnham had seen it as his plain duty to stuff, as it were, lit firecrackers up our arseholes, stand back and watch in the hope of seeing living consequences. And I had been with him all the way in these endeavours. Shove Roman candles up my harris, aristotle, bottle, bottle and glass, you have it, Mr B., do, but pray do not be miffed, smiler, if in return a rocket comes whizzing your way.

He had vision, too, little Teddy, with a love of language and an intelligence palpable about him. So much so that, although he barely admitted it, he knew that I knew that he knew that I knew that were Tom Wrench one of his pupils, gleefully would he light up an entire bonfire under the glum bastard. Still and all, the curtain was due to go up, it was my business to act the part and it was down to me to see that I did my best for him. 'Let us make up our minds to scrub it legitimately, with dignity.' Yes, Tom Wrench can't think that he himself is a great prat. Cannot know that his true bent lies in polishing up the handle on the big front door, locksmithry and retirement to a wooden dish in the laughing academy. Above all, must believe that all he does and says is both good and weighty. 'If we are set to scrub.' Here goes.


Although the Little Theatre at the RADA truly was a little theatre, the snag for me had been that when we did our final rehearsals on its stage the theatre didn't seem to be all that little at all. Not at all. Indeed, my voice had sounded to me so thin and tinny that I was scarce sure that it would pierce out over the floats, travel into the void above the seats and arrive where Sir Kenneth would be sitting in his box at the back. I had asked the Capone broad if she would be good enough to place herself in the auditorium, as far away from the stage as possible, and to give me her soundings on my audibility. She did. 'You'll have to pitch it out more, Pete,' said she, 'you sound kind of squeaky.' Squeaky? Lord love me. 'Tom enters with a pair of scissors in his hand. He is a shabbily dressed, ungraceful man of about thirty, with a clean-shaven face, curly hair, and eyes full of good humour. "My own, especial Rebecca!"' Nerves and effort had brought to my voice a satisfyingly penetrating yelp and though I was fairly sure I could be heard by the audience I was far from sure that anyone at all in that audience was in any way interested in either hearing or watching any item in the matter of what I had to say or do. There was an audience, of that we were sure. Hadn't we stood, made-up and costumed, in the wings or on the stage, in those dreadful minutes before the kick-off, listening to that audience cackling and banging seats and chattering? Now the curtain was up and we were acting a play for them. Acting? Hollow it all seemed, disappointingly pointless and with no sense of communicating into that black rustling and coughing hole. Jilly or Jenny or whoever was playing Rebecca gabbled at me, her eyes staring wild and glassy and all I knew was that when she stopped talking it would be my turn to start. Rebecca has to give Tom a playful thump. She nearly drove the shoulder off me. Next came the business of her trimming off with the scissors the frayed edges of Tom's collar. From the audience there came a sense of an audible smile. A warmth; attentive; a connection. A chuckle. A generous laugh. Secret receptors which unknown to him an actor owns set deeply into his personality heeded this communion with the body of an audience and bade me complete the circle in this mystery of communication by acting for them and for my brother and sister actors and actresses the part of Tom Wrench in Pinero's play *Trelawny of the 'Wells'* with all the determination and the confidence that I could muster. So it went on, as for the first time I could feel what before I had felt when a member of an audience: a oneness in the fiction made by the trinity of audience, actor and author. What had alerted this mechanism was nothing that Jilly or

Jenny or I directly had done: it was when Pinero has a landlady in his play take a pair of scissors to cut off the frayed edges on the collar of an actor, and so spruce him up a little.

Our curtain calls taken, the applause from that scattering of folk who had made us an audience hearteningly enthusiastic, costume, makeup taken off, you could have found me wandering up from backstage to the body of the building. Puzzled, yes, elated, considerably, bemused, not half, gasping for a pint I was blundering up dimly lit more or less unfamiliar stairs and came to a doorway. Framed by that doorway stood the silhouette of a man wearing a large-brimmed hat and a long overcoat. The dark, featureless outline contained a someone not particularly tall, not especially broad, substantial in girth obviously but not inordinately and yet unaccountably that figure was big. Grand. Mighty. Unnervingly, a field of force came shuddering towards me from out that being bulking up before me. The bumper shadow spoke. Its rich and powerful, precisely articulated voice said to me: 'Take the crucifixion out of your voice, and put some cock into it.' Nimbly, the great dark shape banged out of view. The mixture that is me had been given another little shake. I passed through the doorway where the figure had stood and met Clifford Turner on his way down the stairs from the airy, well-lit hall.

'Well done, Peter,' said Clifford. 'Well done, well done, indeed. Very good, very good, very'

'Who,' says I to Clifford, 'was that?'

'Oh, that was Robert,' says Clifford to me. 'Yes, that's right, Robert, Robert, Robert'

'Robert?'

'Yes. Robert Atkins. Yes. That's it. Robert Atkins. Yes.'

YES. It is unlikely that you will have heard or read much about Robert Atkins because little about him has been written and in these times of ours even less is said. To be sure, he exists in the many often sobbingly funny stories of him that the actors and the actresses of my generation relish telling to each other and our patient wives or husbands or lovers or friends or acquaintances or strangers whom we meet and fancy would enjoy their telling; sure it is, too, that in his book on the Old Vic E. G. Harcourt Williams, after penning down a brief synopsis of Robert's work at that theatre, calls him the King; it also is sure that another king, George the Sixth, in his Birthday Honours of 1949, graciously recognized the services to the theatre that had been rendered by his loyal subject, Atkins, R., and made him a Commander of the British Empire; and surely enough that noble gentleman Tyrone Guthrie tells us in his autobiography that it was due to the great talent of Robert Atkins that the Old Vic began regularly to stage the plays of Shakespeare; that, you may be sure, is about the size of it.

If you would seek to know on whom the great credit for translating the Royal Victoria Hall and Coffee Tavern into the Old Vic and so into the heart of all that was excellent, daring and joyous in the English-speaking theatre, then you must look, and rightly so, to the doughty person of Lilian Baylis, sole manageress of the institution from 1912 until her death in 1937. A temperance worker, devout Christian reformer, ardent supporter of working-class colleges and adult education, during her years at the Vic she became Dame Lilian Baylis, Companion of Honour, and the University of Oxford conferred on her the honorary degree of Master of Arts. Variously described as having been a brute, a devil, affectionate, courageous, saintly, ugly, ignorant, humorous, friendly, tyrannical, faithful, stingy, divinely inspired, it seems she had extraordinary forces both of personality and of physical energy and throughout the later years of her life she regularly was festooned with all manner of fine medals, orders, ribbons, and several portrait oils were painted of her in cap and gown suitably adorned. After her death a number of books were written about her and many others directly refer to her and to her work.

Robert famously was a womanizer, drank whiskey by the bucket, could curse blisters on granite; a martinet at work, he was a rollicker at leisure; erudite, theatrical, godless, practical, his industriousness was boundless, his will and determination invincible, his phrasemaking raw, plangent, packed with salt and wit, his fists and boots available for those who fancied a taste; he was a loyal, generous friend, he feared no one and no thing. A primary source is uttering these qualities to you: years after my first and alarming meeting with him, fate sent me out to work with Robert as colleagues in a play. He was Pumblechook and I was Jaggers in the stage version by Alec Guinness of Dickens' *Great Expectations*. Only the trivial matter of his death in 1972 at the age of eighty-six ended our physical friendship. He moved into my mind shortly after this event and lives on there permanently, an hilariously provocative nuisance to all my other lodgers.

A student at the Academy of Dramatic Art before it became royal, in 1905 Robert became interested in the ideas of the actors William Poel, Harvey Granville-Barker and their efforts to stage Elizabethan and Jacobean plays with fluency of action, minimal scenery and a respect for both the speaking and the integrity of the texts. In 1906 the founder of our academy, Herbert Tree, took him into his company at His Majesty's. Playing many parts, he stayed with Tree for three years. Next came a year in repertory at Glasgow, after which he joined the company of Martin-Harvey. Martin-Harvey had been one of Henry Irving's young star actors. Robert toured with him for two years. Subsequently, Forbes-

Robertson signed him up. For almost three years he worked with Forbes-Robertson, touring England and the United States and acting with him at London in plays by Shakespeare and Shaw. 'Bernard Shaw? A very fine playwright, that poor old darling, and a nut-eating virgin.' Forbes-Robertson, as ear-achingly I would learn, became and remained for Robert the man who was a matchless mould for all that was fine in acting and in actors.

A few cheerful months with Frank Benson then followed. Benson, classical scholar, actor and superb athlete from Oxford University, founding father of the Shakespeare theatre at Strat-ford-upon-Avon, a great lover of cricket, he always fielded an eleven from his company, stage management and associates. Indeed, it was difficult to get a job with Benson unless you played at cricket. One time he put an advertisement in the *Stage* newspaper. 'Wanted useful change bowler to understudy Bassa-nio'. Robert batted at eight and was a meaty smiter of the ball.

Mr Atkins joined the Old Vic company in 1915. He played Iago, Jaques, Sir Toby Belch, Prospero, Cassius, Macbeth, Richard the Third, then he listed away as a soldier and went to fight in the First World War.


On the halls in London during the late eighteen eighties an infant prodigy fiddle player name of Lilian Baylis used to scrape her bow. Little Lil was the eldest child and most consistent wage earner of a failed vaudeville act called Newton and Liebe Baylis, respectively baritone and soprano. Hoping for better fortune, Dad and Mum Baylis shipped the act out to South Africa. Billed as The Musical Baylises, they bumped their act by bullock cart around the veldt, eventually fetching up in the frighteningly tough, rough mining city of Johannesburg. The act folded. Now aged sixteen, Big Lil once again became the bread provider. Gamblers and whores and gunfighters and prospectors and diggers and dudes trod the same footpaths that Lil did when she took her mandolin along to the room she'd rented to give dancing lessons to miners.

In London, Lil had a distinguished relative: Aunty Emma Cons, managing director of the South London Dwellings Company, a philanthropic organization with a board of distinguished, rich, influential and titled persons, whose aim was the amelioration of the poverty, squalor, drunkenness and violence in the slums south of the river across the Waterloo Bridge. Aunt Emmy persuaded the board to buy the Old Vic, which was then a gin palace and knocking shop whose cover was its function as a bare-arsed red-nosed bawdy music hall. First Emma Cons closed the place, had it washed, disinfected, painted, and then reopened the theatre but with a new and splendidly virtuous title to it: Royal Victoria Hall and Coffee Tavern. The policy of the theatre was that it would offer a purified entertainment and that no intoxicant drinks would be sold. String quartets, magic-lantern shows, science lectures, poetry recitals, jugglers, ballad singers, temperance crusaders, no filthy jokes, no tits, bums, gin, whores, fun, excitement, well, the punters simply steered away from the purity and the temperance and went to where they could find some good cheer. Wealthy benefactors, particularly Sam Morley the teetotal textile magnate, pumped money into the building to keep such a worthy enterprise alive but it was very much touch and go with the place. Eighteen ninety-five came and Aunty Emm had an inspired idea. She dropped a note to her bustling, enterprising young niece out in the badlands of Johannesburg suggesting that the girl might like to join her in running a theatre. Twenty-one years old, the unstoppable young Lilian Baylis arrived back in London, took up the job of assistant manager to her aunt and the old place once more began to live.

Mandolin Lily, the whole of her young life one long hardship, knew only that pure or impure, temperant or intemperant, drunk or sober, what all classes of working men and women wanted from a night at the theatre was to be entertained. Opera, vaudeville, Shakespeare, decided Lilian, would be the three staples of the fare on offer at the Old Vic, as she always called the place, and in an amazingly ramshackle manner those items began to appear on her stage. Distinguished singers, dancers, actors, actresses, composers, writers, vaudevillians roamed across the river to help out when they could. Few asked for pay; those who did were given bus fare or a chop cooked by Lilian on a gas ring in the wings prompt side of the stage. Nineteen twelve, Emma Cons toppled off the twig. Lilian Baylis took on full managership. Nineteen fourteen, the war came and took away the young men, many for ever. Still Lilian and her allies battled on. For me, Sybil Thorndike still exemplifies the determination shown by performers to put a show on the stage: Sybil played men's roles in Shakespeare, being, it is said, particularly dashing as Prince Hal. The war ended. To the dismay of many, Lilian Baylis carried on her old tinpot ways of throwing productions on the stage and concerned admirers urged her to have a clearly discernible, planned and practical artistic policy. 'I'm waiting for Robert,' is all the lady would say.

You see, in Palestine, after three years of slaughter and destruction, fighting in General Allenby's big push against the Turkish Ottoman Empire, one day in 1918 found my friend Robert Atkins desolate with melancholy and ill forebodings. Against his death or maiming, Robert wrote a long and a detailed letter to Lilian Baylis. In that letter he demanded of her that she heed his proposals on what should be her scheme of productions at the Old Vic. He insisted that although the work at the Vic substantially should consist of plays by Shakespeare, that substance vitally would be leavened by performing works of playwrights ranging from the medieval to those of the twentieth century. He provided a list of authors and plays. To the matter of how Elizabethan or Jacobean works should be staged and played, he wrote detailed

instructions on how, with minor adjustments to the stage apparatus in existence at the Old Vic, a platform could be provided
which would support a flowing simplicity of production and be of
benefit in terms of sense, artistic merit and financial cost. In
regard to the company, Robert was convinced that actors and
actresses of worth would seize this chance to enrich and deepen
their imaginations, techniques and reputations by playing over a
nine- or ten-month season four or five roles in masterpieces.
Acting and the speaking of both verse and prose? Deep from
within himself issued standards whose value had been confirmed
and tempered by years of performing with masters and mistresses
of his profession. In methods of approach and of practice he had
observed and had absorbed the panache of Herbert Tree, the
singular flair of Martin-Harvey, the athleticism and classical simplicity of Frank Benson; above all, the power and the beauty in
the acting of Forbes-Robertson, and the melodious grace and
clarity of that actor's speaking. It is true, I fancy I must add, that
my nut-eating, greenwhiskered mentor had long ago suggested
that Forbes-Robertson, whose speech he declared was unchal-
lengeable in every English-speaking land, should make a phono-
graphic recording of *Hamlet* and that the Academy Committee of
the Royal Society of Literature could justify its existence by
undertaking this work.

'I'm waiting for Robert.'

At the Old Vic in nineteen twenty, having survived the war,
Robert Atkins arrived. In the season of 1920–21 he put on stage
fifteen plays by Shakespeare, the medieval morality play *Everyman*,
*The Hope of the World* by the Reverend Andrew, and *Warriors Day*, a
verse recital, J. M. Barrie's *Pantaloon* and *The School for Scandal* by
Sheridan. Robert acted in most of the plays and produced all of
them. From 1921 to 1922, Robert staged *Wat Tyler*, a new play by
Halcott Glover, Goldsmith's *She Stoops to Conquer*, *Everyman*, Strind-

berg's *Advent*, a frivolity called *Vic Vicissitudes*, thirteen Shakespeare plays and, with Grieg's music, the first production in England of Ibsen's *Peer Gynt*, an event for which, since 1890, commentators on the English theatre had been clamouring. With the exception of *She Stoops to Conquer*, Robert staged all these productions, acted in practically all of them, and designed the settings for *Peer Gynt*. Russell Thorndike played Peer. Robert staged fourteen Shakespearean plays in the 1922–23 season, including *Henry the Fourth, Parts One and Two* and *Henry the Sixth, Parts One, Two and Three*; Dickens' *The Cricket on the Hearth, A New Way to Pay Old Debts*, by Massinger, two plays by contemporary poets, *Britain's Daughter* by Gordon Bottomley; *King Arthur* by Laurence Binyon, with music by Elgar, which music Robert persuaded Edward Elgar to conduct himself, *Everyman*, of course, and, of course, Robert acted in most of the plays and staged every one.

Audiences at the Old Vic by now were enormous, seats were coveted and had to be booked months in advance, the public and the profession knew that what they were seeing on the stage was both original and startlingly good; the newspapers agreed. Samuel Morley, temperance reformer and benefactor to the theatre, had been using a deal of the backstage area as a college of higher education for the working class. After a little prompting from Atkins, Lilian Baylis persuaded Morley to move his college to other premises on the Waterloo Road. Robert suggested to Lilian that she found a wardrobe, this the lady did; in an old public house round the corner in Oakley Street; new dressing rooms, a paint dock, a carpenters' shop were built backstage at the Vic and along came the 1923–24 season. Sheridan's *The Rivals* was staged, the evergreen *Everyman, She Stoops to Conquer*, a version of Dickens' *A Christmas Carol* and the first textually correct version, written by Tristan and Graham Rawson, of Goethe's *Faust*. Robert also produced twelve plays by Shakespeare; the performance of *Troilus and Cressida* on 23rd November 1923 being one of considerable significance. With exquisite timing, and building on the work of his predecessors, the actors Lang, Thorndike, Greet and Foss, Robert made sure, on the eve of the tercentenary of the publication of the First Shakespeare Folio, edited by Shakespeare's colleagues John Heminge and Henry Condell, that in nine years the Old Vic had produced on its stage the entire canon of thirty-six plays contained in that book, an achievement which had never been equalled nor attempted by any other theatre.

Yes, of course he acted in most productions; of course he staged them all.

Lilian Baylis was fond of saying that God never let the Vic down. When in 1915 the Luciferian figure of Robert bustled through the stage door to give her and the audiences a taste of his talent, the lady, I fancy, must have sensed that in order to perform a wonder God was moving in a particularly mysterious way. After reading the letter which Robert had written from Palestine, Lilian, again I fancy, must have realized that God was on the right track: Atkins was the man for the Vic, Baylis would be waiting for him. What is certain is that Robert knew well what he was doing, knew well how to do it, and did it well. Unstintingly supported by Lilian, the efforts of the company, his own talent and colossal labours, Robert Atkins, in the words of E. G. Harcourt Williams, had placed a red mark opposite Waterloo station in London and put the Old Vic on the map of the world. No doubt this extraordinary achievement would have pleased Robert, but if my assessment of the man has any merit, the difficulties to be overcome would have been his first and abiding interest. Anyway, the job wasn't finished: he still had to do the 1924–25 season. *Everyman*, *She Stoops to Conquer*, a new play *Hannele*, eight Shakespeares and, after five years as governor there, what was to be his final production at the Old Vic: a revival of Arthur Wing Pinero's play *Trelawny of the 'Wells'*.

Ever of thee I'm fondly dreaming,
Thy gentle voice my spirit can cheer.

Sentimental old ballad from the 1860s, sung five times in *Trelawny*, played once on a barrel organ, its sweet sounds still drift around in me, and forty years after first having heard it I am of a habit, often at wholly inapposite moments, of croaking out the only two lines of the ditty that I know, which words often are followed by creaky but tuneful, surely, dee dee de dees. The theme song of that play, it weaves its gentle way through the acts, is an indispensable plot point and brings to the piece much of its nostalgic charm. Two productions of *Trelawny* have I seen since our own efforts at the RADA; in the first, scant care was given to the honeyed warbling necessary to the song living on for ever in the hearts of the singers and the audience; scant, I tell you; in the second, well, came the cherished moment when for the first time in the play we are to hear Rose sing 'Ever of Thee', the chubby lass playing the part suddenly erupted into shrieks, hoots and whoops of such violence that I was sure she was either in the grip of cureless hysteria or that some cruel joker had shoved a white-hot poker up the child's botty. Alarmed, I was about to grab a fire extinguisher, rush on to the stage and put the unfortunate creature out, when my companion at the show, Pickering, D., gently restrained me and whispered in my ear, 'You'll find that she's not an actress, she's a singer. The number's probably been cut so that she can rip off a scale or two and give us a flourish of her talent.' This reasoning escaped me then, it escapes me now, but, aghast, I accepted it and grimly held my peace. In both productions fragments of the tune wafted their way from the stage but in neither cases were they integral parts of the whole and in both cases the playing of the barrel organ had no merit. None. Word once came my way that not long ago a musical was made of *Trelawny* in which the number wasn't heard at all, wasn't in the show. In days the musical died the death. Suicide.

In Mr Edward Burnham's two productions of *Trelawny of the 'Wells'* at the RADA in that spring of 1954, on each of the five occasions in which the dainty song is sung, why, in both perform-ances our girls gave full and tuneful tonsils to the melody, and the playing of the barrel organ was superb. The credit for the mastery of this difficult instrument, its ability on cue to hurdy-gurdy the sounds of 'Ever of Thee' from its station in the street through the window of the drawing room in Sir William Gower's house where our Rose sits, unhappy among civilians, unstintingly must be handed to that member of our household at Muswell Hill, the Hopi Hebrew. Not only is my darling savage acting in these productions but also is she stage-managing them and Burnham, E., wisely has left the composition of sound effects for the play in her deft and capable hands.

Pete. We need a piano, a pianist who can handle this number, here's the sheet music, and a couple of newspapers, right? Right. The dear crone who at whiles tinkles the instrument for Stretcher Fletcher is commandeered. Yes, the dear can and will play the piece. Two newspapers are found. Enter Pocahontas lugging a tape recorder the size of an attaché case, big, yes, but a novelty in those dear days, rich and rare. Would I lift the upper lid of the upright piano? Certainly. See that slim strut between the hammers and the strings? I do. OK. Now carefully slide two sheets of newspaper behind that strut so that they press against the strings, you got that? I got that. Easy, Pete, easy, you there yet? I'm there yet. Fine, now hold the newspaper against the lid, don't drop it and neither pull nor push. Neither will I, nor pull nor push. OK. Now, honey, says she to the sweet crone, will you play the piece really slowly but with meat, you know, ponderously, right? All right. First, though, please play a few bars so I can make a test. Plank, plank, plunk, plank, plunk, plunk, plank, plunk. Two large spools on the recorder slowly spin round, recording, testing, as toneless notes bump out from the piano. We're there, honey, we're there. OK. Fire away. Echoless, flat, funereal, 'Ever of Thee' is thumped on to the piano and into the tape recorder. Great, we have it. Thank you very much. See you in the pub in about half an hour, Pete.

An hour later, the Hopi having done splendid things to the playing speeds, tone, amplification of her recorder, a heap of us sat sucking our drinks in Momma Fischer's, listening for the third or the fourth time in admiration and not inconsiderable wonder to the jingle-jangle sounds of a barrel organ rolling out its hurdy-gurdy version of 'Ever of Thee I'm Fondly Dreaming'. You may not be surprised to learn that I and the Hopi, creator of this stage magic, by this time had become practically inseparable. Life for the pair of us was rich, was good. Rejoice!

Playing Molloy in the second production was a gas. Appearing only in the fourth act of Pinero's Original Comedietta, the setting into which he appears is the stage of a theatre; naturally, the stage of the Little Theatre became the setting. A stage manager, Irish, bumptious, Molloy, a man who, when all is hushed and quiet, bellows for silence; who, after apologizing on behalf of the absent call boy, his own elder brother, recently made a widower, presently burying his dead wife, himself calls to their places actors and actresses already standing on them; who tries to bar from the theatre the man who is the sole source of finance for the production in rehearsal; and who gave me the chance, liberated from my duties as guardian angel for Tom Wrench, merrily to clatter about a stage which the day before initially had been a place of anxiety and uncertainty for me. The first three acts I'd spent hovering in the wings, with pleasure watching the Hopi give life and humour to Mrs Mossop the landlady, admiring our beauties giving their Imogen, their Rose and Avonia, but in particular giving great heed to Bob whose turn it was to play Tom and who, although he saw merit in Wrench's ideas for plays in which chaps sat in clubs smoking cheroots and speaking in brief sentences made up of short words, before sallying out to dally with simple maidens in muslin frocks, found Tom Wrench himself to be a tedious bore, a capital fact which Bob felt should be advertised by the manner in which he played the character. Demeanour glum, posture slack, weary, voice an unremitting nasal monotony, he tried at all times to be seated, his face turned away from the audience; occasionally, alas, the dictates of the play demanded that he rise and move, this he did with a sluggish reluctance which pricked tears of joy into my watching eyes, and his most vivid actions came from chain-smoking small cigars whose butt ends he pressed into the large ashtray which he carted about with him whenever he was called to slouch about the stage.

Later, in the boozer, his eyes shining with a rare immodesty, Bob announced that of all the dull performances seen at the academy in the half-century of its existence, no performance could possibly have been duller than the one he had just had the pleasure of giving. One wonders.

---

EDMUND! Sweet Ned, listen me. You're in *Trelawny*, did you know that? At least your spirit is. Yes. You appear in a way which I think would please you for it's bold and simple and theatrical. This is the way of it. In the third act, Albert Finney visits Rose at her digs. Albie is playing Sir William Gower, a querulous old sod who avowedly detests the theatre and all actors and actresses. 'Gypsies,' he terms us, Ned; blimey, the old sausage doesn't know the half of it. Anyway, Gower's grandson has himself tangled up in Rose's briar patch, has gone missing, and the old boy has creaked round to Rosie's pad for a general natter and a sort-out. He is giving her poor earhole a horrible pounding about luring his grandson away to herd with troubadours and harridans and gypsies when suddenly out of Rose's mouth pops your name. 'Kean?' says Gower. 'Which Kean?' 'Edmund Kean,' replies Rose. 'My mother acted with Edmund Kean, when she was a girl.' Ned, the effect these few words have on Gower is beautiful theatre. The grumpy old dodderer loses his bluster and says, 'With Kean? With Kean?' When Rose tells him yes it was with you that her mother had acted, Gower whispers to her that when he was a young man he had seen you act. 'Kean,' he says, 'he was a *splendid* gypsy!' The pair of them begin rooting in a theatrical skip for props which, the playwright tells us, you had given to Rose's mother. One of the props is a sword you wore when you played Richard the Third. 'Lord bless us!' says old Gower, 'how he stirred me.' Into a strange reverie goes Gower, talking of you, muttering a snatch from Richard, buckling on the sword. The scene touched us all, Ned: cast, audience, and young Finney played old Sir William very well indeed.

Larry Olivier had a sword of yours which you used when you played Richard. John Gielgud told me that the sword came from your old strolling mate Chippendale who, apparently, handed it on to someone who handed it on to John's family, the Terrys, who handed it on to someone and it somehow wound up in the grip of Larry. He showed it to me one day at his house in Brighton; he let me hold it; he kindly let me give it a great swish; a fine toasting iron, Ned Kean, hilt and blade all beautifully wrought. Could that weapon have been, I wonder, the sword you wore as Richard in the days of your disgrace? When it must have seemed the world had turned against you and had flung you into infamy and rot. For why? Technically, for being found guilty of having had 'criminal conversation' with the wife of Alderman Cox, Charlotte. Weren't you the gormless git indeed to go and get yourself involved with that wormy little trollop, leave alone its cunning and complacent hubby, the worthy Alderman. But, then, you ever had your brains between your legs. One knows the feeling. All right, caught with your trousers down, adulterer, guilty as charged, weighed off, Coxes paid off, adults make public twots of themselves, matter should have ended. It didn't though, my dear little Flyblown, it didn't, did it? Mob got you. Mob the beast. Moved by forces so small, this brute, nothing so resembles its violence as the big sea. Into the court you'd swanned, you dateless little pillock, if not wholly confident of winning, surely careless of losing. Yes, respectability was a word coined at the time of your birth, had become common currency, but what of that? In the gamey circles, high or low, round which you moved, drunkenness, infidelities, fornication had players of as much zeal and more than ever you did hazard. Rakehells of the Regency were now monarch, court and courtiers but the rules hadn't changed. Before dumping her, Clarence, the future king, Sailor Bill, had fathered double figures of bastards on your colleague Dora Jordan. Poor or rich, low caste to high caste, London had a citizenry lewd and sottish as any on earth and brazenly so. What harm, then, in being nabbed for slap and tickle with the dimpled missus of Cox? Might even be a lark, let's pop in to this courtroom, see what's up. Wrong, Kean, wrong. Ever gaudy, prolix, your letters to the wife of this wronged Alderman of the City of London were read out in court by the Common Sergeant and you were damned. 'Dear imprudent', 'Sunbeam through prison bars', 'Little breeches', 'Bitch', good comical listening for jury, judge, spectators, there wasn't a dry seat in the house. Also, the deceit and hypocrisy unavoidable in shadowy affairs came into the light and there you stood, five foot and four inches of you, liar, homebreaker, humbug. The cast of characters too, Ned, think of it. Sobbing and chastened, Charlotte of the little breeches; Mary, the genteel wronged wife; Alderman Cox, gold-chained, upright councillor, horns sprouting on his blameless head; the Great Kean, mummer in doublet and hose, man of ease, arrogance and display. Irresistibly newsworthy, Ned, and the press went for it in screamers. Cartoons, songs, jokes, vaudeville sketches, the aftermath of the trial produced an industry. *The Times* took a grave and a weighty tone, its moral thunder rumbled,

It appears that Kean is advanced many steps in profligacy beyond the most profligate of his sisters and brethren of the

stage. It is of little consequence whether the character of King
Richard or Othello be well or ill acted; but it is of importance
that public feeling be not shocked, and public decency be not
outraged.

That was fair warning, Ned. Do a Byron, it implied, do what your
friend and champion Gordon the Gimp had done nine years
earlier, push off to sea, go bobbing about on a boat for a month
or four, come back quietly, play the provinces, by the time you
reach London the newspapers, the caricaturists, the sleaze pedlars
may have some other poor sod in the pillory, above all it will be
old news and old news is no news.

No. Not your style, Ned, was it. It was announced that you
would be appearing in a week's time at Drury Lane, where the
public could see you play Richard the Third. The town went
mad. Newspapers, castigating your effrontery, warned you off.
The Society for the Suppression of Vice took to the streets.
The prigs and the prudes were aghast. Decent folk worried. The
nobs and the hobbledehoys smelled blood. Magistrate Birnie, by
the direction of the Secretary of State, Robert Peel, requested
that the performance should be postponed until popular excitement had quietened down. No. You weren't having any, thank
you. You would be there. Eleven years of a success unparalleled
in theatrical history; four years as boy wonder, nine years of
apprenticeship, most of which years had been times of unremitting toil, hardship, starvation, humiliation, want, neglect; and for
all the tosspotting and the frolicking the preparation and the
performances of your acting had been at all times incorruptible
and you had made many enemies, Kean. Enemies who wanted
you down and grovelling. Enemies who wanted you gutted. Our
imperfect human nature, too, Ned, not only in newspapers or
enmity, can find glee or disgust in fallen idols we ourselves raised
up to worship. Yes, we who love you, who have read of you, seen
the paintings, held the properties, we players who yearn to

emulate you, we know that acting of the scale and the detail
and the power which you gave in your performances came only
with the mightiest of efforts; that you studied and slaved beyond
any actor that your wife and colleagues had known; that it was
usual after the performance of any of your principal parts to find
you stretched on a sofa, retching violently and throwing up blood.
We know that. The mob who mustered in their thousands at
Drury Lane seven days after the Cox v. Kean trial, they didn't.
Nor should an audience know or concern itself with what has
gone on in the making of a performance; an audience properly
goes to a playhouse to be entertained, to be thrilled, amused,
engrossed; if fortunate, to be inspired. True, a number of sup-
porters came that night at Drury Lane to give you heart, to cheer
you on; the mob came for derision, for disgrace, to see you
broken. On to the stage you bowled; mayhem and insanity
became the rule. Ructions, rows, fist fights, missiles flung at the
stage, missiles flung around the auditorium as factions in the
audience pelted other factions, bottles, hats, oranges; the lowing
of great jeers, bellowings, screams, fury, savage mockery; three
hours of this, not a word of the play heard, on you went with your
part, my sweet Ned, nor did you at any time so much as flinch.
Hostility was the tone of reports in the newspapers which printed
their versions of that evening's events; hostile, indignant, gleeful.
When it was announced that four days later you would be
appearing on the same stage as Othello, Jesus but the clamour
was hysterical. Did you read *The Times* on the morning of the
show, Kean, my old flower pot? 'That obscene little personage is,
we see, to make another appearance this evening.' That evening
you appeared as Othello. It was Rafferty's rules all over again but
midway through the play the temperature dropped a few degrees,
just enough to let you say a few quiet words to that audience,
anyway, didn't it, great Edmund Kean. These are the words. I
value them.

I stand before you as the representative of Shakespeare's heroes. If this is the work of a hostile press I shall endeavour with firmness to withstand it. But if it proceeds from your verdict and decision, I will at once bow to it, and shall retire with deep regret and with a grateful sense of all the favours which your patronage has hitherto conferred on me.

Those brief few words resolved the issue, Edmund. No justifications for private conduct, no begging, neither did you surrender nor retreat. You did not budge an inch and by that stance the true nature of the obscenity was revealed and your enemies were routed. Yes, the papers were shrill from time to time after; yes, occasional claques in the audience occasionally hooted and derided, but it was pipsqueakery of no substance or matter. Bold boy, Edmund, but then you always were. You would accept the public's opinion of you as an actor but nothing more. On tour, well, city after city after city, uproar after uproar after uproar. By then, though, the mob had forgotten why they were being uproarious. Mobs do. Mobs still make uproars. This bred anger in you, didn't it. Not pain. Not hurt. Not disbelief. Anger. An old ally. In one city the audience was making a nuisance of itself. Playing Richard you were, you became deeply irritated. The sword flashed from its sheath, down to the front of the stage you shot, and, incorporating a Keanian amendment to Shakespeare's text, you belted out, 'Unmannered dogs! Cease ye at my command.' The audience began to hush. You stood there with your sword peeled until there was quiet. The play continued and you played your part.

By doing what was right, what was good, what was brave in that hideous year of 1825, Kean endured. Emotionally, it near wrecked the man. Among commentators on Kean, Giles Playfair is a man who has tried to remove much bunk. Kean's friend the Irishman Thomas Grattan wrote a short sketch of Edmund which Playfair refers to as: 'Perhaps the only faithful and sympathetic portrait of the great tragedian that has ever been painted.' Shortly after Kean had seen off the mob, Grattan went to see his friend in London. He writes:

> I never saw a man so changed; he had all the air of desperation about him. He looked bloated with rage and brandy. He sat down at the piano, notwithstanding the agitated state of his mind, and sang for me 'Lord Ullin's daughter', with a depth, and power, and sweetness that quite electrified me.

It seems to me that in effect Kean was saying to his old chum Tom Grattan that, yes, he'd had a shocking bump, was fit to sing the blues, but after a sniff of sea air and a pot or two down the Coal Hole he would be more than able to get on with his business. For eight more years Kean would blaze on.

Yes, Ned, the sword Olivier let me handle in Brighton. Was it the one you pulled when you cowed the mob on tour? If it was, it's quite safe now. Larry had it buried with him.

---

NOR WAS IT ever so humble, our home, mine and Joe's, the household we shared with the three bonny lassies in half a house at Muswell Hill. Territorial Imperative. Squirt. Squirt. Tom Cat, Tom Cat. Roomy, we had privacy when we wished; cosy, when the mood was on us we would cluster in larky human society; our hospitality was famed and between the five of us the mutual look showed hearts sure of each other, our friendship was easy, rackety, we each knew where to sit, we each had our own door key. Breakfast, I recall, was a feature of which daily I grew more fond. Eggs, toast, coffee, slivers of bacon cooked by the women into thin and crisp and crunchy slices; delicious, novel, nutritious. A meal,

too, over which one at whiles could linger, for the business of
bleary gallops to be at the academy by ten a.m. in order to ram
one's little coloured slab into its appropriate slot at Rainbow
Corner, thus signalling that one was punctually present there, had
been taken over by the extraordinarily punctilious, attractive
females of our household, who took upon themselves the helpful
task of bunging our slabs into our slots and so satisfying inquisitive
eyes that Joe and I were indeed purposefully bustling about the
premises. Resourceful, accomplished, the Hopi also could pick a
tune on a guitar. Tutored by her, a further two chords were added
to my repertoire. Six chords could I twang now and she taught
me a Western song about fieries and snuffies being raring to go
while little dogies were encouraged to ride around 'em real slow.

It was the fridge, though, that, for many who mustered at our
pad, became a totem, a household god. Yes, its novelty intrigued,
what was in it delighted, but, more, its potential for preserving
numerous forms of matter prompted in some of our guests
fanciful speculation as to its uses. Jenny, for instance, felt that had
the device existed in the early nineteenth century, the tears of
Keats might have been kept in a little bottle. O'Liver, once again
giving London the benefit of his presence, had secured a position
as dishwasher at a vegetarian restaurant. The scraping and mopping of plates which had held carrots and nuts and cabbages
disturbed him not at all; that these edibles previously had been
transformed for the customers' delight into the forms and savours
of ducks, lamb chops, beefsteaks, gravy and all outraged his
aesthetic sensibilities and had moved him into a wish to plonk a
person whom he called the One-eyed Lyle into the fridge, let him
firmly set, take the frozen form out, break it with a hammer into
wee fragments, tip the bits into the grinder at the vegetarian
restaurant, abide below by his sink until luncheon and dinner had
been both served and eaten, after which he felt reasonably sure
that a calmer state might return to his disordered sensitivity.

Hardtack, call him, viewed the refrigerator with a discerning and a practical eye. He had digs in a basement which was at all times damp and nippy. A gas fire was his sole source of heat and cheer; the meter for it ate money; your copper pennies, your bright shillings, your substantial silver florins. Coins pressed into their various slots depressed a trigger which in turn activated a mechanism that released gas commensurate to the money inserted. A florin bought a healthy flow of flame. Hardtack mused to me on the possibilities of making a mould shaped to contain a number of objects which would be of a uniform circumference and thickness. One would then just pour water in the mould, shove it into the fridge and the following morning one would scoop out a number of discs in shape very like ice florins. Oddly enough, in the past I'd heard of cold folk who had with occasional success used objects such as fairground tokens, metal washers and the like to gain for themselves a flicker of warmth from gas fires. The snag had been, of course, that these objects stayed in the meter, proof that coin of the realm had not been used. Awkward, that. Florins of ice, however, would melt away, leaving no trace. One simply does not know if Hardtack did ever put his ingenious theory into practice. The most one can say, and it is impossible to know whether or not this has any bearing on the matter, is that from time to time Hardtack would be seen approaching the fridge, at whiles clutching a large bar of soap, at others bearing a Thermos flask.

> My father makes counterfeit money,
> My mother brews synthetic gin,
> My sister sells kisses to sailors,
> By Christ how the money rolls in.

---

'YOU ARE TELLING ME to have a bath with my trousers on. Carve it any way you wish, blossom, that's what it boils down to.'

Do you see, all that I'd done was to ask of herself why it was that her jeans were blue, blue as was the colour of the, what, two or three other pairs of jeans which, enpeopled, I'd seen sauntering about the streets of the city, while my jeans were dark grey. Who, I ask you, could have anticipated the fair rhapsody of instruction, advice, guidance, nay, lyric exhortation that this mild enquiry concerning the comparative hues of heavy duty sailcloth trousers would cause to ripple in streams from out her sweet red kisser? Who, again I ask you, could have anticipated that what began their lives as goldminers' breeches would move on to enwrap the seats of frontiersmen, labourers, dockers, students, slobs, the casual of dress, the swankily fashionable, men, women, children, families, would become the uniform of a country, of continents, of the world? Not I. Bewildered had I listened to herself tonguing out a litany of the labours done successfully to induce these trousers into yielding up from within their grey their bonny blue. Friends of hers back in the States had, said she, stewed their trousers in large pots over slow fires, stirring the while with ladles. Some had with hot water wetted their breeks, sprinkled them o'er with soap flakes, taken stiff scrubbing brushes to them and then scoured and rubbed and scrubbed away for hours at the sturdy articles. Others had gone down to the sea in ships, lashed lines to these strides, heaved them overboard, and in the wakes of speeding motorboats foamingly had trawled them along. Better by far, said herself to me at our home on Muswell's hill, was a way she knew of persuading one's jeans both to loose their blue and to grab your shape. Grab my shape? Fit real snug, tight, stretch like another skin over your long legs, show off your cute buns. Buns? Your fanny, your tush, your bottom. Madam, I neither wish for another skin nor to exhibit my harris, I wish merely to cover my nakedness, from the loins even unto the thighs, beyond, even, down to the trotters. What you have to do, unheeding went she on, is put on your jeans, climb into a hot, salt and soapy bath, massage your jeans against your body, slow, easy, just a little soap, rub strong but gentle, relax, lie back, smoke a cigarette, have a beer, read a book, give it a while, let out all the cruddy water, fill her up with fresh, clean hot water, make sure all the soap's gone, you know, wriggle about, rinse yourself, let out all the water, fill her up again with hot water, relax, do voice exercises, make like you're Clifford Turner, from the diaphragm, darling, the diaphragm, the diaphragm, the dia-frigging-phragm, keep that up but really religiously, in a couple of weeks, Pete, why, you'll be striding around in the neatest, trimmest, bluest pair of blue jeans that anyone ever saw, but ever.

'You are telling me to have a bath with my trousers on. Carve it anyway you wish, blossom, that's what it boils down to.'

———

GET YOURSELF a comfortable berth, say I, young man, young woman, student, stranger, lonesome in a strange city. Find, say, half a house up a hill in northern London, one stocked up with rooms, beds, Joe, furniture, the fridge, guitar, cooker, a trio of gorgeous young American women, you'll find yourself on a winner and better able by far for the toils, the troubles that the days may bring knowing as you will that the nights promise ease, companionship, tap dancing, grub and the matchless benefit of a long cosy snore. Depend on it, such diggings are highly to be recommended. True, these present times differ much from the days of my young studenthood, rackrenting landlords and landladies alone are of a sort that gave the late Chairman Mao a bad name, but as an ideal, while with no educational grant you pine in your costly bed-sitter, as an aspiration, a cherished notion of spiffing lodgings, cleave to the fancy, go out and seek for to find. Chances are you will come unstuck. Times are hard. That is the alley; go weep; we had the best of it.

*

None of us had much money; one of us had not a tosser. Did we moan at Joe's inability to contribute to the household exchequer? Scoff at his busted conceit of thrift, the sudden demise of his soldering empire, his lucklessness as an instrumentalist seeking gainful employment? Certainly not, we merely pitched the bastard on to a corner of Oxford Street and Soho and there bade him twangle his banjo as a street musician. A profession of pedigree, busking, its practitioners hope honestly to scrape a crust by offering for the delight of passers-by on the streets of a city skilful entertainment worthy of reward. You'll find your fire-eater, your glass-shattering songster, your one-man band, acrobatic dancer, percussionist of the spoons, sword-swallower, other novel turns of din or daring and, on those mild springtime evenings of 1954, Cotton-eyed Joe plucking his instrument, warbling his ditties, not a note or a word of which could be heard, blasted away quite by the great growls and exclamations of motor vehicles and the trudge and chatter of citizenry jostling along the pathways of the street. Defeated? Not a bit of it. There was a world elsewhere. Underground. Down the tube station. A quiet hum only here deep below, echoing resonance from vaulted stone, a steady stream of wayfaring potential customers, courtesy of an efficient, inexpensive public transport system. Twang those strings, Joseph, lovey, let the vocal cords spring up and sound. This, to give the man his due, he did do. Indeed, he did more. Didn't he pluck the kerchief from around my neck, tie it around his own neck but in cowpoke fashion, hammer blazes from the steel gut of his guitar, tilt back his napper, let rip a yodelling yippee-eye-ay, and in an approximation of a voice redolent of the Wild Western prairie, sagebrush, buffalo, tumbleweed and all, howl out a number wherein no lavender cowboy but a blue-chinned Jack of Diamonds had at once, it seemed, both lamentable and enjoyable doings with old paint, old smokey, rye whiskey, the Queen of Hearts, rambling, gambling, fires, pork, beans, boots, hat, bones, saddle, and around whom endlessly roamed omnipresent little dogies?

Bet your ass. This, mind you, from a young English former artillery officer heavily under the influence of American Forces Network broadcasts and his present female companions; which companion crumpet stood with me as we whooped and we hollered on this inspired member of our household.

Then it happened. The pitch we had chosen for our Yankee ballad singer stood in the tunnel a yard or so down from where tube train passengers having been transported down the down escalator spilled off to head for their various platforms. To their eyes, ears, and rightly so, the Ninas, the Hopi and I would have formed a surprised, enthused audience for this doodle-dandy banjo-plucking song grinder. A brace of travellers, music lovers clearly, paused a while to join us, to inhale these authentic tones from the great plains of America, to tap their toes, to hum along, to admire, and before going their ways, dull care banished, to poke blessed hands into pockets, purses, to scatter copper coins into the receiving, open guitar case at ragtime Joe's feet. Admirable. Here's a smiling stroller come along to pitch a chunky threepenny bit into the clinking collection in the case. A bright sixpence spun from a bowler hat and brolly chimes among the funds. Better yet and better still. 'Might it not prove a good idea,' says Woody Joe Guthrie in the carved vowels and tinkling consonants of your cultured, home-counties English gentleman, 'to pop across the way to where people are going up the up escalator? They'll be arrivals and less likely to be dashing f'  Smothering his mouth in a soothing half-nelson, urgently I whispered to him that probably it would prove a splendid idea to pop across to where folk would not be haring for their trains; where they would be sauntering to ride up the up escalator; but that what was of maximum importance to the success of our enterprise would be, as gringo hobo minstrels usually did not speak in the crisp rounded accents of former British subalterns, at all times other than when croaking out lyric canticles from the States to cork up his cakehole or we would be banjaxed. Point made. Point taken.

Point allowed. His. Pitch shifted across the way, many of our customers indeed dawdling up before going up the up escalator. Profitable too this pop across the way: a fair haul of coinage piled inboard. Better by far, though, proved to be the notion we had, to which Joe nodded in mute assent, of moving four square on to both escalators. Yes, acoustically we lost the vibration that a stone tunnel can give but what of that? Joe was hot, was heaving, was relishing his role as lead-bellied Orpheus of the underground and appreciators of song going up the up were invited to rejoice and be glad for the springtime has come as those coming down the down were advised to throw down their shovels and go on the bum. The Chicago chick had the cap off my head; in best Capone fashion did she approach our ever shifting audience, hold out to them the receiving headpiece, hot dark eyes smoking with the desperation of vicious poverty, wordlessly she implied: 'The kid's starving. Fill his belly. He sings to live. You got money, he don't got none. Ever been garotted?' Nina Von's turn with my cap. Breasts heaving, hips revolving, eyes imploring: 'He's my man. Singing so we both may eat. Just a coin or two. Fail me and I will have to sell my poor body. Then he'll kill me. Help, please, generous handsome stranger.' Nina Van. 'A fallen angel stands before you; forlorn, modest, hungry. My loving partner plays his harp in hope of pennies to get us through the night. You will help. Your eyes are kind.' Me. Well, my work was to make myself useful in any way possible. To form an audience with the Ninas when the Hopi was collecting; with the Hopi and a Nina when a Von or a Van was carting round the hat; when the coast was clear to pluck money from the guitar case, and when the coast was crowded enthusiastically to toss it back in again; in short, to bring enthusiasm to the endeavour and to keep out a weather eye for anything in a blue uniform with brass buttons that might want to put an authoritative block on the concert.

An hour or so passed merrily, merrily, and then we skedaddled, first to the Burglar's Rest where a lubricant pint was poured down the minstrel's throat, the audience, collectors and look-out man moistened their aridity, then we hopped on the bus and went on up to our comfortable house on the hill. Cosy there, at ease, we had a count-up. Joe's busking had earned us more than a stripe and a half. That meant meat and drink for five in a restaurant, or cinema tickets, bus fare, and a couple of packets of fags. Elected.

> I ride an old paint,
> I lead an old dan,
> I'm going to Montana
> To throw a Houlihan.
> They feed them in the cooleys,
> They water in the draw,
> Their tails are all matted,
> Their backs are all raw.
> Ride around, little dogies,
> Ride around real slow,
> For the Fiery and the Snuffy
> Are raring to go.

———

BEING INVITED to discontinue my work as shover-in of the spaghetti, that night when Nina Von held her celebrated dinner party, came as no hardship to me. Not at all. To the contrary. Usually game for a lark, I, the hazards of fires, of roasting ovens, of seething pots, of frying pans, of boiling or grilling or scalding or devilling, cutting, carving, slicing, chopping hold only terror for me who find wholly admirable the valour, physical robustness and the art indispensable to those who, with no Factories Act to indemnify them against the hideous disfigurements at hand, unprotected save by a pinny or a glove yet set about in kitchens for to cook. Bravo, say I, toodle pip, well done, cheerio, here we go, thanks awfully, delicious. No, unburdened of dangers I had been quite content to let Nina Von do her own shoving in nor, these four decades on, do I precisely recall what had prompted our seductress to throw a dinner party of spaghetti and meatballs, garlic bread, wine, and to arrange about the place bottles with candles stuck in their necks. Could have been that her dosh had come in. Yes, a likelihood right enough. Do you see, our household in the half a house we shared up Muswell's hill, what loot its members had coming in, from an allowance, a grant, a scholarship, when Joe had a gig or earned a commission hawking 'ladies' fragrances', yes, almost invariably the stuff came in at differing times: end of term, beginning of term, half term, once a month, now and then, but it had been our way that when these rations of readies arrived, the one who struck pay dirt would but immediately blow a fair chunk of it on the other members. Modest, this liberality, its charm lay in the pennies seeming to arrive at the right moment. Yep. That could have been it: the bonny Von was flush. Whatever, that night she was driving the cooker.

Joe was her assistant. Joe the cheesemaker. That's right. Hadn't he intercepted on its way to be dumped a bottle of milk gone sour, sniffed it, inspected it, murmured a mantra of waste not, want not, thrift? Decanted the stale milk into a pint pot and with that dread light of ingenuity glistening in his eyes hadn't he pronounced that he would translate that reeky bilge into a fine, mild cheese? He had. Days ago. Rancid, now, the milk, soaplike, noisome, hasn't the lump it's in been slipped entire into a sexy nylon stocking, property of Von, and doesn't it now hang dangling from a hook in the kitchen? It does, Lord love you, and though my knowledge of the mysteries and the perils which the preparation and the cooking of food involve is scant, there is one thing I know: if matters shape up as in the past they have done, our guests tonight will surely be served up spaghetti, meatballs, garlic bread, wine and a footful of homemade mousey.

Right. Chicago and Van are out haggling in shops, Von and Joe are planning and preparing, the time is right for me to bolt myself in the bathroom, flop into the rub-a-dub, scrape off a few clinkers, dangleberries and soak away the grime ingrained from scampering up and down from nine in the morning till six in the evening the five floors at the RADA. And the basement. And the roof. That's seven. Yes. For the students who keep on the pace, and more and more are falling off it, who go up and down the stairs to rehearsals, discussions, lectures; attend voice classes, fencing classes, diction, movement, technique and ballet classes; enter speech, accent, verse competitions; perform the set pieces and the plays, all on different floors, why, in that building we go up and down up and down more often than a young whore's knickers. Yes, and now I'll lie me down to steep me in a hot and soapy tub.

Last time we had a celebration of note was when Roger Bannister galloped round four laps of the track in the park at Iffley Road, Oxford, to win the mile race for his university and immortality for himself by becoming the first man ever to run that distance in under four minutes. Everest conquered but on the flat, so to speak.

Proprietorial, of Roger Bannister, Pocahontas and I felt. For, do you see, under the terms of the Anglo-American scholarship that she had won and which afforded her to live and study in England, twice a term my dusky little plum was required to attend on her benefactress, a charming woman who lived close by Richmond Park at London, and to give this lady an informal account of how she was applying herself to her work and general doings while studying at the academy and living in the smoky city. These visits proved cheerful, relaxed and chatty affairs during which tea was taken, cakes were munched, the cross-fertilization of cultures between Great Britain and the United States would be discussed, and whose endings invariably held the bounding happiness of Pocahontas scooping up a generous wedge of lettuce. This was very good for the nerves. This allowed my sweetheart to pay her rent, buy her beans on toast, her books, her gallery seats at theatres and to sprinkle a little joy on to the members of our household. Naturally, to bring tone to these occasions, to give demonstrable evidence that at least in little there existed harmony between the peoples of these two continents, and in one of those startlingly absolute turnabouts of which women are supremely capable, the Hopi would invite me to discard my Army and Navy surplus store gear, to deck myself in my own and proper natty gents' suiting and thus, all goofiness of wear and wearer obliterated by feminine quirk, gaily bedight to accompany her on these excursions to Richmond.

Our benefactress had a relative who in some way had an association with Roger Bannister; over the months we had heard of how this young medical student, Bannister, was determined to have a crack at running a mile in under four minutes; of his exceptional athleticism, his rigorous training, his planned and timed pacing, his determination, above all of the young man's conviction that the four-minute barrier to the mile would be broken as much by the human spirit as by his body. Yes, a truism around since miles and minutes have been by man measured but remarkable to Pocahontas and me by our coincidental association with a woman who had a relative who in some way had an association with this young fellow who had uttered these thoughts and who heroically was going to put himself to the test believing that he would not fail.

Breaking four minutes for the mile had been on since 1924 when Paavo Nurmi the Finn, meticulous, melancholic, and eventual suicide, had turned in a time of four minutes and ten point four seconds; the little English lawyer, Sidney Wooderson, bespectacled, spindly, in 1937 brought the time down to an agonizingly close four minutes and six point four seconds; between 1942 and 1945, turn and turn about, the Swedish runners Gunder Hagg and Arne Andersson, by seconds and fractions of seconds, pounded away at this magical quartet of minutes for the mile: four minutes and four point six seconds, four minutes and two point six, four minutes one point six, four one point three.

That last was timed in July of 1945; it is now May 1954, we know the result but the heavy firm are sitting packed tight among the excited punters crammed into the cinema on the Tottenham Court Road, all eyes fixed on the newsreel showing us the run at Iffley Road. Crack goes the starter's gun, away in the lead Christopher Chataway bursts, great chest thrusting in shape in purpose rounded as the bent bow of an archer and for two laps in graceful burliness he leads the field, Brasher takes it up, again we have a bespectacled Englishman galloping the mile, his face a savage mask of determination, of ferocity in effort as he runs at the head of the bunch and here comes Bannister! Long frame, long face, long strides, the final few yards, a human fully extended, head thrown back in a grimace of suffering he breasts the tape. 'The time was three minutes an'   The cinema exploded in roars and whooping yells. He'd done it. Three minutes and fifty-nine point four seconds. Superb. Yes, proprietorial, that's how we felt, I and Pocahontas, that great day. Nor, I imagine, will you be surprised to learn of my pleasure when, later, Chataway went on to break the world record for the 5,000 metres and Christopher Brasher won Olympic gold over the 3,000-metre hurdles.

So, I shall leak a little more hot water into this here tub, soak, luxuriate, pick a little lint, a little wax, what appears to be a little gravel out from the deep dimple of my belly button and croak a line of verse, no one can hear.

> They said to me it couldn't be done,
> So, with a smile I got right down to it,
> And I tackled that thing that couldn't be done,
> And I couldn't do it.
> Tooralooralay. Tooralooralay.

Kean's buried at Richmond. There was no tombstone. No grave-marker in the graveyard at the old grey parish church of St Mary Magdalene on the Green. That was irritating, that was perplexing. Sure enough, what we in time would call Victorian Society had been by no means unhappy that the whoreson little bastard was dead and laid in the grave, unmarked neglected and unmourned but, still and all, it would have been nice to know in which grove of the bone orchard there had the old sod been planted, just so one could have placed down one's jam jar of dandelions on the spot, paid one's respects. Untouchable Griffith, when making in the early seventies one of his singular, cracking documentaries, one on the life of Kean, became irritated by this absence of a tombstone for his subject, became perplexed. Marshalling the vicar at Richmond, local historians, archivists, undertaker's records, beavers, moles, voles, sundry burrowers, the interested, the helpful, and generally behaving in a manner best described, surely, as being thoroughly Welsh, Griffith began searching for Ned's old bones. He found them. Underground, right enough, but not in the earth: wrapped up in a leaden coffin and put in an antechamber to the charnel house at the back of the church. Grandchild of a stone mason, Untouchable G., he had a tombstone carved up but promptly, whistled for me and, inside the church, in memory of Edmund Kean, together the pair of us laid it down. That ended our irritations, our perplexities, that was right. Tread softly.

A fine place, true enough, when the summer's days came, the roof of the RADA. True, too, that rain or shine or when bitter winds blew, since first I set an exploratory hoof on it an eternity ago, for me the roof has ever been a present and a splendid arena. Bubble, bubble, bubble. 'Don't forget the diver, guvner, don't forget the diver. I'm going down now.' Bubble, bubble, bubble. 'Surface.' 'Midships your helm, if you please.' 'Midships it is, sir.' 'Steady as you go.' 'Aye aye, sir.'

I grabbed a squeegee,
She grabbed a broom,
We chased the bastard lobster
Round and round the room.
Singing, Row tiddly O,
Row tiddly O,
Row tiddly O, tiddly O,O,O.

Turn off the hot tap. Some there are who can control the spars of
the tap with a trotter, with a heel, but I could never learn the trick
and have no wish to cop yet another blister in the trying. A tweak
or two with the hand. There. She's off. Lie back. Better. Lovely.
Soak. Stew. Aquatherapy. These warm days, in the sun, high over
Gower Street, a few more souls than have done in the past come
up to join in our society of the roof. Not many, mind, just the odd
handful, the occasional couple, the investigating solitary. Nor do
many stay for long. A quick squint and then they're off back down
again. Odd that, I find, for the roof is a spacious spot on which to
potter about, to stretch limbs, to take one's ease, to mutter lines,
practise moves, mope over matters gone wrong, skip around when
they've gone right, and we have an abundance of nifty crannies in
which those who fancy a cosy cuddle may in comparative privacy
tuck themselves. Herman the boilerman, who's been here for
donkey's, tells me that it was ever thus. Many hundreds of students
have in his time crowded into the building but dozens only have
bobbed up on to the roof. Access is simple enough: go to the
canteen, you'll think you're at the top of the academy, you're not.
Slide round the corner at the entrance to the noshery, you'll find
a further flight of stairs, up you go, there's a door, give it a shove,
out on our roof you'll find yourself. Also, if we like the cut of you,
you'll find the society has much which may be of interest to you.
We offer trips which, by nimble way of fire escape, boiler room,
platform, duckboard, and without once entering the building let
alone using a conventional corridor, will take you from Gower

Street to Malet Street. We can whisk you in seconds from the canteen to the Vanbrugh Theatre while your fellows are in many minutes plodding down and along and through and up and down again. Fancy a visit to Great Heap or Luscious Robert, the scene designers, in their fancy new habitation above the Vanbrugh? Done. A way into the academy which avoids the searching eyes of Sergeant? This way. Yes, through that gate, along the garden a few feet, that's it, now, hop over the wall. There you are. Done, dusted, and the same way takes you out. Where we keep the whiskey, though, well, that's not generally known, not, as it were, splashed about. A sip when stressed, to be sure; fortification against the agonies of a ballet class, certainly; a nip for Herman who's fond of a drop and whom it keeps sweet, your health, brother boilerman. For those of the society in need of a haircut, Nina Van's our woman. Yes. Surprising this talent she has for shearing hair, our beauty of the yellow tresses, and even more surprising for me is her real relish for the job. Up on the roof, deft and dainty, cut and trim and nip and snip, Nina Van's scissors snap in the sun. As you might expect, what with its remoteness and all, during the day from time to time when he's in town, up on the roof is where O'Liver stashes himself. Handy he finds it, these balmy days, for to sketch, for to preach sedition, and for to prey upon the female student body.

Disbanded, now, the heavy firm, divided, scattered, our ways dispersed throughout the academy; other classes, other plays, different teachers, differing times; Albie and Honey Sal, splitted away; Slim Mac and Jilly, split and gone; Bob and Pocahontas, split. True, we all meet up Muswell's hill, and if not there then in Momma Fischer's, if not in Momma's then at Olivelli's, if not up the hill, in the boozer, at the café, we muster on the roof. Fine it is for us who joined together to fill in one another on our separated doings, to introduce new classmates, to gossip, to yarn. That Hopi's gone very grand on us. Under the terms of her scholarship wee Minnehaha is required to be responsible for the staging and production of a play. The savage is doing an English version of a Spanish play by Federico García Lorca called *The House of Bernarda Alba*. It's an all female cast and Sir Kenneth has rounded up women to appear in it from all over the academy. Very grand. My little plum is fair buzzing and hugely enjoying herself. She'll be gone soon. Back home to America. When in a few weeks the term ends and her year of study in England will have been done. Yep.

''Tis but fortune, all is fortune.' That's right. My new class is rehearsing scraps and patches from *Twelfth Night*, which choice chunks will be performed in the Little Theatre, I'm giving slices of Malvolio, our teacher is the Cisco Kid. Known to you and me as Mr Ernest Milton, our fantastical man has taken to sticking his hands in his trouser pockets, lodging his hat on the back of his head, swaggering around the shop and, in the most exaggerated tones of West Coast United States that you ever could hear, is pronouncing such rich gems as, 'Toots. Time may come when you'll be the finest goddamned actress ever did grace the stage of an opry house. Ain't a dang sign of it yet but, what the hell, I'se just a kid from Cisco.' Or. 'Buddy boy. Stead of rootin, tootin, elocutin like what you is trying to do, did ya ever consider makin a livin ropin critters or wieldin a brandin iron?' He's wearing specs most of the time now. With the clearer sight these goggles give him, his view of the acting talents of most of his charges is indeed dim. Odd fact is that Ernie truly does hail from San Francisco. He arrived at London in his early twenties, strutted straight into a hit play in the West End, played Ibsen, played Shaw, moved over the water to the Vic, astonished all with his interpretations of Shakespeare, became especially dear to Lilian Baylis, and of course from time to time was with Robert Atkins during the big years of nineteen twenty to nineteen twenty-five. 'Ernest Milton? A very fine actor, Ernest, and with an off-stage manner which suggests that he fucks spiders.' The Cisco Kid. Have a banana.

Highest of high comedies this play *Twelfth Night*; love is found to be a verb in deed when as reader, audience, player we enter into its world, merry as it is sad, lyric as it is boozy, magic, theatrical. The work supplies half the total of Shakespeare's plays to which scholastically I have applied myself. *Julius Caesar* makes up the other half of the sum. The whole being the result of a decision made by my generous former masters at the *Yorkshire Evening News* to send me at the age of seventeen to a commercial college for a bit of a bone-up on English literature. On the paper's time. Hugely kind, that, hugely enjoyable were the studies, and I'm stewing nicely into a huge pink prune as I wallow and ruminate in this here hot tub. One minute more.

Marlon Brando, though, in the film of *Julius Caesar*, playing Mark Antony, by God but that's a performance of rare scale. Subtle or violent or still or cunning, immense energy pumps through every living moment he's on screen. Mighty. At home in a toga, he's at home with the language. Not surprising. His tongue shaped up clean and clear each nuance and complexity in the writing of Tennessee Williams when as Kowalski in *A Streetcar Named Desire* the dialogue flowed from his mouth as though it were crude vernacular merely. An actor, Brando. A master. That Burton bloke's not too dusty, neither. And the range the man has! The Bastard, Coriolanus, Caliban, Hamlet, Toby Belch. Over and over and over again, splendours have come pelting at me these many months from that Old Vic stage. Richard Burton, Michael Hordern, Fay Compton, Claire Bloom, Robert Hardy splendidly leading the company in production after production after production. *The Tempest* was too fussily staged for me, a bit overwrought, but simplicity of staging, of setting, colour and cut of costume chiefly has been the rule, with flowing movement, magnificent speaking, beautiful acting, the traffic of the stage, and *Twelfth Night* was a daisy. Claire Bloom, sad and lovely Viola, feigning malehood as the page Caesario, all legs and swells and sweet sexuality in doublet and hose, when she announced, 'Then Westward ho!' to Olivia, who plainly fancied her as him, the wonderful womanliness in her attempt at a long-legged butch male stride brought each time I saw it a yelp of pure pleasure from her audience. Burton, Sir Toby, burly, rubicund, hugely pleased with his belly, the vigour of his limbs, hell bent but in no hurry, merrily a rascal and at all times religiously pissed, a total transformation from all the other parts he has played. Good on you, Taffy! Well done. Well done, too, Michael Hordern. Prospero, King John, Polonius, every one a winner all right, but his Malvolio, Lordy, a comic masterpiece. The majesty he's shown us, the torment, the sly, ruthless courtier, the lyricism and authority replaced quite by this spindly great lugubrious prat of a pompous arsehole. Giddy from the height above mere mortal man to which stewardship of a noble house has elevated him, hilariously this jack in office rapidly scuttles about, brooking no delay here, no deny there, save for her ladyship, no peer nor match nor fellow anywhere. Gulled into festooning himself in yellow cross garters and to stretching up into a terrible smile the crumples and the dewlaps of his emaciated bloodhound's face, the while rattling out his prattle, why, time and again Mr Hordern has had me weeping with laughter, one among many audiences privileged to have seen his sublimely funny Malvolio. My old teacher at our commercial college said once that in her view excellent performances of *Twelfth Night* and *Julius Caesar* afforded one, both in drama and in comedy, the supreme delight that Shakespearean acting can give. Brando, John Gielgud, James Mason, Louis Calhern, Edmund O'Brien, Deborah Kerr, Greer Garson and all in the flick of *Julius Caesar*; the Old Vic mob fair humming on the green in *Twelfth Night* down the Waterloo Road; you were right, ma'am, true delights, ma'am, supreme ones God wots.

> Three merry men, and three merry men,
> And three merry men are we.
> I in the tub, and thou on the ground,
> And Jack sleeps in the tree.

Kid Milton, though, Cisco's very own uncle Ernest, he played Malvolio in the young years of the century and apparently blew the town down with it. At rehearsal, when it's my turn for a twirl, Hordern-influenced it is true, the moment I open my cakehole up pops Ernest and, looking, sounding, moving as though slowly he is bleeding to death in his shoes, doesn't he give me a demonstration of the one true way in which the part properly can be played? He does. Fascinating it is too, grotesquely comic and strange, but I tell him it's a load of old bollocks. This ignites him. Up he flares. The howling begins. I join in. The windows rattle. Fury, curses, then all subsides, calm returns, back to work we go. Later, the pair of us meet for a jug in the Burglar's Rest. He's given me his novel to read. *To Kiss the Crocodile.* It's bizarre. I love it. Get out of this bath. Stand by to submerge. 'After one more quart of brandy, like a daisy I awake', Pal Joey at the Princess. Marvellous. Bubble, bubble, bubble. Surface. Spume. 'With no bromo seltzer handy, I don't even shake,' Carol Bruce, edible, 'I'm vexed again'. Out, you bastard, out. 'Zip. I was reading Schopenhauer last night. Zip. And I think that Schopenhauer was right.' Out.

---

LIKE ENOUGH the green suit would have been the outfit that we had chosen to wear at Nina Von's spaghetti and meatball bash. Thought of as gaudy by some, my green whistle, whistle and flute, suit, those times, one had merely considered the flowers of the field, of the forest, the skies, the seas, the mountains valleys and the meadows, and then one had smiled at all glum disapprovers wrapped as they had been in browns and blacks and the dark greys, uniform with that decade of dinge and shadows following the '39–45 war. Yes. Chicago had been of a view that in cut in cloth in colour there was in my wardrobe no item in which I had looked more dandy than my green suit, and so let's fancy that that's what I had worn at our frolic in those long years ago. With, of course, the green white and gold tie, another lurid eyeful for the more grimly clad. The jeans would have stood where they had been parked, stiff and grey and standing in a corner of the room.

Other than our regular noshers and bibbers, who would have been our guests that evening? Mikey O.? Possibly. Black-haired, blue-eyed, Welsh-reared Irish stock, a tough little nugget of a chap, practically since the off an easy and a cheerful chum, one whom I'd often met in bars boozers and after-hours shebeens and who had to his considerable astonishment found himself playing Toby Belch in scenes from *Twelfth Night*, all under the tutelage of Mr Ernest Cisco Milton. Mikey, who fancied himself playing hoodlums in gangster movies, on the whole had found the RADA to be a puzzling place, one where the very quantity of classes he had to attend was bothersome to him, where the subjects taught in those many classes seemed to him to be barely comprehensible, where he wondered if all that dancing and fencing and poncing about was in any sort necessary or even useful and where that business of learning lines was irksome to a degree. That he had yet to perform with distinction in a play was a matter for which he didn't care a toss. Getting through the bloody thing and remembering all those bloody lines had been quite enough of a bloody hurdle for him, thank you very much. Still, the academy did have its charms and about the place he had wandered, a mischievous smile on his kisser, bemused but untroubled, at all times chugging with an infectious sense of the absurd. Also, in order to add a cheering jingle to his pockets, Michael had secured a position at a West End playhouse: scene shifter to Her Majesty's Theatre, Haymarket. First for *Paint Your Wagon* and then attending on *The Teahouse of the August Moon*. Yes, that evening perhaps Mikey O. had been with us. Tristles, too. Mr Tristram Jelinek. A flying officer recently demobilized from the RAF, Tristram had joined the merry heap rehearsing *Twelfth Night* and immediately had made a dottily elegant fist of Sir Andrew Aguecheek, impressing me, Uncle Ernie and, had they wit or sense or sight, the rest of the class. Slim, tall, angular, a demeanour scholarly and grave, Tristram Jelinek of course had known of the comical possibilities sounding in his surname but had rather preferred that others should be aware of them, not he. Tristles' chief concern had been getting a surer grip on this business of being a drama student. Surprisingly, he had also a love of revue, and a knowledge of the business which matched his affection for it. Rehearsing two scenes only from *Twelfth Night* had taken not overmuch of our time and in short order Tristram had put himself, Mikey B., Hardtack and me through sophisticated paces, warbling and cavorting to Noël Coward's 'The Stately Homes of England', 'Lord Elderley, Lord Borrowmere, Lord Sickert and Lord Camp.    Our ancient lineage we trace    Back to the cradle of the race    Before those beastly Roman bowmen bitched the local yeomen.' We had performed it in public too, at the RADA annual knees-up. I was Lord Camp. A good actor, Tristram, a gifted man, he doesn't depend on the profession for his wages but relies more on a healthy income from his successful antiques business. If, however, the mood is on him, and the part is right, from time to time he appears on our stages and our screens. Yes. Could have been Jelinek, could have been the wrinkled Pringle.

Pringle, B. Brian. For forty years a distinguished member of our profession, an actor of real worth and a stayer, able for your classics, your burlesques, your moderns, as a young man at the academy in the long ago my friend Brian had had this astonishing knack of appearing always to be deeply worried and elderly. A cheerful sprig, not yet twenty, it had seemed that many years had dug deep grooves, deep whorls onto a countenance burdened with troublesome ailments. And yet. Recently, chance put the pair of us together in one of the dungeons which, it is reported, when open sells food and drink at the Fourth Reich, National Theatre, London. With neither a cellophane sandwich nor a plastic cup of beer available, we found a crack in the cement which led to a joyless balcony overlooking Checkpoint Charlie. As we trudged along and back and back and along the bleakness, chuntering of this and of that and of t'other, what became and remains remarkable to me was the quaint fact that Pringle, who has chalked up a good six tenners, looks now more youthful and more healthy than he did those forty years ago. Fancy. Older now he seems much younger than when he was young for then he seemed old indeed.

To be sure, as professionals, when year after year he grew ever more young, we have enjoyed working together, but never having been together in the same class during our RADA days, old Pringle and I had met only for a jaw or a pint or a fling of the limbs in pubs, at parties, at cafés and often enough in the tavern at Lords cricket ground. The merriest of huts, that old alehouse opening on to the green and sacred acres of that cricket field of all cricket fields, Villiers, J., of course, often was there; Fraser, R., Finney, A., Mikey O., Bob, enthused, wrapt, thrilled among the many scores of men who during the weekdays had in some manner arranged to be absent for a brief while from their places of employment or study and present at Lords for the hour or so before or after the luncheon interval in the hope, say, of a sight of Titmus, F.J., graceful action flighting up the ball, guileful, accurate, deadly; Edrich, W.J., putting the sweet spot of his bat to the cherry and pugnaciously, bravely punching her away either side of the wicket; Compton, D.C.S., our cavalier, hopping down the track to on drive, changing his mind, shaping for a smack through the covers, readjusting his intentions, dropping on to one knee and with his right hand only on the stick, late cutting the ball to where we had stood shouting in the tavern.

Yes, most certainly it could have been ancient Pringle, or Alan Bates or Brian Bedford or Johnny Stride or Frank Finlay, contemporaries of mine at the RADA, young students all who had begun already to excel at the game. A thought. Whatever the worth of

Stanislavski's theories on acting, when applied to playing at cricket, though in principle sound, unless one is a useful bowler or batsman and on song, one will find, alas, the system to be a washout. Do you see, what with Malvolio and my creakings of Lord Camp not taking up all my time, and what with the time that Pocahontas had been given to boss about the women folk of *The House of Bernarda Alba* being limited to a couple of hours a day, little Tiger Lily had thought it fit, as these lashings of surplus time had come our way, that they constructively could be used on a thorough squint at *The Seagull* by Anton Chekov. Up to a point, you will understand, I was game. Up to a point. That the weather was fine, Lords a few stops away only by bus, minutes by taxi, was a snag; Mikey O.'s having a relative who was a wheel in film trade unions and who had given him a card which could get us into cinemas for nothing, that was a snag; the roof, or, if the sun was intolerable, a pint or two in a pub or a drinking shop, a peep at a painting, a frame of snooker at Leicester Square, a stroll through the streets of the city, away from all that acting and prating and buggering about, serious snags; perhaps just as serious a snag, perhaps even more serious, was that as neither Tiger Lily nor I had Russian, the work which she was keen that we examine would be an English version of *The Seagull* by Anton Chekov; a translation. Truly a whopping snag. For me.

The word, you see, for me, not only was in the beginning but also it is my end. As the music and the magic in the arrangement and the meaning of words had lit in me throughout my childhood the spark that would in time light my way to becoming an actor, so now, as it has been throughout my professional life, the sounds of thoughts set down with pen and ink on paper by a master dramatist, the singular diction of his characters, the richness of his stories, the cunning of his plots tell me not only how to play my parts but also at last it is the expression of these thoughts by speech and movement which forms my purpose in being an actor. You may, though you will find me ferociously reluctant in allowing you to do so, take from me my perquisites, my properties, my plush playhouses, all finery, flim-flam and gorgeous show; take them, say I, wreck them should you begrudge my having them, or should you judge them to be cheap, unnecessary, worthless; leave me though, you meaner sods, one entity only and gladly shall I go on: leave me the word.

Came the other day, you could have found me in a chirpy mood, idly flicking through a book on Victorian song. A chapter on the eighteenth-century genesis of some of the songs sung in that period briefly had my attention; I turned a page, there singing up at me in black ink were the words of a song whose tune I have known and heard for most of my life: the Scots dialect words of 'The Flowers of the Forest'. Grief lilts through that lament which pipers play for the dead and for many of us there is a great sadness in the aching skirl of it. The song was written around 1750 by a young Scotswoman, Jane Elliot, a girl of nineteen and after whom my mother had been named. My mood did not remain chirpy, neither did it become glum; for a brief while I was touched, and I was silent.

> At e'en, at the gloaming, nae swankies are roaming
> 'Bout stacks wi' the lassies at bogle to play;
> But ilk ane sits drearie, lamenting her dearie –
> The Flowers of the Forest are a' wede away.

'Words, words, words.'

As to the nature of acting, of playing, of making a character, well, I've read a number of epistemologies on the lark and, such being the way of books purporting to reveal the very essence of the matters about which they have been written, be their subjects, say, dancing or painting or copulating, I have often found in them some merit, clear and demonstrably sensible, much platitude, inflated and decked out in fancy ribbonage, and heaps of effort-fully ground battered old axes. Nor is the present-day practice, pursued with varying degrees of intensity by many of my col-leagues, of scrutinizing at first hand persons with traits, quirks, conditions which match those of the characters whom they are to play on stage or film to be considered any new thing. The better part of two centuries ago, why, Kean, of course, for example, when preparing to play King Lear, was to be seen at Bedlam, wandering and talking with the insane; while, later, Irving's interest in murder and murderers, disturbing enough to his playmates, seems not to have done him any harm when playing that tormented man Mathias, the Jew-slayer in *The Bells*.

Then there's the business of a character's owning special skills such as, perhaps, bus-driving or unicycling, and of players apply-ing themselves to achieve at least an outward show of competence at these arts. Kean, perhaps you didn't know, useful with his dukes from childhood, acquitted himself so well at the nose-busting business of bare-knuckle boxing that, in time, he would give exhibition scraps with professional prizefighters; his mettle and mastery at swordsmanship was such that serving soldiers at arms regularly invited him back to their barracks where he would fight with them in private bouts at épée and at rapier, buttoned, to be sure; and the triple hornpipe, skipped up on a slack wire, can be counted among his many bye-the-bye accomplishments.

An observer, Ned Kean, a listener, acuity of both eye and ear sharp, one time in a pub he was asked by a young friend how he studied. Answering that he was studying there and then, he pointed to a chap who although indeed heavily pissed and with scarce a leg to put under him was yet somehow arranging himself for an attempt at getting from the bar to the door, and Kean said to his chum that the secret of playing drunkenness was in the endeavour to stand upright when it was impossible to do so. True.

Those words turned the trick nicely for me when playing Alan Swann in *My Favourite Year* and Jeff in *Jeffrey Bernard is Unwell*. That and quite a lot of not necessarily related practice.

What, however, in my view cannot be overstated is my proficiency at riding a racing camel. That's a jolly caper. That hadn't been on the syllabus at the RADA. That's a feeling no seeker of the novel sensation should miss. There's woeful bumping to be had nine feet up on the hump of one of those brutes, and when the great beast blunders about at thirty miles an hour, as the wooden saddle first hammers into disbelieving buttocks you may be sure that if the upright nail-like pommel at its front doesn't ram itself into your breastbone its brother at the back will certainly crack into your spine, and the splintering of bone, the rending of flesh will be enough, surely, to satisfy the heart of the most sincere appreciator of bloodsport.

Flying a Grumman seaplane had its moments of thrilling strangeness. Heaving back at full throttle the three-foot-long steel joystick to take off and to propel the mighty machine up into the air had proved a manoeuvre that I could successfully master, as had buggering about in circles through the wide blue yonder in the monster, but putting back the hugely mad great animal on to the dip, do you see, that, so I'm told, had been an exercise which I did not manage smoothly to conduct. It was, a witness told me, as though he had seen some demiurge playing at ducks and drakes with a winged and roaring double-decker blue bus. For my part, yes, there had been an unevenness about matters, an unusual lurching about and goutings up of water but, really, what otherwise could one have anticipated? You may admit that at best the sea seems to be an unlikely choice of stuff on which to land an aeroplane. It was ever frisky.

Quite a number of Chinamen were spilled out to try a mouthful of the Salisbury Road, Hong Kong, too, that time when I had been learning how to pull a rickshaw, but what of that, but what of that, these are merely examples of the handling of properties and the simulation or even mastery of difficult abilities which during our professional lives all us actors and actresses at whiles must learn how to do; what the more sententious of acting theorists will tell you are our 'externals'. Bollocks. Is one to consider the actress opposite whom one is playing as an external? The play in print on the page, the stage on which one struts, the costume and wig one is wearing, the American accent one has assumed, the paying customers of the audience, the theatre in which one is playing; these, too, are they externals? Dig up dead Joe Ferrer; tell him that the endlessly long nose he stuck on to play Cyrano was an external; and the camera as well before which matchlessly he played his part. About as external as Joe DiMaggio's bat when he played at the ball game, or Louis Armstrong's cornet when he blew his jazz. Internal, external, thinking, reacting, interacting, feeling, handling, moving, speaking, timing, listening, connecting, projecting: when acting all these factors indissolubly are one. This I began to learn at drama school, began to understand more fully during years in repertory theatre, and as my private study became more efficient, my study of technique more mature, the business of simply getting on with it more customary, with increasing skill I began to realize the oneness to this acting and could with more confidence put it down at rehearsal for performances in a playhouse or before a camera in a studio.

All for the delight of our paying customers, there are those souls among us professional actors and actresses who, in seeking a bright light of insight into the beings whom they will act on our lighted stages, in the hope of inducing, unearthing, of gouging out from within themselves emotional and intellectual veracities which will fit pat with the parts they are to play, often do set themselves to introspective labours, to complex exercises of debate, of improvisation, to the erection of a psychological scaffolding that will support conscious quests to seek out sources from the subconscious mind. Fine and dandy, say I, if those of my

colleagues minded to undertake these troublesome approaches
find they assist them in a more confident attitude to the work and
believe that they have found in these practices true allies in the
terrifying battle of making contact with an audience. All can be
well indeed so long as a resolutely hard distinction has been made
between the prattle and excitements of amateur classroom drama
and the exacting grind of rehearsing a play in a set limit of time
for presentation in the professional market, for it is a distinction
complete as that between a child at play with its spinning top and
a highly trained competing athlete hearing the bell for the last
lap. So, set yourself to whatever scrutinies and examinations of
yourself and your part that you list, you players who cleave to such
bents, but then leave that work in the study where properly it
belongs and go to rehearse dead letter perfect in that part, waste
no one's time and be ready to combine over and over again with
your fellows in the repetition of a dramatist's work as practice
before the public appearance of that play. That is the proper
business of rehearsal on a stage; it is no occasion for dabblings in
the inexact science of the nature, functions, and phenomena of
the human soul and mind. The muses are lovely elusive bitches,
and though memory is their mother, their father is time and it
concentrates the mind wonderfully to realize that in two weeks'
time one opens in Brighton. As to the question, what is acting? It
is my pleasure to remind you of the words spoken by Fats Waller
in reply to a woman who had asked him what was swing. Mr
Waller said: 'If you has to ask, madam, you ain't got it.'


Green sprigs of notions only, in those young student days, had
been sprouting up in my mind, on acting, on plays, on playhouses;
nor on matters theatrical was I even halfway sure of any damned
thing at all. In truth, other than feeling that I could last for ever,
I was fierce short of dead certainties on practically any subject
whatsoever. In common with the barometers of Ireland, change

was my only constant and, God Almighty, but my life had been tumbling about in dozens of directions.

Fingernails stained a filthy brown by darkroom chemicals, I had begun my working life as an apprentice photographer on a provincial newspaper. Night-school, optics, fieldwork, and no sooner was I getting the hang of this clicking of snaps but my interests shifted; tolerance from my employers with the heavy woollen Yorkshire voices and I was encouraged to become a Pooh-Bah of the paper, now with the sports, now with the features, now at day school, now in the news room, now in the library, now with a camera, now with the cartoonist, the commercial editor, the engravers, circulation, sales, compositors, printing presses. Then mutinous and unhappy in a sailors' barracks in Pompey, opaque of brain in my studies at a naval school snuggling deep in a rural southern county, with a trudge through the pigsty and a hole in the hedge my illicit way in and out of that baffling establishment; motor torpedo boats, a survey ship, merrily on the *Montplonk*, mother ship to a submarine flotilla, big seas, foreign ports, Civvy Street, steeplejack, demolition man, amateur actor, vagrant, Cod War, corvette, Icelandic waters, a student in London, an academic year almost done. Physically also I had changed a good deal. Less than two years ago there had been thirteen and a half stones of me packed into a burly lad standing five feet ten inches; one hundred and eighty-two pounds of mustang on the hoof. At twenty-one, my height had stretched up four more inches and I had become six foot two of apprentice actor weighing in at about a hundred and seventy pounds, twelve stone and a bit of elongated me wondering much as to what this acting caper was all about.

Blind instinct had been my guide, one who led me into no grievous wrong, into a good deal of what would prove happily to be right and on whose silent counsel I had put much faith but, wouldn't you know, it was that gentleman with the green whiskers, GBS, long ago under the stairs, at present and forever goading away in my mind, who, with vision and with words, pointed me in a direction which immediately I knew I wanted to go. Shaw had written: 'No frontier can be marked between drama and history or religion, or between acting and conduct, nor any distinction made between them that is not also the distinction between the masterpieces of the great dramatic poets and the commonplaces of our theatrical seasons.' Between acting and conduct no frontier can be marked. Yes. Off a short-pitched viciously fast lifter, five and a half ounces of corkwood and leather cricket ball has just thudded into one's ribs. Jesus. Now, it's pointless pretending that it didn't hurt, it did, the point is how next one conducts oneself. Whether rubbing the cracked bone, cursing the bowler and the God that made him, or disdaining to acknowledge either the pain or its perpetrator, what is of supreme importance lies in the composure with which one faces the next ball. One cannot feign, nor counterfeit, nor simulate composure, one either is composed or one is not. It is a conscious act. It is a way in which one has chosen to conduct oneself. Yes. Just as when a boy I would give at least three accents to the way in which I spoke. One for school, one for play, and one for home. Yes. The manner of a teacher, a doctor, a lawyer, a priest, a policeman, a judge, an employer, an employee. The rituals of courtship. Sergeant at the door. Sir Kenneth in his study. Father. Mother. Son. Daughter. Yes. Bad conduct, good conduct, conduct unbecoming, distinguished conduct, the whole world acts the actor, a face to meet the faces, how are you in yourself? Oh, yes. That how when set at tasks or in the varying circumstances and situations of our lives we choose in one sort or another to conduct ourselves should have been by Bernard Shaw thus linked in kind to acting a part in a play, came to me as solid ground on which to walk, to trot, to run. Obvious, you might think. True. True is it also that the obvious often is most difficult to spot and although Shaw's words on the matter did not come as a blazing revelation, they yet held to my mind a quality kin to a Jim Joyce epiphany, a sight into the 'whatness' of a subject, a glimpse which for me connected acting not only with the arts of, say, singing or dancing or music-making but also with that protean capacity we all have of striving to adapt our personalities into fitting whatever positions or duties or needs that in our lives we may encounter. Of course, there are some better than others at conducting these shifting manifestations of the human spirit; a few of whom even take up acting as a profession.

For all that and all that, though, for me the beginning and the middle and the end of all one's performances are to be found in the writer's text. All good writing, be it in a poem, a history, a guide book, is alive on the page and talks to me. When the work is a play, I hear the voices of its people, I inhabit their persons, live in them throughout their conflicts, interactions, divisions, reconciliations, and above all know which is my part almost from the moment he opens his mouth to say his first words or puts himself to his first deed. How come? You will find me with Sir Andrew Aguecheek on that score, for as that dotty knight found he had no exquisite reason for wishing to set about a certain action but felt that he had reason good enough, so is it with me and the part which I know to be mine: it is less my choosing the part to play, more the part choosing me to play him. Nor is it given to me to have much say in the business. A part is born in the mind of an author, forms in his being, travels down his arm, into his pen, transforms itself into ink, is set down in writing on to a page, and sits there, alert, waiting. Along come I, pick up a play, read the scenes, the narrative, the argument, hear the voice and see the actions of a particular character, the words formed in ink flow up from the page, through my eyes, into my mind, become recognizably the image of a man, he insists that I give him human form, human speech, and a few weeks later, if all goes well, I find myself acting him on a lighted stage. That simple; that difficult. Also, there is much more sweat in these processes than there is magic; but there is magic; actors and dramatists well understand this, well enough to know never to explain what can only be understood; well enough to know these glimpses of magic will be found only in much sweat.

And yet. Somewhere deep and deep within me, disguised as an old man or a cripple or a washerwoman, Robin Hood steps out from the greenwood daringly to walk around the pathways of the town, while all unknown to me, joyful, dangerous, wicked, Loki fits on my soul to any size he may wish and knows by the fading smell of rotting teeth and hot iron that Merlin the shapechanger has passed by.


As to the matter of reading, examining, discussing, with Tiger Lily, a version in English of a Russian play, *The Seagull*, by Anton Chekov, well, to be sure, there had been snags; the more whopping of which had lain heavily in the hard fact that the work was a translation and that this, even accepting the efforts of the translator to have been both commendable and worthy, effectively would have excluded me from the sounds of the dramatist's voice. That the voice in which Chekov spoke was Russian, and thus would have been incomprehensible to me, had been in my view, in those days, neither a great deal here nor not a lot there: it was the thing itself that I would have wished to hear, the nature of the poet speaking through his characters as they acted out the drama of his plays. Translations, it had seemed to me, may give us the sense of the words spoken in another language, but they cannot give us their tongue. It is what is meant by the words that we hear, not the sounds of their saying. But still. 'We should so render the original that the version should impress the people for whom it is intended just as the original impresses the people for whom it, the original, is intended.' Thus quoth the Poe, E. A. With you all the way, Edgar, with you all the way. However, many there are, and have been, who vehemently will gainsay us. Think of the Bible. Awful fusses were made over the translations into English of that book. 'Thy navel is like a round goblet, which wanteth not liquor: thy belly is like an heap of wheat set about with lilies. Thy two breasts are like two young roes that are twins.' Well, if those words are only limp or impudent or irreverent echoes of the ancient Hebrew, one can only surmise that the clay or the skin or the papyrus on which the original had been set down must have been fair fireproof. True is it too, old Poe, that the one who will render that original in such a wise that its language impresses the reader, the audience as forcefully as did the language of the original must be such a one whose poetry matches the voice of the original poet. Divinely inspired?

Whatever, no such being had set his or her hand to this English version of *The Seagull*, a comedy in four acts by Anton Chekov or Chehov or Tchekov, the play to which Tiger Lily had proposed we give our one hundred per cent attention. It is true that I have forgotten how the poor sod's surname had in English been rendered; it is true too that I have forgotten who it was did the rendering; it is also true that I have not forgotten how the translator chose to render some of the dialogue: Trepliov, of Trigorin who doesn't fancy fighting a duel with him, 'When he was told I intended to challenge him, his honour failed to prevent him from cowardly behaviour. He's leaving. Ignominious flight!' Trigorin, the writer, to Nina, whom he fancies something horrible and has arranged to meet in Moscow, 'Oh, how happy I am to think that we shall be seeing each other soon! (*She leans her head on his breast.*) I shall see these wonderful eyes again, this indescribably beautiful, tender smile, these sweet features, the expression of angelic purity!' Ignominious flight. Expression of angelic purity. Exact literal translations from the Russian of Tchekof or Chehov or Chekov they may well be but to my mind they have all the urgency, passion and soul of a Speak-your-Weight machine.

Apart from which, why should I yet again be bolted into a classroom for yet another session of yammering and staggering about and acting all over the place when for yet months and

months and months these doings have been my daily fare? Two
slabs of Malvolio and *Twelfth Night* have been given to me by the
academy as my portion and, believe me, my little sizzler from
Chicago, they do demand the best chewing I can muster. And
think, do, of the alternatives. Poised in my stance over a meadow
of green baize, sink a red, sink a colour, sink a red, sink a colour,
smoothly my cue follows through the struck white ball, sink a red,
sink a colour. Or. Sink a pint of porter, black and foaming, the
ale when it is yellow, sink it down. 'Will you lend me your wife for
an hour and a quarter?   Oh, the brown and the yellow ale.    I
said I will do anything that is fair.    Oh, the brown and the yellow
ale.' Blue smoke, beer, tobacco, chuckling voices, quiet, cool,
'Another?' 'Just the one.' Or. Should the sun not be a torment,
boiling up the asphalt of the roads, a saunter through the leafy
squares of Bloomsbury, a peep up on the RADA roof to see
what's blooming there for, yes, the flowers are made of woman-
kind. Grim, indeed, the togs that men do wear in the summertime
but not those worn by the bonny lasses. No. Pink and petals and
bunches of colours wrap around the buds and stems and bodies
of the women in their muslin, cotton, linen, bloomy frocks of
summer. Yoicks! 'Happy little hunt boom boom ting horn.' 'Tis
only a roam through gardens, Chicago, only a sniff and a savour
of blossoms, an eyeful of desirable, pickable, pluckable dear and
dainty daisies and why not? Why so? Minnehaha, pray, who is
leaving whom? Is it I who as summer is a-coming in shortly will be
a-going out? Answer no, Pocahontas, answer no. Here will I be
found where we met a year ago. You it is who will be pissing off
back whence you came. You know that. I know that. Both spoken
and tacit we both know that our loving friendship will have
ending. So. What harm if I prowl about and seek out a flower or
two to gaze on when you are gone.

Meat and drink to moral rhetoricians a union of man and
woman such as ours; leave it to them to suck and guzzle on for we
are matched equals and so are wealthy. A hell of a lot of

cuddlesome attraction for one another, certainly, but other than that hell of a lot it was only great to find someone who disliked the same people I did. No better foundation, surely, than that for a fine friendship. Why, from time to time probably we disliked each other somewhat; we are so constituted by nature that we couldn't all the time possibly approve of each other. Sensitive of one another's faults, you seldom hesitated to whisper in my ear the odd disagreeable truth, nor did I fail to mutter out to you aught of your ways and manner which irked me, and in consequence of which our affection for each other grew and we liked one another the more. Yes. What we have can never be lost. No. Vicious right jab you have, though, no telegraphing, unexpected, sudden, straight from the shoulder, pop, right on the mince pie. Eye. Twice I've carted about bright shiners. Wary, now, am I. Shall be till you leave. Which shortly you will be doing. Yes. Opinion in politics, say, religion, literature, when we differed, well, it wasn't important. You have no winning ways in which you try to please me, nor I you, we are little concerned whether we please each other or not, certainly we don't try wangling one another, and so we know much pleasure.

Sublimely ridiculous moments, too, we've known. The eclipse of the sun? Biblical. Perfect, that time, to suggest to me that I convert to Judaism. 'Sun, stand thou still upon Gibeon.' Would you have had Joshua make him a sharp knife and circumcise me upon the hill of foreskins? You agreed, though, as you sat on the pavement sobbing with laughter, that to sit down by the waters of Babylon, and to weep as he remembered Zion, might be considered an odd thing to do by a chap whose name was O'Toole. Jealous? Of course you've made me jealous, young men easily are made jealous and I'm only a man, and young, and easily made jealous. Consider that fucking Norbottle, or whatever his name was, that spy from the windy city, out on the town with him you tottered, dolled up in your dainties and buzzing like a bee. True, that what with his being a former serviceman and all gave him access to a special store in London where goodies could be bought for astonishingly little bread and that you returned home bearing bottles of booze and cigarettes by the carton but, still and all, I wanted to bite off your nose and then cheerfully break that bastard's face. My tootling around town with the beauty queen from Sweden had those black twinklers of yours go green as seaweed though, didn't it? One thumping great Nordic nymph in my view was fair exchange for bleeding Norbottle, liquor and smokes and all, but that's not it, Chicago, that's not it. From our early days right to these our last few weeks before you board that boat and we shall part, it has been and is and perhaps ever will be your calm and smiling certainty at all times that in me there lives a true artist and actor. That's it, Chicago, that's it. And just think. There's you, a passionate interest in theatre since girlhood now informed by years of study and knowledge and practical experience. There's me, quirks of chance, of happenstance tumbling me on to the boards, and who only in this last year has become as much as a regular theatregoer. It both amused and bewildered you, didn't it, sweetheart, when first you found that this bloke whom you thought did the business very well had indeed not the ghost of a notion about the business he was doing and who until fairly recently had entertained no thoughts of ever doing the business at all.

Yes, occasionally I would go to the theatre but I went only when the play and the players were reckoned to be special, for, do you see, jazz and vaudeville and cinema were nearer my mark, little one, and boxing and big bands and singers, cricket, comedians, rugby. That's changed. Without deserting any of my old loves, I'm now onions deep in plays, actors, acting. Yes. And throughout this change, there or thereabouts, watchful, critical, helpful, there's been you. A word, a gesture, a look and often when matters were going astray you've set me right again. True, over the last two years I've had minor successes, had encouragement, won a scholarship to this RADA, have been from time to time led to believe that, all things considered, given the will and the wish and the want, there was a possibility, with luck, of my, perhaps, having enough talent maybe to consider the idea of chancing my arm and giving this acting a try. But you. From our beginning. Never a doubt. That's bred in me the beginnings of a confidence that could increase, a trust in my abilities that might flourish, a self-belief that may endure.

For my part, well, I did give you Eli Wallach for your birthday. Had they been in my gift, I would have given you one or some or all or any of the many other actors and actresses whom we had seen and admired act, but I wasn't able to wangle it. No, not Alec Guinness or Wilfred Lawson in *The Prisoner*, Paul Scofield, Gladys Cooper, Mary Hinton, Pamela Brown in *Question of Fact*, Sam Wanamaker, Rene Asherson, Frederich Valk, Diane Cilento, George Coulouris in *The Big Knife*, no, nor Dorothy Tutin in *I Am a Camera*, Robert Morley or Wilfred Hyde White in *Hippo Dancing*, Diana Wynyard, Robert Fleming, Ernest Thesiger in *Marching Song*, A. E. Matthews, Marie Löhr in *The Manor of Northstead*, and, alas, I couldn't give you one member of the cast of *The Dark Is Light Enough*, not John Moffatt or Peter Bull, Hugh Griffith, Peter Barkworth, Margaret Johnstone, Edith Evans, Peter Sallis, unable, too, to come up with Trevor Howard or Gwen Ffrangcon-Davies or Robert Eddison or Esmé Percy from that English version of *The Cherry Orchard*.

You will allow though, surely, that as a gift Eli Wallach came rare and unexpectedly. Mikey O.'s doing, really, for he'd sneaked me in backstage at Her Majesty's and there from the wings I'd had, as it were, a scene-shifter's eye-view of Mr Wallach peerlessly performing the part of Sakini in *The Teahouse of the August Moon*. After the curtain, Mikey had introduced me to him and a good-humoured, tolerant and a kind man Mr Eli Wallach had turned out to be. Having listened to me tell of my being a drama student, of having a girlfriend with a birthday coming up, of how as a celebration I was going to take you to see his play, and of my wondering if after the show we might knock on his dressing room door in the hope that he might say hello to you, Eli chuckled his merry chuckle and said we would be welcome. Came the night, you enjoyed the play, thought Eli was superb and afterwards we drifted towards the stage door where Mikey was waiting. Through the door we went and, saying nothing, I steered you down a corridor, up a flight of stairs, came to a door, knocked, the door opened, there was Eli Wallach. 'Hi, honey,' said Eli to you, eyes brimful with fun, 'I'm your birthday present. Hope you enjoy me.'

All right, Baby, all right, here I come, lay it on me, it's all for my own good, that's understood, this our scrutiny of *The Seagull* by Chekov or Chehov or even Tchekoff, better for me by far than my lounging at no cost at all on a comfy seat in a plush and fuggy cinema, puffing a cigarette while deluding myself into a belief that the Hollywood trash flickering up there on the screen is hugely enjoyable, it has to be rubbish, I realize that, so let's get down to a serious inspection of a dramatic work of worth, one which will endure, this here *The Seagull,* in an English translation, yes by Christ, oh, let's to it in this boiling RADA classroom, yes, my sweet little Alice Capone, by inviting me to join you in this exciting enterprise, you really could have chosen no better man. Selah.

Now, you should I think know that preparatory to this generous and unexpected effort to move me up a further ratchet on the evolutionary cog-wheel of my education as an actor, I had made it my business to seek out solid counsel on both the playwright and the play. For, do you see, O'Liver had acquired a Russian poet with a cleft palate, name of Vinoskolnikof, 'snear enough, who, in an English of a remarkable sort, emphatically had marked my card on the author and his work. That the malformation in Vinoskolnikof's cakehole did cause him when he spoke to utter out his matters in an amazing twang of great noise which in fierce bursts of metallic clatter sprang from out his nostrils, in no way had deflected me from scooping up the gist of his drift. It may be true to say however that, uncomprehended, the odd phrase or two had exploded about my head but, if you will be good enough to bear in your mind's ear that the nearest Vinoskolnikof could get to pronouncing 'O'Liver' or 'Peter O'Toole' was 'Nolly' and 'Eater No Nool', you will have a hint of the plot. So, homework done, a vital source tapped, I was ready to contribute in any way that I could to this our examination of a Russian play.

You'll be well aware, says I, I fancy, to herself, sitting pretty at a table, all earnest and bossy and luscious, that this cove Chekov, when late in his little short life he coughed up blood and took to writing plays, made sure that one facet of the many that his genius as a writer owned was put to singular use: his capacity to fashion human speech into an art form; to scratch down dialogue whose apparent simplicity yet was woven thick with the complex stuff out of which the people who spoke it were made; simple speech, right enough, but shot through with quirks of tongue, stray remarks, the casual, the odd, the unusual, revealing the deeps and the shallows and the unique self of the individual who was speaking; diction so felicitous that be he or she or they the speakers peasants or professional class or serfs or servants or bourgeoisie or upstarts or landed gentry their positions in society of late-nineteenth-century Russia would after a couple of sentences immediately be identifiable; more remarkable still, no clutch of words, no matter how straightforward and unadorned the words, could it be imagined coming out of the mouth of anyone other than the character whose words they were. Rare that, my honey, my Hebrew humdinger, ripe lips stuck shut as I rattle on, rich and rare, and our not speaking his language means that we are deprived, really, outcast from Chekov's world. The cardboard sandwiches that this version in English gives us to chew are intolerable. That's what I have read on the subject. That's what, with extravagant emphasis, I have been by Russians informed. That, baby, is about the entire size of it. Now, it's three p.m.; afternoon closing time; that means the back of Momma Fischer's will be opening; shall we trot round for a sip of something against the dehydration?

Fair play to Chicago, the broad wouldn't budge an inch, not a fraction, nor, I reflect, had my mouth music seriously fluttered a feather on her, had been, in fact, I further reflect, in some wise probably anticipated by her. Possibly, it seems to me now, positively welcomed by her. Yes. Hip to my ways, it is more than a likelihood that the clever cow had led me on to let me empty myself of my contents and when all my matter was shot had deftly but firmly and resolutely sandbagged me. Thud. Infuriating, you will agree, to have been so used, to know that one had been a dope, a sucker, a patsy. Always wary of that right cross, swift, meaty, body behind it, I had been ready with my parry when she had unbalanced me quite by not only leaving the punch unthrown but by quietly agreeing with me that our not speaking Chekov's lingo and all effectively had excluded us from the very pith and soul of the play, that we had been left with only these, at best, inadequate English paraphrases of his characters' speech, which was a damned shame but hardly the fault of Chekov, and, so to speak, the husk of the work, the frame of the play, its structure. Was it beyond the scope of a pair of dumbos like us to put aside our players' disappointment at being unable properly to act any of the roles and just to content ourselves, you know, like make that we were kind of serious students of drama and just take a light-hearted peek at the carpentry of the play, the way the guy had shaped and laboured and built his work? How had I put it? Yeah. Facet. Good word, on the money, facet. Did I think it would be a frigging great yawn to bother ourselves with another facet of the guy's genius as a writer, his craftsmanship, the way in which he had constructed the play's shape? She was cool, if form was of no interest to me, only content, groovy, let's split the scene, go to Momma Fischer's, have a drink, and beef about what bad shit it was not speaking Russian and all. Appalling, isn't it? The word is not too strong. One is appalled to recall that practically half a century ago one had been so toyed with, manipulated and bamboozled.

Thus were the serpentine ways of Miss Wrigley from Chi that from afternoon until late in the evening, deeply into the fiction that we were examining structure, I found myself wholly engrossed in being Konstantin Trepliov, Chekov's febrile young suicide, my naivety exploited so fully and so ruthlessly that any number of times throughout the four acts I tossed aside the stiff, unbudging translation and grunted out improvised approximations of what a young failure at love, at writing, at manhood even might utter in his agonies, manoeuvred into these excesses with a chilling artfulness and banjaxed utterly by that merciless young woman.

Came the following day, my delusions intact, believing still that we were considering the carpentry of the play, I was giving Trigorin a walloping, Boris Trigorin, Chekov's famous, obsessive writer, and the pair of us were inspecting the long scene at the close of the second act in which the author character speechifies at length, prompted to it by the posh and lovely young Nina. Why, says the Hopi to me, do you think he chooses to talk about his compulsion to write? Don't question fiction, sweetheart, me, just accept it, unless the fiction is sloppy, clumsy, badly done, then it becomes questionable. If, however, my mother cut my father's throat, well, then it's altogether probable that I would ask her why. Should she tell me, 'Because I was fed up with the ratty old bastard,' I should have to ask myself whether or not I thought that was a satisfactory explanation. If not, well, my old mum and I could go on prattling about it for hours. But this isn't a police station we're in, nor a coroner's inquest are we at, nor are we under oath as witnesses in a court of bleeding law, we're just a couple of green mummers prodding this old Cossack Comedy about. OK, says she, all prickly now, a slight flare to the nostrils, could mean the right hand, no, determination, composure, articulate speech. What then, she says, when Trigorin tells Nina, goes she on, of having his own moon, as an image of his obsession with writing, write, write, write, is the subtext of his speech? Don't give me any subtext, sweetness, subtext me no subtexts, I've heard that word used dozens of times in this last year, used, mind you, as though the word exists, there is no such word as fucking subtext, no dictionary I know entertains it, whatever number of parrots use it the word does not exist. You know, Pete, you're so brave, such a gallant defender of the Queen's English, your valour gives me goosebumps; give us a kiss, me; nuts, she, more, it's only jargon, it's only actors' shorthand; it's cant, me; OK, how's about undertow, below the surface of what he's saying; fair, say I, and the words for that undertow are the drama; OK, the drama, what do you think is Trigorin's objective?; objective?; objective; do you mean what is he up to?; kinda; he's up to having Nina fair pasted on to the dogshelf with himself stapled to her and giving her a ferocious seeing-to that's what, in my view, he's up to; your view, crass as you are, crudely as you put it, may, in the long term, be a correct one, but I was thinking in more subtle, immediate and realizable acting terms, this being the Royal Academy of Dramatic Art, you should excuse my folly; give us a kiss; nuts; give us a kiss; buy me a drink; certainly; read this, Pete, tell me what you think.

*An Actor Prepares.* Constantin Stanislavski.


Later, Lord love you, later. Fancy.

'Well?'

'Unreadable.'

No. Anger came there none from my dusky little plum at this my red-eyed and mind-punished assessment of the work in question, not a flicker, rather from her tasty lips there followed a short discourse flowing with that serenity and reasonableness which one may note in those blessed with a faith wedded fast to revealed and unshakeable truths. Stanislavski, purred she, when labouring at his book, never had been so immodest as to believe that he would present us with a deathless work of literature, not at all, far from it, and a scornless phooey to all who had set about his work hoping to find in it matter so banal as to be considered merely a 'good read'. Such error in approach was, of course, as understandable as it was quaint but one rapidly should be disabused of such a sentimental expectation. In *An Actor Prepares*, Constantin Stanislavski has done what no worker in the theatre ever before had attempted to do, which was to codify and to systematize what we actors and actresses actually do when we study a character for performance in a play. She would allow, condescended that dear little chick, that by avoiding the textbook angle, by structuring the book in a way that had an immediacy and a pertinence to all who studied acting, his device of creating a fictitious drama teacher conducting classes with a group of fictitious drama students did, at times, seem to ramble a little, even, occasionally, appearing on some points to be inconclusive, but so trivially what? This rejection of arid rules and regulations in favour of a more pliant, a more human approach, where we are invited to participate in the dynamic of the pupil–teacher process, allows us, when we identify a specific problem, to set about solving that problem in its exact context by working it out in parallel with an equivalent problem which we will find the students and the teacher addressing in *An Actor Prepares*. There's one hell of a difference between being rigid and being exact in your preparation but you have to identify the precise area which is proving difficult before the book can be of value to you, it's no use just picking it up, settling down in an armchair and expecting to be entertained and informed, you have to know what you need, know what you lack, the approach has to be methodical and you have to work.

For the first time in the whole year my sweetheart was being pompous; pompous, smiling, softly speaking gibberish and in a manner so superior that it made mortal me want to cough.

'What do you think?'

'I think that those unfortunate students Grisha, Sonya, Kostya,

Masha, Larry, Curly, Mo should one by one visit Commissar
Tosstoff—'

'Tortsov—'

'That Larry, Grisha, Curly should one by one visit Commissar
Torstov—'

'Director Tortsov—'

'That Mo, Masha, Sasha, should one by one visit Director
Torstoff and hit him on the head with a hammer. No, baby, 's my
turn. It near broke my poor brain it did, trying to read this
bookful of gobshite's tosh and I've just now listened to you
burbling away as though all you said made perfect and holy sense.
It doesn't, honey, it doesn't, and it smacks nastily of Looselips
Tosteroff's blatherings in this here King Farouk.'

'King Farouk?'

'Book.'

'That's not a good rhyme.'

'It is in Dublin.'

'Groovy.'

He's a lulu that Looselips, isn't he, and you won't find him
using ten words when a hundred and ten will do. And is there
anything that the great pillock doesn't know? Is there? Any
fucking thing at all? And in his omniscience he never fails to be
an ill-mannered crucifying bore, does he? 'When I ope my lips let
no dog bark' isn't in it. Hark! 'I know, unquestionably, that that
was a great mistake for you have just admitted a mass of incoher-
ence and lack of logical sequence to your actions.' What does that
mean? That in his great view some poor sod got something wrong
and can't explain why he did so? Why should he? What's with all
these explanations, explications, dialectics, scrap-heap philosophical speculations? It's less sensible backstage counsel than it is
Young Marxist Association gabfest, which, coming from Stalin's
Soviet Union, shouldn't, I suppose, surprise one. It's a theatrical
fucking Show Trial. Talk, talk, talk, talk, natter, natter, natter, it
would drive a man stark raving sausage. Painting, loving, writing,

you can stifle the life out of anything with too much talking about it and it's only acting that's on the menu here. Acting, mumming, farting about in disguise. To act. To do. So let's have more action and less chunter. So, please, spare me the sight of that ghastly book and the sound of all that canting codswallop and squeeze me out some of Looselips' points, if he has any.

Again and again fair play and fair play to herself. Realizing, as I think she must have done, that what for her had been an extension only of the years and years of all her study all her care, for me had been a year of tumbling among new notions, new activities, new sensations, had been, indeed, a year which had seen me stumbling into a completely new life, the darling chose to address me in the tone and the manner with which, one imagines, the merciful and saintly do speak to the heretical and the godless. It is also possible, although far from certain, that my sweetheart had realized that little was left of the third month of the cricket season and yet here was I stuck in this poxbottle of a drama school. Ever articulate, Pocahontas that time talked to me in a way so calm so sweet so fluent that her poise and purpose drew from me the best of what was left of my sorely rattled attention. Thus. It was true, she fluted grave and quietly, that Stanislavski in the person of Tortsov often was verbose, was arrogant, was infuriatingly repetitive, discursive, often laboured points that were simple and easily understood by anyone with an imagination, a sensibility open and aware but nevertheless, went she on so hushed so holy, he had selected and emphasized a handful of points, clean, clear, valid and strong, which were constructive, were practical and which could be of a positive use not only in acting but in many other areas of human endeavour.

'The gist, baby, the gist, for Christ's sake bung us the gist.'

'Relaxation. Tension in the neck, the throat, really screws up the voice. We can learn consciously to relax the muscles binding around the vocal cords. Same with the face, the shoulders, the hips. Name it. We just concentrate on specific zones of the body and by relaxing those zones we make sure our muscles are not strangling us or physically inhibiting gesture, expression, movement, the free play of emotions and the frigging blood supply.'

'Nothing worse, right enough, than sitting padded up in the pavilion. Next wicket down and you're in. Made a duck last match so you're due a score. That, or you find you'll not be picked. Dropped like hot shit. Lads look set but you never can tell. It's cricket. Funny old game. Blimey, that was streaky! Got away with it, though. Jammy bastard. Twenty minutes to tea. Hang on lads, do. Don't fancy going in now. There's a crack on this bat below the splice. Needs taping. Tense. Yes. Tension. Mouth dry. Quick sip from the tap? Yes. Where's the tap? Howzat? Mother of Jesus, he's gone. Castled. You're in. Fifteen minutes to tea. Anyone seen a right glove? It's at those moments, sweetheart, that one could do with being able to relax every tensed-up zone in the body that you've ever heard of. "Middle and leg, please, umpire." There can be no doubt, lovey, that as far as relaxation is concerned Stanislavski is absolutely sound. Next.'

'Concentration. He has Tortsov set up a pretty nifty light display in order, literally, to illuminate for the students a number of areas on which, during rehearsal or performance, actors must learn to concentrate their attention. For example: what Tortsov calls Solitude in Public. He has a lamp throw a bright pool of light around one of the students. In effect this isolates the guy from the others but the guy feels great, he feels special, he feels he can more easily observe objects and communicate with his buddies because he's doing it from his own exclusive circle of attention, circle of concentration.'

'Circle of concentration. I like that. Yes. There you are, do you see, you've been at the crease for, what, thirty minutes? You've chalked up only a dozen or so but, remember, the first ten are the most important runs you'll make in an innings and, anyway, by blocking when it's been there or thereabouts and prodding away the loose ones for ones and twos, you've knocked the shine off her and seen off their quick. Right. You're set. Feet are moving nicely, you're seeing her round and red and big, the stick's swinging sweetly up and down the line, timing's coming, you're middling her, it's the moment to start giving it slipper, smack a few through the covers and there are acres of vacant pasture on the on-side for anything straying down leg. It's all down to luck, picking the right one, and, above all, concentration now. Circle of concentration. Standing in the middle of an imaginary circle. Concentrating. It's growing on me. Between deliveries, do you see, it's usually my habit to shift off my stance, plod a couple of paces towards square leg, gaze at the green of the grass, mutter to myself, "You're here to bat. Bat, bat, bat. Nothing but bat," and then back I go, set my feet, wiggle the toes, and be ready to face the next ball. Oh, one gets used to their keeper telling you filthy jokes as the bowler starts his run-up, the quiet non-stop commentary coming from the slips on one's appearance, probable sexual proclivities and the lamentable state of one's batsmanship. That's no bother. No. Nor are the host of other distractions. The weather's moods, the field changes, the bowling changes, one's partner not backing up, no bastard on the scoreboard, some bastard wandering across the sightscreen, you know, the infinite variations and vagaries of cricket. No. It's this damned business of having to have absolute concentration and on tap. Circle of concentration. Stay within it. Calm. Face. Ball, ball, ball, feet, feet, feet. Here he comes. Don't blink. There's the cherry. Head over it and in line, body will follow, pitching up outside off stick, to it with the weight on the front foot, lean into it, watch her right on to the blade, follow through. Tonk. Through extra cover. A four spot. That's most interesting. Circle of concentration. Yes. I think I like it. Yes. Next.'

'What Stanislavski calls units and objectives. Units are more or less the plot points in which a character finds himself, but objectives, Pete, objectives are the active verbs which bring shape, bring impetus, bring definition and purpose to a performance.

When Hamlet comes across Claudius praying, his objective becomes "to kill". He must first think and then feel that that is what he will do. But then his objective alters, changes, turns into "to think". And we see him "sicklied o'er with the pale cast of thought" as once again he becomes irresolute and ineffective. Also, these objectives become incorporated into a super-objective. The energizing principle which defines the thrust of a character within the context of a play. Take Valentine in *You Never Can Tell.* Off the top of my head I'd say that his super-objective was "to be his own man and to prosper". And look what happens to the poor dummy. He finishes up under the boot of Gloria. Ironic. Right?'

'Snag is, baby, at cricket, when batting, one's sole objective, one's only active verb, is to put bat to ball. Certainly, there is your forward defence, your back-foot dead-bat defence, your straight drive, off, on, and cover drives, your hook, your pull, your square cut, late cut, leg glance and sweep, but at all times your governing principle, baby, simply is to put bat to ball. Super-objective? Prod out a fifty, I suppose, a gentle hundred, a big hundred, but, no, on the whole, there seems to me to be no place for these objective animals, none at all. Pity. Next.'

'As the heading for one of the later chapters in his book, Stanislavski chooses an interesting word, he uses the word Communion, and it's my belief he uses it in the sense of participation, of holding and sharing something in common, that thing being the rehearsal and the performance of plays. I believe also, Pete, that both directly and indirectly the word communion connects with practically all the subjects under discussion and experimentation throughout the book. Action and interaction between players, the ability to adapt to the given circumstances of an actor's working life, an understanding of oneself, an understanding of one's fellow performers, an understanding of plays, of scenery, lights, costumes, props, et cetera. To be responsive to all the stimuli of the backstage theatre world. To commune face to face with other actors and actresses. Generally to be aware of what is going on, to be affected by your circumstances and be able to make an imaginative and a positive contribution to those circumstances.'

'There you are, do you see, and the track's a greentop, sticky, drying, spiteful. Bound to be turn, bound to be grubbers. Before taking guard, even, you've spotted the keeper standing up, a forward short leg, backward short leg, slip, gully, silly point, silly mid-off, a deepish extra cover for the lofted drive, a man at cow catch, another patrolling the rope on and off. Has to be a legger, doesn't it? The bowler's follow-through has gouged a Passchendaele out of the strip. Right on a length. Need to be nimble on the trotters, baby. Going to have to skip up and down the strip. Soft hands to smother and it's tricky stuff to get away, leg spin. Hit against the turn and it's easily goodnight nurse. Pad away's an answer but we need quick runs, so must push on. Leg stick guard, I fancy. Yes. Now, he'll be trying to pitch into that rough and you can expect a diet of bread and butter leg spin mixed with the arm ball, top spin, a google or two, the flipper, flat leg cutter—'

'Halva!'

'How many?'

'Halva!'

'Halva? Oh, that's the song that your lot with the Homburg hats and the curly whiskers sing, isn't it, when they wear those amazingly long double-breasted hacking jackets and shuffle along doing the Hassidic conga.'

'Schlemiel of schlemiel of schlemiels! Schmuck of all schmucks! My God, what did I do to you that you should pitch me into the arms and danger of this goon goy from Cricketsville who's telling me from curly Homburgs and congas of the Hassidim? Oi! Oi! Oi! Oaf! Degenerate! Pigsmeat! God forbid you should die but in His mercy couldn't He for a couple minutes just break your collar bone in eighteen places and nail your dum dum tongue to a sticky cricket bat for an hour so's to let you feel the suffering that the wretched thing inflicts when it wags at a poor person trying to be helpful, trying to be patient, trying, I must be demented, to be your loving friend. God knows I should smash you in the puss but I'm too unhappy, already, and anyway you're used to it now and the inside of my arm hurts from your blocking my little punches. My God, but no one deserves this, you hear me? No one. Listen I'm just a little joosh girl far from home who wants to eat a piece joosh candy. That's what halva is, you dumb yok, it's a candy, a sweety, a bonbon. Joosh girls, joosh boys, joosh families, since the di-frigging-aspora, have enjoyed ruining their teeth on a little chunk halva. Dr Pepper's celery soda! God Almighty, but do I ask too much? Lend me your hanky. Then lend me your fancy kerchief, it used to be mine.'

In rapid order, wrapped round one another, the pair of us were bowling in a flounder down to the East End and the street market at Whitechapel. A Jewish quarter since the late 1600s, the very Jewishness of the area was a tangible matter in which my little Hebrew sweetheart could revel and could match by delightedly revelling in her own Jewishness. Quick and noisy, tough and chuckling the street traders hawked their wares from open stalls spilling along the cobbles in the din and banter and bustle gusting about the booths and the barrows and the customers and the costermongers as we trod and squeezed our way all along the stretches of the wide and sunlit lane. Shoes, crockery, hats, books, flowers, mousetraps, skittles, birdcages, cutlery, brooms, clocks, turnips, trousers, armchairs, record players, ashtrays, all these and a multiplicity of much, much more was being sold and bargained for and bought and it was said that you could feed a family, furnish a house and plant a garden from Whitechapel Market. We found halva, of course, dense, nutty, sweet and oily, wrapped in thick tin foil but, alas, Dr Pepper's celery soda was that day unavailable in this Eastern bazaar. Her craving in most part mollified, however, a green shirt with white stripes, one in which she thought I'd look nifty, took her fancy and with a rough and bulky man the haggling began. The trader's position, one from which God knew he could not budge, was that as the day was lovely, his customer beautiful, the shirt pure cotton, his heart tender, for thirty shillings, which was the value of the very buttons on the garment, he would for her, and her alone, practically give away the splendid shirt. Could he not tell, wondered the Hopi, hurt by this stance, this obduracy, that she was poor, was a student, was a stranger? Did he not care that with only the jingle of a few coins in her purse she had the responsibility of putting beans on toast into the mouths of four people other than herself? Was the shirt to be a gift for herself? She should be so profligate. Wasn't it to be a peace-offering to her boyfriend with whom she'd had a brutal row? On her life it was and couldn't the man understand her need for love and reconciliation, forlorn as she was and desperate in London. Twenty-seven shillings and sixpence. Stung now by the salesman's deliberate over-estimation of the worth of a shirt evidently bleached already on one shoulder by the sun and marked with what appeared to be ineradicable stains in the creases where the shirt had been folded, hotly she demanded to know if it was his habit always to take advantage of the naïvety of young women and didn't the fact of her being Jewish entitle her to a discount?

Twenty-six shillings went one way, a green shirt with white stripes came another, the curve to her nostrils sensed through the myriad odours and pongs of the market place a particular whiff, and within seconds the pair of us were slowly wandering through the gorgeous aromas of a kosher restaurant. Behind the counter, well fed, vigorous, bright of eye, a woman wordlessly beckoned that we should come to her. We did so. As my lips opened to bid good day to our hostess, gently she popped a spoonful of flavoursome grub into my mouth, repeated the favour to my dote, and as the lovely stuff melted on our tongues before tastefully slipping down our throats, knowing that we had been baited, hooked and caught, we sat down at a table and got dug into a serious bout of nosh.

\*

You should know, I do believe, that during our days together in 1954 Chicago and I had wandered much. If London owned a stone of note, brickage of distinction, metals ably wrought; a tower, a tunnel, a structure, a street to tread, a stair to climb, a bridge to cross; spots historical, spots aesthetic, spots remarkable and it had been her fancy to cast a peeper on such places, tread a trotter in such purlieus, to inhale, as it were, the antiquity, mystery, singularity attendant on seekers in the flower of cities all, then cut my throat but hadn't the cow hauled me out of the pub, shoved me on to a bus or a boat or an underground or an overground railway train and then by foot had she not had me with her to go roaming, wandering, loitering, gazing at many a distinguished nook and significant cranny? Too right but she had. Also, it had been on one of our dinky excursions when my phrase about her, 'a Red Indian over here to learn the language', had first tossed itself out of my mouth. Thus.

Near to a hatter's in St James's Street there runs a little alley, on one wall of which you may see a sign nailed up proclaiming that you are standing in the precincts of the embassy of the Republic of Texas. Howdy. Perceiving itself to be from all points of the compass vulnerable to oppression and tyranny, in 1840 the recently formed Texan Republic had suggested to Queen Victoria that she adopt the young country and place it under her care in the huge family of empire over which she was great white mother and Sovereign Queen. Her twenty-one-year-old Majesty, perhaps believing that with most of the continents of the great world already under her plump little sway she had quite enough cactus and prairie and cowboys and Indians to be going on with, thank you very much, made it known that she was disinclined to accept this suggestion. The Republic of Texas exists now only on a sign up an alley close by a hatter's in St James's Street, London SW1, and one wonders, when in 1901 the Lone Star State saw the black roses of Spindletop gush and flourish upwards, if gracious old

Queen Victoria had thought that sixty years earlier the advice she had been given by her ministers might possibly have been not tip top.

One of history's quirks only, a matter for the mouth music made by me and Pocahontas that day when we moved down from the hatter's to explore what we could of St James's Palace. Originally built in the fifteen hundreds by Henry the Eighth, and with many subsequent modifications, extensions, reductions, as royal palaces go it is an astonishingly unassuming building. With no wall at all to separate the palace from the main street, one could, having remarked the soldier wearing his enormous bear-skin helmet and bearing his musket on sentry go, with ease aplenty pry and ponder at the exterior of this royal residence. Which is what, that day, we were doing. Perhaps noisily, for that was one of our ways, perhaps having a bull and a cow, row, for that was another of our ways, perhaps silent, perhaps laughing, perhaps kissing, perhaps talking about this, wondering about that, questioning, giving, answering, taking, perhaps just wandering on our way when a window above us shot open and didn't an elegant man and an elegant woman stick their elegant frames through the aperture and begin a wholly unexpected conversation with the pair of us? They did. What points were made or not during the first exchanges I no longer can recollect but in short order elegant man asked me who I was and what did I do. 'O'Toole is my name,' said I. 'I'm a drama student at the Royal Academy. This is my girlfriend, Pocahontas. She is a Red Indian over here to learn the language.' Seconds later and the pair of us were within the palace, in a lovely room, seated on comfortable chairs, taking tea with half a dozen elegant men and elegant women and making elegant small-talk about, say, Father Murphy, appendec-tomies and the price of turnips. Thirty or so minutes later, our host and hostess courteously walked out with us to the spot whence we had been invited in, lingered to chat a little more, and then we shook hands, and bade farewells and Chicago and I continued wandering on our way. We had been treated right royally.

Another fine time, up-country, I saw with pleasure my juicy little plum take a bright smiling shine to the woodlands and the great gilded sweeps to the green broad acres of northern Yorkshire and felt the swift quickening of her sensibilities when hand in hand through the massive medieval arch of Micklegate we entered into the ancient city of York. All along those narrowest of alleys there, lined on either side with timbered houses of the Middle Ages, sloping inwards, nodding to their neighbours, we followed the thread of the thoroughfares as they wove their winding ways through the lovely old town and sent us spinning towards the immense Cathedral of Saint Peter: The Minster. 'Beautiful enough to be the gate of Heaven,' Arthur H. Norway, traveller and writer, tells us. Yes, sir. Up, then, the pair of us on to the great fourteenth-century walls. To walk their two-and-a-half-mile circuit of York; to gaze at what had been Roman Eboracum; capital of the Kingdom of Northumbria; garrison town to Vikings, Normans, Plantagenets, Tudors, Stuarts, Cromwell's Republicans; to wonder that the city had escaped destruction by Hitler, to realize that we stood on what in medieval days was the military centre of all England, to see, at last, that what for over seven hundred years had been a capital city of Christendom yet still stood and was by men women and children ordinarily inhabited. Beautiful, indeed. Nor did we visit the racetrack at Knavesmire; neither did we sell any balloons.

Anon, picking them up, laying them down, going against the grain of the Great North Road, irresolutely hitch-hiking our way back to London, we had allowed ourselves to be diverted from the highway by taking up the offer of a lift in a car which, though it was travelling southerly, would be doing the job in a roundabout manner, sideways, and in a half-circle. I think I had thought that we would at least be getting a fair bite out of the mileage and

anyway it would give herself the chance of copping an eyeful of
the rurality stretching about in England's lower Midlands. So it
had proved but, after remarking the clover, the duckponds and
the cow shit, our efforts to get back on the main drag had been
fruitless and we had found ourselves stuck luckless with our
thumbs in the vicinity of Lesser Cold Bottle. Or somesuch. The
day had had enough itself, evening was nigh, thoughts of grub
and snore were teasing our minds, our tummies, and though the
prospect of beer and pork pies in a pub to be followed by a kip in
a ditch was not yet on the cards, you should perhaps know that in
the early fifties cheap lodgings, bed and breakfasts and the like
were, as it were, strangers to rural England. A small shooting
brake, was it, a modest station wagon, a little van, it is not easy for
me exactly to recall but, anyway, a four-wheeled article of some or
other sort heeded our gestured importunities and came to a halt
for us. At the wheel a woman in a headscarf, forties perhaps, frank
blue eyes, listened to my wishes, chuntered to her right calmly, of
getting to where there would be traffic, southbound traffic, of
thumbing a lift there, and somehow, maybe, that night, being
lucky enough to hit the Big Smoke. We were invited to hop in, in
we hopped, Chicago in the back, me in the front, and, while
hopping, I spotted in the space at the rear of the vehicle horse-
feed, tack, brushes, a bucket and gumboots. Murmuring that if we
hoped to get to London that evening, without our own transport,
we had left it somewhat late, from within the headscarf there
came a voice that easily managed at once to drawl and be quite
clear, to be softly pitched, confident, cultured, and hard as nails.
The voice wouldn't be going to London, it said, and I saw that its
headscarfed owner had a fine profile, feminine, strong, was
wearing a stout, waterproofed jacket, light khaki trousers and
gripped the wheel with leather-gloved hands, but it would be
driving quite near to where the main road ran, now, it wanted to
know, who were we, where had we been, what had we been up to
and, when we weren't hitching lifts all over the place, what did we

do with ourselves? 'My name is O'Toole. I'm a drama student at the Royal Academy. This is my girlfriend, Pocahontas. A Red Indian over here to learn the language.'

What, thirty minutes, three-quarters of an hour, there or thereabouts, later, we were being driven past a gatehouse and its large, formidable, open iron gates, along a ride of lime trees, round a bend and pulling up before a graceful Queen Anne manor house.

To be sure, the meal we'd had of stew, chunks of bread, cheese, a couple of glasses of red wine, taken in the vast kitchen with our driver and hostess, had been welcome, flavourful, unexpected to the point of astonishment; indeed, the bed which to my amazement I'd been invited to occupy for the night was deep, downy, passing comfortable, but my chief concern as down this creaky corridor I creep is to recall which door it was that would lead me in to where herself had been parked. This one? Think so. Try it. Worst way you can always say you'd gone for another squint at the Reynolds, got lost, and blundered into the wrong dosser. Wouldn't cut any ice with her ladyship. Nothing would. Kind, though, bloody kind. Here goes. There she is! Blimey. A dot only. A little dark dot in a positive architecture of four-poster, pillows, bolster, covered all with a vivid red bedspread and lit by a bedside lamp on its table. 'Hello, Cheeky. Give us a kiss.'

That was the night when she had first introduced me to the short right jab. A wicked punch, expertly delivered. When you consider that to throw a good punch ideally one should be balanced on the balls of one's feet with one's legs braced and that my sweetheart merely had been sitting upright in a bed you will appreciate, surely, just how impressive that punch had been. Body, shoulder, behind it, travelling a few inches only but ramrod straight, full of snap, pop, flush on my left mince pie. Eye. Jesus Christ, but my honey was a savage.

\*

After our scrumptious nosh in Whitechapel it had seemed to me meet that I should take her for an amble around that square mile there within which, over twelve weeks stretching from the August to the November of 1888, with a precision surgical as it was horrifying, the killer we call Jack the Ripper first murdered and then butchered six forlorn women.

At cricket, later that summer, going in to bat, no tension at all in my frame or face or limbs or fingers, securely ringed in my circle of concentration, communing with my given circumstances, as I neared the square my assessment of the situation was this: three slips and a gully, the keeper standing back, deep fine leg, a man at point, one in the covers, a forward short leg, a man at sloggers but deep, chances are the bowling will be quite brisk, off-stump line swinging away. 'Two please, umpire.' Right. Bit of shrubbery in the middle of the track but bare as a biscuit on a length. Watch for the one that comes in, or gets big. Face. Feet, feet, feet. Ball, ball, ball. 'Good night, Charlie!' Saw it all the way, pitched well up, came down late on her, she slipped under the bat, castled, there's timber all over the shop. Out. Do you see, unless one is a naturally gifted cricketer, with a good, constantly honed technique, Mr Stanislavski, confident and on song, the objectives of putting bat to ball or pitching the ball on the spot turn into a raffle, Mr S., a bugger's muddle, nor can any systematic approach to the job, not only yours, my old segocious, however sound in principle, prove to be anything other than a washout. Saw it all the way, you know, swung in late, just too rusty to get wood on it. Fuck. A duck. It would make you weep.

St Veronica's towel, yes, John Barrymore's startling image of how he perceived an actor's face and body should be, that's what I fancy I had thought about that Whitechapel night, as Pocahontas

343

and I swayed home on the rattler, a blank ready to receive an impression that the bloodied Jesus of his part in a play presses on to it.

The soft leather desert boots, do we think, bought for buttons only from my bootmaker, the Army and Navy surplus store, tested during the North African campaigns by Montgomery's Eighth Army, guaranteed to give miles upon miles of hard slogging wear, noble articles needing no blackening, polishing, buffing, just bung 'em under the tap, a sluice, a dart with a nailbrush, they are fit for wearing, for baffling inspection by any critical eye, and which comfily wrap themselves around my pale, patrician trotters? Yes, indeed, arches may fall yet cosily shall we be shod. Sniff. Into the nose an air that thrills, odour of spaghetti and meatballs drifts around our half a house up Muswell's hill. Listen. Rustles and bustles and chatter tell that skirts and trousers and mouths are assembling round the trough. Nina Von's bash is on. Time for me to leave my ruminations, neat, trim as I am, chin new reaped as it is, greet our guests, and, do you not think, make myself useful in any way that I possibly can? Absolutely.

> My uncle's a slum missionary.
> He's saving young maidens from sin.
> He'll save you a blonde for a fiver.
> By Christ, how the money rolls in.

---

'DIMPLES FROM the deep herself, Aphrodite, among other calls on her precious time, goddess of whores and sailors, one fine day this luscious chick was swaying around Olympus on her lonesome, giving out with the cosmic generative force that pervades all nature, hot diggedy doo dah, yeah, when who should the winsome broad softly bump into but the king of the road himself, Hermes, among other calls on that cat's precious time, God of thieves and other physical jerks, also on his lonesome and the day was hot, brothers and sisters, right heavenly hot. Hallelujah!' It is the voice of our Theatre Major, Hardtack, I fancy, stuffed with meatballs and spaghetti, awash with red plonk, sitting up on top of the enormous chest of drawers which stands in our living and loving and dining and dancing and drawing room, flanked by lit candles stuck in bottles, and, in circumlocutional response to a query from Jeannie, giving out with erudition. '"Hi, Herm," says Aphrodisiac. "How's tricks? Cute hat." "Thanks, Myrtle. Things is slow. Being a quicksilver guy who needs to connect, that ain't good. How're you, babe?" "Feeling kinda lonely and restless and fertile." "Come back to my grot, honey, I'll take out my lyre and we'll have us a pluck." "Lead on, Swifty."'

Littered about the room, sitting at table, on chairs, the sofas, the floor, our customers fork and swill down the grub and the wine even as in varying degrees of attentiveness they absorb Hardtack's drift. Scattered hither and yon among the regulars, we have welcome newcomers to our leery old digs: two particularly pretty young women; two, I'm quite sure, most interesting young men. The Ninas and Pocahontas serve up second and third helpings. Joe and I slosh out more booze. We munch, we glug, our Theatre Major continues.

'The consequence of this encounter up on top of old Olympus, my brothers and sisters, was that unto this god and this goddess a child was born, yea, unto these ding-dong deities a son was given. Aphroditus was his name and his mom had him brung up a mere mortal man among the timberlands and high hills of Ida ho! Yo! By age fifteen, naked, bearded, wild and beautiful this kid just lived for to hunt. Bow, arrows, knives, spear, hatchet ready, this natural child roamed the land a-hunt-hunt-hunting. Came a day, our hunter boy all muscled and sweating and heaving in the heat, why, the kid was dangling his hot tootsies in the cooling still waters of a lake. Peeking up at him through the water lilies, and boiling with desire for the boy, was Big Sal, the sauciest nymph of the region. Out of the water rose this gorgeous figure of lustful womanhood and right politely she introduced herself to the kid. Aphro was real glad of her company and it came into his mind that Nympho might like to be took. Kid was on the ball, for Nympho wanted nothing more than to be took by Aphro. So, brothers and sisters, they took one another and they took one another and they took and took and took until, after hours of being taken and taking and being took, our boy figured it was time to mosey along and maybe prong a wild boar for supper. "You ain't going nowheres, lover," says Big Sal, "you is all mine just as I is all yours and I pray to the gods never ever to separate you from I or I from you. Hotcha!" That done it. But immediately, he into she and she into he both their bodies were united as one. Yes, folks, this beautiful guy and this luscious doll fused together and lived on in one humdinger of a sexy frame. And that, my friends, is a-how the androgynous came to be. Praise it!'

Approving grunts for Hardtack's dissertation emerge from the masticating mouths of a few of our munchers, gargles from the throats of two or three suggest no dissent, all is well, quiet is the chomping, the supping is smooth, words are few again as we guzzle, as we chew. Jeannie and Sal it was who had prompted Hardtack into his singular elaboration of a Greek myth. Was, they had wanted to know of him, Viola, in *Twelfth Night*, when dressed as a man, when conducting herself in manly manner, supposed to be believable?

From his candle-lit eminence up on the chest of drawers, Hardtack gently had asked them by whom was this suppositional belief of which they talked to be or not to be entertained. The cast? Unlikely, for other members may have read the play, met the actress playing Viola in the street, at rehearsals, the stagedoor, in a dressing room; may have watched her play the woman in the earlier and the later scenes; may, it was possible, have contained a male who was a lover of the actress. The cast, on their part, had to act that they believed she was a man. But what of the audience, our lovely Jeannie had wanted to know, what of them? Precisely that question from the darkling beauty it had been which had sparked the Theatre Major into his folksily contrived version of an event from mythology, pronounced to tease and amuse his listeners, and to give an oblique, sensual answer to the darling enquiry. Honey Sal had seemed wholly and quite sexily satisfied with Major Hardtack's parable and, it further had seemed, having gained another dimension to the gender which she so confidently inhabited, happily returned her blonde head into its dinner pail. Jeannie, though, intrigued but at ease, felt moved to offer one more discursive thought.

'To an audience, then, when being a man, Viola doesn't have to be plausible.'

'Viola has to be a plausible androgyne. With the elements so mixed up in her that the audience, men and women, might stand up and say to all the world, "Jesus. What a dish!"' Laughter from Jeannie, no sadness that night, none at all, rather a sustained and an even merry note.

'That,' she says, 'is more or less what I thought. But so many literal-minded people around do bang on so, talking of how Shakespeare wrote the parts for men and boys.'

'The modes of his time,' says Hardtack, 'insisted that boys and men, at least in public performances, played Viola, Rosalind, Desdemona, Ophelia, Cleopatra, Doll Tearsheet, Mistress Quickly, but Shakespeare wrote women. Matchless women. Round and deep and filled with women's flesh and spirit. As for prosaic bodies, those with literal minds on both sides of the footlights, if they can't accept the theatrical it would be better for them to stay away from the theatre.' Delighted with this, reassured, gaily

347

Jeannie replaced her sweet snout and her dainty trotters back into the trough.

Quietly a cheerful geezer, Hardtack, a scholar from the States, one of distinction and academic pedigree, he had been one of the first guests to arrive that evening when Nina Von held her illustrious dinner party. Shining clean, combed and nattily suited I had presented myself to the other members of our household, peered through the kitchen door at the wonders being prepared there, inhaled splendid aromas, spotted a brace of hefty saucepans in which fine fat balls of meat simmered in savoursome juices, realized that one of these thick, toothsome balls had found its way into my mouth and had given the tasty chunk a thorough chewing and swallowing, noticing as down it went a tang to the meat that was not familiar to me. Not that I, nor indeed practically anyone else in the England of that decade following the war, had been overly familiar with the various tastes of rich red meat. Far from it. Hadn't meat at times been more severely rationed than it had been during the bloody conflict? Too right it had, making one wonder, making this one wonder, me, who, after all, Lord love us, had won the fucking war. No matter. Delicious was the meatball and just as another discovered the right way into my receiving mouth, what did I spot but Joe's homemade cheese. Decanted from its nylon stocking, it squatted on a plate, a greying, living, formless and a loathsome thing.

Would I, please, instead of criticizing the labours of others, while making a pig of myself, lend a hand to the immediate preparations of the dinner party by lighting the candles, uncorking a number of bottles and pouring the wine into the jugs? Certainly. Nothing to this business of unscrewing corks from wine bottles. Practice aplenty I've had; on the boat, at the soldering factory, in sundry gaffs, drums, digs, chambers, crash pads; just twist in the corkscrew deeply through the cork's centre, so, grab a handful of the bottle's neck, so, and slowly ease her up and out. The mercy is that when the cork splits and splinters and the corkscrew comes away leaving most of the cork stuck in the bottle, one merely sticks the corkscrew on to the cork where it is least damaged and then one rams the bastard hard down and into the bottle. Mop or lick or ignore the gout of liquor which during this action almost invariably squirts up the sleeve, for one will find that the way out for the wine has been unplugged and the wrecked cork bobs about in the bottle. True, this may somewhat impede smooth pouring but a poke with a little finger, a ballpoint pen, one finds that eventually the wine will flow, while spitting out little bits of cork when drinking is scarcely troublesome for teeth make fine strainers and ashtrays are handy animals. Yes, of course I'll answer the door. Hardtack. Tumbler of wine would you care for? Sal, Bob, Jenny, Mikey O.? Cheers.

My duties during the next thirty minutes or so proved not to be too burdensome. Just loading up the bafflingly ingenious little electrical record player with its ammunition of 45 r.p.m. small and jazzy bendable discs and letting her rip; lighting candles stuck in bottles, handing out slugs of booze from my jug to Minnehaha, Joe and the Ninas as they finished dressing and titivation; hopping up and down the stairs to let in customers when the doorbell rang out their arrivals, Jilly, Mikey B., Jeannie, Albie, Pringle, Sweetheart, Tom, Dick, Henriette and Gorgeous; talking, smoking, listening, drinking, with my chums, and quizzing Hardtack as to what, when majoring in theatre at colleges in the States, exactly it was that one did.

Reserved in manner, reticent in opinion, unapt for monologues, a cultured young man, he yet contrived, when the doings were right, always to be there or thereabouts, managing somehow to seem more an observer than a participant, but that night at Nina Von's celebrated bash, warmed no doubt by red wine from the jug, tickled maybe by the present promise of hot, solid grub, and perhaps aware that the vehicle of his year's study at London

349

rapidly was nearing its terminus, fine in fettle, in utterance, he started the party as he meant to go on.

Came the earlier years of the twentieth century, he explained to me, several institutions of higher learning in the USA had decided that the study of theatre literature, history and practice was worthy of being considered an academic discipline leading to a degree. Being himself, he went on, unable to act, even at gunpoint, and incapable of writing plays or designing sets or costumes but having already taken degrees in history and English and owning an affection for both the theatre and a student's life, he had signed on for a further stint of study and had majored in theatre. More, yes, he'd like another tumbler of wine, he had excelled in his studies, so much so that he'd been awarded a scholarship to further these studies and that's how come he'd skidded over the ocean and settled down for a year's frolic at the RADA.

What form, I asked him, had these studies taken? Well, he answered, we sat around and read plays from all periods and many countries. Then we discussed them. Then we wrote essays on them. We studied the history of the drama, from the Greeks to the present day. Then we had discussions. Then we wrote essays. We went to lectures on administration, acting, masks, design, playwriting, criticism, et cetera. More discussions. More essays. Occasionally, why, we even put something on. Not, he added, reaching for the jug, that he'd ever taken a part in these productions, he'd usually just written blurbs for the programmes.

It sounded a delightful way in which to while away a few years at college and, aloud, one wondered whether or not at some university somewhere some enlightened someone might yet see fit to suggest for inclusion as an academic study the noble art and sweet science of pugilism. Think of it. A history reaching back three thousand five hundred years to the isle of Crete when boxers wore soft leather thongs wrapped around their fists and forearms. The inclusion of the art as a competitive event at the

23rd Olympiad in 688 BC. The dramatic switch to hard leather gloves in the fourth century BC. The lethal use of iron-studded gloves at gladiatorial games in ancient Rome. The days of bare knuckles. The present-day use of six- to eight-ounce gloves. The literature, for hadn't Homer, Virgil, Byron, Shaw, Hemingway hymned these bloodsoaked single-combat contests? Broughton's Rules, Chambers' Rules, Queensberry Rules. Discuss. Essay. The roped, square prize ring of 1839. Discuss. Essay. The role in the ring of the English, the Americans, the Irish, the Jews, the Blacks. Discuss. Essay. As for boxing practice, well, there's always room, surely, for a master of ceremonies, timekeeper or, if skilled, a cutman. That one's degree as a graduate Boxing Major might not well equip one to go the distance in the ring at the weights was, of course, academic. The Theatre Major took the point, grinned his grin, swigged his drink, hollered for more, and then announced that when he returned to the USA, he fully expected to get a job in a drama department at a college, teaching theatre to prospective theatre majors.

Are we all met? Yes, we all are met, well met, gamesome, noisy, hungry and clamouring for food. Here come the Ninas and Capone bearing great steaming pots of spaghetti, sauces and large, succulent meatballs. All hands to the swill! Plates are heaped up, spoons and forks shimmer in the candlelight, mouths more used to the dingy fare cooked on gas rings in digs wrap themselves around this pasta, this juicy flesh, and a great calm descends as the hubbub of chatter gives way to the civilizing sound of molars rhythmically chewing and chomping at the nosh. Unwanted and unlovely, Joe's cheese squats hideous and untouched on its solitary dish.

Lolling about the room an hour and more later, the forking and the feasting done, crockery and vessels clattered into the kitchen sink, bellies filled, cigarettes lit, tumblers charged, by candle's light in the smoky fug with the gramophone softly playing its jazz, its swing, its croony tunes, satisfied our customers lounge or prowl or perch or stretch as with unstopped mouths the prattle and the chatter rattles out. My heap, the heavy firm, having enjoyed Hardtack's sermon on the nature of the androgynous kind, and being a horny lot, insist that he continue, and in like vein. So, from his high place on the chest of drawers, the Theatre Major does. Of a certain dude, name of Tiresias, he tells, who one day when goofing off down a boulevard came across a couple of snakes, a mamma snake and a pappa snake, and my eyes roam round the half-light of the room, the men and women in it, and my mind, fired with wine, finds matter more elemental than earlier it had seemed, in the sprawling bodies, the music, the mood, around each other, all a-twisting and a-twining, why those two snakes were having carnal knowledge of one another, Frances is her name, that dimpled darling sitting pretty in the armchair, the buzz in the canteen is that she's filthily rich, or rich or poor she's taking lots of no notice of me so I'll plod across with my jug to give her a squirt of sherbet, Tiresias lifted up his walking cane and he brought it down with a mighty whack on to those two copulating reptiles and that put an end to their unseemly shenanigans, lovely eyes and a sweet shy smile she has, Miss Frances, now where's that Augusta child, she of pedigree and a distinguished family, yes, nobbled already by Bob, immediately, but immediately, Tiresias found himself transformed into a woman, a real live female lady, brothers and sisters, with all the concomitant appendages and apparatus, so she went her way and had herself a full life in her spanking new gender, Pocahontas, sweetheart, what's with the glowering, who, you must ask yourself, and do not stay for answer, will be departing from whom, will it be I, no, not I, you it is who will be across the bounding dip, I, I shall have not budged an inch, will be here or hereabouts, you'll be gone, Lady Tiresias one fine day turned the corner of an alley and there before her eyes two other snakes were wrapped around each other and coupling, Tiresias lifted up her parasol and swished it down right hard on the tails of those two shameless slitherers, that ended their misconduct on a public highway, Nina Von may not be coming back after summer, but Nina Van will be, there she is, draped on the sofa, lovely young woman, seen her on stage a couple of times, in the Little Theatre, for a few minutes, graceful creature, presence, true quality, timid, though, no attack, that will come, Canadian, she can work over here, a few more months at RADA, a rough and a tumble in rep, she'll be there, yellow hair, nothing propinques like propinquity, Ah well! immediately, but immediately Tiresias found herself transformed into a man, a real live male gentleman, brothers and sisters, fully equipped, so away down the road a piece he scuttled to have himself a full life as a man, Jeannie chuckling at the Major, beautiful girl, no shadows over her, not this night, when they're gone it's as though they've never been, transformation, by Jesus, in a year from gawky convent schoolgirl to that fine young woman before me, parked on the floor, now with her dark head thrown back, now smiling at me, warm, open, now sipping her drink, Ah well!, Mrs Zeus, Hera, got to hear of the goings on going on with this Tiresias and she said, Tiresias, Baby Doll, Lover Boy, in which way when you has it does you like it best and want it most, when you is a man or when you is a woman?, when I is a woman, Honey, says Tiresias, and by nine whole times more, that's supposed to be a secret only woman knows, says Mrs Zeus, getting real mad, from now on, Blabberpuss, you is going to be blind, there, and from then on Tiresias couldn't see nothing.

'Very like a prawn,' says Bob, temporarily disengaging his full attention from Miss Posh. 'The humble prawn that you and I like grilled or fried or with a little mayonnaise on. The prawn comes into the world either male or female. For a span it is, say, a male. It then becomes neuter. Then it has a span as a female. And so on. Male, neuter, female, neuter, male, neuter, female until it finds itself one day being washed down my throat with, preferably, a little Chablis.'

'Guess what?' It is Nina Von, entering from the kitchen, eyes wide, brimming with a strange accomplishment. 'Tonight we had real Châteaubriand. I had to go to a special place right across town to get it. Did you guys know that real Châteaubriand is made of horsemeat? That's right. When you cook a real Châteaubriand steak, you must use horseflesh. So tonight we ate meatballs I made out of horsemeat. Cute, eh? Horseballs!'

There came a silence one could photograph. Lord have mercy on us. We had eaten a gee gee.

---

SKULK. That's favourite. When one's performance on the stage has not been infused with a divine afflatus but rather has been flat as a fart at a funeral, go skulk. That, in my view, is favourite. That's what I do. Skulk. With a huge indifference towns and cities in two continents have harboured my skulking form when, after giving some sham of a show, some strut and fret of lifeless wretched bogus acting, I have slunk through shadows away away from stage doors of theatres, have addressed my steps and my shame towards a riverside or dockland boozer, called for a bowl of liquor strong and peculiar to the region, stuck my sorry head in it, and there got pissed as a rat.

This glum, drear business of giving a performance absent from inspiration, hollow, mechanical is a dispiriting circumstance lived through by every actor and actress I have ever worked with or known, all of whom, in the hours following this dying the death in public, needs must and do cope, in their fashions, with that awful sense of worthlessness which arrives always. Some there are who kick the dressing room to bits and splinters. Some go home and savage a spouse, a lover, a domestic pet. Others fit on faces of resolute bravery, receive visitors, tittle, tattle, insist on keeping the dates they made for supper at charming little spots, nor flinch at compliments made about their acting. Some others, after weeks of no performance owning so much as a spark of truth, of buoyancy, vitality, realize at last that they must either cut their throats or take up dealing in antiques. Yet others, in my view the more sensible, balanced personalities, quit their stage doors with all convenient speed, find themselves comfortable holes wherein they may safely skulk, and there get pissed as rats.

Joycey it was who defined for me what I did when disgusted with any of my own performances. Joycey, whose mum, Dame Lilian Braithwaite, had been one of our greatest theatre ladies; whose dad, Sir Gerald Lawrence, had when a young man cradled the head of the dying Henry Irving; yes, Joycey, Miss Joyce Carey, if there has been a wittier, more accomplished, more versatile and poignant actress than Joycey this century, then how come I've never heard of her? In her twenties Juliet to the Romeo of Basil Rathbone, life-long friend and colleague of Noël Coward, who could scarce write a play without penning a part just for Joyce, first choice for decades as an actress for many authors and actor-managers, Miss Carey played leading parts in dozens of plays staged both in England and the United States, made dozens of films and televisions, acted with great success the leading part in her own play *Sweet Aloes,* and in her and the century's later eighties topped a long, long and a distinguished professional life by giving a performance of great beauty in Michael Palin's play for television *No. 27.* That Joycey.

At the age of ninety-three, Joyce Carey popped in to see a play running on Shaftesbury Avenue at London. After the show, dark eyes sparkling with fun, she downed a couple of glasses of champagne with the delighted cast, and then went home to her elegant apartment in Belgravia where, quite shortly after, peacefully she died.

One time, Joycey and I were touring in GBS's *Man and Superman.* Joyce was playing Mrs Whitfield and I Jack Tanner. During a performance in Wales, or Scotland, or the north or the south or the midlands of England, you will please forgive my uncertainty, it is difficult after a tour precisely to recall where it was that one went, just as when touring it is often tricky to know where one is, has been, or hopes to go, anyway, it seemed to me that Joyce was a little down, her timing a hair off its usual knifing precision, her supple, springing voice a wee bit chalky. So what? Touring is a tiring lark, the play a difficult, demanding beauty, Joyce is over eighty but with a vitality and a technique so formidable that any sag in the tension of her playing is unlikely to be spotted by any of the younger members of the company leave alone the audience which, as ever, is seeing this production and these performances for a first time. Tomorrow evening, as usual, the lady will come on striking twelve. Curtain down, the calls taken, I was halfway in, halfway out of my dressing room, blathering with chums of this and t'other, arranging where to sup, dabbing off makeup, when rapidly down the corridor came Miss Carey, wrapped in raincoat and headscarf, hurriedly aiming for the stage door. 'Blimey, Joyce. You've been sharp. Where are you off to?' Pausing not at all, but flicking at me an eye livid with a self-loathing anger, with biting emphasis as she passed by her voice snapped back at me, 'To skulk!'

So that was what, after giving shoddy performances, many times in many years, it was that I had done: I had skulked. Yes. Ever since that afternoon at the RADA when, well, do you see. As Sir Kenneth grimly had promised at the beginning of the year, all students would be required, wearing full fig and makeup, to perform solo in the Little Theatre speeches or set pieces from plays and there I was, Lord love me, obedient to the typewritten letter of the paper pinned up on the noticeboard listing those souls who, one every fifteen minutes, had been called upon to stand alone on this stage and perform their pieces. Four fifteen p.m., the noticeboard had declared, Peter O'Toole. Malvolio. *Twelfth Night*. Act Two Scene Five. The letter scene, well, that should have been all right. It was one of the numbers I'd performed with the class when only a few days ago we'd done scenes from this play and on the very same spot. They'd gone quite well, too. Bedight in Elizabethan costume we had played with a rattling gusto, our reception from the audience had been cheerful, my own performance as Malvolio had not displeased me, and afterwards in the dressing rooms even Uncle Ernest had unwreathed his face from its weary agonies briefly to bestow on us congratulatory beams. That was then. This is now. Here stand I. Dressed as Malvolio, made-up, wigged and whiskered as Malvolio, sickeningly realizing that no nerve or sense or tissue of me feels in any way at all like Malvolio. There is just me. Wrapped in a ruff, doublet, hose, chain, wig, moustache, beard, my memorizing and speaking motor rattling on alarmingly, my acting engine refusing to start. It's horrid. Worse. The more dreadful matters become, so, astonishingly, the clearer becomes my awareness of all about me. Jenny, clearly Jenny, is pumping out cues from the prompt corner, 'Bolts and shackles!' There's a cigarette butt stubbed out lying by the letter. It's the same letter we used in the performance a few days back. Might even be one of my old fag ends. Across the floats I can see a few bodies parked in seats, audience to my rubbish, up above in the gallery a couple whisper, there's a cougher, and at the back of the auditorium, lighted in his booth, Sir Kenneth Barnes sits rumblingly sound asleep. The letter. 'By my life, this is my lady's hand.' Every word I speak, I can hear myself speaking them, even as the words lifelessly flop out of my mouth. Sometimes my voice sounds like Ernest Milton sounding like me. Other times like me sounding like Ernest Milton. Michael Hordern's joining in now. The hollow awfulness of it all is becoming more and more awful. '"I may command where I adore."' 'Why, she may command me: I serve her, she is my lady.' Peter Ernest Hordern is beginning to jabber even more rapidly. Slow down. Bollocks. Babble on. Get the bloody shameful thing over with. I've an appointment with Hugh Miller at five thirty. Senior cheese of the academy, Miller. Scooping up sinners for a production he's doing in the London Parks. Play called *The Trial of Mary Dugan*. Read it. My part's the doctor. Five words in

357

the witness box at the beginning. Five words in the witness box at the end. Don't fancy it. Jenny's prompting: 'You might see more detraction at your heels than fortunes before you.' I hear you, Jenny baby. '"M.O.A.I." This simulation is not as the former: and yet, to crush this a little, it would bow to me, for every one of these letters are in my name.' I should never have looked in that fucking mirror. All done up but dead in the dressing room I'd felt before the kick-off. Suddenly felt a glow of Malvolio beaming in me. Stuck my kisser in a mirror for a square glare of what he looked like. El Greco figure passing a hard stool. Tried to stick on that expression before I entered. Remember how it felt when I looked. How it looked when I felt. Outward show, I thought, few seconds only. Malvolio will come. You'll be home in a hack. I thought. Know what thought did. Thought stuck a feather up its arse and thought it could fly. 'I will wish off quaint agrossment.' That's not right. No. Jenny's falling about the prompt corner hooting. 'I will wash off gross acquaintance.' Christ. 'I will be point-device the very man.' Get it over with, Peter, before Sir Kenneth wakes up. And to think of that poor sod I saw playing Lord Foppington the first time I came into this place. Fuck him. Amen. Hallelujah. 'She did commend my yellow stockings of late.' Gabble, Hordern, babble. 'I thank my stars, I am happy.' Babble, Milton, gabble. 'Jove and my stars be praised!' Gibber, impostor O'Toole, splutter. 'Jove, I thank thee, I will smile, I will do everything that thou wilt have me.' Exit.

Off with the plumes and the paint before you could say 'knife', out of the damned building, despondently, beadily, to trudge through shadows in Malet Street, up and down, down and up, brooding, smoking, lighting fags from the butts of chain-smoked others, avoiding human communion, killing the hour before I had to meet this Miller geezer, cursing myself for a presumptuous eyes front: that's right. Act? My false whiskers had acted their part in Malvolio with more truth than I had. Actor? At the start of the year, a bungle I'd made of Oliver; at the death, a whore's knickers

of Malvolio. Lamentable. Here come folk known to me. Avoid
them. Scrutinize interesting cracks in the pavement. Head away
to Dillon's bookshop. Look through the windows, feign an interest
in the titles of books. *The Trial of Mary Dugan.* Dr Welcome.
London Parks. I should cocoa. Besides, through my professional
contacts at the Mother Redcap in Camden Town, haven't I already
secured an engagement for the summer season? Too right, I have.
On the stones there will be me and Barney McGee, with Tyrone
Grogan and Johnny McGurk on the sand. West Meath Malone
will roll the wheelbarrow, Slugger O'Toole hump the cement, yes,
while Hogan from Clare and Fighting Bill Brady will be driving
the mixer. Ten loads an hour, ten hours a day, thick wages, we
shall be performing north of London and our show will be laying
the concrete foundations for yet another huge electrical power
station. McAlpine's Fusiliers. Not to be missed. Much nearer my
mark than this acting lark. Acting? I shall try acting my way to the
Tottenham Court Road and buying myself a newspaper. Twenty
minutes to go. Slowly shuffle back to the premises. Consider. In
its fifty years, this old academy must have seen an awful lot of very
bad acting. You are at one with a great tradition. Get in there.
'Good evening, Sergeant.'

Tall enough, Hugh Miller, the first time I met him he'd seemed
taller. Erect yet easy, pliant, the way in which he'd carried himself,
may have given me that impression, it's possible. Slim, spare,
silvered wavy hair, a sculpted head, his face handsome, graven
with lines at once severe and deeply humorous; his eyes not large
but big with wisdom, intelligence, mirth, the first thing I'd noticed
about Hugh was how spankily polished were his neat fine shoes.
Reading the sports page of the newspaper, I'd been; sitting,
smoking, thinking of not a lot, paying no heed to the prattle of
the half a dozen or so other students in the room, when I side-
spied this nifty pair of shiny shoes standing a few feet from where
I sat but, as in time I would discover, my being in skulkdom had
meant that I couldn't be bothered to look up at their occupant.

Most of the twenty-seven parts in this American courtroom drama which Mr Miller was producing for a tour in the open air of a number of parks in London already had been cast and indeed the play was deeply into rehearsal. The production, however, still lacked a few courtroom attendants, newspaper reporters and, of course, the expert witness whose testimony virtually topped and tailed the piece, Dr Welcome.

My fellow students in the room were yapping away, eager to snap up these bits and pieces of parts, and it had been when I'd felt moved to growl at one or some or all of them and make plain my view that, even if practically every page of my engagement diary for the coming period were not already densely inked in, the matter of my playing, or not, Dr Welcome was of absolute insignificance because, really, it was only a small part, that a voice from above the polished shoes came slicing into my heart saying, 'There are no small parts there are only small actors.' Looking up for the first time at this man so trimly shod, my look was held in challenge by the eyes of the tall man who so erectly stood before me. I said, 'That's Stanislavski, isn't it?' Hugh Latimer Miller said, 'The saying was a commonplace aphorism in the theatre before Stanislavski's great-grandfather invented the machine which translated ingots of bullion into gold thread.'

Yes, I didn't know that Stanislavski was the Polish stage name adopted by an eccentric, filthily rich Russian merchant and amateur actor called Konstantin Sergeivich Alexeyev. No. Nor did I know anything of Hugh's long and distinguished professional life as an actor and producer in both the United States and England. Neither did I know a sausage about his love of film, of literature, of engineering, of wine, of painting, of poetry; nor of his deep and abiding interest in economic, political and social reform; nor of the ranging width of his reading, knowledge and interests in a whole host of subjects. In time, though, it would become my good fortune to know him. As a pupil with my teacher,

Hugh; as a colleague of my colleague, Hugh; as a friend to my friend, Hugh Miller. If it rightly can be said of a man that he was the one who turned the key that unlocked and set free whatever abilities as an actor were held inside me, then let me happily with love and gratitude say it of Hugh.

Nothing of this did I know then, though, did I? There I was with this rangy old cove beadily staring down at me, one second he was dishing out baffling information, the next he was telling me of the authority that needed to be brought to the part of Dr Welcome, an authoritatively convincing professional manner had to be given to the doctor by the actor who played him, he said, or the surprise ending to the play would be dissipated. Did I think I was up to it, he wanted to know, if so, then these were the dates when we would be playing the parks. The final date was two days before the day of my recruitment into McAlpine's Fusiliers.

'I'm on for it, sir.'

'Good,' said he, and he smiled and then he turned away.

Feeling lower than whale shit I slunk out of the academy. The fiasco of Malvolio was heavy on me and I'd just been made bits of by this bloke Miller. The thirst on me was a dreadful thing and I could have murdered a pint but, no, not for me Momma Fischer's, the Burglar's, the Baskerville, there would be people in those places who knew me, I wanted none of that. No. Nor a woman near me. Nor familiar friends. Down towards the river I roamed out, away along the twisting lanes, the crooked alleys, through the dark closes, the narrow ginnels, drenching the parched being of me with sweet pints sucked down in dim anonymous boozers, lurching past black churchyards, through seedy squares and market places, fetching up at last in Edmund Kean's Coal Hole, above the river beyond the Strand.

Deep it was down there and safe for me, so I sat there a long while, skulking, drinking, convincing myself that to fail as Malvolio in *Twelfth Night* was a grander destiny than to be adequate as Tom Wrench in *Trelawny of the 'Wells'*, and got pissed as a rat.

---

MIGHTY LOFTY stands the giant pylon of Ally Pally, and slightly to the south-west of where one great foot of it prods into the receiving earth, could the demi-paradise we had known for much of the tumbling academic year of '53 to '54, living as we did at Muswell Hill in half of that red-bricked house with the fancy Edwardian timber and plasterwork twiddly bits, for ever untroubled roll on? We will, I fancy, let our landlady, Mrs Chubb, tell you exactly what's what.

'A priest, young ladies, is absolutely beyond. Absolutely. I'm shocked. My Jack's shocked. After all, I mean to say, a priest, it's shocking. Absolutely. Not that I'm saying that you young ladies are behind it, my Jack suspects, and so do I, that it's Mr Peter or Mr Joe what's behind it. Who else would know a priest? They're both barmy enough, both of them. Now you young American ladies have a free way with you that's very taking, very taking indeed. Very friendly, very affable and Jack and I aren't no prudes, you know. We've children of our own, your age, grown up, gone from home, so we know what young people are like. And we was both in the war, you know. My Jack was a sapper and when the babies was evacuated I did part-time driving with the ATS so we've both seen a lot, Jack and me. We don't shock easy. Now, you pays your rent always promptly in advance and the accommodation is yours to do with what you like but a line has to be drawn somewhere and my Jack and me have drawn it. And you have to admit, young ladies all, that we've put up with an awful lot and never said overmuch about it not never. The smell of bacon and eggs cooking night noon morning dusk and dawn. I ask you. There's clouds of bacon and egg smells drifting from this house all over the street. You all must live on them. You'll all be turning into bacon and eggs. That Mr Peter, bold as brass he is and daft as a brush, the other morning he's only walking out of the front door with a dirty great bacon and egg sandwich in one hand and a big mug of tea in the other, that's all. Going to have his breakfast on the bus, I suppose. Jack and me did have a laugh. And I have to admit there's what you might call a vein of pleasantry to Mr Peter and Mr Joe that's very very agreeable, very affable indeed. But the tap dancing. Be fair, ladies. That ceiling's been thundered on. Tap dancing, square dancing for all I know, reels and jigs and hornpipes but it's tap dancing what makes that horrible clatter. All right. I know. One night Mr Joe and Mr Peter came in all light-hearted, all high-spirited, there I was and before I really knew what was happening, Mr Joe's sitting on the bottom of the stairs playing his ukulele and Mr Peter's got me waltzing all around on the lino in the hall. When I got back to our sitting room Jack smelt the whiskey on my breath so I gives him the little bottle of it Mr Peter give me and we both wound up drinking it and toasting all your good healths. Oh, we're not against a bit of fun, not Jack and me. Take that fine, strapping young lad with the ginger hair, Albie I think you call him. Months ago, the first time I ever saw Mr Peter, let alone know he was living here, he had that Albie with him. I asked them who they were and what were they doing here, and I could see an idea coming into their heads that they'd have a bit of fun with me. Mr Peter puts on this strange, weird, very peculiar voice and says his name was Milton. Ernest Milton. Then young Albie puts on the same voice and says his name is Milton as well. Ernest Milton. Then Mr Peter says they have an eccentric father whose name was also Ernest and that he'd had both his sons christened Ernest to match. Three Ernest Miltons. Really, I had to chuckle. A couple of days later what happens? There's young Albie and Mr Peter outside the front door mincing about wearing ladies' hats. Your hats, I presume, young ladies, your hats. When I asked them both what they thought they were up to, they both puts on that same peculiar voice, only much higher, and then they tells me that they hadn't told me the truth, that they really was women, both called Ernestina. Ernestina Milton. I mean, I ask you, what can you say? Now, young ladies, you are three really beautiful girls, as lovely young women as ever I've seen, and God bless you for it, with hordes of young men crashing round here with their tongues hanging out and as for the garden drainpipe, Jack and me aren't fooled, you know, that drainpipe might as well have rungs fitted to it the number of young men, and women, who use it as a way in and out of this house. You'll have to pay us for the broken drainpipe. Then there's the Risen Christ. That's what Jack calls him, and he has reason I can tell you, that O'Liver creature, that friend of Mr Peter's, him that's so tall, with all that hair and the potty eyes, a painter he calls himself. Painter? He comes in here with those big canvases of his, all weird colours of paint, all splashy blotches sploshed higgledy-piggledy, all runny and with red arrows painted on them pointing all over the place. He comes in the other night, as much paint on him as there is on his canvas, looks at me with those eyes of his all lit up and staring, and he yells at me, "King Jesus rides a milk white horse!" The Risen Christ is right, you'd want nerves of steel with him. And if it's not the Risen Christ it's that young man with all the wrinkles, Sprinkle or Tingle or Pringle or whatever he calls himself. The other morning, I wasn't prying, I just went up the stairs to your part of the house, to open a few windows, to let some fresh air in and the smell of cigarettes, beer and bacon and eggs out and as I passed that big Edwardian chest of drawers I saw that the middle one was pulled out. I was pushing it in when, Lord love a duck, what did I see but that young man with all the wrinkles sound asleep in the bleeding drawer! Excuse the language. In the drawer. Asleep. I nearly had heart failure. Up he sits, face all dreadful crumples, and says to me he says, still sitting in the drawer, "What am I doing in here, lovey? Is the party over? Could I have a cup of tea?" I didn't know what he was doing in there, did I? Could he have a cup of tea, my foot! He could get out of there but sharpish. And yes, ladies, the party is well and truly over. I mean, how would you like to walk into your own house and find a wrinkled young man sleeping in a drawer? We've put up with an awful lot, Jack and me, and I will admit at times what you might call the flow of high spirits has been very enjoyable, very amiable and affable indeed but, Jack and me are both agreed, enough is enough. It's the priest what has broken the camel's hump.'

Mrs Chubb's troublesome priest was my friend Father Leo. Father Leo had rambled into London to annoy the authorities of the one true holy apostolic faith, to take the Ninas, Pocahontas, Joe and me to see *The Wages of Fear* at the Curzon cinema and had then come back with us to Muswell Hill for a glass of something cheerful and a knees-up. Yes. Father Leo.

———

I WAS ON the body and blood, Pongo on the ting-a-ling, we were to do the seven a.m. shift, the cathedral, as is the way with awesome great stone edifices, was decidedly nippy and the war was still terrible months away from its bloody end. The stout black thread, exchanged with Craggy Tom the cobbler's son for a fag and a look at my *Film Fun*, plied with a darning needle liberated from my mother's sewing box, had worked a treat. My task, one I'd set myself and to do which had meant my arriving early at the sacristy, had been to sew together, at a point just below where I'd estimated his knees would be, a wee section of the back and the front of Pongo's black cassock. Mission accomplished. Obstacle to a successful wearing of the article undetectable to the eye. Ever a last-minute artist, Pongo will come puffing in, jabbering of the film he'd seen, cricket, the gorgeous bird he saw leaving the Children of Mary social; his usual old prate. He'll go grabbling at his cassock, which is unbuttoned down to below the waist, he'll be prattling twenty to the dozen, he'll step into it all of a rush, he might get one leg in all right, he might even get both legs in, he might, who knows with him, even start buttoning up the flaming thing. Then he'll twig. He won't be able to walk, you see, waddle, yes, but he won't be able to walk, he's been well stitched up. Chances are he'll spot the stitches but, should he try to snap them open with his hands, so strong is that thread and so densely have I needled it in, it's a hundred to plenty that the gormless prat will only tear his cassock into tatters. His best bet will be to abandon it as hopeless and grab another cassock. I've hung up two cassocks on the hooks either side of where his stitched-up one dangles. Long ones. He'll be able to get into whichever one he picks but when he tries moving, so long are the buggers, he's bound to trample straight up inside it and, with any luck, stumble about, fall over, and break his face. Failing that, he'll have to hitch up the long cassock with both hands and float towards the altar as though he were some dozy tart in a long dress walking over mud. And he has the bell to carry. Could be a lark. Not, you might understand, that I have anything against Pongo, far from it, we are great mates, it's just that the mood came on me to see that the bastard gets stuffed. Here he comes, grunting, flushed, he's been running, his eyes are wide, he looks alarmed, he says to me, 'Have you seen the new priest?'

'No.'

'You will.'

At his cassock now he is, that's a boy, go on, you red-haired pillock, flounder about, that's it, he has both legs in, well done, he's heaving, hello, he's twigged. He's spotted the stitching. He looks at me as I stand here all shining and combed in my clean cassock and crisp white surplice. 'You did this, didn't you?'

'Did what?'

'This. Put stitches in my cassock.'

'Me? Can't sew.'

'Don't come that, you lanky git, wait till mass is over then I'll murder you.'

'You? You'll need artillery, my fat friend.'

'No friend of yours, you Irish snotrag.'

At that point, there or thereabouts, it was a while ago, through the door from the presbytery, into the sacristy stepped Father Leo.

Well over six foot of him looming up there, vested head to foot in the long white alb, amice over broad and powerful shoulders, stole wrapped around a strong neck and secured under the cincture roped around his waist, with his black hair and fierce dark eyes set wide on his eagle's face he seemed to me to be an altogether huge and mighty man. Priest. Blimey. With Pongo struggling and buttoning his way into the right wrong cassock, silently Father Leo placed the chasuble over his head, draped the maniple over his arm and, his vesting completed, stared hard at the pair of us, sparing Pongo not at all but rather watching with a severe interest as my good mate finally managed to heave himself into his surplice. We were ready. In solemn procession of three, through the dim chill of the arched and empty early-morning cathedral, we set off for the Lady Chapel.

The mass was going very well indeed. As ever, we had few customers for this seven a.m. shift. Just the cleaners and the odd Knight of the Blessed Sacrament eager to keep up his quota, but our new celebrant was bringing pleasing vigour to the sing-song Latin of the liturgy and it's my belief that his acolytes' responses were amply echoing this vivacity of tone. Mine were, anyway. Pongo's too, when he remembered where we were up to. Pongo was not having an untroubled morning. He'd taken a fierce tumble at the High Altar. We had paused there to genuflect before the tabernacle. As our procession rose to continue its progress to the chapel, Pongo's genuflecting legs unravelled themselves up his cassock, he stamped down hard and over he went like a struck skittle. Poor sod. He's all right now, though, but his movements are a bit impeded because he's chosen to wear a cassock that's far too long for him. His face is a billiard-ball red, his hands are bruised from breaking the fall but, when he finds his place on the response card, he honks out lustily. Well done that man. It would be a cheerful morning all round if it weren't for this vicious draught blowing in bitter cold from a window open up at the side of this little chapel. This big Father Leo bloke puts himself about with real style. Time for me to stand close by him at the altar, and to be handy with the cruets.

'Dominus vobiscum.'

'Et cum spiritu tuo.'

'Oremus.'

Here we go. The host. The water. The wine. Now, this the Offertory verse for some reason is always said inaudibly by the priests but sometimes I catch the odd word. 'Suscipe, sancte Pater,

'circumstantibus,

'vitam aeternum. Amen.'

The water. 'Deus, qui humanae substantiae dignitatem.'

The chalice. 'Offerimus tibi, Domine'.

The bread and wine. 'Veni, sanctificator'.

The washing of hands. 'Lavabo inter innocentes manus meas'.

One of my favourite passages will shortly be coming up. When the priest says in silence a Secret prayer. They surely must be great secrets that a priest has, to say them in silence just before the most sacred parts of the mass, the elevation and consecration of the host. Great. I always earwig. You never know, something might slip out. I wonder what secrets this big fellow has. Maybe he's like that bloke from *The Playboy of the Western World*. Maybe he, too, killed his da with a belt of the shovel. Coming up. 'Orate, fratres'. He's leaning over the altar. It's all hushed. I'll listen like mad. 'For pity's sake, please shut that window or we'll all perish.' What? It sounded as though he said, 'For pity's sake, please shut that window or we'll all perish.' Blimey! He has me on the end of those piercing eyes of his. They're stabbing at me, and then at that open window, and then back at me, and then again at the open window. Blimey. He must really have said, 'For pity's sake, please shut that window or we'll all perish.' This is what Daddy would call a 'notable first'. This sort of thing never before has happened to me, not at a mass, not ever. This is only wonderful! One shut window coming up, Father. Yes indeedy. On to a chair with me. Ram down the perishing window. Off the chair. Back to the mass. Great. No stopping. Important passage coming up.

'Dominus vobiscum.'

'Et cum spiritu tuo.'

'Sursum corda.'

'Habemus ad Dominum.'

'Gratias agamus Domino Deo nostro.'

'Dignum et justum est.'

I enjoyed that. Now. Shortly, Father Leo will say, 'Sanctus, Sanctus, Sanctus.' I will hold the tail of his chasuble; Pongo, three times, will ring the bell. Coming up. 'Cum quibus et nostras voces ut admitti jubeas, deprecamur, supplici confessione dicentes'. Now. 'Sanctus, Sanctus, Sanctus.' 'Ting-a-ling-a-ling.' That's no bell. That's a voice. A quick peer backwards under my arm. Yes. Pongo has forgotten the bell. But Pongo being Pongo, having no bell, eyes shut, Pongo himself is being a bell. 'Ting-a-ling-a-ling.' Glorious. Father Leo's shoulders are shaking. Should you wonder? 'Ting-a-ling-a-ling.' Good man, Pongo! And there's consecrations and elevations to come, and more bells to be rung. Glorious, Glorious, Glorious.

---

'ARE YOU TELLING me that my boss is a conman?' Yes, it's himself, it's Father Leo. On a bright day shortly after Pongo had been for our delight an unexpected but expert, mind you, expert ringing bell, I was leaving the cathedral by a side door and there before me was Leo. Clad in priestly black, the brim at the front of his hat turned up, long bicycle-clipped legs straddling his James autocycle parked at the kerb, his voice wrapped in a metallic, wholly bogus American accent, he was putting to the question a portly, prosperous-looking large gentleman who, in answer to his interrogator, was responding with deep purple flushes and the odd vehement splutter. Again. 'Are you telling me that my boss is a conman?' A low incoherent mutter rumbled out of Portly Prosperous; he turned and in a huff and a puff the fellow stamped away. From under the upturned brim of his black and dusty hat, Leo turned on me a darkly burning eye: 'That guy,' he said to me, 'was telling me that my boss is a conman.' His boss, I thought, who's Leo's boss? I knew what a conman was, all right. He was a bloke who would sell you lumps of lead painted to look like gold bricks, or the Brooklyn Bridge when he didn't own it, what Daddy calls a flannel merchant, a geezer who runs a bucket shop, but who was Leo's boss? Monsignor Gunga of the sermons flaming with the fires of hell? The Bishop, occasionally seen at High Mass flinging with a little mop holy water at the bent heads of worshippers? The Pope, who, it was reported, personally had blessed the gross of Bakelite rosary beads which lately had fetched up in the presbytery?

'Who, Father,' I said to Leo, 'is your boss?'

'My boss,' answered Leo, neither altering the tone and tenor of his voice, nor damping down the smoulder in his eye, 'is Jesus of Nazareth.' Blimey, I thought; just blimey. 'And that guy,' Leo continued, 'was trying to tell me that when Jesus spoke of His kingdom He didn't really mean what He said!'

'When, Father, Jesus spoke of His kingdom, what, then, Father, did Jesus mean?'

'You're young,' said Leo, softening not at all, cooling not by a degree, 'but know this. The kingdom Jesus spoke of, whatever of this world, that world, the next world, the other world: the kingdom of Jesus is on this side of death.' Leo started up the little engine on his James autocycle, and off he pop pop popped about his parish.

Leo's words on the whereabouts of the Nazarene's kingdom,

words which never had I heard before, implied to me that day not only that I already inhabited that kingdom, but also they put into my mind, for reasons that I did not then well understand, a slowly forming idea of a Jesus as an actual figure in a real world: human, in fact. This inhabitant of that kingdom went thoughtfully whistling on his boy's own way.

A sturdy old bike with a wee engine on its back wheel to assist up hills both bike and biker, that really summed up the composition of the James autocycle on which Leo rode around, but the popping sound of the vehicle and the cheerful sight of its rider brought much gladness to the hearts of the Catholic community of the city. A learned seminarian, an educated man with a wide range of secular interests, you may be sure that on points of scripture, both with the laity and with his colleagues in holy orders, he relished combative debate but, very like his boss before him, he was not overwhelmed by scripture, rather he found in it much that invited speculation, much that could accommodate the altering circumstances of human life. Again like his boss before him, Leo had his own line of country, his own views of conduct, which he then quoted scripture to support. Annoying, that. To some. Overtly, then, being an ordained priest chiefly meant to Leo that he was another of his boss's apostles. An apostle from whom oozed no odour of sanctity, who eschewed religiosity as he did pomposity, whose vitality, authority and common humanity were startling, and who had determined that by thought and word and deed the well-being of his parishioners would be his golden priority. Amen. That he was a card also is true. Nor, you should know, did he neglect the war wounded.

Imagine. You are a serviceman. You have been wounded. A bullet or a shell or a bomb got you. Your body has been burnt, split, gashed, broken. You have lost a leg or an arm or your sight. Stomach or liver or kidneys or lungs are wrecked. You are in hospital, now, deep in rural north-west England. Your wounds have been tended and bound with bandages. Wearing your light blue pyjama-like injured serviceman's uniform, you have walked or hobbled or been wheeled or carried to the sunlit recreation room and there you are having a smoke, a cup of tea or coffee, and a chat. No blasts of battle are about you, no firestorm rages, no clamour of attack, foray, raid, encounter. Wounded, yes. Maimed, perhaps. You know a kind of peace. Skirling, droning, shrieking, wailing, sounding through the flung wide doors of the quiet room, in streel the kilted bagpipers of Lord Kilmorey's Own Hibernians, Donal MacBruin at the head, Big Hamish, Pongo and I blowing hard behind him. It is only lamentable. From my pipe-playing position at the back of this honking squealing hideously shrill quartet, I could see on the stricken faces of those wounded warriors, flabbergasted and deeply unhappy, great winces that shuddered through their battered bodies and shook into the remainder pith of their tormented souls. My view was that we should skedaddle pronto. A prudent notion not shared by The MacBruin. Not him.

Made mad by God, Donal the Gael, for whose race the sainted G. K. Chesterton tells us all wars are merry and all songs are sad, even as our opening burst of 'The Wearing of the Green' came mercifully to an end, didn't the man step forward and begin to pipe up a solo number? He did. What tune he piped that day no longer can I remember. 'The Truetodeedle Song', perhaps. Who knows? All I can tell you is that seldom if ever on a bagpipe has a tune been more swiftly played. Flicking, releasing, blocking the stops, in a rippling blur his fingers flew and hammered up and down, down and up, fair blistering his chanter and ever more rapidly a profusion of notes came tumbling out of his instrument. Then it was over. The deed was done. A terrible silence filled the room. Donal turned, Hamish, Pongo and I turned, and with all convenient speed Lord Kilmorey's Own Hibernians scarpered through the door.

That from our kilted rear a murderous fusillade of false legs, false arms, glass eyes, walking sticks, crutches, wheelchairs, false teeth and piss-pots was not flung to cut down, bludgeon and slaughter us into bloody bits upon the spot will to me for ever remain a mystery and a mercy. But, Lord love a duck, it was so. Leo moved swiftly. No longer would the convalescence of injured servicemen be so violently assaulted. No more would our band be put to piping peril. No. He had formed a Boy Scout troop at the cathedral, he wanted bold musicians to lead this troop on their marches, Lord Kilmorey's Own Hibernians were by Leo dragooned into the service of his Scouts.

'Joy cometh in the morning,' says the psalm, and it pleases me to believe that on that chill yet cheery morning more than fifty years ago when Leo and I first met at mass in the cathedral, to the nature of the sacrament which that morning he ministered, to the pure and unblemished essence of its mystery, two scamps of schoolboys and a young Irish priest brought with them an earthly joy in merriment and so blessed the beginning of a friendship between two flawed vessels, Leo and me. In Moelwyn Merchant's beautiful novel *Jeshua*, Gamaliel the Pharisee tells James the brother of Jesus that throughout time Adonai has been content to use flawed vessels. Well, you couldn't hope to find a better pair of flawed vessels than Leo and me: half a century after we first met, cracked, antique, our friendship still creaks on.

---

'GIVE US A LOOK at the paper, Daddy.'

12th April 1945. On Pine Mountain in Warm Springs, Arkansas, in his bedroom in a small bungalow, at 3.35 p.m. today, Franklin Delano Roosevelt died. He had been having his portrait painted

373

when a severe headache suddenly struck him. Two hours later, he died of a cerebral haemorrhage. The news of his death was telephoned to Mrs Eleanor Roosevelt who was attending a charity function in New York. President Roosevelt was sixty-three.

30th April 1945. Shot by their own countrymen, tied by the feet to the front of a garage, side by side in Milan, the bodies of Mussolini and his mistress Clara hang head down in the Piazza Loretto.

30th April 1945. Hitler is dead. At 3.30 p.m., ten days after his fifty-sixth birthday, sitting on a sofa in his underground bunker in Berlin, Adolf Hitler shot himself. By his side was the body of the woman whom on the previous day he had married. Eva Hitler had poisoned herself.

7th May 1945. In a small red schoolhouse at Rheims, General Eisenhower, the Allied Supreme Commander, received the instrument of unconditional surrender which General Alfred Jodl, the German emissary and Army Chief of Staff, had signed. General Bedell Smith signed for the Western Allies. General Ivan Suslapatov was witness for Russia. The war in Europe was over.

Bells ring out, bands play, voices sing and laugh and shout; flags are waved, beer drunk, streamers chucked, cardboard bugles and squeakers blown, and through the streets of the city on this sunlit day of May the thirteenth, nineteen forty-five the happy men and women and the children of the town stream along in carefree celebration. It is Victory in Europe Day. From morning to early afternoon, I had wandered alone about the city, watching the fun as soldiers, sailors, airmen, civilians climbed up lamp posts, rode the town-hall lions and danced the hokey-cokey down the broad thoroughfares but, though I enjoyed the clamour and the gladness all about me, and truly felt the shared relief that after five years and eight months for us the war was over, within me there roamed a deep sadness and from the hullabaloo of happiness I walked apart.

At home in the afternoon I had listened to the wireless and had heard that mighty spirit Winston Churchill, whose defiant courage and eloquence had inspired his nation to endure and to fight and fight again, broadcast his victory speech and say, 'Long live the cause of freedom,' to the people of England, and then I had quit the house. A street party had been rollicking on outside but, although I had lingered there a while, drunk my lemonade, eaten my cake, watched a couple of the turns being performed on the open back of a furniture removal van, parked there on the cobbles for the purpose, what I had wanted was to be quiet, away from crowds, from noise, and so I had walked away, through the ginnel across the railway lines, over the wasteland, past the mills and the factories and now I sit on the bank of the old canal, gazing down at the still, brown water, watching a patch of oil float and bob, slick with bright colours. For a half an hour or so I had bowled a stone at a crack in a wall. One, two, three, four, five paces, leap on to the delivery foot, six, head still, eyes on the crack, fling the left arm from the right ear to cut over and down at the target, swivel the body and mill round the right arm high and straight, seven, away at the crack flies the stone, follow through. Again and again and again. But I got fed up with that and so I sat myself down by the canal.

Peaceful enough it is here, right enough. In the sunshine. Going hither and yon, the odd sod passes by; the sound of revelry can still be heard, all right, but far away; on the whole, I have the canal and its banks to myself. Yes. Look into the waters. 'I was at home    And should have been most happy – but I saw    Too far into the sea'. Aye, me and all, John Keats, and if it's only a slimy old brown canal I'm looking into, it will do as a sea, it will have to. 'Where every maw    The greater on the less feeds evermore.' No maws here, John Keats, no jaws, no waves, just a sludgy bubble or two with here and there the odd suck and ripple, but they come, but they go. 'But I saw too distinct into the core Of an eternal fierce destruction,      And so from happiness I was far gone.'

Aye. Not altogether, though, John Keats. Not, at any rate, me. Glum a bit today I am, but it will pass. After Churchill's broadcast, I had watched my mother and father walk down the street and they had been walking hand in hand. I'd never seen that before. To be sure, the four of us, my parents, my sister and me, we were forever kissing and cuddling, but not until today had I seen my mother and father walking together holding hands. They had looked young. And my little sister had danced. To what music I can't say: a wireless playing in a house, perhaps; a gramophone in the street, a band passing by, a mouth organ; maybe to a music within her only she could hear, that could have been so. Beautiful she'd been on the back of that old furniture van. Mop of black curls, to which from time to time she'd give a haughty toss, back arched, small slim figure erect, relaxed, blue eyes now open, now closed, alone up there, heedless of onlookers, heedless, it seemed, of the world, nimbly, gracefully, formally, casually, heeding surely rhythm, melody, harmony, my little sister Pat danced; and serenity was in her face. We were at Peace.

>
> You haven't an arm, you haven't a leg, aroo! aroo!
> You haven't an arm, you haven't a leg, aroo! aroo!
> You haven't an arm, you haven't a leg,
> You're an eyeless, boneless, chickenless egg,
> You'll have to be put with a bowl to beg,
> Johnny, I hardly know you.
> With your drums and guns and guns and drums, aroo! aroo!

---

THIRTY MILES and more from Inchgoole, I'd reckon, and that across the bog where there's gyrations to the road would have you twisted, tracks off the road, easily taken, rambling away to nowhere at all, chunks of it gone entirely, all of which must be put into the addition, and so I'd say that, from Inchgoole to here, a roundish figure of about thirty miles and then some would be approximately fair. Golden gorselands behind us, Patrick Pearse's cottage there across the bay, over the swing bridge, through Ballydangle, past where Horseface has the boozer, beyond the quarry where Maurteen Bawn hews out the pink granite, away along down the lonesome road to the isles, into miles of silence and a place of stone under the sky, that's where you find Pocahontas and me, the pair of us among the stones, both staring out over an immensely still Atlantic, and while clouds brood above us as the bright sun lurks behind them, in the hazy blueness of this day the sea and the sky seem indivisibly to be one.

Jaunting off to Ireland on the night boat from Liverpool, tumbling down the gangway at the North Wall in Dublin, land legs firmly on the cobbled quays and immediately the Hopi is Molly Bloom and I, of course, Poldy. 'Dublin has a Jewish Lord Mayor? Bobbie Briscoe? Groovy hallelujah!' Breakfast gulped down and away we go to saunter along the banks of Anna Livia Plurabelle, the niffey Liffey, the loved river running its life through Dublin's old heart. O'Connell Street and bullet-pitted post office next. Site and symbol of the Easter Rising in 1916, the rebellion whose eventual outcome was the end of England's eight-hundred-year dominion of Ireland, that alone surely made the building worth a visit but as my savage urgently needed to post off to London an essay she had written, a fair copy of which for much of the pitch and toss in the eight-hour crossing I had laboured on her portable typewriter to produce, its ordinary function as a working post office would suit us very nicely, too. In through the scarred columns, past the black statue of Cuchulain, emblem of the rebels, the raven of death on his shoulder, and with stamps bought and licked, an envelope addressed, off to England goes the essay.

Out in the street again, I am Sean McBride, Pocahontas Countess Markievicz. 'A Countess? I love it. Markievicz? She Jewish too?' Into the middle of the road, to where Pearse read out the proclamation of an Irish Republic. 'In the name of God and of the dead generations'. Away again back down O'Connell Street. 'Who's the guy on top of this high column?'

'Nelson.'

'The English Lord Nelson? Trafalgar, all that?'

'That's the man.'

'What's he doing in Dublin?'

'I don't know, keeping his eye on the place, I suppose.'

Across the bridge over the Liffey, past Trinity College, up Grafton Street to Stephen's Green, through the dusky green, twist round to Baggot Street, and into a snug in a pub for a pint of Threble X with a creamy thick head on it a man could rest his face on. Captain Jack, me, is in fine fettle; Juno, herself, purring with happiness. Gathered in a neighbour snug, giving their tongues a fling, an assortment of men sip and blather. As happens in pubs in Dublin, the group is made up of, say, a docker, a physicist, a jockey, a taxi driver, a bank manager and an under-taker, all of whom in intricately strung sentences, are giving their views on the comparative merits of, say again, the nineteenth-century poets Ferguson and Mahoney and which horse will piss what race at Leopardstown. Drawn by the twangle in the sound and sense of these voices, round the corner of our snug and into theirs drift that Hopi and I, the better for to earwig the mouth music being made there. Charmed by the sight of a neat little dark-looking judy in the boozer, and don't mind the long bollix that's with her, we are made welcome to this morning assembly, are told that our money is useless in this pub, are kindly bought drinks, a small Irish for that handsome young woman, a pint for the long hoor, same again all round, Jack, and the rich prattle sounds on. Our companion taxi driver sports on an eye a fine shiner. There is a pause in the chat.

'How did you get the black eye?' Pocahontas wants to know.

'I swerved to avoid a child,' says the driver, 'and fell out of the bed.'

Where to doss, where to doss? Oh, I know a spot, a dilapidated little spot, just come along a me, and after passing eight clocks showing times differing wildly from each other, and all wholly at variance with what ticks neatly on my sweetheart's wristwatch, we reach that spot, where they are glad to see us, in about, what, call it fifteen or so minutes, give or' take, and there we park our rucksacks, pay up for two nights' kip and rashers in the morning, and with some disbelief but certain determination herself riffles through a guide book, optimistically to plot out a timetable for the afternoon which, it is not to be doubted, we will spend visiting art galleries, museums, libraries, statues, places of historical interest and buildings of architectural merit. Come the shades of evening, though, it also is not to be doubted, we shall both be plushily seated amongst the marble and mahogany and etched glass of the Dolphin, chewing prawns, munching beefsteaks until, replete with grub at last, we shall go tripping along the quays, up a crack, and into a gorgeous hole I know where there's rakes of gargle, chunter, and the crack is mighty.

*Twenty Years a-Wooing.* Expectancy, disappointment, surprise, pleasure. A roll around of sensations, right enough, for us to have had in one night at a theatre. The play's title had seemed familiar to us. Was it a Lennox Robinson, a Brinsley Macnamara, a T. C. Murray, a play we'd heard of but didn't know? Whatever, we had expected from the ring in its title to see an Abbey perennial. Not so. *Twenty Years a-Wooing* turned out to be a new play written by a John McCann. Hadn't heard of him. Disappointed, really, because truly we'd hoped to see an O'Casey, a Synge, a Yeats, a Gregory, you know, one of the Abbey's Gods, but not being greedy but liking a lot we'd settled for an earthling only: but John McCann?

A fire having burned down to ashes the old Abbey in 1951, the company was playing at the Queen's Theatre, a vasty barn in Dame Street. Up went the curtain and we'd been completely surprised to see a skilfully crafted, well-acted play, which looked evenly but keenly and compassionately at Ireland in our time of 1954; the measured cadences of a Yeats changed utterly by tough and abrupt comical tones of the street; old themes of love and trouble played by no Cathleen Ni Houlihan or Niall of the Hostages but by young lasses with perms and high heels and young lads wearing zoot suits and playing saxophones. Pleasing, that, to the pair of us, and, after a quiet and a lovely day in which we'd trundled out by bus to Ireland's garden, Wicklow, and had glimpsed her meadows, streams, woodlands, waterfalls, vales, rivers, her mountains beyond; had walked between the two lakes either side the unearthly majesty in the ruins of the old monastic city, gazed up at the soaring high round tower, wandered by graves, we had then hopped on a bus back to Dublin city. Yes. Pleasing that Mr McCann and the Abbey had had a crack at grabbing stuff from the flux and fixity of contemporary life and putting it in play form on a lighted stage.

A man of parts, the writer John McCann: although not a Jew he, too, had been Lord Mayor of Dublin, and by John out of Margaret, there came naying and yeaing into this world Donal McCann. Pound for pound, and that fellow carts a load of those around, as fine an actor as any this world knows, Oscar O'Flaherty Fingal Wills McShant, my name for him, oh don't ask why, oh don't ask why, for almost thirty years Donal and I have been friends and colleagues. You may have seen him playing Conroy in John Huston's final film, his appropriately elegiac, supremely realized version for the cinema of James Joyce's *The Dead*, and the other night, sitting in the audience, I saw McCann with matchless passion and a superbly honed technique, move and shake to laughter, tears and sad silence all of us in the auditorium. The play was *The Steward of Christendom*, by Sebastian Barry, an astonishingly beautiful work. Larky lad, McShant; a brainy bugger whom I love, skilled with the inky pen, the brush, plays the mouth organ, has no big toe on his right foot. That's about the size of it.

Connacht, girl, over the Shannon and into the Fair Land. Aye. Tuck it away carefully, sweetheart, we'll pick it up when we get back to Dublin. That's it. You see, what with her being a Red Indian over here to learn the language and all, and our arriving early at the Queen's Theatre, where we'd somehow found ourselves having a bit of a chat with members of the company and the administration, who found her to be charming and knowledgeable and articulate about Irish theatre, don't mind the long bollix with her, hadn't she been with great kindness given a dainty present? She had. A programme from the first night that the Abbey Theatre Company opened its doors on the twenty-seventh of December nineteen hundred and four.


We would have been heartily welcome, the policeman had assured us, to sleep the night in a cell at his police station but unfortunately he already had hens and chickens in one cell and a sow with her litter in the other. However, if we were so minded, his wife's sister's husband had an aunt who lived only a mile or so down the road and she, he was fairly sure, from time to time, for a few shillings only, did provide bed and breakfast for wanderers to the isles. Would he, he'd wanted to know, as night was fast falling, walk the step with us? Scragged by winds, bone weary from tramping rocky roads, awed by the fields of stone, treeless, houseless, the sea hushing deeply around them, gladly we'd gone along with our policeman's suggestions and sure enough as dark came tumbling down that noble officer, whose jail sheltered pigs and poultry, had found for us a place where we could lodge for the night.

Bright morning, now, and well rested, well fed, Pocahontas perches on a boulder, I sit on another, and here among the Rocks of Bawn we both gaze out over the broad Atlantic. From east to west, from sunrise to sundown, from Dublin to Connacht, good fortune the whole while with us, from coast to coast we had hitched lifts across the breadth of Ireland. At Eamon's pub in the county of Mayo, beads in her old fist, his mother knelt behind the bar saying a decade of the rosary. Eamon was at the pictures. Icy Icelandic waters, sailoring for England's Queen, protecting her Royal Codfishes from Ingelrica Bloodaxemansdotter's predatory countrymen, as we lurched about the bridge on our corvette, Eamon and I had yarned together, telling one another what, should we survive the perils of the Cod War and when we no longer would be salt-water sailors, we hoped to do with our lives. He'd listened to me tell of my wish to become a drama student and then had said, 'My father died last year. He left me a pub in Mayo. I'm going to drink myself to death.' Scraps of memory only, you understand, but in that pub, among the Hail Marys, the fumes of shag and plug, and the quiet solitary men supping their pints, in the dim light the Hopi and I sit at our ease, through the door sways Eamon, a year only into his life's ambition, his eyes telling me plain he has determined that one day he will complete this task he had set himself, and we are made welcome.

Twenty-five years it took him but, constant to his purpose, seldom entirely sober, rarely straying far from those licensed premises, whose modest profits mostly went down his throat, at last Eamon did not fail. One night he set off to climb up the stairs in his pub and he never got to the top.

In those young years, though, apprentices both to our hard trades, taciturn and undemonstrative Eamon had in no way been displeased to see again his former shipmate, had been charmed by my rare companion, and with his guidance, by Lough Conn, below the Ox mountains, before Killala Bay, for a couple of fine days Pocahontas and I rambled around this stretch of the wild and lovely ancient kingdom of Connacht.

Pegeen Mike, herself, among barrels and brisk with a broom to the flagstones outside the pub; Christy Mahon, myself, seated atop a barrel, cooling drink to hand, approving of this work, and J. M. Synge much on both our minds. 'I knew a party was kicked in the head by a red mare, and he went killing horses a great while, till he eat the insides of a clock and died after.' Yes, *The Playboy of the Western World* country it is that we're in, the very stuff of the poets' play living all around us, Chicago and the Royal Academy of Dramatic Art far, far away, our senses plugged in to sounds, sights, sensations immediately with us. Eamon pokes his head round the door. 'I've a friend inside drinking his breakfast. He'll be off in his car to Galway shortly and can give you a lift. He's a decent man and mad. Will I tell him it'll suit?'

Look, do, at any good map of Ireland. You may perceive that of the roads which run from Killala Bay to Galway City there's none cannot but jink, sidestep, swerve its way around mountain, lake or crag. What your good map of Ireland will not reveal to you is the staggering number of pubs lying in wait along each zig and zag of your chosen road. That, at any rate, those long years ago, is how matters had seemed to the Hopi and me. Do you see, Galway City and from there by boat to the Aran islands was where next we had hoped to travel. Eamon's friend's offer to us of a trip there in his car did indeed suit. A husky man, our driver, and silent, and smiling, we stowed our kit in his old black car, thanked Eamon, wished him well, and leaving him at his pub, glass in fist, busy about his life's work, off to Galway in the motor we bowled. We'd gone, what, five miles? Ten? Hardly more, when our amiable man at the wheel pulled up the car at the side of the road in a small village, turned to us, beamed gently and said softly, 'We'll have a sup of black porter.' For our journey to Galway, the City of the Tribes, one knew that, quietly, inflexibly, a crazy pattern had been set. Dear laminated Jesus, but don't ask me for details for I have scarcely any for you. Depending on the way that one went, on the Irish roads of nineteen fifty-four, one's journey from A to B, that time, should have been anything from a neat seventy-five miles or so, to a rambling hundred and odd, give or take; with a mean time for the trip, either route, or a differ, allowing for essential stoppages, hunger, thirst, fuel for the vehicle, a visit to Red Dan, collision with a restive beast, of, say, four and a bit hours to five or more. When not hurrying.

Dawn it was when we arrived at the outskirts of the gaunt, grey city of Galway. We had set off from Eamon's before noon on the previous day. 'We'll have a sup of black porter', that had been our theme. Fond of the stuff, me, new to the brew, she, unquenchably thirsted, he, for thirty or so minutes, more or less, we would in our car roll along the roads in purposeful locomotion, our quiet man at the wheel, smiling the while as he drove, a left, or a right, or a little further on, the car would halt, on with the brakes, switch off the engine, that friendliest of lunatics would turn to us, he would beam. And. Pubs, hotels, shebeens, shops, farmhouse kitchens, garages, back rooms, cellars, attics, offices, premises of all sorts, licensed or otherwise, did we call in for to sup down black porter, diversifying these visits with unlikely but certain progresses by motor vehicle, clutches of miles at a time, south-east, south-west, southerly down the road.

Awash with bottled bogwater, stiff in the driving seat, Smiler sits; snoozy in the back, similarly disordered, the pair of us cuddle up cosily; and in a parked car on the edge of that City of the Tribes, for a few hours we three travellers from Mayo slip easily into untroubled coma. We are at Galway.

> My shoes they are well worn
> And the rain comes tumbling in.
> My old coat it is threadbare now

And I'm leaking to the skin;
But I'll rise up in the morning
All for the clear daylight to dawn,
And I know I'll never be able
To plough the Rocks of Bawn.


'Flowers on the fisherman's field.' White breakers run foaming
on the sea swelling high, and that version in English of a dainty,
laconic Irish saying tells us that this day no fishermen will be
putting out their boats into the water's danger. No, by God. Nor
will the Aran boat be sailing. Disappointing, that, for the Hopi,
who had wanted very much to sail out to those remote, stone isles;
to wander in the winds among rocks and the limestone houses; to
hear Irish spoken by people whose ordinary tongue it was; to see
for herself what she knew of only from books, plays, films; the
hardy islanders living out their own ways of life on Inishmore or
Inishmaan or Inisheer, since recorded time islands inhabited by
Aran folk, and lying off this jagged edge to the north-western
seaboard of the continent of Europe. But. I know a spot. A lonely,
a desolate, a beautiful place. Scantily populated, and that by Irish
speakers, stony flatlands running with waters and lapped by the
sea, where meagre patches of shallow poor soil yield spuds and
turnips, home to the solitaries, the heron, the bittern, where
seaweed is harvested, and which, though linked to the main by
stone-built causeways, by swing-bridges of iron, still remains a
cluster of small islands, entire of themselves. Shall we go there,
girl, shall we go? Surely. We can go most of the way there by bus.

And that is where you find us, Pocahontas and me, seated on
boulders, apart, smoking, thinking; the sea before us still as the
stones about us, and greatly all around us a silence broods. Of a
sudden, having all that morning sulked up behind white cloud,
the sun rolled out from its cover, lolled lazily in the bright sky

and, brazen as you ever did see, leered down on us a flaming great grin. Well, the response from this melancholy shore and the sombre deep sea was immediate and unrestrained. Paint pots of colours spilled out from the stones, the ocean, the rock pools, bog drains, kelp bunches, tufty scrub, the flinty walls, the isolated houses, and the air itself shone gorgeous over the lonely isles. Revelry in the wilderness, bright-hued, jaunty and brave.

In his painting *Clown of the Ocean*, Jack Yeats shows us a tall figure, dressed in motley, standing on a crude raft rigged up from the timbers of a broken circus wagon, and setting out to sea from a sunlit stretch of the western coast of Ireland. For me, that painting has a myriad meanings: it also holds all the colours and the mood of that our time on the isles of South Connemara. So swift, so unexpected, was this switch in aspect, that when what had seemed timeless, grave, eternal, turned round to become immediate, frolicsome, and grandly beautiful, why, a rip of laughter fair chuckled out of me. The Hopi looked over at me, nodded her head, smiled in happy agreement, plucked out a lipstick and a mirror from her satchel, faced again the old blue sea and, ever one to be at her best for fine occasions, began carefully to make up her lips. That was when I said goodbye to her. No, she didn't hear me for the words were unspoken. Yes, there would be the return to London, a night or two on the razzle in the town, the spiffing news that her essay had won first prize, the flapping of hankies as her boat left Southampton for America, but with herself on a rock, me on another, lipstick to her mouth, a cigarette to mine, in the sun, by the sea, in the holy land of Ireland, that was when we parted. Farewell and adieu to you, dark little Jewess. Farewell and adieu to you, sweetheart of mine.

---

RED AS HELL, the sunset, that time when one evening on a waterfront I stood watching as a setting sun bloodied the tide running swiftly into the bay. Fishing boats, restless, uneasy, chafed at their moorings, tugging, heaving, and with smacks and spanks angrily their sterns slapped hard at the red and streaming indifferent water. Or so it had seemed. Presently, the sharp steel in that north wind which from the Sea of Japan stabs cold into Nagasaki, knifed through my greatcoat and, chill, contemplative, I shuddered my way back to our hotel above the fishing village. Ahead of me, trudging up the same path and similarly wrapped up against the raw cut of the wind, was a Japanese chap, a man of about my own age, and whom I recogized as one of a party of us who that day had flown down from Tokyo. My visit to the country was a business trip, only indirectly connected to films or filming, and I'd found myself blundering about among the rituals and formal graces of corporate Japan, a sore thumb to an efficient body of businessmen. During the various meetings and discussions that we'd had, I'd noticed that the man who was sharing the slope with me up to the hotel had always spoken quietly, paternally, had been deferred to by the others and clearly was an authoritative figure in the group. We reached the entrance. He kindly held open the door for me. Passing him, I nodded a thank-you and saw that I was looking into eyes that were unguarded, sensitive, and questioning. 'Nagasaki,' I said.

'Nagasaki,' he answered.

Two or three hot drinks later, seated at a table in the bar, an interpreter attending, and having established that we were both indeed more or less the same age, he asked me what I remembered of the days when the atom bombs had fallen. Having been often though inadvertently impolite in his country, it seemed to me meet that I should, as it were, this time open the door for him, and so I asked him what he remembered. He had been in the countryside north of Tokyo, I learned, and in common with most of the population of Japan, had heard nothing of the bombings. Tokyo's devastation by air raids and firestorms, that news had come his way, but it was only after Emperor Hirohito had broadcast that Japan would unconditionally surrender did he learn of Hiroshima, Nagasaki, and of their obliteration by atom bombs. Me?

Plunge with me into the belly of this dark river. That's a wetting, nippy and a delightful shock. Thrust and kick and pull and breathe and coil and thrust and kick and pull and breathe and coil. That's the way of it. The upthrust of your river is not what it is in the tiled and diving-boarded, shallow- and deep-ended chemical waves of your municipal swimming pool. By no means. All below you and about you is a power running deep running stealthy running wide running strong. Dark she is, and for all the sunbeams bouncing on her, she won't buoy you up, no, she'll hug you right down. Here's stealth. Here's no clatter, no commotion. Here sound plops and sucks and chuckles. Steady for a second. Paddle. Feel the current tug your body and push against your face. Right. A hundred yards upstream against that current, up to where the wire-bound logs hang stretching across the river. Big breath. And. Thrust and kick and pull and breathe and coil and thrust and kick and pull and breathe and coil. Swim, you bastard, swim. Two and a half minutes only, and you'll be there. Thrust as though you were a battering ram. Kick waves against either bank of the river. Pull your shoulders right out the water. On you go, boy, on you go, on, on, on. Swim, you bastard, swim. Upstream, upstream, upstream. Where are those fucking logs? There! On. On. On. Double efforts and redouble efforts. On. On. On. Thrust and kick and pull and breathe and coil and thrust and kick and pull and breathe and coil and thrust. And grab the logs. Puffed, by God, puffed. Swallowed half the river. Prob'ly swallowed a trout. Have a good splutter. Breathe in through the nose. Exhale. That's the way. Breathe. Exhale. Puff's coming back. Breathe. Exhale. Blow your nose in the river. Snot's good for trouts. That's what I reckon. Good swim, that. Good rhythm. Good time. A drop in the tank at the death, too. Least, that's what I'll tell anyone who asks. Now for the best part. Now for the glorious part. Now for the super-dooper river ride. Away with you, you droopy old logs, for here we go. Effortlessly to cruise along downstream in the river, and the current propelling you. Float. Drift. Flow. Manoeuvre a little with the hands, the feet. Stay in the river's middle. You'll feel the depth to her drive as she glides you along. It's only bliss. No grind, no slog, no ache, just ride along on the river. Yippee! A good trick is to swirl around and, lying on your back, bob along down feet first. To be sure, it takes a bit of effort, but you'll find it's well worth it. It's as though you're sitting on the river looking at the view. The greenwood either hand, a summer's sky blue above. Luxury. Getting stronger. Every swim. I feel it. Good feeling. Captain of swimming, now. And we're scooping up pots and gongs, team and individual. And at thirteen I'm a year younger than anyone else in the team. Good feeling. Dear God, but I love swimming in rivers, and kissing girls. Hello. Here's my stop. End of the ride. Out you scramble. Belt along to the tent. Towel down. Scramble into shorts, a shirt, shoes. Scamper down to the country town. Buy a glass of pop. Gobstoppers. Wander by the pubs and round the market. See what's up. The Mother Shipton pub. There's the stream that runs through a trough from a spring. Pop anything into the trough, it will turn to stone. Honest. There's a pair of gloves in there petrifying nicely. Here's a newspaper van pulling up at the newsagent's. Out from the back of the van the driver's lad heaves a big heavy bundle of newspapers, tied with string, on to the pavement. Let's have a squint. Huge headline. 'Atomic bomb. Japanese cities totally destroyed.' Huge photograph. A vast funnel of debris, dust and fires shooting up into the sky and then spreading out in an enormous boiling knob. Jesus. The newsagent's cutting the string on the bundle. Grab a couple. Here are my pennies. Thanks. Hurtle back to the field by the river where we're camping. Trotting, reading, gasping. One bomb flattens a city and kills eighty thousand people. Trot. Read. Gasp. Another bomb flattens another city and kills another eighty thousand people. Trot. Read.

Gasp. Five miles high, that cloud, five miles wide. Hiroshima. Nagasaki. Japan must surrender. A million lives will be saved. 'Great news, lads! The atomic bomb. Look at that picture. Was there ever a bigger bang ever? The Yanks are blowing Japan up into shite!'

Father Leo grabs a newspaper. Stares. Reads quickly. Hands the paper to Donal MacBruin and says, 'Pity the poor devils under that cloud but, please God, let it put a stop to this accursed war. Hallelujah!'

All of us boys are buzzing and whooping. Everyone wants to look at the picture in the newspaper. Faces flush and excitement whooshes around like fire.

'Five miles.'

'That's high as Everest.'

'Eighty thousand with one shy.'

'A gross or two of them fellers, you'd make bits of the world.'

Here's Donal MacBruin playing blazes out of the Irish warpipes. 'Drop an atomic bomb on the hairy little Scotch bastard.'

There's joy and jumping and commotions.

Slumbering, grumbling, and farting under canvas that time by the river Nidd in those summer days of 1945, the heap was composed of cathedral Scouts, whose number was augmented by several young persons who had for the occasion disguised themselves as Scouts; a pile of hard chaws from Father Leo's home town in Ireland, a handful of whom were Scouts, the rest, the majority, having signed on for the crack in the trip to England merely, disdaining even to feign solidarity with that tenderfooted brotherhood; Lord Kilmorey's Own Hibernians, that's me, Pongo, Hamish; and our adult supervisors, Father Leo, Donal MacBruin, Michael Kenealy, a couple of others, they will forgive me, I have forgotten their names. Pubescent adolescents, most of us, the news of the atom bomb and the imminent end of the war released in us fantasy, ebullience, high jinks, high spirits, high hopes, but as the days turned over and time ticked on our moods levelled out even as our testicles descended and soon all was normal again as we set to brawls and songs and robbing orchards; cricket, smoking, masturbating, hurling, swimming, gabbing, swapping, breaking bones, and, knowing nothing of the incertitudes nature had woven into the coming years, just got on with the aching business of being boys.

Different, though, for the adults with us as more news came to them from radios, newspapers, the talk of the town, and their minds in vain tried to ingest reason from the magnitude of what had happened.

'One hundred pounds of chemicals produced an explosion the equivalent of twenty thousand tons of TNT. Why, that's twenty thousand V2 rockets landing on this field.'

'Five thousand four hundred degrees Fahrenheit. Isn't that half the heat the sun gives out?'

'Yes. But the sun's ninety-three million miles away. The suns at Hiroshima and Nagasaki fell on the heads of the inhabitants.'

'Uranium 235.'

'Splitting the atom.'

'Little Boy.'

'Fat Man.'

'People and buildings melted.'

'At the epicentre, people turned into vapour.'

'Some were fired into shadows on the stone.'

'It had to be done.'

'It won the war.'

'If the Nazis or the Japs had had the atomic bomb, do you think they would have had any scruples about dropping it?'

'That's the point. Who in the future will have scruples?'

Yes, I heard scraps of the adults' talk, saw the occasional shadows fall over their features, understood the tone, at least, of their speculations, prefigurations in little, I suppose, of the

anxieties, the concerns, the intellectual, rational, moral delibera-
tions that would come and be ever present with us, but at the time
truly was I heedless of those grave matters, occupying myself more
with matters of great moment such as from whom would I be able
to cadge a cigarette, my wonderful swims in the river, and the
torment brought to me by the farmer's daughter who, having
pretended to be picking blackberries, bent over to wash her hands
in the brook, hoisted up her skirts to leap over the trickle and
thus brought to me fierce trouble in the trousers.

MacBruin alone in the woods, playing on his pipes 'Lament for
the Children', the pibroch that holds agony, composed in the
eighteenth century by McCrimmon, after he had returned home
to find that his eight sons had been murdered.

---

### KING HENRY THE FOURTH, PART TWO, ACT III, SCENE II
*The Open Razor's chambers*

Comfily parked on his sofa, fine goodies to hand, the Open Razor
addresses me, even as I settle into my usual seat on the big old
armchair.

RON: Don't, Pedro, for fuck's sake, my treasure, start on that
who's dead palaver, or we'll be here till sparrow fart
chuntering on about who's brown bread. 'Death, as the
Psalmist saith, is certain to all; all shall die.' So leave it out
because all the mates are dropping like flies, Pedro, like flies
they're dropping, lovey, the mates, the contemporaries, it's too
depressing. I totter to the boozer for a pint of lager at
Christmas. Wallop. John Osborne's dead. First thing the

governor told me. Before I'd even dipped my lips into the brew. Disagreeable toad. 'Wouldn't it have been more civil of you,' I suggested to that oaf, 'to have considered before apprising me of such glum tidings, that it were better to wait until after the festivities?' 'Sorry, Ron,' he muttered, 'thought you should know.' Shortly after Christmas, into the same boozer I pop, am about to sip my sherbet, up behind the bar strolls that beast of a landlord. 'Didn't mean to upset you before the festivities, Ron. John Osborne, and that. All right if I mention passing away now?' 'John Osborne,' I said, 'his nib inked a fine text. Your *Look Back in Anger, The Entertainer, Inadmissible Evidence.* May he rest in peace. Right next to the three of his wives who predeceased him. Happy families. Your health.' 'Too right,' said that jolly landlord. 'And while we're talking of passing away, two days ago Peter Cook died.' Well, Pedro, my old flower pot, I could hardly Adam and Eve it. Jesu! Jesu! Peter Cook gone. And young, old Pedro, young. Only in his fifties. Osborne was only in his sixties. But Cooky. Was there ever a more witty, more intelligent, funnier, kinder, more difficult bastard than Cooky? Scores upon scores of writings and performances, wickedly comical, wholly original, fairly poured out of him. And the fountain is stopped. By the Rood, a' shot a fine shoot. At the golf. We did, Pedro, from time to time, lurch around the links together. Once, having found he had an impossible lie in the rough, he only set fire to the bushes round his ball, that's all, claimed a concession for a hazard not considered under the rules, dropped down a new ball, whacked the pill into the pond, threw his clubs in after, and went on the piss, official! Jesu! And Falstaff in shape and in quality he was turning into the last time I saw him and we've many of us heard the chimes at midnight with Peter, Pedro, haven't we? And a's gone. Goodness gracious, fuck me pink, but I dreaded going into that boozer in case that horrid landlord would lay on me even more heavy info. Anyway, petal, the other day I wander in there for the one. The landlord has a hideous grin on him. I order a pint. He waits until my lips are kissing the froth and then says, 'Sad about Robert Bolt.' Really! It's dangerous to go in there for drink. Someone will have dropped dead and the landlord can hardly wait to tell you who. Robert Bolt. That's three on the trot, lovey, that's a threble up, that's a trio of the best. John. Peter. Robert. Jesus, the days that we have seen. Robert was your mate, Pedro, not mine, but when we met he always seemed an engaging fellow. And a' scratched a fine scrip. Your *Flowering Cherry, A Man For All Seasons, Lawrence of Arabia*. And, by the Rood, a's brown bread. Someone once showed me a newspaper article in which Bolt's missus said that, believing it to be beneficial, she drank her own wee wee. One wouldn't, when wanting a slug of apple juice, want to go rummaging in her fridge, would one? So, don't, Pedro, for fuck's sake, my treasure, start on that Jesu is a' dead lark. We are all dropping like flies. Though some of us, our heap, despite the mad days that we have seen, and to the bafflement of medical science, still have a pulse. There's old Bletchley. What a spark! Of all the rambling men, Jack the Lads and prowling Tom Cats that we've known, petal, it has to have been big odds against that old scoundrel entering, let alone winning, in the domesticity stakes. How long since we were at his wedding? Ten years? A dozen? There he is with lovely Sarah, in that prettiest of pads they have in Pimlico, three bonny, strong children crashing around the place, jumping on his head at dawn, and he loves it, loathes being parted from his family for even a week. He knocks out what bobs he can at the mumming. Sarah clicks away at the typewriter. He's a good dad. She's a good mum. They're a good team. That's a result, old Pedro. Dancing Johnny Bletchley copped himself a snorter when he fell across Whizz, as he calls her. Lang may their lum reek. As for Griffith the Untouchable. What a geezer. I hear of him in South

Africa, keeping faith with his Zulu friends, marching with
them to Jo'burg. Then the shooting starts. Real bullets, mate.
Dead bodies everywhere. And there's Griffith. Unharmed and
talking fifty to the dozen about what's right and what's wrong!
A Welshman the size of two penn'orth of copper and he must
be seventy. Then he's back here for the publication of his
autobiography, *The Fool's Pardon*. He knew what he was doing
when he chose that title, all right, but still he must be fearless.
Then I hear that, being a Republican, he's only skipped across
to Belfast to be at the sharp end of matters, that's all. Peace is
declared and so he's off to India to give officialdom a
bollicking about the way they mishandled his film on Pandit
Nehru. In London, he is, for five minutes, and now I hear he's
flown off to Russia. What mischief is he up to there, Pedro?
Don't suppose you know. Don't suppose Griffith knows. So
long as there's a fuss being kicked up, he's content. Jimbo,
though. Mr Jim. Big Jimbo. Under the cosh. Well under. He
only upped and got married, didn't he? A year ago. Kept it
very quiet and would you wonder? After all the screeds of
naughty text on the subject that for decades he's been dishing
out to friends, relatives, strangers, passers-by, he only wobbles
into the holy state of wedlock, that's all. The newspapers get
wind of it, ring him up, and he tells them that he only has the
faintest recollection of the event. You can hear him saying it,
can't you? A guinea a minute, our old mate Jimbo. Let's wish
him well, Pedro. Let's wish his wife well. A young thing, for my
money she deserves the Victoria Cross, the Croix de Guerre
and the Congressional Medal of Honour with oak leaves and
bars. Gentle time we had down in Gloucestershire doing the
P. G. Wodehouse film, didn't we? Lovely location, Sudeley
castle, that deep gold Cotswold stone, the rose garden, the yew
trees. Reeking of history, too, didn't you find? I could see
Crookback Richard scuttling out of there and riding off to
fight at the battle of Tewkesbury. Tudor intrigues. Catherine

Parr buried in the little church. And not separated from her
head. Rare, that, for one of Henry the Eighth's wives.
Cromwell gave it a fierce walloping, though. My word, didn't
he just. Remarkable that five of us from the RADA days of '53,
'54 should have been working together on the same film,
wasn't it, my old sausage. Five who've remained pally, too. The
Parfitt. Jude. Must have been a baby way back then. Splendid
mummer. Handsome woman. Gigglesome lass. You reckon her
one of the best Shavians you ever worked with, don't you. Not
too dusty at the Wodehouse, either. Or anyone else, for that
matter. Dickie. Richard Briers. Hasn't changed at all. Bookish.
Irreverent. A great curser. Crazy the way our dodgy old
profession works, though. Dickie flogs away on the flashbox
for twenty years doing sitcom after sitcom after sitcom. Along
comes that bold Irish lad, Kenneth Branagh. Reckons Dickie
to be the best thing since toilet paper. Pop. He's on stage
playing Malvolio. Pop. Pop. Films of *Henry Five* and *Much Ado*.
And then big Pop. Dickie tours the United States playing King
Lear. A mad world, my masters. Indeed. Then, of course, there
was Pringle. The unstoppable Pringleissimo! With that
amazing face. He had me pissing myself with laughter. But
then he always did. I'll tell you what, Pedro. Pringle looks
much younger now than he did forty years ago. How did that
happen? When he was eighteen, he played Abraham Lincoln
without makeup and won the Bancroft Gold Medal! Oh.
Lovey, it's all too comical. And you. And me. Parsloe and Lord
Emsworth. In one way it's a pity we didn't have more to do
together but in another way it was quite a good thing because
you can't get away with any of your old rubbish with me and I
can't get away with any of my old rubbish with you. That's how
it's always been and no bad thing either. Tell me, Pedro, those
three gorgeous birds you lived with in '53, '54, what became of
them? What became of the big sexy dark-haired vamp?

ME: Fiddled about with the business for a year or so and then turned it in and got married.

RON: And the tall blonde? Beautiful girl she was, an angel.

ME: Came out of the blocks flying, Ron. But blew out, so she turned it in and got married.

RON: And your bird? She was an attractive, gutsy little darling, full of devil.

ME: Pounded doors and slogged around to auditions for a couple of years or so. Taught for a year or so. Then turned it in and got married.

RON: Yes. That's often the way of it. Oh! That young Arab boxer whom we both think will be the world champion, Nazeem Hamed. I've a video of his fight with that bloke who'd never been on the deck before. I'll shove it on the television. The good news is that the old trout down below has snuffed it, so she won't be round in the morning complaining about the din.

---

DECEMBER THE FIFTH, 1813, and the new candidate for admission into the company at the Theatre Royal, Drury Lane, Mr E. Kean, stood relaxed and composed before the committee. Politely he listened to what the members had to say and when he was invited to answer sundry questions, he answered them in a voice of sweet accent and charm. Mr Kean's shortness of stature was notable, as was his self-possession, the paleness of his face and the black brilliancy of his eyes.

Five weeks earlier, he had been acting in rural Barnstaple. His four-year-old son Howard became ill, coughing violently. Dorchester was where he would be acting next. Money was needed for medical attention to his son. He'd paid the coach fare for Mary his wife and their ailing child and then he'd walked the ninety

miles from Barnstaple to Dorchester with his two-year-old son
Charles on his back. They'd arrived on November the fifth. On
November the fifteenth, after playing Octavian in *The Mountain-
eers*, Mr Arnold, the manager of the Theatre Royal, Drury Lane,
had called backstage to see him. They met again the following
day, November the sixteenth. Arnold told him that at the behest
of Dr Drury he had travelled to Dorchester to see him perform
and that he could offer him terms as a leading actor at the
Theatre Royal. He had accepted the terms. On November the
twenty-second, Howard died.

'Kean don't have that Apollo-like symmetry of figure,' said one
committee member loudly to another committee member, 'which
could alone furnish a passport to the footlights of the national
stage.'

'Bless me,' cried another, 'he's a puny little man.'

'Pygmy.'

Nine years a stroller, he had played in practically every theatre,
public house, barn or village hall in England, Scotland, Wales and
Ireland, acting and honing many of the major parts in the canon
of English dramatic literature and excelling at dozens of them.
Constantly, insistently, his want of inches had been made known
to him.

Dressed in black, dark curls tumbling in a mane about his lean
pale almost femininely beautiful face, the candidate for admission
into the company of the Theatre Royal, Drury Lane, said nothing.

'Kean!' A voice from a member of the committee sounded out.
'Recite something for us.'

Incledon had been his voice and singing tutor; Angelo had
taught him fencing; d'Eggville had instructed him in dance. Aunt
Tid had paid for these lessons which had begun when he was
nine. He had regularly practised and taught those disciplines ever
since.

Moving softly towards the members, quietly he rebuked them.
'I am engaged at the insistence of Dr Drury. You are not to judge

my capabilities, but the public, by whose verdict I shall abide.'

The confabulation of committee members confabulated further. An idea was floated, discussed, and presented to the candidate. 'Would it not be wise, Mr Kean, to, as it were, take the pulse of that public and initially to come out in secondary or tertiary parts?'

Eighteen nine to eighteen eleven, they'd been golden years for him. Leading actor with Cherry's company in Wales and Ireland, his acting had been widely admired. His adored Howard had been born. As Acting Manager, he had conducted rehearsals of all the plays. Skilled in stage carpentry, able at handling theatrical machinery, he'd also been the Getter Up of shows needing complex scenic effects, dance, song. A wonderful two years. He'd taught himself rudimentary Latin. Charlie had been born. His engagement ended, he'd written for work to many theatres. Not one had replied. For the next eighteen months he'd drudged in the west of England and the Channel Islands. Back in London, destitute, he'd written to Drury Lane and Covent Garden, offering himself to them in third- or even fourth-rate situations. No reply. He'd set off strolling again.

'No,' said the candidate to the committee. '"Aut Caesar aut nulles" is my text. Caesar or nothing.'

Yet more confabulations by the confabulation. 'Very well, Mr Kean,' said the chairman. 'We have decided that you should come out as Richard in Shakespeare's *Richard the Third.*'

'No. Shylock in *The Merchant of Venice* is my choice.'

'Out of the question, Mr Kean. Stephen Kemble will be playing Shylock for us in a matter of days. And Mr Huddart from Dublin has been booked to act that part on the twenty-ninth of December. Out of the question.'

His determination to play Shylock was founded solidly. It was a part that over the years he'd acted many, many times and in which he excelled. At Dumfries, in 1806, old Moss had instructed him in the nuances, the stage business and the huge emotional range of the part. Moss had been a pupil of Macklin, whose acting of Shylock had drawn from the pen of Alexander Pope the famous line: 'This is the Jew that Shakespeare drew.' Also, the long Jewish gabardine robe he wore for the part did much to conceal his littleness.

'Well, gentlemen,' said Mr Kean the candidate, 'Shylock or nothing.' He inclined his head towards the members of the committee, and then he withdrew.

Later, and reluctantly, the committee of the Theatre Royal, Drury Lane, accepted his terms. Mr Kean, they agreed, would come out for them in the part of Shylock.

'No, no, no, Mr Kean. We can't have that. It is an innovation.' This from Raymond, the Acting Manager, at rehearsal on the day of the opening night, January the twenty-sixth, 1814.

'I wish it to be an innovation.'

'It will never do. Depend upon it.'

'Well, sir, perhaps I may be wrong but, if so, the public will set me right.'

At six p.m., as Kean left his lodgings for the theatre, he looked at Mary and said, 'I wish I were going to be shot.'

He didn't wear the red Judas wig that was customarily worn by actors who played Shylock. Nor the large hooked false nose. His wig was black and groomed and severe. The beard he wore was short and trim. His cue came. Edmund Kean walked on to the stage of the Theatre Royal, Drury Lane, and became immortal.

---

'O'TOOLE MUST GO.' Taters can stay. That, one is sure you would agree, is a mercy. He downed a spoonful of Kit-E-Kat yesterday, he licked dry his saucer of milk, and he took a wobbly but successful turn right around the room. Chances are he'll survive. Scarcely thinkable, that, when Taters and I moved in here. Emaciated scrap of bones, when first we found him lying shivering beside the dustbin and carried him inside, the only sustenance we could get into him was by taking a rubber ink holder from a fountain pen, filling it with milk, pricking a hole in it and squeezing out drops into his gasping mouth. Yes, one feels that Taters should be all right, but O'Toole must go. That's the gist of the letter to Tristles which his father wrote to him. The pith of the matter. The nub. To be sure, one reads of his disquiet on learning that I was sharing the flat with Tristles, the catalogue of his views on youth, on the artistic temperament, on irresponsibility; the quaint sentence on how the law of contract is applied even to actors, the mentions of sub-letting, of vigilant landlords, but, of course, he saves the best till the last. Papa pays his son a monthly allowance; therefore Papa has a sanction at his command. 'It all comes down to this,' stabs his pen, 'O'Toole must go or else I shall instruct the bank to stop your allowance forthwith. I'm sorry if this seems unkind. A single man can surely find a room or stay at the YMCA. Better still, why doesn't he give up being an actor and start in an honest job. Kindest regards. Yours, Papa.'

That's me out, then, that's me gone, that's me away into the street as November drizzles in to smack one in the kisser with fog thick as pig shit. Just as one thought one had found and settled into a comfortable berth of the sort one feels to be beneficial to the welfare of a young student in London. Ah well! Nice of Tristles' father to be sorry for being unkind. May he get all that he would want from his life, and may he die roaring. I shall go tonight. There's the rehearsal of *Alice in Wonderland* to attend, and though a little of Carroll's flapdoodle goes a long way with me, playing the March Hare, the Carpenter and the White Knight is a larky caper and I do enjoy annoying Edward Burnham, our teacher. Then I'll pop into the Army and Navy store, buy that camp bed with the slim metal struts which rolls up into a slender sausage about two foot long, come back to the flat, ram the camp bed into my knapsack, shove in a toothbrush, a shirt, knickers, socks, a french letter and a five-pound note, then away I'll stroll with my bundle on my back, kipping wherever I drop, wherever I'm let, which is what, you should perhaps understand, I did during the first week of term.

Do you see. Summer had been an altogether fine season for me. Touring London parks with Hugh Miller's production of *The Trial of Mary Dugan* had been a gas. Playing an American courtroom drama in the open air of leafy parklands to audiences of ducks, Chinese nurses, courting couples and the odd retired colonel who, with his wife, had paused in their perambulation for a gander at the unlikely proceedings, had been as truly enjoyable as it had been totally eccentric. At first, one's voice, one's performance, even as they were uttered, had seemed to evaporate, to float away up into the air, but eventually one got a better hang of it and had felt a sense of projecting out to our modest clusters of disparate non-paying customers. Learning, indeed, of the huge but bridgeable gap between acting and performing.

Away with me then to moil at the mixer with my pack of wild Paddies. Ten hours a day, shite or shine, ten mixes an hour, six days a week, for six weeks we churned out lashings of cement, poured it into wheelbarrows, tipped the ugly issue into the pit, and so did our bit to form the foundations of yet another sub-power station in England's rural heartland. Stones, you should know, were what I and my shovel had been assigned to scoop up and dump into the barrow. Shove in the blade, they'll roll on to the shovel more easily than the sand and they heave into the barrow more smoothly than does the sand, too. Last year I'd fallen for the cement sack trick. Not this year. Hump those buggers ten mixes an hour ten hours a shift you'll find you've humped five tons. The effect is cumulative and like to crack one's spine.

A thick wedge of green wages in my pocket, I'd then scooted up north to kiss my parents, tool around with old mates and had even managed to get in a couple of matches at cricket. Healthy, strong, unattached and twenty-two, keen to tackle whatever might come my way and certain sure I was ready for any bloody thing, I'd bowled me down to London for to begin my second year at the RADA. My little dumpling's gone, fact, I'd thought, as the rattler chugged along down the line, but, scoop up both the Ninas, we'll collar Joe, find a nook, far away from our reputation, in short order we'll replicate our Muswell Hill household. Yes. And the good times once again will roll.

'No.' That, I reflected while sucking down my pint at Momma Fischer's, is what Patsy the secretary had told me in her office. 'Neither Nina Von nor Nina Van are coming back to the academy. Both of them wrote to say that their studentship was ended.' Well, now, there, then, but, you may appreciate, one hadn't been ready for that. Bob had just left the pub to go up to the Gardens. We'd cracked a couple of jugs together, we'd swapped old news, new news and such news as you have never heard of, and Joe, I'd learnt, had moved in with a girlfriend and was living south of the river. That's a lovely bubble burst. A rearrangement of what at best could be called notions was very much on the cards. So, for a week I went out rambling. Yes, from time to time I called into the shop to say hello to the mates, to call on Sir Kenneth, Nana Brown, Clifford, Denys, Madame Fletcher, Amy Boalth, Professor Froeschlen, Hugh, Willy, Ernie, to mingle with old lags, newcomers, and to find out who would be with whom and in what class, but mostly I stayed resolutely on the piss.

There's a jumble to the week which makes quite dodgy a precise recollection of events and the sequence in which they occurred but I do recall meeting at Olivelli's a sturdy dark-haired man, pugnaciously good-looking young man, George the Greek, a new student who, before we both fell into a bucket of whiskey, had told me in a singularly charming speaking voice that he wanted to get together a group who would share a large apartment that he'd been put on to in Notting Hill Gate and that he, the Goritz, would do the cooking.

One evening I tumbled into the buckle, bracelet, torque and ashtray factory Rough Harriet was running in King's Cross. The darling was welcoming, she fed me, we made good cheer and she tucked me up cosy for the night, scrumptious lady. Mikey O.'s mother's carpet gave me on another occasion solid support for a deep snore. Albie? Yes, Albie and I bumped into each other somewhere, I believe, though it's not certain. Soho, with the Norwegian, Jan, yes, we wound up singing opera with a choir of whores at Scoop's place off the Haymarket. Jeannie. Slouching along the Tottenham Court Road I was, a voice called out my name. Jeannie. Running towards me, arms outstretched, beautiful Jeannie with the sweet sad smile. She'd broken out from that awful hostel, was, temporarily, living with friends, but hoped to find a place, preferably with RADA chums, where she could be independent, live her own life. That silver crucifix she always wore, its chain was round her neck, but the cross wasn't hanging down to her breasts, she'd tucked it inside her dress. Tristles, in Olivelli's, and would I consider going half the rent and sharing his flat with him?

A bedroom each, a bathroom, a kitchen, living, dining room and the pad was in a little alley off the north end of Gower Street, a short trot only from the academy. Elected.

Fencing, singing, voice, dance, rehearsal, a long hard day at the RADA behind me, my new-bought rolled-up camp bed under my arm, I went back to what had been my very comfy flat to pick up some of my effects. Yes, the threads could stay but I must go. 'Here's a funny thing. And this is a funny thing. I went home last night. There's a funny thing!' Max Miller, I fancy, at the Old Met. That's nice, Maxie. In the flat, silent, solemn, stand Mikey B. and Tristles, both downcast, both staring at the floor. 'What's up?'

'Peter,' says Tristles, 'this is awful. Really awful. Taters is dead.'

There's the little creature. Frail black body. Lying in his basket. He seems to be half curled up, but his head is thrown back, his gums stretched away from his teeth. A goner, right enough. Poor little sod.

Right. Let's bury him. Where? There's a loose flagstone by the area steps, every time I step on it it rocks, hand me that poker. Out I go. Yes, it's very loose. The light from the window's fine. In with the poker. Lever up. Here's Mikey B. with the sharpening steel. Good man. I'll stand on the poker, that'll lift it up, then you ram in the sharpening steel. Right. In they both go. OK. We'll both lever together. Easy does it, the stone's loose. Up she comes. Right. Stand on the steel and the poker, you. That's the way. OK, I have it. Lift, you bastard. It's not very heavy. It's all right, I'll twist it on a corner and then lean it against the steps. There. Yes, there's plenty of earth. Don't have a shovel on you, do you? Let's see what's inside. Spoons. They'll do. Come on. Three spoons, three pairs of hands, we need to get down about a foot. Three spoons dig. Three pairs of hands scrape and dig and cup and dump. Right, that'll do. In we go. Tristles has the cat wrapped up in a pillow case. Let's have a look at him. Goodbye, Taters. Out we go. Yes, you carry him, Tris. Lay him in the earth. What's that, Mike? Tin of Kit-E-Kat? Why not. Why not, indeed. No, just scoop a couple of handfuls of this wormy bloody earth over him, then get a broom and sweep the rest back in the hole. Good man, Mike. That's the way. Stamp it down. Help me with the flagstone, both of you. That's the way, just stand it upright where it came from. Right. Leave it with me. I'll just let it drop down back. So.

Washed, changed, knapsack on my back, the camp bed in it and sprouting up funnel fashion. Outside there's drear drizzle, there's filthy fog. Lying high, though. Scraps and patches only scud around low. Navigable. Enough, surely, to get from this here A to whichever B may be my destination. Now. Options.

Church of Turkey? Perhaps, but the company of sailors can lead to lively doings. Think.

Mikey O.'s? Sound idea. Mike's good news. His mum likes me. Wants to fatten me up. Possibility.

Bob? He's rid of the thistles in his bed but he might have a rose there, or a leek, or even a palm tree, one never knows with that fellow. Doubtful.

Rough Harriet? Nothing would suit me finer. That's one luscious woman, by God. Snag. From time to time, H. is stepping out with a finger from Islington. A promoter. He puts on events. Comedians. Skiffle groups. Singers. Boxers. Don't think I very much fancy appearing on one of his bills.

Tone and Stan's at Ladbroke Grove? The word is O'Liver's there. We could all get involved in a little burglary, sedition, arson. Think.

George the Greek's at Notting Hill Gate? Take Jeannie. Jeannie's keen. I hear a still small voice but what it is saying is indistinct. Favourite, though.

I shall wander down to the river and there I might make up my mind.

Under the flagstone, safe from all harm, Taters he sleeps sound.

> The rain it raineth every day,
> Upon the just and the unjust fellow,
> But more upon the just, because
> The unjust hath the just's umbrella.

On!

# Acknowledgments

My thanks are due and happily given to Richard Mangan, of The Mander and Michenson Theatre Collection, for his constant support throughout the writing of this book, and for his generosity in allowing me to dip into the many riches stored in that unique establishment; to the London Library for indispensably being the London Library; to the RADA for allowing me to sift through its archives; to the distinguished journalist, Jack Crossley, for his counsel and practical assistance; to old friends and colleagues for their help and good humour; and to Hazel Orme who expertly took me through the task of editing this book, and whose disinterested sympathy for the work was as remarkable as her professionalism was a joy to share.

## Publishers' Acknowledgments

The author and publishers have made every effort to trace the copyright holders of all text and photographs used in this book. In the event that any have been inadvertently overlooked, please contact the publishers so that the situation can be rectified in future editions.

The author and publishers are grateful to the following for kindly granting permission to quote:

Irving Berlin's 'White Christmas', Copyright © 1940, 1942, 1995 Irving Berlin Music, USA; Warner/Chappell Music Ltd, London. Reproduced by permission of International Music Publications Ltd; Warner/Chappell Ltd for Cole Porter's 'Kiss Me Kate' and 'Pal Joey'; Faber & Faber Ltd and Harcourt Brace & Company for 'Sweeney Among the Nightingales' and 'Mr Eliot's Sunday Morning Service' by T.S. Eliot; Constable Publishers Ltd for Patrick Hamilton's *Rope*; Michael Imison Playwrights Ltd for *The Stately Homes of England* © 1938 The Estate of Noel Coward; David Higham Associates for Louis MacNeice's *Suite for Recorders*.